MODERN ENLIGHTENMENT AND THE RULE OF REASON

**STUDIES IN PHILOSOPHY
AND THE HISTORY OF PHILOSOPHY**

General Editor: Jude P. Dougherty

Studies in Philosophy
and the History of Philosophy   Volume 32

Modern Enlightenment and the Rule of Reason

Edited by John C. McCarthy

THE CATHOLIC UNIVERSITY OF AMERICA PRESS
Washington, D.C.

Copyright ©1998
The Catholic University of America Press
All rights reserved
Printed in the United States of America

The paper used in this publication meets the minimum requirements of American National Standards for Information Science–Permanence of Paper for Printed Library materials, ANSI Z39.48-1984.
∞

LIBRARY OF CONGRESS CATALOGING-IN-PUBLICATION DATA
McCarthy John C., 1955–
   Modern Enlightenment and the rule of reason / edited by John C. McCarthy.
      p. cm. — (Studies in philosophy and the history of philosophy ; v. 32)
   Includes bibliographical references and index.
   1. Enlightenment   I. Title.   II. Series.
B802.M29 1998
190'.9'032—dc21
97-40889
ISBN 978-0-8132-3052-8 (pbk)

Contents

Introduction	1
1. ALAN CHARLES KORS, Just and Arbitrary Authority in Enlightenment Thought	22
2. RICHARD KENNINGTON, Bacon's Reform of Nature	40
3. PAMELA KRAUS, Method and Metaphysics: The Foundation of Philosophy in the *Discourse on Method*	55
4. ROBERT P. KRAYNAK, Hobbes and the Dogmatism of the Enlightenment	77
5. JOHN C. MCCARTHY, Pascal on Certainty and Utility	92
6. PAUL J. BAGLEY, Spinoza, Biblical Criticism, and the Enlightenment	124
7. PHILIPPE RAYNAUD, Leibniz, Reason, and Evil	150
8. F. J. CROSSON, Hume's Unnatural Religion (Some Humean Footnotes)	168
9. TERENCE E. MARSHALL, Poetry and Praxis in Rousseau's *Emile:* Human Rights and the Sentiment of Humanity	187
10. KENNETH L. SCHMITZ, Lessing at God's Left Hand	213
11. JOHN R. SILBER, Kant and the Mythic Roots of Morality	232
12. NICHOLAS CAPALDI, The Enlightenment Project in Twentieth-Century Philosophy	257
Contributors	283
Bibliography	287
Index	303

MODERN ENLIGHTENMENT AND THE RULE OF REASON

Introduction
JOHN C. MCCARTHY

WHAT WAS TO BE MODERN ENLIGHTENMENT?

That we usually speak without qualification of "the Enlightenment" is a testament to those who inaugurated that epochal transformation in human understanding. After all, notable scholars of Greek antiquity have accorded to the Sophists the honor of having introduced enlightenment to the world, the same honor the Sophists heaped upon themselves.[1] And although he took pains to distinguish his activity from theirs, Socrates has often been depicted as the hero of an Athenian enlightenment, especially because of, or despite, his celebrated apology to his city.[2] Or turning our eyes to still more distant shores, we observe the reverence shown the Buddha or Zoroaster, to say nothing of other great religious figures of antiquity, by the many souls who credit them with having first revealed the path of enlightenment to humankind.[3] Indeed, when and where has light not been invoked as a metaphor for the most important truths subject to human inspection, and the daybreak, for our initial access to them?[4] But whereas the same sun rises in the east and sets in the west, the sheer number of ancient schools of enlightenment supplies ample proof, if any proof were needed, that none has yet managed to

---

1. Cf. W. K. C. Guthrie, who looks back to Zeller and Jaeger, in *A History of Greek Philosophy*, vol. 3, *The Fifth Century Greek Enlightenment* (Cambridge: Cambridge University Press, 1969), xiii, 48–50; and Friedrich Solmsen, *Intellectual Experiments of the Greek Enlightenment* (Princeton, N.J.: Princeton University Press, 1975), 3. And see *Protagoras* 316d–317a.

2. Consider *Apology* 29d–30b, 36c–e with 31d–32b, 38a–b.

3. Both Judaism and Christianity have generally declined to present themselves as paths to "enlightenment." Despite their differences, they are one in their insistence on humility or obedience, born of an awareness that "autonomy" is not a coherent human possibility. Correlatively, they both distrust anything remotely "gnostic," i.e., the belief that mankind can be set free through the possession of some teaching attainable through human efforts alone. In this sense Hans Blumenberg's claim that "[t]he modern age is the second overcoming of Gnosticism" is plausible only if the modern age has no interest in "enlightenment." See *The Legitimacy of the Modern Age*, trans. Robert N. Wallace (Cambridge, Mass.: MIT Press, 1983), 126–36.

4. But see *Republic* 516e–517b; *Metaphysics* 993b 8–12; *Summa theologiae* 1 q.1, a.5, ad 1.

bring humanity to a common illumination. For this reason among others, we the reading public have not pledged our allegiance to any ancient pedagogy. We show no such hesitation about the recent past, however, speaking as we do of "*the* Enlightenment." Given the record of competing "enlightenments," our use of the definite article must be meant to identify the paramount instance, the individual that defines the class. Or since the promise of enlightenment has, everywhere and always, been of a liberation from the heteronomy of misleading opinions and errant attachments, one is compelled to conclude that "*the* Enlightenment" designates what we suppose to be a conclusive victory after a series of draws at best, a class with only one qualified member. Not even Jean le Rond d'Alembert had hoped for such acclaim.

On the other hand, one must immediately concede that our commemoration of the Enlightenment, nowadays cursory and lackluster, is not much in keeping with our habits of speech.[5] Whatever ordinary linguistic usage signifies in this matter, it is doubtless true that public opinion accords far greater esteem to the Buddha, or even Socrates, than to any Enlightenment thinker one might care to mention. When the Enlightenment is pondered seriously, it is by "scholars," and not by adepts, disciples, or partisans, and in their thinking about the Enlightenment it is characteristic of scholars to reduce it to one among several "periods" in the "history of ideas." Or to speak with the precision that is the fruit of the most advanced research, it is not a matter of "ideas" strictly speaking, but of a "metanarrative" serving to legitimate a particular, and therefore passing, set of interests and practices.[6] In effect, the scholars have come progressively to suspect that the aims of d'Alembert and company were not nearly so rational and public-spirited as they themselves had professed. Thus scholarly interest in the Enlightenment concurs with nonscholarly neglect of it. Both stances betray the conviction that we have surpassed our enlightenment, that we are superior to it, that we are so to say more "enlightened."

Why, then, have we not abandoned our customary tag for this particular moment of our past? Why has it not simply been absorbed into the "dark ages" that the Enlightenment had termed the era preceding its own? Laziness surely does not explain our continued use of the epithet, still less does cowardice. And while scholarship sometimes resorts to the typographical irony available through quotation marks, still there are few to be found in the academy whose historical sense detects a regress

---

5. Consider how attenuated is the American public's interest in its own Enlightenment heroes, figures such as Benjamin Franklin, Thomas Paine, and Thomas Jefferson.

6. Cf. Jean-François Lyotard, *The Post-Modern Condition: A Report on Knowledge*, trans. Geoff Bennington and Brian Massumi (Minneapolis: University of Minnesota Press, 1984).

in the march of time from the Middle Ages, the *medius aevum*, until the present; by the same token, nostalgia for things Greek has never been so marginal to the cultural life of modernity as it is now. It appears likely, then, that we continue to speak of "the Enlightenment" because we remain persuaded that what it sought to replace deserved replacing, and because we are satisfied that the replacement it effected was, as it claimed to be, an improvement. If our praise for the progress brought about by the age is muted, that is simply due to its being but a forerunner to our more luminous present. By our willingness to regard the Enlightenment as belonging to our past, we honor what we suppose we have buried.

In truth, our confidence in having surpassed the Enlightenment is among the clearest signs of our debt to it. For the idea that we are wiser than our ancestors is of Baconian origin. Bacon labored mightily to free men from what he believed to be the leading conviction of his day: that authoritative judgments about the most decisive matters lie ready to hand in tradition, in the things handed down from one generation to the next. In persuading his readers that "the old age of the world is to be accounted the true antiquity," and that "this is the attribute of our own times," he ensured that a reverence for antiquity, which he took to be an "enchantment" by it, would, in time, subside.[7] As a matter of course, then, Bacon's own novel authority would seem destined to be sublated by "history." Yet our adoption of Bacon's philosophical chronology has cost us something of his youthful élan.[8] For while we are fully as certain as were our enlightened precursors that no prior age was so much in the know as are we, such is our sophistication that we cannot regard our advance toward the light with anything like the assurance we credit to those who first embraced the Baconian doctrine of progress. Witness all the weary talk of late about "postmodernity." Postmodernism accepts the Enlightenment's teaching that we have nothing substantive to learn from premodern thought, which is to say that its doubts about modernity are modern, not ancient, doubts. That it cannot summon the nerve to be forward-looking marks its divergence from the "optimism" inculcated by Enlightenment progressivism. The postmodernists suppose themselves to

---

7. *The New Organon, and Related Writings*, ed. Fulton H. Anderson (Indianapolis, Ind.: Bobbs-Merrill, 1960), 1 §84 (see also "The Great Instauration," 8–10, and *New Organon* 1 §56). It is true that Bacon entitled one of his writings *The Wisdom of the Ancients*, but as is clear from its contents, which are often strikingly "modern," he meant by its title only to subvert the authority of certain ancient authors by appeal to others; in this regard, see *New Organon* "Preface"; and 1 §§31, 32, 56, 61, 71, 72, 122, 125. It goes without saying that Bacon does not ever mistake the sheer passage of time with a demonstration of truth, for which see 1 §§84 and 93 together with §§71, and 122.

8. See the "Great Instauration," 8, 10.

see more clearly because they believe that they peer through a darker glass.[9]

By way of countering the suggestion that postmodern gloom is representative of our age, one might point to the surprising resurgence of the claim that we have attained "the end of history." Does not the vigorously "Hegelian" response to the fall of the Berlin Wall demonstrate that enlightened optimism has never been stronger? It is clear that for the advocates of this thesis, the steps we have taken beyond the Enlightenment amount to the perfection of it. In our age, they assure us, the global realization of its deepest hopes has become visible. Without pausing to consider the stiff resistance the world continues to show to this gospel message, it suffices to note that the sunny partisans of history's "end" cannot avoid the dark ambiguity of their chosen terms. If human existence is essentially historical, that is to say, unnatural, then however much our being at the end of its history is a culmination, that end must also spell our termination. The apocalypse of all progressivist history, whether "liberal" or Marxist, must be the cessation of human life as such.[10] In sum, deference still shown toward the Enlightenment at the dawn of the twenty-first century seems unable to mask the sense of melancholy superiority characteristic of those who regard their innocence as a thing forever lost.

However that may be, the pride we take in having put behind us that part of our past most oriented toward the future is surely not unfounded. To a considerable degree that pride is justified. What justifies it is our having negotiated a serious difficulty within the Enlightenment, a difficulty its principal exponents themselves had already felt acutely. To put the problem simply, if mankind was ever, by daring to think for itself, to emerge from its self-imposed immaturity, that could only be because

---

9. Cf. *New Organon* 1, §92, 120.

10. The Enlightenment might almost be said to have begun with the utter rejection of the Aristotelian doctrine of *energeia*, i.e., of a being at an end conceived as the being at work of a being's natural and proper capacity. On history's being at an end, see the letter of Leo Strauss to Alexandre Kojève of July 22, 1948, in *On Tyranny*, revised and expanded edition, including the Strauss-Kojève correspondence, edited by Victor Gourevitch and Michael S. Roth (New York: Free Press, 1991), 236–39, together with Kojève's letter of September 19, 1950, pp. 255–56, and the long footnote to the revised edition of his *Introduction to the Reading of Hegel: Lectures on the "Phenomenology of Spirit,"* assembled by Raymond Queneau, trans. James Nichols Jr., ed. Allan Bloom (Ithaca, N.Y.: Cornell University Press, 1950), 158–62.

Kojève was both remarkably candid and remarkably cheery in conceding the brutal connotations of his prophesy concerning the realization of man's historical "end." Francis Fukuyama's "liberal" retrieval of Kojève's Hegel, which recently enjoyed a flurry of attention, looks to be a classic case of wanting to have one's cake and eat it. On this point, see Peter Augustine Lawler's able discussion in his "Fukuyama and the End of History," as well as the essays by Joseph Knippenberg, Victor Gourevitch, and Timothy Burns, in *After History: Francis Fukuyama and His Critics*, ed. Timothy Burns (Lanham, Md., and London: Rowman and Littlefield, 1994).

some bold, enterprising, and mature mind had led the way by doing our thinking for us. Otherwise stated, the origin of modern enlightenment depended upon a qualified continuation of the very pedagogy to be overcome by it. A way had to be found to create and sustain a traditional hostility to tradition.[11] In fact, the Enlightenment's founding fathers themselves proposed not one but several devices to address this problem. To mention only two, Bacon recommended that an aggressively modern natural science adopt the trappings of a high-church liturgy, while Locke, following Hobbes, advised that the legislative power, which enacts nothing more than "the consent of the majority," should nevertheless be held by all to be "sacred and unalterable."[12] These examples suffice to indicate that it is not only gratifying to us but consistent with the plans the founders of the Enlightenment made for us that we should have forgotten our reliance upon their thoughts in order to rely exclusively on our own. Our post-Enlightenment wisdom necessitates a certain ignorance.

Before the Enlightenment came to think of itself as either postmodern or modern past-perfect, the typical way we made it serve our, and its, purposes was to deem it to be shallow or superficial. On the basis of such a judgment, we could readily acquit ourselves of having to consider what exactly we owed to it, and what we might have misappropriated, or missed altogether. A variety of routes to this conclusion can be traced. We might simply have fixed our eyes upon the philosophes, the most visible and enthusiastic proponents of the revolution set in motion by their philosophical predecessors, and wondered at their naiveté. In light of the astonishing brutality that followed in the wake of 1792, to say nothing of the political crimes committed in our own century, the philosophes' sublime confidence in progress could be seen even by those of the meanest intelligence for what it was: a terrible delusion. Superficiality need not be an indictable offense, however. If, despite its own warts, one insisted that our age marked an advance over the many centuries that led up to it— and who would deny that the lot of human beings has improved in significant respects, or that our knowledge of the whole has been extended in ways that no earlier age could have anticipated?—one could continue to salute the Enlightenment as an age of great prophets and pioneers. For

---

11. Prior to Marx, no modern thinker had ever supposed that enlightenment could possibly occur simply as the result of spontaneous combustion, the leading principle of his "materialism." This was, of course, the one point of his physics that everyone ignored, his most able students above all.

12. *New Atlantis*, in *Selected Writings of Francis Bacon*, with an introduction and notes by Hugh G. Dick (New York: Modern Library, 1955), 545–84, and esp. *ad fin*; *Second Treatise of Government*, in *Two Treatises of Government*, rev. ed., ed. Peter Laslett (New York: New American Library, 1965), §134, 401.

example, we know far more about the workings of the human brain than La Mettrie ever did, yet the intellectual audacity of his *L'homme machine* was and remains something to marvel at.

What were until recently the standard assessments of the Enlightenment's achievement did not necessarily depend upon historicist premises. The most sophisticated judgments regarding the Enlightenment's alleged shallowness correct or complement earlier approaches on precisely such grounds. Thus some have suggested that superficiality be taken neither as a pardonable shortcoming, best not dwelt upon, nor as a sign of overweening pride, but rather as an invitation to scrutinize the Enlightenment's authors more intently. What everyone had come to know as the face of eighteenth-century literature is construed by such readers as a mask hiding from view a much more intriguing contest of psychic forces than we had hitherto appreciated. According to this thesis, adverted to earlier, the Enlightenment was not the result of sober, if also fallible, deliberation. Nor did it arise from hubris, a sin that might have been avoided. The Enlightenment was rather an expression of the will to power, as is every human undertaking. Its self-understanding must therefore be construed as a superficial display of mysterious depths. Nevertheless, the superficiality of Enlightenment pretense is not a reason to put this part of our past simply out of mind. To the contrary, we are advised to exploit the age, or its relics, as a whetstone upon which to sharpen our analytical or diagnostic skills. More precisely, the school of interpretation to which we are adverting would have us exercise our wills through the verbal task of deconstructing this (and all other) past formations of the will. The truth of the Enlightenment, which it did not quite see for itself, was that there is no essential connection between the surfaces of things and the depths of things. Accordingly, we pay it our respect by invoking its willful depths to obliterate its rational surface.[13]

A second, somewhat different, reassessment of the Enlightenment's significance has issued from those who favor an American rather than a continentally inspired "postmodernity." The most pragmatically minded among self-styled postmoderns also urge that we expose what in the Enlightenment's very self-display had lay hidden from sight, but their school intends its hermeneutic to a contrary purpose. Whereas their European counterparts are ambivalent about the Enlightenment's outcome, they

---

13. Cf., e.g., Michel Foucault's Gallic revamping of Machiavelli in *The History of Sexuality*, vol. 1, *An Introduction*, trans. Robert Hurley (New York: Pantheon Books, 1978), 92–97, along with his account of the "purpose" of his historical analysis in *The Archeology of Knowledge*, trans. A. M. Sheridan Smith (New York: Pantheon Books, 1972), 199–211; also see "What Is Enlightenment?," in *The Foucault Reader*, ed. Paul Rabinow (New York: Pantheon, 1984), 32–50.

gladly endorse it. And while continental postmodernity faults modernity for not quite thinking through to the anarchy of the depths, American postmodernism would have preferred an Enlightenment that was more thoroughly, which is to say, "democratically" shallow. In their estimation, the onset of modernity was, for all its glory, colored by a lingering attachment to the Greek philosophical and Christian theological outlooks the Enlightenment professed otherwise to reject. Let us have more of the *Discourse on the Method* and less of the *Meditations on First Philosophy*, such critics advise. Enlightenment is best assured not through ontological or analytic investigations of "subjectivity," but through manly (or womanly) "self-assertion," whereby the "self" endlessly posits itself without ever pausing to wonder what it is, what it is doing, or why it is bothering—presumably because the self is for this school a nonentity, and because nonentities, being nothing but surface, lack the stuff necessary either to do much harm to, or to receive much harm from, other selves.[14]

Internecine disputes concerning the Enlightenment and what it should signify for us now afford us the opportunity to restate some obvious questions: How did modern enlightenment understand itself? What did it intend to be? What did it want for us and from us? Notwithstanding the variety of positions taken lately regarding the advantages and disadvantages of the Enlightenment, the scholarly consensus has gradually come to acknowledge that its precise "historical" meaning, what it meant on its own terms, cannot be disclosed on the basis of a reading of the philosophes alone. To make proper sense of the *siècle des lumières* most competent authorities now concede that we must begin any study of the eighteenth century by looking back a full century at least. This is, of course, to do no more than take the most scientifically minded of the editors of the *Encylopédie* at his word. In the "Preliminary Discourse" d'Alembert openly admits that it was Francis Bacon and René Descartes who first drafted the plans for their revolution.[15] It goes without saying that the Enlightenment has had ramifications in every area of human life—technical, economic, aesthetic, moral, political, scientific, and religious—such that an

14. Cf., e.g., Richard Rorty, "Habermas and Lyotard on Postmodernity," in *Essays on Heidegger and Others*, vol. 2 of *Philosophical Papers* (Cambridge: Cambridge University Press, 1991), 164–76; and "The Priority of Democracy to Philosophy" in *Objectivity, Relativism, and Truth*, vol. 1 of *Philosophical Papers* (Cambridge: Cambridge University Press, 1991), 175–96.
15. *Preliminary Discourse to the Encyclopedia of Diderot*, trans. Richard N. Schwab (New York: Bobbs-Merrill, 1963), 50, 52–53, 74–77. This admission did not prevent Citizen d'Alembert from claiming the laurels for France (80, 85, 87–89). See Voltaire, *Philosophical Letters*, trans. Ernest Dilworth (New York: Bobbs-Merrill, 1961), letter 12, 52–60; and Rousseau, *First Discourse*, in *First and Second Discourses*, trans. Judith R. Masters, ed. Roger D. Masters (New York: St. Martin's Press, 1964), 62–63, for rather different continental assessments.

adequate history of it would require, if possible, the cooperation of a great legion of scholars. But on the testimony of many of its protagonists, the story of the Enlightenment is essentially the story of the birth and growth of modern philosophy. Whatever the superficiality of the most public or "enlightened" expressions of modernity, modern enlightenment can rightfully be accused of shallowness only if modern philosophy itself proves superficial.

One might observe in this regard that the hallmark of modern philosophy has from the start been its great distrust of surfaces, and its preference for what it supposes to lie hidden below them. Thus the Florentine secretary counseled that effectiveness requires that a prince not be "taken in by the appearance and the outcome of a thing," still less by what men say about that thing.[16] Similarly, Hobbes ridiculed the Aristotelian notion of species, itself meant to vindicate the visible looks of things, and our speech about them, in order to make room for his hidden causes.[17] Examples of this sort could be multiplied indefinitely, for as regards both human and nonhuman affairs, modern philosophers are almost unanimous in their hostility to what first greets the eye. These two suffice to indicate the casuistical skills that would be necessary to demonstrate that modern thought is to be blamed (or praised) for its lack of depth. That such a charge continues to be made about modernity suggests how much we continue to be in its grasp. One might well argue, instead, that if modern philosophy were to be faulted, it would be on account not of its neglect but of its distortion of the depths of things, a distortion owing, in turn, to its inability or unwillingness to give surfaces their due. Pace Foucault and Rorty both, does not the Enlightenment's penetrating beam, which is indifferent to the daylight of ordinary human experience, threaten to blind us by its brightness?[18] Here is not the place to debate such matters, however. Let us turn, rather, to consider some of the obstacles facing those who would gain clarity about the philosophical and historical basis of modern enlightenment.

16. *The Prince*, trans. Harvey C. Mansfield Jr. (Chicago: University of Chicago Press, 1985), chap. 18, p. 71; chap. 15, pp. 61–62.

17. *Leviathan*, ed. C. B. Macpherson (Harmondsworth, U.K.: Penguin Books, 1968), 1, 86, 695–96. For some splendid indications of the obvious deficiencies of Hobbesian "epistemology" from a phenomenological point of view, see Robert Sokolowski, *Pictures, Quotations, and Distinctions: Fourteen Essays in Phenomenology* (South Bend, Ind.: University of Notre Dame Press, 1992), esp. 125–26, 159–61, 288.

18. Consider Descartes's inversion of the traditional optical metaphor for knowledge in the opening "rule" of his *Regulae ad directionem ingenii*, in *The Philosophical Writings of Descartes*, vol. 1, trans. John Cottingham, Robert Stoothoff, and Dugald Smith (Cambridge and New York: Cambridge University Press, 1985), 9–10; together with Leo Strauss's statement of the defining principle of his "phenomenology," in *Thoughts on Machiavelli* (Glencoe, Ill.: Free Press, 1958), 13.

In the first place, while it is possible to locate the temporal origins of modern enlightenment with more or less accuracy—early modern philosophers took pains to make plain the novelty of their teaching—just what made this philosophy "new" has never been a subject free from controversy. Here it would be useful to restate the obvious. "Modernity" is a term of distinction, having meaning only in relation to that with which it is disjunctively paired. Therefore, it is only by attending to the protracted quarrel between modern thinkers and their ancient and medieval predecessors that we will be able adequately to appreciate what belongs to modern enlightenment as such. Needless to say, we cannot entirely rely upon the moderns' characterization of their opponents' position in order to grasp just what they reject and what they are the first to affirm. Despite the best efforts of the Enlightenment's authors to put the past utterly behind us, then, modern thought can be accurately understood only if we conjointly pursue a sympathetic understanding of its "other."[19] The need for such wide-ranging historical inquiries is not lessened, it is magnified, in view of a thesis advanced by some of the greatest of our contemporary authorities, namely, that modernity is at heart not really new at all but merely the continuation of antiquity by other means. The same need obtains should we contend with a very different, but almost equally respectable opinion, namely, that modernity owes its principal innovations to philosophical and theological aberrations of the late medieval period. Whatever the case proves ultimately to be, we cannot attain clarity about the specific philosophical difference constituting modernity until we familiarize ourselves with the tradition or traditions that preceded it. Our memory of the Enlightenment is not entirely to be trusted if we should be standing entirely within the shadow that it casts.[20]

The sheer temporal stretch of modern philosophy itself is, secondly, a sign that it is not nearly so monolithic a thing as the tag "the Enlightenment" generally suggests. Already at the outset, agreement between early modern philosophers provided the condition for serious disagreements. Witness Bacon's extreme moderation of Machiavelli, or Descartes's real or alleged improvements upon Bacon. Furthermore, over time a series of radical attempts emerged to adjust the course of modern thought, while remaining faithful to essential modern commitments. These successive revisions of modernity invoked Greek philosophy and occasionally

---

19. See David R. Lachterman, *The Ethics of Geometry: A Genealogy of Modernity* (New York: Routledge, 1989), 2–5.
20. Friedrich Nietzsche, *The Advantage and Disadvantage of History for Life*, trans. Peter Preuss (Indianapolis, Ind.: Hackett, 1980), §1, 8.

even medieval theology as course correctives, precisely in the service of a more thoroughgoing modernity. Thus that quintessential Enlightenment figure, Leibniz, could, by appealing to Aristotle and Scholasticism, be every bit as severe in his judgment of Descartes as that implacable foe of modernity, Pascal. It is not by accident, then, that we typically employ the gerund "enlightenment," "*Aufklärung*," to name this moment in the history of human thought. Modern philosophy is something of a moving target.

The use of the gerund is appropriate for another reason. Verbal nouns do not sharply differentiate subject, action, and object. This fact of grammar mirrors the historical truth that the Enlightenment largely took hold under the cover of innocence and anonymity, according to no clearly defined procedure, and yet in a remarkably rapid and diffuse fashion. Accordingly, one does not go far wrong in describing it as something of a conspiracy.[21] The conspiratorial temper of the Enlightenment is especially pronounced in what may well be its most characteristic institution, what we may loosely call "Freemasonry," itself recently a topic of several useful studies.[22] The grave purpose animating what may seem to us now rather a comical device is the thing that unites all parties committed to Enlightenment: opposition to the established authority of Aristotle, of "hereditary principalities," and of the Church. Because these three, despite their real and profound differences, had generally managed to observe an entente cordiale, the Enlightenment was forced to adopt the classic practice of dividing in order to conquer, and the terms of such practice necessarily made its opposition to the old ways appear, at first, less comprehensive than it was. What is more, given the institutional entrenchment of the old authorities, especially at the dawn of the

---

21. D'Alembert, for one, does not hesitate to employ the term. Cf. *Preliminary Discourse*, 80. Tocqueville appears to ratify this characterization when he observes of the most momentous political event of the Enlightenment, the revolution of 1789, that it took the ancien régime completely unawares. As he presents that occurrence, the old orders did not at first know what happened, they did not know whom to blame, and they did not know that their own ability to respond had effectively been compromised long before the alarm was sounded. See *L'Ancien Régime et la révolution*, in *Oeuvres complètes*, vol. 2, ed. G. Lefebvre and J. P. Mayer (Paris: Gallimard, 1952).

22. See Margaret C. Jacob, *Living the Enlightenment: Freemasonry and Politics in Eighteenth-Century Europe* (New York: Oxford University Press, 1991), along with her earlier study, *The Radical Enlightenment: Pantheists, Freemasons, and Republicans* (London: George Allen & Unwin, 1981). For a consideration of the protohistory of this institution, see Frances A. Yates, *The Rosicrucian Enlightenment* (London: Routledge & Kegan Paul, 1972), esp. 111–129, 179, 192. On the properly philosophical significance of "Freemasonry," see Lessing, "Ernst and Falk, Dialogues for Freemasons," trans. Channinah Maschler, *Interpretation: A Journal of Political Philosophy* 14 (1986): 14–49, along with Maschler's introduction, 1–13; and Leo Strauss, "Exoteric Teaching," in *The Rebirth of Classical Political Rationalism*, ed. Thomas L. Pangle (Chicago: University of Chicago Press, 1989), 63–71.

modern era, and granted the conviction widespread until very recently that "error has no rights," it was inevitable that the founders of the Enlightenment would prepare their assault "silently in the shadows" as d'Alembert almost noisily proclaims.[23] The implications of these facts for our understanding of modern philosophy have yet to be fully digested. We are alluding here not only to the decision sometimes made by early modern thinkers to publish their thoughts anonymously or pseudonymously or even from the safety of the grave. We refer especially to the willingness of some modern thinkers to dissimulate, a practice recognized more than two generations ago by the young Gilson, in his studies of Descartes.[24] Of course, the Platonic Socrates long ago forced us to concede that speaking ironically does not necessarily entail a violation of philosophical virtue, indeed, that in the dialectical encounter between philosopher and nonphilosopher irony is all but inevitable. Unfortunately, the necessary corollary to this discovery is not so often conceded, namely, that it is in the nature of such practice that its precise extent can be determined only by those able and willing to expend the necessary exegetical energy: obvious irony is oxymoronic. It should go without saying, then, that the possibility that modern thinkers have not always disclosed their thoughts with the utmost candor or frankness introduces yet a third obstacle to any easy understanding of the meaning of modernity.[25] In this regard it is worth noting that virtually all early modern philosophers appear to have thought the bid to achieve a universal or unadulterated "enlightenment" to be unrealistic and so undesirable.

This leads us to a fourth problem. If it is true that the eccentric core of "the Enlightenment" is modern philosophy, then we must summon the courage, or resolve, to confront the rare ambition of the modern philosophers. Bacon's celebrated remark to his uncle, Lord Burghley, is no idle boast: "I have as vast contemplative ends, as I have moderate civil ends:

23. *Preliminary Discourse*, 74.
24. *La liberté chez Descartes et la théologie* (Paris: J. Vrin, 1913), 436–38. One might recall here the motto Descartes adopted from Ovid: *bene vixit bene qui latuit*.
25. The controversy surrounding Leo Strauss's rediscovery of "esotericism" is notorious, classical statements of which are to be found in "Persecution and the Art of Writing," in *Persecution and the Art of Writing* (Glencoe, Ill.: Free Press, 1952), 22–37; and "On a Forgotten Kind of Writing," in *What Is Political Philosophy?* (Glencoe, Ill.: Free Press, 1959), 221–32. Whatever the particular merits or failings of Strauss's work, only unyielding dogmatism could lead one to assert a priori that modern philosophers did not make use of an "art of writing" well known in antiquity. In such matters let Francis Bacon, again, be our guide and shining instance; consider, inter alia, *The Works of Francis Bacon*, ed. J. Spedding, R. L. Ellis, and D. D. Heath (London: Longmans and Co., 1857–1870), 3.248; 4.50–52; 5.31; 6.377–78, 387–89, 428–31, 456, 695–99, 701–2. That aspects of Strauss's rediscovery are gradually gaining in academic respectability is suggested by the work of David Berman, among others. Consider his *A History of Atheism in Britain: From Hobbes to Russell* (New York: Croom Helm, 1988).

for I have taken all knowledge to be my province."[26] Whatever the final judgment of his accomplishment is to be, philosophy's only lord chancellor attempted something extraordinarily daunting, a truly comprehensive science, a science that would account for what lies both above us and below us, and for the space we occupy in between. Hence we find in his writings sustained reflections on nature and supernature, physics and psychology, economics and politics, language, morality, the arts, and history. By the same token, his most capable successors, for all their divergences from him, perpetuated his ambition. Now, whether modern philosophic aspirations should prove to be Promethean, or whether they remain in their own way "erotic," we cannot understand the modern philosophers as they understood themselves, we cannot understand the Enlightenment in all its profundity, unless and until we ourselves have abandoned our egalitarian skepticism, on the one hand, and, on the other, suspended our everyday human allegiances: because such detachment from ourselves and our opinions is the condition for an impartial science of the whole, rational assessment of any putative science of the whole requires the same studious indifference. Admittedly, postmodernity, in the name of either democratic or antinomian "difference," would command us to distrust all "globalizing solutions." Yet it is by no means certain that the comprehensive investigations of Bacon and his peers suppose themselves to be reducible to a "solution"; and in any case, postmodern suspicion of philosophy lays itself open to the charge of self-contradiction, for the dismissal of any understanding of the problem of the whole involves either an overt or a covert substitution of one's own understanding of that problem. As recent experience attests, few things are so intolerant nowadays as postmodern tolerance. Moreover, we have even in our own century the example of a handful of thinkers whose activity suggests that a comprehensive reflection on the whole remains both possible and necessary. We would, therefore, be ill advised to reject a serious engagement with modern philosophy on the grounds that ours is a "postmetaphysical" age. Anything less than a philosophic judgment of the philosophical animus of our Enlightenment is doomed to inadequacy. But if this is true one must face the question of our competence to pass such a judgment.

Someone might object that the reduction of enlightened modernity to a philosophical achievement is laughably high-flown. The history of Europe since the seventeenth century has surely been too sprawling, too complicated, and too tumultuous to be explained by appeal to the theorizing of some few thinkers, however great they may have been. As a man

---

26. In a letter dated 1592. See *Selected Writings of Francis Bacon*, 3–4.

possessing a different sort of greatness, the Emperor Frederick, famously observed, should he desire to punish a province he would send it a philosopher to rule over it. Philosophy seems, in its abstractness, incapable of attending to the endless and unforeseeable details that seem to make up human existence and human history, and surely do require our constant attention. To put the objection another way, treating modernity's enlightenment as essentially a rational achievement appears to require that we analyze a temporal event as though it has escaped the confines of time. As the young Nietzsche might have put it, such an approach would make a monumental "effect in itself," an effect without a sufficient cause, from what is in fact the result of a tangled network of causes, itself finally indecipherable.[27] Or to state the objection in a still more radical way, can we even be sure that the Enlightenment is finally a human accomplishment at all, and not rather a mysterious "destiny" sent us by Being in its self-display and self-withdrawal?

There is no doubt that properly historical studies of the Enlightenment contribute immeasurably to our understanding of the period, and that there is ample room for further scholarly activity in this regard. But we need look no further than the present moment to see how urgent is the need to engage in careful study of the modern philosophers. For what we do is largely governed by what we think and say; and what we say and think draws heavily from a borrowed vocabulary, a vocabulary we have learned largely from them. To mention only the most obvious examples, examples that must also surface in any examination of the Enlightenment, no political discussion at any level is possible nowadays that does not appeal to the notion of "rights," even though we almost never stop to ponder just what rational basis, if any, our rights enjoy. Or again, scientists and nonscientists alike take it for granted that modern science employs the only reliable "method" for cultivating the truth, despite the fact that the things any of us know best, including whatever knowledge we may possess of "the scientific method," have been apprehended by no method known to human beings. Our use of such terms as "rights" and "method" indicates that our own modernity is defined to a profound degree by philosophical doctrines whose meaning has been subject to a lengthy process of sedimentation. Key teachings of modern philosophic enlightenment have over time been cut off from the original insight and argumentation that lends to them what truth they may possess, leaving us captive to a strange hybrid, philosophically inspired opinion.[28] It is for just this reason that close study of the philosophers of the modern era is

27. On the Advantage and Disadvantage of History for Life, §2, 14–17.
28. See Jacob Klein's masterful description of the first stages of this process of sedimen-

indispensable, for our sake, and perhaps also for the sake of philosophy itself. Apart from such labors we seem destined to talk without really knowing what we are saying, a prospect that bodes ill for our action.

Paradoxically, the gap we have been describing between pivotal modern doctrines as they were originally conceived, and our muddied appropriation of them, points to a second objection to the argument advanced here concerning our access to the truth of the Enlightenment. To interpret modernity as the project of a small but brilliant band of conspirators appears to depend upon presuppositions of the most "enlightened" sort. It seems to beg the most obvious and important question: "Was '*the* Enlightenment' truly the source of *an* enlightenment?" There can be no doubt that some of the greatest minds of modernity intended a novel alliance between science and society, for a novel purpose or purposes, and to be effected by novel means.[29] But did such an alliance really come about? Were the "ideals" of the Enlightenment truly "effective," to use Machiavelli's preferred terms? Did they generate, not another "imaginary republic"—for everyone can see that "the Enlightenment" names a real occurrence, and one that has transformed the whole planet—but something truly "useful" for all parties involved? The fact that we the reading public have not generally understood or even sought for the philosophic nerve of modernity, that we have so readily embraced philosophical teachings cut loose from their reasoned moorings, indicates that whatever else "the Enlightenment" has done for us, it has not turned our prephilosophic darkness into dawn. As for the modern philosophers, who, if words are to mean anything, truly share with their ancient and medieval predecessors the ambition to understand the whole above all else, what evidence is there that the enlightenment they disseminated brought them any closer to realizing that ambition? Indeed, given the many differences between them, in what sense can we speak about a common Enlightenment teaching?

This second objection has the merit of reminding us of something hidden in plain view, namely, that the expression "the Enlightenment" names a reality that posed itself as an answer to a question. The question for which it meant to be an answer is a Socratic question. It follows that we

---

tation in *Greek Mathematical Thought and the Origin of Algebra*, trans. Eva Brann (Cambridge, Mass.: M.I.T. Press), chap. 9, "On the Difference between Ancient and Modern Conceptualization," 117–25. Klein builds upon the analysis of modernity provided by Husserl, an analysis that culminated in *The Crisis of the European Sciences and Transcendental Phenomenology*, trans. David Carr (Evanston, Ill.: Northwestern University Press, 1970).

29. For this characterization of the meaning of modern "enlightenment," see Richard Kennington's essay on René Descartes in *History of Political Philosophy*, 3d ed., ed. Leo Strauss and Joseph Cropsey (Chicago: University of Chicago Press, 1987), 421–39.

cannot really begin to understand the historical and philosophical reality of the Enlightenment, in itself and for us, unless we put that same question to ourselves. What may be said to be the defining question of the Enlightenment concerns the relation between reason and rule. Is it possible for philosophy, the life devoted to reason, to exercise rule over human affairs generally without compromise to its own proper purpose? At the same time, can philosophic rule do justice to those human desires that fall short of philosophic eros? Either way, what necessity or desire could move the philosopher to take up the exercise of rule? And if the rule of philosophic reason is desirable, or necessary, either for those ruling, or for those ruled, or for both "parties" together, what would be its terms? If properly philosophic rule were to be what Aristotle calls "political rule," that is, ruling and being ruled in turn, what would it be that rules philosophy, if not the whole? But would this not amount to rule of superiors by inferiors, that is, unjust and unreasonable rule, insofar as the whole includes both the nonphilosophic many and a natural order that seems largely indifferent to the distinction between superior and inferior, and is to this extent itself inferior to philosophy? What becomes of "enlightenment" in such a case? Contrarily, what would it mean to speak of philosophic rule over the whole? Setting aside the question of the intelligibility of human rule of the extrahuman world, if the rule of modern philosophy were not political, if the philosopher were to rule the nonphilosophers without himself being ruled by them, how would his rule be distinguishable from tyranny, surely one of the principal targets of Enlightenment thought generally? Finally, how could the rule of philosophy ever overcome the abiding political problem, the problem not of attaining to rule, but of preserving it? How would philosophy ever surmount the problem of succession?[30] This question, or set of questions, offers one way at least to begin to adjudicate the contest set in motion by modern philosophy in its quarrel with Greek antiquity and the Christian Middle Ages. It may also be said to unify the essays that make up the present collection.

THE ESSAYS IN THIS VOLUME

This volume has its origin in a lecture series held at The Catholic University of America in the Fall of 1991 under the aegis of the School of

30. On this question it would be most useful to consult Francis Slade, "Rule as Sovereignity: The Universal and Homogeneous State," in *The Truthful and The Good: Essays in Honor of Robert Sokolowski*, ed. John J. Drummond and James G. Hart (Dordrecht and Boston: Kluwer Academic, 1996), 159–80; and his unpublished essay, "Was ist Aufklärung? Notes on Maritain, Rorty, and Bloom," which is to appear in *The Common Things: Essays in the Thomistic Philosophy of Education*, edited by Daniel McInerny (Washington, D.C.: American Maritain Association, forthcoming).

Philosophy and its dean, Jude P. Dougherty, and with the financial assistance of the Franklin J. Machette Foundation. In order for the following collection to provide a fuller consideration (although inevitably a still partial consideration) of the Enlightenment's principal protagonists, several papers were solicited from authors who did not participate in that series. Hence the contributions by Paul Bagley, Pamela Kraus, Terence Marshall, and Phillipe Raynaud.

Alan Charles Kors provides an overview of the Enlightenment's engagement with its antecedent tradition in his "Just and Unjust Authority in Enlightenment Thought." By focusing on such public initiatives as inoculation against smallpox and penal reform, Kors shows that the Enlightenment was not opposed to authority *tout court*, but merely to inherited authority in its various forms, that of the received religion above all. Against such authorities modernity raised the standards of the happiness of the individual, the evidentiality of what is present to the senses, and the ultimacy of nature; its conception of these standards quite naturally gave rise to a new kind of authority. Kors's presentation helps to remind us why the battle waged by men like Voltaire must have seemed and must seem an undertaking at once necessary and noble.

In "Bacon's Reform of Nature" Richard Kennington takes us back to the dawn of the Enlightenment, and to the founding of the most powerful modern authority, natural science. Whereas modern political life has witnessed titanic struggles between fascism, liberalism, and communism, all three modern political "forms" are as one in the deference they have shown to modern "physics." No modern regime denies that our lives and our fortunes are dependent to an extraordinary degree upon laboratory "results." (The temporary stature Lysenko's "biology" enjoyed under Stalin is, in its very ephemerality, proof of this reality. One might also note that in marked contrast to Lysenko, the efforts of opportunists and ideologues to unseat the authority of the great twentieth-century revolution in physics got nowhere under Stalin.) Nevertheless, it remains a question whether, as some hold, the essential purpose of modern science is, to use Bacon's phrase, "the relief of man's estate," or whether such a purpose is accidental to its deepest intentions. Kennington turns to Bacon for clarity about the precise origin of the modern bid to "master" nature, because Bacon articulates the mastery goal in relation both to the Bible and to Greek philosophy. The essay goes on to discuss the links between the end of Baconian science and the "method" Bacon devised to lay bare the "laws" of nature. Finally, Kennington argues that Baconian science, in requiring a novel sort of institutional "tradition," and in clothing itself in the garb of Christian humanitarianism, brings about a reconfiguration of the relation between philosophy and history.

Pamela Kraus reexamines that great charter statement of the Enlightenment, Descartes's *Discourse on Method*, the work in which Descartes's debt to Bacon is most apparent, and the only Cartesian writing really to provide a synopsis of his thought. As indicated earlier, Descartes's celebrated ontological investigations have recently been derided by some as compromising the legitimacy of the modern age. Kraus's "Method and Metaphysics: The Foundation of Philosophy in the *Discourse on Method*" argues that the literary unity and hence the philosophical integrity of the *Discourse* cannot rightly be understood by forcing that writing onto a grid derived from subsequent Cartesian publications. In this way she furnishes an important clue regarding the unity of Descartes's philosophy. On the way to showing in what way the *Discourse* forms a whole in its own right, she explores the implications of Descartes's use of architecture and legislation as metaphors for his "work," and provides some indication as to how the certainty of the Cartesian "I am" furthers the "foundations" of the method. Her reading discloses a Descartes who is much more modern than is generally acknowledged.

"Hobbes and the Dogmatism of the Enlightenment," by Robert P. Kraynak, assesses the achievement of Descartes's most famous English interlocutor and Bacon's most successful amanuensis. Kraynak argues that Hobbes's seemingly reasonable distrust of all "dogmatism," a distrust that is with us ubiquitous, is itself subject to insoluble difficulties. For Hobbes's campaign against dogmatism amounts in fact to a denial of any scientific worth to prescientific opinion, a point that appears to divide ancient and modern science; yet Hobbes himself relies considerably on premethodological experience, much of which cannot readily be squared with the results of Hobbes's own theorizing; furthermore, in Kraynak's view, Hobbes cannot do without certain dogmas of his own, such that his "positivism" begins to look suspiciously like a matter of convenience. Kraynak concludes that Hobbesian science is a progenitor of a new sort of dogmatism, characteristic of the Enlightenment as a whole, and that in light of its limitations a serious reconsideration of ancient and medieval thought is the sort of skepticism of which our age stands most in need.

In "Pascal on Certainty and Utility" John C. McCarthy examines the thoughts of one of the greatest of the counter-Enlightenment skeptics. Pascal's quarrel with Descartes is often taken to be a family feud, the bickering of a lesser Cartesian with a greater. It is true that the young Pascal was, through his father, privy to the most progressive scientific circles of his day; he probably met Hobbes, and he encountered Descartes in person on at least two occasions; given his intense theological convictions, it is easy to forget how much he was at odds with the academic, political, and even ecclesiastical authorities of his day. But by appealing to a wide range of texts from the *Pensées*, McCarthy makes a case that Pascal's celebrated gibe, "Descartes: useless and uncertain," is meant as a dismissal of Cartesian philosophy root and branch. He directs our attention again to both the mastery of nature theme, and the "clear and distinct" foundations of Cartesian method, in order to argue that, for Pascal, Descartes is useless because his understanding of the good is uncertain, and uncertain because his conception of the true is useless. Pascal proves to be such an enduring critic of modernity because he had, already at the outset, thought through many of its presuppositions.

Paul J. Bagley argues in "Spinoza, Biblical Criticism, and the Enlightenment" that the lens-grinder identified by subsequent generations as one of the heroes of the Enlightenment was in fact not terribly sanguine about the possibility of an enlightenment broadly conceived. There can be no doubt that Spinoza was among those most responsible for what Bagley terms the Enlightenment's "new theology." This theology seemed to preserve the noble reverence human beings had always maintained for God or the gods, but was unencumbered by the requirement that it submit to the peculiar terms of the old religious institutions. Enlightenment "theology" was meant, in short, to promote a religion within the limits of reason alone, whose principal target was biblical "prejudices," and whose intention was to serve both a more humane politics and the new natural science. But while Bagley's Spinoza advocates an enlightenment of sorts, and precisely in the service of these ends among others, he continues to insist on the distinction between the vulgar and the wise, and makes the cut between them much differently than his most enthusiastic adherents supposed. The bold Hobbes, commenting upon his counterpart across the Channel, observed that he "durst not write so boldly." Bagley demonstrates that Spinoza's boldness does not require him to cast all caution to the winds.

Leibniz read Spinoza carefully, and had even talked with him at length. Despite their common debt to Descartes, however, he professed alarm that Spinoza's writings (as well as those of Hobbes before him) were "dangerous to piety." In his "Leibniz, Reason, and Evil," Phillipe Raynaud outlines the first modern "theodicy," which seemed to vindicate the Providence that Spinoza had, apparently, denied. Nonetheless Leibniz's work in theology is by no means a simple restatement of Augustine, as this essay shows. Raynaud also indicates how Leibniz was able, in sympathy with Descartes, to advance a mathematical physics—which had appeared to spell the end of Aristotle's philosophy of nature—partially on the basis of a rehabilitation of Aristotle's conception of certainty, over and against Descartes. On the other hand, Raynaud contrasts what he takes to be Descartes's rational caution with Leibniz's speculative audacity, which, he argues, paves the way for the absolute science of Hegel. Finally, Raynaud suggests that Leibniz is also a source for the irrationalism of Nietzsche, insofar as the doctrine of the monads turns on a reduction of appetition and awareness to subrational "entelechies."

F. J. Crosson's "Hume's Unnatural Religion (Some Humean Footnotes)" again takes up modernity's response to the theological question, as regards both the "positive religion" embraced by the nonphilosophical many and the "natural religion" endorsed by some of the philosophical few. Crosson argues that the *Natural History of Religion* and the *Dialogues Concerning Natural Religion* form a pair, which together set out Hume's view of the logical and rhetorical necessities governing these two forms of religiosity. In Crosson's analysis, Hume's "history" of religion both advances and withdraws the claim that theism is morally and politically superior to polytheism. The *Dialogues* as Crosson lays them out go even further, proposing that there is no rational basis for religion of any form apart from "custom, the great guide of human life." Crosson concludes his investigation by comparing Humean skepticism with the understanding of faith offered by Thomas Aquinas.

Terence E. Marshall discusses Hume's erstwhile friend in "Poetry and Praxis in Rousseau's *Emile:* Human Rights and the Sentiment of Humanity." Marshall holds that Rousseau's critique of the first phase of the Enlightenment led him to rethink the question of the principles of moral and civic life, and also that Rousseau's answers are intentionally concealed in the literary style he adopted, a style well illustrated by his most comprehensive work, the philosophic novel, the *Emile.* As Marshall presents him, Rousseau believes that the advocates of Enlightenment have not adequately fathomed, in their natural philosophy, the problem of human cognition and appetition, and that the upshot of this would be "nihilism." Rousseau's reexamination of the Enlightenment's premises again resuscitates a version of "Providence," and anticipates German critical philosophy, by conjuring a novel sensibility, which he calls the "sentiment of *humanité.*" Transmitting through the *Emile*'s pedagogy the sort of poetry or aesthetic needed to inculcate this sensibility, Rousseau hopes thereby to promote a more effective and public-spirited attachment to human "rights" than could be maintained on the basis of "enlightened self-interest" alone. Marshall concludes his essay by considering the paradoxical significance of Emile's "humanistic" education, leading to the oblivion of that natural perception his mentor seeks, and adumbrating Kant's critical rationalism, displacing the primacy of Enlightenment science in favor of moral practice, but also supplanting practical reason and the quest for wisdom as they had been explicated in ancient constitutional philosophy.

Kenneth L. Schmitz explores Lessing's ambiguous relationship to Deism, to the Christian orthodoxy of his day, and to the Idealism just ahead on the horizon, in "Lessing at God's Left Hand." What did Lessing mean when he claimed to prefer to strive after truth than actually to possess what truth God might hold in his right hand? And what does his preference say about his understanding of the human condition? Schmitz presents Lessing as a proponent of the religion of humanity invented by Rousseau, a figure who struggles to free himself from the contingencies of history, above all biblical history, in order to make space for the liberating but also logical developments of modern history, anticipating in this way the notion of history as an unfolding of the human subject in its inwardness or self-relation. On that basis Lessing can, contrary to much of modern rationalism, welcome the Bible's contribution to human self-development even as he dismisses it.

"Kant and the Mythic Roots of Morality," by John R. Silber, takes up the problem of the form of education appropriate to an enlightened age, again with respect to the older theological tradition. The essay begins by describing the principal task Kant set for himself, namely, to provide a rational basis for moral conduct that would satisfy both the stringencies of modern scientific reason and the exacting demands of the properly moral good. Having sketched Kant's theoretical solution, Silber goes on to ask whether it could ever succeed on the practical level. The difficulty with Kant's solution, Silber argues, concerns whether it possesses sufficient "motivational force" to promote moral conduct, especially since it rejects any appeal to what Silber calls the "mythical" character of Christianity in its traditional expressions. This leads Silber to ponder the place of "moral incentives" within Kant's thought generally. He concludes by explaining why Kant thought it necessary to do without the sort of poetic devices Socrates invokes in the *Republic*, and Rousseau appropriates—for somewhat different purposes, and in quite a different manner—in the *Emile*.

Finally, Nicholas Capaldi demonstrates the resiliency of many key Enlightenment notions in his "The Enlightenment Project in Twentieth-Century Philosophy." Capaldi provides a kind of resume of the thought of the philosophes, which he characterizes as a simplifying distortion of the modern philosophy they claim to be executing. His purpose in retrieving this history is to shed light on twentieth-century philosophizing in the English-speaking world, and on the Scholasticism it has generated. He identifies both in the philosophes and in prominent thinkers of our own day a commitment to scientism as a substitute for metaphysics, a politicized skepticism in place of a reflection on soul, and an ideology in lieu of a doctrine of natural right or natural law. Common to all three commitments, Capaldi claims, is an unwillingness or an inability to mount or entertain substantive arguments about the deepest human questions, which is to say that Condorcet, for example, or Quine, must ultimately fall back on a kind of rhetoric to advance their program. Without a doubt there is a place for rhetoric in philosophical protreptics. How else is the philosopher to speak to the nonphilosopher or to the potential philosopher if not in language commonly accessible? In Capaldi's presentation, however, the Enlightenment rhetoric of analytic philosophy papers over serious logical difficulties; by the same token it has had rather distressing consequences for public life. To the question, How "enlightened" are the Enlightenment's analytically minded heirs? he answers, Not very.

1   Just and Arbitrary Authority in Enlightenment Thought

ALAN CHARLES KORS

I shall address the Enlightenment in its eristic mode by focusing on its most fundamental attitudes toward a criterion of legitimate authority. I say "attitudes" by choice, because to discuss "the Enlightenment" is to discuss a family of thought that was far less a specific set of formal philosophical positions than a general set of attitudes about humanity's relationship to natural phenomena, and, above all, a general set of attitudes toward inherited authorities: intellectual, religious, moral, social, and political. The heart of this essay concerns the close relationship in Enlightenment thought between intellectual authority and authority of all other kinds. My claims here are wholly historical, involving no other claims whatsoever about the substantive issues of just and arbitrary authority.

Enlightenment authors, in their own minds and in their explicit and implicit self-presentations, shared an essential common denominator: they rejected the presumptive authority of the past. This was not a sufficient mark of new and rightful philosophical thinking as they saw it, but it was a necessary one. Specific debates about what that past had or had not been, although related both to their iconoclasm and to substantive issues of what they took to be a new critical scholarship, were in the final analysis surface waves upon a tidal current of much more epic and culturally significant character. That deeper current was a shift in attitudes toward past and present whereby *inherited, traditional* beliefs and practices received no presumption in their favor from the acquiescence or repetition of the ages. Indeed, for most Enlightenment authors, given what they understood to have been the phantasmagoria of human history, there almost

---

I am grateful to the faculty of the School of Philosophy of The Catholic University of America, and to their dean, Dr. Jude Dougherty, for their kind invitation to speak on general issues of the Enlightenment. As someone who works almost always at the monographic level, I deeply appreciate this opportunity to speculate on broader themes.

was a special burden of proof upon those beliefs and practices that had belonged to centuries defined as benighted, tyrannical, and cruel.

Enlightenment polemicists presented their opponents as perhaps the final defenders of an outlook that identified tradition with wisdom and that modified the term "innovator" by the adjective "rash" or "presumptuous." Their own texts, on the whole, tended to equate tradition and "prejudice," and to identify innovation with the possibility of remedying human ignorance and helplessness, and of rewriting some sorry scheme of things. The Enlightenment's campaign for inoculation against smallpox in France was in many ways emblematic of its vision of the whole issue of tradition and innovation. Both the Faculty of Medicine and the Faculty of Theology in Paris voted more than once against the practice, each agreeing—if I might simplify the complex—that it violated the tradition of medicine to give a disease, whatever the intention or outcome. Each cited appropriate inherited texts from each tradition to the effect that the physician could not play such a role.[1]

A major clerical review condemned Voltaire's first plea for inoculation—in the 1730s—as an assault upon Providence (even then, you see, a fear of physicians playing God); the doctors-regent of medicine cited the Hippocratic oath and its implicit ban against giving any disease.[2] For Enlightenment authors, this putative authority of past beliefs and practices was categorically nondispositive of and, indeed, irrelevant to their own essential claim: toward the absolute moral end of reducing natural pain and increasing natural well-being, empirical knowledge of nature should be applied to the natural causes of human suffering. In light of that claim, the beliefs and practices of the medical past were unjust and therefore arbitrary authority. Further, given the harmful outcome of the ban on inoculation, one could condemn as arbitrary authority all of the intellectual and moral criteria, the institutional and social structures, and the very attitude toward custom and innovation that had led to such a prohibition.

Contemporaneous critics tended to depict the new philosophers as assailing the very principle of authority per se. Voltaire's *Lettres philosophiques*, which would seem mild before long, elicited reviews that so depicted him. The Jesuit *Journal de Trévoux* declared that it was "a book that attacks religion, morals, the government and all good principles." One

---

1. For informative accounts of the debates over the issue of inoculation in eighteenth-century France, see Arnold H. Rowbotham, *The "Philosophes" and the Propaganda for the Inoculation of Smallpox in Eighteenth-Century France* (Berkeley and Los Angeles: University of California Press, 1935); Charles Michael Davis, "Contemporary Reactions to Smallpox Inoculation in Eighteenth-Century France" (Ph.D. diss., Canadian Theses on Microfiche, National Library, Ottawa, 1979); and Genevieve Miller, *The Adoption of Inoculation for Smallpox in England and France* (Philadelphia: University of Pennsylvania Press, 1957).

2. Ibid. Concerning Voltaire, see below, note 3.

abbé wrote, "I am appalled by the tone of contempt which is manifest throughout. This contempt extends to his nation, to our government, to our servants of the Crown equally, to all that most deserves respect, in a word, to religion." A Jesuit reviewer was particularly offended by Voltaire's criticism of mandatory tithes: "M. de Voltaire does not know that the custom of paying tithes to priests dates from antiquity, indeed, from the time of Abraham.... A wit does not understand traditions and historical facts. M. de Voltaire has sounded an invitation to sedition and brigandage. Happily, the French people know how to live wisely and to respect their superiors." Another cleric explained the "philosophical" in Voltaire's title: "And what precisely is a *philosophe*? [He is] a kind of monster in society who accepts no obligation toward its mores and morals, its proprieties, its politics, or its religion. We can expect *anything* from their kind."[3]

In its own minds, however, the Enlightenment was not challenging the notion of authority per se in any sphere, but seeking to redefine the criteria of just and illegitimate authority. Inoculation was just because it met certain criteria; its prohibition was arbitrary because it violated those same criteria. The past itself could be judged by these criteria, which was why for all of their positive use of "innovation," most Enlightenment authors indeed viewed diverse aspects of the past—ancient philosophers, institutions, and practices—as worthy of admiration or even restoration. Ultimately, authority based merely upon the presumed moral authority of tradition was arbitrary; ultimately, authority that increased natural pain and decreased natural well-being was unjust; ultimately, authority, wherever found, that increased such well-being and decreased such pain was just. The essential debates about authority lay not on the plane of attitudes toward the past per se, but on the plane of the ethical criteria by which the past itself could be judged.

The anti-philosophes exaggerated the Enlightenment's love of innovation qua innovation—while the latter actually rejected a great deal in the name of more classical standards. The Enlightenment exaggerated the reverence for the past qua past among their critics. Both orthodox apologists and heterodox Enlightenment authors tended to claim the genius of the seventeenth century as their own, for example. On the whole, of course, they all arose, lest we forget, from the same Catholic education and learned community, with its pas de deux of infinite complexity between Christian doctrine and natural (above all Greek) philosophy.

3. *Journal de Trévoux*, January 1735, 95–111 and February 1735, 316–38; Abbé Jean-Baptiste Molinier, *Lettres servant de réponse aux Lettres philosophiques de M de V**** (Paris, 1735); Pierre-François Le Coq de Villeray, *Réponse ou critique des Lettres Philosophiques de Monsieur de V***. par le R. P. D. P. B.* (Reims, 1735); *Journal Littéraire* (1734), 350ff.

Both accepted a fundamental commitment to the principle of non-contradiction, which is why they indeed could argue with each other throughout the eighteenth century. Both claimed to believe in *évidence*, demonstration, and the resolution of the objections of error by the logical presentation of truth. It had been the Church, of course, not the state, that quite literally had educated the authors of the Enlightenment. It had been the Church (often to the alarm of the monarchy) that had insisted upon the exponential growth of education throughout the sixteenth and seventeenth centuries, demanding a more learned and intellectually discriminating clergy and laity. It had been the Church, thus, that had brought into being the secular reading public that would provide both authors and audience for the movement of the eighteenth century and beyond that would challenge the Church's intellectual, moral, and, eventually, educational hegemony. The Church had educated France to secure traditional, in its mind apostolic, authority from the specious but seductive claims of Protestant critics. It staved off French Protestantism, but it educated the Enlightenment! The same drama, with different ecclesiastical loyalties, was being played out throughout the European world.[4]

For Enlightenment authors, history had changed qualitatively in that educated seventeenth century: the human mind had acquired, for the first time, a sound *method* by which to seek natural knowledge of the world. Bacon's metaphor of right method as the path toward natural truth informed fundamental Enlightenment thought. For Bacon, the speed of the traveler—individual genius—was not the critical variable, because on the wrong path it merely led one more quickly away from the truth, and even the plodder on the right path reached sound knowledge more quickly.[5] The Enlightenment's sense of a triumphant seventeenth-

---

4. On the educational revolution in early modern France, see François Lebrun et al, *De Gutenberg aux Lumières*, vol. 2 of the *Histoire générale de l'enseignement et de l'éducation en France* (Paris: Nouvelle Librairie Française, 1981); M.-M. Compère and D. Julia, *Les collèges français: 16e–18e siècles* (Paris, 1984); J. Lelièvre, *L'éducation en France du XVIe au XVIIe siècle* (Bruxelles: Institut National de Recherche Pédagogique, 1975); G. Snyders, *La pédagogie en France aux XVIIe et XVIIIe siècles* (Paris: Presses Universitaires de France, 1972); F. de Dainville, S.J., *L'éducation des jésuites (XVIe-XVIIIe siècles)* (Paris: Les Editions de Minuit, 1978); W. Frijhoff and D. Julia, *Ecole et société dans la France de l'Ancien Régime* (Paris: A. Colin, 1975); J. de Viguerie, *Une oeuvre d'éducation sous l'Ancien Régime: Les Pères de la doctrine chrétienne en France et en Italie, 1592–1792* (Paris: Editions de la Nouvelle 1985); R. Chartier et al., *L'éducation en France du XVIe au XVIIIe siècle* (Paris: Société d'Edition d'Enseignment Supérior, 1976); S. Guénée, *Bibliographie de l'histoire des universités françaises des origines à la révolution*, vol. 2 (Paris: Picard, 1978); G. Rigault, *Histoire générale de l'Institut des Frères des Ecoles chrétiennes*, 8 vols. (Paris: Plon, 1937–1953): and L.W. Brockliss, *French Higher Education in the Seventeenth and Eighteenth Centuries: A Cultural History* (Oxford: Oxford University Press, 1987).

5. Francis Bacon, *The New Organon and Related Writings*, ed. Fulton H. Anderson (New York and London, 1960), 78–80, 92–93.

century method was eclectic, involving Descartes's belief that natural philosophy should assume no prior authority; Galileo's marriage of the inductive and the mathematical; Locke's empiricism, and, as an essential part of that, his bounding of human knowledge by human experience; and the Newtonian paradigm, as they understood it, of an inductive search for general, ideally universal laws of nature that revealed the will, dominion, and design of God.[6]

For Enlightenment authors, there was a strong analogy between intellectual, above all natural philosophical, authority, and all other forms of authority, and it would be difficult to exaggerate the influence of that analogy on their self-image and on their thinking about authority in general. As the Enlightenment told the tale, the part of the seventeenth century they admired—anti-Aristotelian, mechanistic, and experimental, culminating in Newtonian physics—had abandoned a model of knowledge based upon received authorities, syllogistic deduction from premises provided by such authorities, and the unsystematic citation of or search for whatever data or observations might lend support to propositions believed before they were examined. Their intellectual paragons all fit that model for them: thinkers who had attacked—in theory, in practice, or both—disputation decided by inherited authorities, syllogisms derived from such authorities, and experience forced violently into support of prejudged beliefs (the Enlightenment's model of what had preceded the intellectual revolution of the seventeenth century). Thus, they celebrated Bacon's *New Organon* not only as a presumed method distinct from Aristotle's *Organon*, but, even more dramatically, as a very act of challenge to Aristotle's presumptive authority. They tended to recall Bacon's analysis of the Idols of the Theater more than his analysis of the Idols of the Cave or of the Tribe. Bacon's sense that, given the frivolity of human thought without proper method, what was weighty probably had sunk in the river of time and what was lightest probably had reached us, could have been the very metaphor for the way in which the Enlightenment tended to regard the entire human inheritance from the past.[7] Similarly, they celebrated a Galileo who challenged Sarsi to look in the book of nature, not in the books of men, for knowledge of physical operations; they sympathized with a Galileo who had written of the Ptolemaic astronomers who insisted that they did not have to look through his telescope

---

6. See, e.g., Jean Le Rond d'Alembert, *Preliminary Discourse to the Encyclopedia of Diderot*, trans. and ed. Richard N. Schwab and Walter E. Rex (Indianapolis, 1963) [The "Discours Préliminaire" was originally published in 1751], and Voltaire, *Lettres philosophiques*, ed. Raymond Naves (Paris: Garnier, 1962), 54–103 [the *Lettres philosophiques* was first published in 1734].

7. Bacon, *New Organon*, 7–11, 74.

because they long had known what was up there; and they suffered with a Galileo who was forced to recant a belief that contradicted the received wisdom. As Enlightenment thinkers presented it, the seventeenth century had dawned in the absolute grip of received intellectual authorities. The minds that rejected the presumptive authority of those received authors and texts had looked to nature inductively and articulated a knowledge confirmed by experience and useful to mankind. Harvey on the circulation of the blood; Kepler on planetary motion; Gilbert on magnetism; Galileo on mechanics; Boyle on gases; Torricelli and Pascal on pneumatics and the vacuum; Pascal on hydrostatics; Huyghens on centrifugal and centripital force; Hooke on elasticity; the accumulated knowledge and theory of the Royal Society and the Académie des Sciences; and, above all, the Newtonian synthesis of terrestrial and celestial physics—these were the fruits, in Enlightenment analysis, of abandoning the presumptive authority of the past in natural philosophy and engaging the world by means of an inductive, natural, and useful criterion of knowledge. Bacon's promiser seemed confirmed to the Enlightenment by the triumphs of the seventeenth century. Bacon had insisted that such a program reserve to faith the things that were faith's.[8] The Enlightenment believed that the new philosophy had disclosed a knowledge of nature, God, and ethics as revolutionary as the transformation of physical understanding had been.

The fruits of the new philosophy were not merely theories or hypotheses for the Enlightenment, but actual discoveries of the real nature of the world. Kepler's sense of his own work in *De Harmonice Mundi*—"Has not God himself waited 6,000 years for someone to gaze upon his work with understanding?"—and Alexander Pope's sense of Newton's work—"Nature and Nature's laws lay hid in night; God said let Newton be, and all was light"—remind us that the triumphs of early-modern natural philosophy were deemed real disclosure of fact.[9] When Voltaire, in the *Lettres philosophiques*, introduced Newton to France, he opined that Descartes had put us on the road to truth, and that Newton had taken us to the end of that journey.[10] In his *Lettres persanes*, Montesquieu unfavorably compared the theologians, who argued for millennia without convincing each other, to the natural philosophers of the seventeenth century, who, without persecutions, could demonstrate satisfactorily to each other the simple laws that accounted for the most universal phenomena of nature,

8. Ibid., 14–16.
9. For these quotations and an excellent review of the accomplishments of seventeenth-century natural philosophy, see Charles Coulston Gillispie, *The Edge of Objectivity: An Essay in the History of Scientific Ideas* (Princeton, N.J.: Princeton University Press, 1960), 83–150.
10. Voltaire, *Lettres philosophiques*, 70–76.

ending, he believed, millennia of confusion. As Montesquieu explained it, sectarian theology (his model, safely, was the Koran) wrongly impressed us by placing the mere thoughts of human beings in the elevated language of God; seventeenth-century natural philosophy had put the majestic thoughts of God—his actual creation—in the simple language of human beings.[11] In the Enlightenment's self-image, it was to accomplish in the whole range of human thought and activity what the seventeenth century had accomplished for natural philosophy: free of the presumptive superiority of tradition and the past, it was to discover and apply a just criterion of authority to the human experience.

That criterion, for most Enlightenment thinkers, had three dimensions: to be just and not arbitrary, authority must be based upon (1) the pursuit of secular, human happiness, (2) inductive experience, and (3) the natural order. Just authority secured natural (and, thus, secular) human happiness by means derived inductively from nature by natural experience. Such a criterion has obvious links to prior philosophical and ethical systems, but to understand it contextually, which is to say, to understand its place in eighteenth-century history, it is important to see how it emerged from the seventeenth century.

First, let us recognize that the three criteria—Did something serve secular, human happiness? Was it derived inductively? Was it natural?—were all equivocal and problematic, and allowed for a profusion of both substantive and theoretical debates within the Enlightenment (and, indeed, well beyond the Enlightenment). What constituted secular happiness? What were the preconditions of secular happiness? What were the status and proper method of inductive knowledge? What were the objects and parameters of inductive knowledge? What was the meaning of "natural," and how was such a meaning derived? The West lives still with the ambiguities and internal disagreements of Enlightenment thought. As positive (as opposed to critical) criteria, secular happiness, induction from experience, and following nature provided the Enlightenment and its heirs with countless thorns of contention.

For some, for example, happiness was categorical, for others relative not only to time and place, but, indeed, to individuals. The chevalier de Chastellux's *De la félicité publique*, which Voltaire termed superior to Montesquieu's *De l'esprit des loix*, sought to mediate among such views by measuring "public happiness" in terms of the time that remained to the individual for the pursuit of a privately conceived happiness after satisfying

---

11. Montesquieu, *Oeuvres complètes* [L'Intégrale edition], ed. Daniel Oster (Paris: Seuil, 1970), 113 [Lettre 97].

the demands of subsistence and the demands of community and constituted authorities.[12] For Rousseau, happiness was above all the awareness of one's virtue in pursuit of the common good; for Voltaire, it was above all the absence of unnecessary pain and suffering.[13] Even the materialistic atheists disagreed in fundamental ways about the happiness human beings sought: for d'Holbach, and, at times, for Diderot, it was above all psychological, *delectatio*; for La Mettrie, and, eventually, Sade, it was above all physical, *voluptas*.[14] Further, all Enlightenment political theory understood that the most vexing problem of all was how to reconcile by legislation—above all, by rewards and punishments—the well-being of the larger society and the well-being of the private individual.

For some, induction offered representation of God's actual creation. For others, induction offered merely a phenomenal knowledge whose prior and underlying causes we never could penetrate. For some, empiricism led to an ontological dualism, for others to materialism, for still others to a systematic skepticism about any knowledge of substance per se. For some, induction led to certainty; for others, only to probability; for yet others, it led ultimately to philosophical doubt. Whatever the confidence that the eighteenth century had in the concrete accomplishments of a seventeenth-century physics, astronomy, pneumatics, or mechanics that it believed linked to empiricism, in matters of fundamental epistemology, to say the least, empiricism and sensationalism left more questions open than resolved.

As for "nature," the eighteenth century needed several words, because it used the term not merely equivocally, but, indeed, in many often mutually exclusive ways. For some, "natural" meant "essential"—this was a commonplace use for millennia—the "nature" of an entity being that which distinguished it from all other entities. It was with this meaning that both Rousseau and Bishop Butler argued that to live according to human nature was to be a rational creature responsible for accepting the

---

12. François-Jean de Chastellux, *De la félicité publique, ou considérations sur le sort des hommes dans les différentes époques de l'histoire*, 2 vols. (Amsterdam, 1772) [It enjoyed a third edition, Bouillon, 1776]. Voltaire's review of Chastellux's work, proclaiming it superior to that of Montesquieu, was published in the *Journal de politique et de littérature*, May 15, 1777, 85–87.

13. Compare, e.g., the "Profession de Foi" in Rousseau's *Emile*, in Rousseau, *Oeuvres complètes* [L'Integrale edition] (Paris, 1971), 3.184–216, and Voltaire, *Candide*.

14. Compare, e.g., Paul Henri Thiry d'Holbach, *La morale universelle, ou les devoirs de l'homme fondés sur sa nature*, 3 vols. (Amsterdam, 1776), and Julien Offray de La Mettrie, "Discours préliminaire," in *Oeuvres philosophiques* (Berlin, 1750), available in a superb critical edition by Ann Thomson, *Materialism and Society in the Mid-Eighteenth Century: La Mettrie's "Discours Préliminaire"* (Geneva: Droz, 1981); Diderot's ambivalence about the nature of happiness is best seen, perhaps, in his *Jacques le fataliste et son maître*; for Sade, any work will do!

dictates of moral conscience.[15] For some, it meant what was not supranatural, such that it was "unnatural" and wrong to seek chastity by putative supranatural command and "natural" and right to live in pursuit of physical love and pleasure. For some, it was simply the statistical norm, such that it was natural to have two eyes and unnatural to have three. For some, it was all that happened by matter-in-motion, such that, as for Diderot in *La rêve de d'Alembert*, homosexuality was as natural as heterosexuality, though less frequent statistically.[16] Again, as with the issues of secular happiness and inductive empiricism, the Enlightenment focus on "the natural" both continued and opened debates that are with us still.

Nonetheless, for all of these equivocations and ambiguities as positive criteria, such touchstones—secular happiness, empirical derivation, and following nature—were all profoundly powerful themes for any eighteenth-century author. They were linked in authors' and readers' minds to what was taken to be the astonishing achievement of the seventeenth century, and, when conjoined above all for critical purposes, they were considered dispositive of claims of authority that failed their test. If a claim could be transformed into one of the following forms—this will increase secular suffering, it is not empirically derived, and it is not based upon any natural need or behavior, but it is legitimate and right—such a claim could be adjudicated unanimously in Enlightenment thought as arbitrary and unjust. Needless to say, the Enlightenment judged many a theological claim in that light. Any intellectual, theological, moral, political, or social claim, however hallowed by time, that could be shown to increase secular suffering, to be unconfirmed by empirical evidence, and to be based on some source other than nature, was arbitrary and unjust. From such perspectives, the Enlightenment attacked both the prohibition against inoculation, the practice of civil religious intolerance, and the privileges of the Roman Catholic Church. By contrast, if one could in some sense conjoin unproblematically a claim for increased well-being, empirical evidence, and following nature, as Voltaire believed he had done in the case of inoculation against smallpox, one had, for the Enlightenment, satisfied the question of legitimate authority. What was legitimate government? Most Enlightenment authors answered, ultimately, that it was any government whose authority was based upon compelling empirical and natural claims to secure secular happiness.[17] No defense

---

15. See Rousseau, "Profession de Foi"; and Joseph Butler, *Five Sermons, and A Dissertation Upon the Nature of Virtue*, ed. Steward M. Brown, Jr. (Indianapolis, 1950), 3–32 [The Sermons were first published in 1724].

16. Denis Diderot, *Oeuvres philosophiques*, ed. Paul Vernière (Paris: Garnier, 1964), 372–85.

17. For my fuller argument that even the most "radical" Enlightenment rhetoric pointed

based upon tradition that could not also be based upon such claims could be more than arbitrary.

Arbitrary authority, then, could be identified by any one of three criteria: it did not serve secular human happiness; its claims were not based on induction from experience; it was *contra natura*. Just authority could be identified by its satisfaction of those criteria. For purposes of analysis, these may be discussed as three discrete criteria, but in the work of most Enlightenment thinkers, the power of eighteenth-century criticism of existing claims to authority lay in the symbiosis of these three demands. That is to say, the etiology, and, in the case of deism, the heart and soul of Enlightenment thinking, was the claim that we knew inductively from our experience and analysis of nature that it was human nature to seek secular happiness and to flee secular pain, and, thus, that to do so was to fulfill God's design and purpose. God himself through nature itself had given human beings such a moral criterion.

How did such a view come to pervade European thinking in the eighteenth century?

Scholastics, of course, would have agreed that it was precisely human nature to seek happiness, *beatitudo*, an end accompanied by delight, *delectatio*.[18] *Delectatio* was not *voluptas*, sensual pleasure, for the Scholastics, but that was equally the case for most Epicureans, Stoics, Aristotelians, Thomists, Deists or, for that matter, Jeffersonians.

Indeed, the *form* of the argument did not change from the medieval to the early modern periods: the end of human nature was the true satisfaction of the natural desire for happiness. As Aquinas taught it, human nature was determined, first, by what distinguished us from all other beings, our rational and morally free soul, and second, by the end toward which we tended, our final cause, namely, the search for happiness. Since no form was actualized without a final cause, we indeed could be defined above all by our common desire for happiness. This was known by natural reason.[19]

If we shift our focus to two English voices of the new philosophy of the eighteenth century, the eminent Christian bishop and moral theologian Joseph Butler and the Deist Matthew Tindal, we shall hear many of the

---

to the end of secular, empirically discerned happiness rather than to any particular form of government, see Alan Charles Kors, *D'Holbach's Coterie: An Enlightenment in Paris* (Princeton, N.J.: Princeton University Press, 1976), 301–29 ("Mastery and Order").

18. For the use of *beatitudo* and *delectatio*, see Aquinas, *Summa Theologiae*, I2 2.1; II.I.1, 2.6, and 4.1–2.

19. Ibid., II.1.2.

same words, but not the same meanings. In 1724, Butler's *Fifteen Sermons on Human Nature* were published to great acclaim, condemned only by evangelical preachers then considered marginal to polite society. For Butler, as for Aquinas, human nature as formed by God was discernible by consideration of the principle that set humans apart from all other beings—for Butler, our reason and conscience—and by consideration of the end toward which our constitution tends, our final cause or purpose—for Butler, as for Aristotle, the pursuit of an inseparable happiness and virtue. This was not, for Butler, our nature in the sense that it predicted how most people in fact behaved, but that was irrelevant. Even if some ignorant people used watches merely as baubles, toys, or weapons, the nature and proper end of a watch remained defined by the ways in which it was distinct from those other things and by the purpose of its interrelated parts, knowledge of both of which could be derived from observation and analysis. Thus also for human nature: "It is from considering the relations which the several appetites and passions in the inward frame have to each other ... that we get the idea of the system or constitution of human nature." For Butler, our nature, from God, was to seek happiness and virtue by means of conscience and reflection.[20]

For the Deist Matthew Tindal, whose *Christianity as Old as Creation* (1730) defined so much of the Deist controversies in England and, by adoption, in France, "the perfection and happiness of all rational beings ... consists in living up to the dictates of their nature." In Tindal's view, "[T]he principle from which all human actions flow is the desire of happiness," and "The happiness of all beings whatever consists in the perfection of their nature." All of these views mirrored not only the concepts but even the language of Aquinas's consideration of nature, happiness, and perfection.[21] It could sound traditional and orthodox enough. Why wasn't it?

When Aquinas sought to know how happiness should be understood, he thought from a Christian supranaturalism, not from a naturalist perspective. He thought in terms of a qualitative universe of degrees of perfection, of God's will being known clearly only through grace, and of the categorical separation of the finite world from the infinite being of God. From such perspectives he explicitly considered and ruled out as the ultimate end of human nature any happiness based on wealth, honors, fame, bodily health, sensual pleasure, inherent states of the soul, or, to put the matter briefly, any created good.[22] Instead, it was union with God that

20. Butler, *Five Sermons*, 6–18.
21. Matthew Tindal, *Christianity as Old as the Creation; or The Gospel: A Republication of the Religion of Nature* (London, 1730), 22–23.
22. Aquinas, *Summa Theologiae*, III.2–4.

constituted the happiness for which our nature longed: on earth, partially; in heaven, fully and ultimately. The pursuit of happiness as dictated by human nature was a supranatural pursuit. Human beings were moved by their nature toward the supranatural, toward the grace of incorporeal union with God.[23] The government that pursued *true* happiness, it followed logically, was the government that assisted to the utmost the achievement of that supranatural end.

The revolution in seventeenth-century natural philosophy radically transformed the culture's sense both of nature and of its relationship to Divine Providence. Methodical inquiry, the seventeenth century's moderns believed, revealed ordered laws of nature, with God as lawgiver. The laws of nature were the will of God. Think again on Kepler's description of his discovery of the three laws of planetary motion: "Had not God himself waited 6,000 years for someone to gaze upon his work with understanding?" Think on Robert Boyle's *Experiments Physico-Mechanicall* (1660), which talked not only about the expansion of gases, but also about how the laws of motion embodied God's wisdom, providence, and purposeful governance. The laws and mechanisms of nature were agencies of God's will, accomplishing his intentions. To touch those laws was to approach the wisdom of God. Think on Halley's introduction to Newton's *Principia*, that nearer the gods no mortal may approach.[24] Seventeeth-century natural philosophy believed that having achieved proper method, it was gazing upon God's handiwork for the first time with proper understanding. How could one not feel the order and providence of God in the work of Kepler, Galileo, Harvey, Gilbert, Torricelli, Boyle, Huyghens, and Newton? As the early moderns increasingly saw it, such natural philosophers had learned God's actual designs from the systematic and experimental study of what God actually had created. They had discerned order and law in the physical motions and relationships of the Creation and they had disclosed the formerly unseen in the particular laws of nature and the wondrous mechanisms of the world. In doing so, seventeenth-century thinkers increasingly believed that they had seen the purposeful intelligence of God. The religious awe of the new science, locating God's providence in these wondrous natural mechanisms themselves, made possible, within orthodox culture, a reconceptualization and revaluation of nature, and, in a manner that would not have been coherent for Aquinas at all, a revaluation of human nature in terms of its ordinary mechanisms. For the new philosophy, it was the mechanisms and laws of the natural order, not its supposed qualities and forms, that embodied divine will, such that

23. Ibid., 2–5.
24. See above, note 9.

following the empirically discernible laws of nature meant following the laws of God. In moral theology, this transformed and naturalized an understanding of human happiness by validating precisely physical and secular pleasure as the happiness we had the right, from God, to seek.

It always had been a commonplace of Western thought to say that human beings, and, indeed, all animals, sought sensible pleasure and fled sensible pain. Given the distance between that goal and the goal of union with God, the governance of mankind by the pursuit of natural, secular pleasure and the flight from natural, secular pain was far removed from Aquinas's discerned end of the human quest for true happiness, and, in that sense, was even the mark of our sin and our distance from God to whatever extent it drew us from the pursuit of beatitude. Our effort to secure earthly pleasure and avoid earthly pain, when it imperiled that pursuit of beatitude, provided subject matter for countless sermons: it was the sign of our depravity and bestial state; to the extent that it governed our lives, it was the indication that we had not raised ourselves or been raised by God to a higher level of being. In comparison to union with God, earthly pleasures were at best trivial if not at times occasions of dangerous distraction; further, it was, to say the least, not impious to accept many of the burdens and pains of life as occasions of a closer relationship to God.

In light of the new philosophy of the seventeenth century, however, such an evaluation was quite thoroughly rethought, and it did not require a Hobbes to rethink it. If the laws and mechanisms of nature were the agencies of divine intention, and if it were a law of nature and a governing mechanism that all living creatures, including human beings, sought earthly pleasure and fled earthly pain, then it followed that the pursuit of such pleasure was nothing less than the divinely ordained end of human life. What could be more "self-evident," as Jefferson phrased it. The commonplace observation that we sought pleasure and fled pain now became an understanding of the very mechanism whereby the will of God was fulfilled: the pursuit of happiness was what God himself had chosen for us and had joined to the good. Happiness, understood as the increase of natural pleasure and the reduction of natural pain, was the very criterion that God himself had instructed us to apply!

Thus, for Bishop Joseph Butler, to say that we should *not* seek our happiness in this secular, natural world was to criticize the very design of God himself. In Butler's words, "The thing to be lamented is not that men have so great regard to their own good or interest *in the present world*, for they have not enough [emphasis added]." For Butler, those who denigrated the moral worth of self-interest, self-love, and the pursuit of earthly happiness, or who sought to separate it from divinely ordained virtue (he had in mind *both* Calvin and Hobbes), denigrated God's handiwork. There was no inconsistency whatsoever, Bishop Butler wrote, between moral duty and self-love or self-interest, "what is really our present interest,—meaning by interest *happiness and satisfaction* [emphasis added]." For the eminent Christian divine, "Self-love then, *though confined to the interests of the present world*, does in general perfectly coincide with virtue, and leads us to one and the same course of life ... under the conduct and administration of a perfect mind [emphasis added]." If it were a law of nature that we were creatures of self-love in pursuit of happiness, then, literally *by God*, happiness was our birthright and coincident with virtue.[25]

The further contribution of Deism was simply to naturalize the religious component of the pursuit of happiness categorically, where a Butler, by contrast, had written of Christ as reinforcing for us our obligation to virtue and of an afterlife as redressing any unpunished vice or unrewarded virtue that might have slipped through the cracks of the natural moral economy.[26] With orthodox culture itself increasingly having located God's providence in natural mechanisms, Tindal made the universal laws of nature, including the human pursuit of natural pleasure and avoidance of natural pain, the sole moral nexus between mankind and God. God required nothing, and thus had created for the well-being of the creatures alone, a fact to which both natural law and reason testified. Given the operations of nature, for Tindal, "It unavoidably follows: nothing can be a part of the divine law, but what tends to promote the common interest and mutual happiness of his rational creatures." This being the case, for Tindal, "God can require nothing of us, but what makes for our happiness ... [and] can't envy us any happiness our nature is capable of, can forbid us those things only which tend to our hurt." We were assured, from rational consideration of nature, that "this supreme being ... had made our acting *for our present* to be the only means of obtaining our future happiness [emphasis added]." Thus, for Tindal, as opposed to Aquinas, the pursuit of happiness meant precisely the pursuit of knowledge, bodily health, and physical pleasures, none of which could offend God. If it gave human beings pleasure to secure "esteem, credit and reputation with their fellow creatures," then surely God had so disposed the world that the requirements of attaining such happiness were consistent with, indeed, synonymous with, virtue itself.[27] Why? Because "the principle from which all human actions flow is the desire of happiness," and God has created us "wholly for our own sake."[28] The neglect of secular

25. Butler, *Five Sermons*, 16, 48–49.
26. Ibid., 49, 64.
27. Tindal, *Christianity as Old as the Creation*, 13–21.
28. Ibid., 22, 44.

happiness was not only *not* religious, it was offensive to God. That God had made us by nature to pursue happiness supplied us with full assurance that he had equated the true causes of natural, secular pleasure with virtue and the true causes of natural, secular pain with vice. As Locke had taught in the *Essay*, we learned our ideas of virtue from happiness and our ideas of vice from suffering.[29] For Enlightenment Deists, this was a discovery akin to Kepler's disclosure of the laws of planetary motion or Newton's inference of the system of universal gravitation. We induced from the study of nature both that the universe was lawful in a manner that only could be divine in origin and design and that we ourselves were governed by a law and mechanism whereby we sought secular happiness and fled secular pain, associating the good with the former and evil with the latter. We had no need for supranatural validation of such a mechanism, for God had spoken clearly in the book of nature itself. God providentially had created a world with a self-sustaining natural, moral economy: we were impelled, when we understood—by proper use of mind—the real nature of things, to pursue a happiness that was coincident with the good. This was categorically removed, for naturalizing theists, from the views of Hobbes and the later materialists, who argued that all that we meant by "good" was what we deemed the causes of our happiness and all that we meant by "evil" was what we deemed the causes of our pains. Nonetheless, it operationally yielded the same criteria—what we know by induction from nature about the mechanisms of our own human nature provided the source of legitimate authority: the pursuit, via applied empirical knowledge, of secular happiness.

Just as inherited principles of medicine, physics, and astronomy had to be reexamined and reconstructed on the basis of legitimate intellectual authority, so, too, did theological, religious, moral, social, and political thinking need to be reexamined and reconstructed on the basis of legitimate authority. Thus, just as practices in medicine or mechanics had to be reconstructed on the basis of rightful authority, so too did practices in these other essential domains of human activity. The antiquity of Christianity or of absolute monarchy was no more a mark in their favor than was the antiquity of denial of the void or the espousal of a geocentric astronomy a mark of their legitimate authority in physics or astronomy. Were the claims of Christianity and of absolute monarchy derived from experience? Were they *contra natura?* Most essentially, did they lead to the secular happiness of mankind? *There is the critical agenda of the Enlightenment!*

---

29. John Locke, *An Essay Concerning Human Understanding*, ed P. H. Nidditch (Oxford: Oxford University Press, 1975), Book 1, Chapter 3; and, esp., Book 2, Chapter 20 [The *Essay* was first published in 1689].

Examine, in this light, the whole Enlightenment assault upon Christian claims. To the extent that those claims were urged on empirical terms—the historicity of Jesus Christ; the historical evidence of miracles and fulfillment of prophecy; the visible evidence of grace in this world—the Enlightenment contested those claims empirically. To the extent that those claims were urged on supranatural terms—the submission of reason; the command of revelation; a supranatural means of knowledge—they were contested on theoretical terms, as incompatible with the means of knowledge by virtue of which the seventeenth century successfully had reformulated the project of human knowledge, and as a violation of the modalities and limits of knowledge as identified by empirical epistemology. Above all, however, beyond responding to particular apologetic claims, the Enlightenment stressed, again and again, the suffering that it believed occasioned by religious belief, conflict, and authority, and the incompatibility of Christian moral claims with what the Enlightenment believed to be the self-evident right of the pursuit of secular happiness as the source of moral legitimacy.

Examine, in similar light, the whole Enlightenment project of social and political criticism. In Montesquieu's fable of the Troglodytes in the *Lettres persanes*, the malleability of political, moral, and social life is revealed by the cycles of Troglodyte society but limited by the empirical reality of how human nature interacts with objective conditions. Thus, the vicious Troglodytes fail as a society because such a society inevitably leads to dysfunctional misery: no one will honor contracts; no one will reciprocate protection; no one will administer fairly; no one will help the vicious Troglodytes a second time. Vice leads to misery and destroys itself in the world as God created it.[30] In many ways, so much Enlightenment political theory was a word to the privileged wise: a vicious society provides ephemeral benefits for the few and real misery for the many; it is inherently unstable, because humans truly seek their happiness; for authority to be legitimate (and, parenthetically, to enjoy the benefits of its status), it must work for the general good.[31] As in Uzbek's harem in the *Lettres persanes*, unjust authority may rule temporarily by terror, but the moment such terror is lessened, as for some accidental reason it will at some time be, nature reasserts her rights, each individual seeks happiness, and all order based upon illegitimate authority ends in chaos.[32] There is not much Enlightenment political theory that cannot be subsumed under that simple message.

Examine Voltaire's, Montesquieu's, and, indeed, in general, the En-

30. Montesquieu, *Oeuvres complètes*, 68–70.
31. Kors, *D'Holbach's Coterie*, 301–29.
32. Montesquieu, *Oeuvres complètes*, 144–48.

lightenment's celebrated criticisms of civil religious intolerance. For the Enlightenment, civil intolerance is secular cruelty inflicted in the name of a God whom the study of nature reveals to will the secular happiness of His creatures. Where defended on empirical grounds—for example, the common apologetic claim that history teaches that uniformity of religion is essential to the peace of the state—Enlightenment authors challenge that empirical premise, with appeals precisely to historical evidence. Where defended on supranatural grounds, however, they attack that whole manner of a claim upon human activity. What human being knows the will of God beyond what we know from nature—the imperative of the pursuit of secular well-being? What evidence supports such a claim? Thus, again and again, until, indeed, the conscience of Europe is changed, they stress the immense suffering present in the history of religious warfare, inquisition, intolerance, and persecution.

Consider in this light a work that is revealing and significant precisely for the virtually universal acclaim with which it was received in the European Enlightenment, Cesare Beccaria's *On Crimes and Punishments*. Its rapid diffusion and its embrace by admirers of the Enlightenment in Northern Italy, Austria, the German states, France, England, Scotland, and the Low Countries signal a work in which the European Enlightenment saw the application of what it had come to believe. More exactly, the Enlightenment saw in Beccaria's work its own argument that institutions reflected models of authority in which the adherents of the new philosophy no longer believed.

The issue was the reform of the criminal justice system—the laws of Europe—and Beccaria first dismissed the claim on behalf of them based on their antiquity. They were "[a] few remnants of the laws of an ancient predatory people, compiled for a monarch who ruled twelve centuries ago in Constantinople, mixed subsequently with Longobardic tribal customs, and bound together in the chaotic volumes of obscure and unauthorized interpreters . . . the tradition of opinions which in a large part of Europe is still accorded the name of law."[33] So much for the presumptive authority of the past! In theory, Beccaria noted, there were three possible sources of law: revelation, natural law, and the conventions of society. Because all three surely were intended "to lead to happiness in this mortal life," he reasoned that the surest path was to seek the causes of that mortal "happiness."[34] So much for claims beyond the secular! Finally, Beccaria wrote, there was only one ground upon which his own claims about

---

33. Cesare Beccaria, *On Crimes and Punishments*, ed and trans. Henry Paolucci (Indianapolis, 1963), 3. [*On Crimes and Punishments* was first published in 1764, and was translated into French in 1766 and into English in 1767.]

34. Ibid., 4–6.

law should be challenged or accepted: were they derived from experience, logical, and productive of human happiness?[35]

For Beccaria, given our human nature—we pursue happiness as the end of our behavior—there was only one conceivable reason by which the state came into being: to provide for that happiness. Since individuals found greater reason to seek happiness in society rather than as isolated individuals, the social contract of the state was for the provision of happiness under terms of equality before the law. The goal of the state, thus, was "the greatest happiness shared by the greatest number," meaning as he already had explained, "the greatest *secular* happiness shared by the greatest number [emphasis added]."[36] Punishment, which caused unhappiness, was legitimate only insofar as it inflicted the minimal possible pain sufficient to achieve the social conditions in which the happiness of the greatest number could be pursued and achieved.[37]

From such criteria, the Enlightenment sought not only a series of particular reforms, such as Beccaria's proposals for revision of the system of criminal justice, but sought to change in general the way a civilization thought about the legitimacy of power exercised upon its members. It followed from such endeavors, with dramatic consequence, that it should seem "self-evident," in Jefferson's foundational phrase, that among the inalienable rights, which government had been instituted to protect, would be "the pursuit of happiness." It was a legacy of the Enlightenment that such a pursuit and such happiness should be discussed above all in secular terms and upon the basis of natural evidence. Indeed, various Counter-Enlightenments, from the eighteenth century to the present day, may be analyzed on the basis of which of these criteria they most or least assail.

35. Ibid., 6–7.
37. Ibid., 10–14.

36. Ibid., 7–10.

2 Bacon's Reform of Nature
RICHARD KENNINGTON

Of all Bacon's successors, it was perhaps Kant who had the greatest insight into his methodology. Kant tells us in the first *Critique* that Bacon "partly initiated . . . partly inspired" the intellectual revolution in natural science of the seventeenth century. The core of that revolution was the change in standpoint toward nature brought about by human reason. "[Reason] must not allow itself to be kept in nature's leading strings," Kant observes, but must devise experiments to "constrain nature to give answers to questions of reason's own determining."[1] And despite the "Copernican" turn he made a commonplace, he indicates that it was Bacon who had been the first to see that nature might be so constrained, which in Bacon's terms means "forced out of her natural state." Bacon had seen the decisive point that inquiry is not primarily a receptive activity but an active compelling of nature to yield up her secrets.[2] But this leads to an aspect of Bacon's argument not quite so salient in Kant's presenting of it. In Bacon's context the compulsion of nature by experiment is inseparable from the goal of philosophy as mastery of nature. Prior to Bacon, the great tradition had regarded the nature of philosophy as predominantly contemplative or speculative in its purpose. The consequence of his reform is visible in Descartes's statement that in place of "the speculative philosophy" of the Scholastics, he would seek "a practical philosophy" by which "we" could make ourselves "like masters and owners of nature." No one doubts that Bacon is the progenitor of Cartesian mastery of nature.[3]

1. Immanuel Kant, "Preface to Second Edition," *Critique of Pure Reason*, trans. Norman Kemp Smith (London: Macmillan & Co., 1956), 20.
2. Francis Bacon, *The Works of Francis Bacon*, 14 vols., ed. J. Spedding, R. L. Ellis, and D. Heath (London, 1857–1874; reprint, Stuttgart-Bad Canstatt, 1963), 1.141; 4.29. Double references are provided, as in the present case, when the original is in Latin, and when the English translation as well as the Latin original are contained in this edition.
3. René Descartes, *Oeuvres*, 11 vols., ed. C. Adam and P. Tannery (Paris: J. Vrin, 1964–1974), 6.61–62. See Descartes, *Discours de la méthode*, ed. E. Gilson (Paris: J. Vrin, 1966), 444. According to Gilson, "ce qui inspire la philosophie de Bacon n'inspire que la publica-

From the outset of the present century, and with increasing urgency since, it has proven necessary to ask: Is the goal of modern rationalism, and especially of its scientific component, truly Baconian? Is mastery of nature the purpose governing reason in modernity? The question itself is incited by the experience we all have of a liberating but also alienating technology; it seems to have been answered in the affirmative by the overwhelming fact of that technology. Premodern philosophy and science was obviously theoretical in character; it produced no technology of any significance. Contrarily, the seventeenth-century exponents of modern rationalism—Bacon, Descartes, Hobbes, and Locke—are unanimous in announcing that it intends the mastery of nature, and a consequent "infinity of artifices," to use Descartes's phrase, that will alleviate the human condition. Surely reason in its post-Cartesian formulation could be said to have delivered on its promise.

Nevertheless, our question about the goal of modern rationalism divides competent observers into two camps. The first camp defends the theoretical purity of modern science, and is comprised mainly of the scientists themselves and their public defenders. "Science, in its pure form, is not concerned with where discoveries may lead; its disciples are interested only in discovering the truth."[4] The scientist qua scientist is not concerned with the applied science produced by engineers, and called "technology" by all. If we ask this pure scientist why there appears to be an inherent connection between scientific theory and technological success, he replies that his science delivers results simply because it is true. If, inspired by Kant's Baconian insight, we ask the scientist if it is always the scientist, and not on occasion the "interested public," say, who selects the questions put to nature, or if we point out that certain questions of apparent interest have not been posed by science, sometimes for centuries at a stretch, he replies that we have raised issues of a historical character, issues that science is not equipped to answer.

The other camp to have considered modern rationalism does not hesitate to affirm that its goals are Baconian in character; but this camp also has its difficulties. It consists mainly of philosophers of the last one hundred years or so, for example, Nietzsche, Scheler, Heidegger, Strauss, and Löwith, among others. While Nietzsche was not the first to have identified modern rationalism as dedicated to the mastery of nature, his

---

tion de la philosophie de Descartes." See the discussion of the alternative view in my "Descartes and Mastery of Nature," in *Organism, Medicine, and Metaphysics*, ed. S. Spicker (Dordrecht, The Netherlands: D. Reidel, 1978), 201–23.

4. Daniel S. Greenberg, *The Politics of Pure Science* (New York: New American Library, 1967), 3.

account is the most influential, for he gives ample sanction to those who want to pursue the most power. "Science—the transformation of nature into concepts for the purpose of mastering nature—belongs under the rubric 'means.'" Nietzsche believes that extremism is necessary and ingredient to virtue; Strauss holds that moderation never compromises what is excellent. Strauss summarizes the extent of the transformation wrought in modern life by the Baconian goal: "The purpose of science is reinterpreted: *propter potentiam*, for the relief of man's estate, for the conquest of nature, for the maximum control, the systematic control of the natural conditions of human life. Conquest of nature implies that nature is the enemy, a chaos to be reduced to order; everything good is due to man's labor rather than to nature's gift. . . ." Heidegger stresses the ontological change in the status of man among all the beings; man now takes on "the role of standard-giving being within beings as a whole." Scheler is especially concerned with showing that the traditional distinction between theory and practice does not apply to modern science, for what it calls theory is already conditioned by demands that are ultimately practical.[5]

Have these philosophers proved their case against modern rationalism? Of course we have learned much of the first importance from them, and much that bears closely on the meaning of the concept of mastery of nature. We recall with gratitude the remarkable studies of Strauss, especially of Hobbes, and the illuminating studies of Heidegger as found in his Nietzsche volumes. Yet there are at least three significant problems still in need of attention. The first concerns the origin of the concept of the mastery of nature. If we are to understand this origin we must first consider the Greek discovery of nature; only then could we begin to assess the subsequent transformations nature underwent in the centuries prior to Francis Bacon; we would then be in position to understand how it was that science abandoned the traditional discussion of nature as the principle of generation. The same problem might be put in slightly different terms. Why was it that out of the two traditions guiding the West, biblical religion and classical Greek philosophy, there arose the one new goal of universal mastery? A second problem turns on the question as to whether or not the mastery-of-nature goal actually determines or conditions the very principles of the new concepts of nature.

5. Friedrich Nietzsche, *The Will to Power*, trans W. Kaufmann and R. J. Hollingdale, ed. W. Kaufmann (New York: Vintage Books, 1967), 328; Leo Strauss, *Six Essays*, ed. H. Gilden (Indianapolis: Bobbs-Merrill, 1975), 88; Martin Heidegger, *Nietzsche*, 2 vols., trans F. Capuzzi, ed. D. Krell (San Francisco: Harper and Row, 1982), 4.86; Max Scheler "Erkenntnis und Arbeit," in *Die Wissensformen und die Gesellschaft*, 2d ed. (Bern: Franke, 1960), 68; Karl Löwith, *Meaning in History* (Chicago: University of Chicago Press, 1949), 203.

For example, does it determine or condition the notion of the "laws of nature" so characteristic of modern nature? Unless such a link has been shown, it is still open to the defenders of the theoretical purity of modern science to say that the Baconian element is just the application of disinterested theory.

The third problem concerns the proper target of inquiries. To which philosophers should our attention be directed? Here, of course, I declare my interest. My theme will be that the problems just raised are most properly put to Bacon, because it was he who addressed them, not only first, but more fully than anyone after.

The plan of my essay is as follows. Its first part treats of the question of the end, and of its roots in the medieval and ancient traditions. Then in part two it considers the manner in which the mastery of nature goal conditions or determines the principles of Bacon's reform of nature. Finally, in part three, I propose to indicate how the mastery of nature includes for Bacon the construction of institutions by which it becomes a nascent philosophy of history.

THE QUESTION OF THE END

According to Bacon, the question of the end of knowledge is the primary question of philosophy, the question with which it begins, and the question with which it remains. The end of knowledge has hitherto been understood in two fundamentally different ways: the way of the Bible, and the way of Greek philosophy. The way of the Bible is considered in the first published statement of his philosophy, *The Advancement of Learning* of 1605. The way of Greek philosophy is presented in the book of his philosophic maturity, the *New Organon* of 1620. In other writings, published and unpublished, he invariably distinguished these two ways, biblical and Greek. We thus have from Bacon a considerable reflection on the two great sources of Western civilization on the great question of the end of knowledge, a question which, we should expect, finds them most at odds. In fact, Bacon implies that the answer to the question of knowledge offered in the Bible and in Greek philosophy is basically the same. All the more important it is, then, that we establish what this answer is, in order to make clear Bacon's modern alternative.

The inquiry proper into the question of the end begins with the assertion "there are two ways of contemplation." This simple statement occurs in almost all of Bacon's major published books. He does not mean by the "two ways" the way of the Bible and the way of Greek philosophy. He shows us what he means by making the demand that "contemplation and action be more nearly and straitly conjoined and united together than they have been."[6] The first sort of contemplation is exemplified by Greek philosophy, which pursued knowledge for its own sake without regard for action or practical results. The second contemplation, conjoined with action for the "use and benefit of man," is Bacon's own philosophy. Yet the way of Socrates, who also sought the useful for man, is not Bacon's. Socrates called philosophy down from heaven to converse upon the earth, leaving aside natural philosophy, whereas Bacon insists that natural philosophy be pursued with the greatest diligence. Thus the difference between the two ways depends upon whether they pursue natural philosophy in order to benefit human beings. Bacon can call both his philosophy and the various schools of Greek philosophy "contemplation" because contemplation in its ordinary nonphilosophic sense means just to consider or inquire into something, regardless of the end.

Bacon does not immediately tell us why he rejects the first way, Greek contemplation. The *Advancement* does help us, however, to understand his answer to another question that has been widely disputed in the last half century. Was the Bible or Christianity the reason why he rejected Greek contemplative philosophy? Since the Bible in Genesis, chapter 1, verses 26 and 28, grants to Adam a certain mastery over the creatures, it has been argued by twentieth-century philosophers and scholars that it is the Bible that is the source of the goal of mastery of nature. But it is important to note that Bacon never mentions Genesis 1.26 and 1.28 in his discussion of God's creation, though he surely knew the verses.

Nevertheless it could be held that Christianity exerted a powerful influence upon the Baconian philosophy. For Bacon says repeatedly, in many books, that the pursuit of knowledge should be governed by charity. Charity he identifies as the first of all virtues. The one thing needful, the Pauline charity of First Corinthians, is necessary because of the Fall. It cures knowledge of the taint that human reason inherits from the rebellion in the Garden against God's prohibition of the knowledge of good and evil. For charity to govern knowledge means that knowledge must be sought for "the good of men and mankind."[7] Presumably the goal of charity is the same as that of Baconian contemplation, for the use and benefit of man. In late writings such as the *New Organon*, in which mastery of nature replaces or enlarges the goal of utility set forth in the *Advancement of Learning*, we still find the requirement that knowledge be pursued for the charitable end. One might easily conclude, then, that it is Christian charity that sanctions and enjoins the mastery of nature. One finds another argument made by Bacon that yields a similar result,

---

6. Bacon, *Works*, 3.294.
7. Ibid., 266.

namely, that the Holy Faith decides against the contemplative life as understood by Aristotle. For the Holy Faith exalts the common good over the private good, whereas the contemplative life surely exalts the private over the common.

But upon closer scrutiny it becomes clear that it is not Christian charity that persuades Bacon to endorse mastery of nature. Bacon's version of charity is much too worldly to be considered peculiarly biblical or Christian. As possible fruits of scientific mastery it features the extremes of pleasure, great engines of warfare, and indeed the pursuit of the immortality of the body in this life. Baconian charity is thoroughly humanistic, dropping the traditional insistence on the absolute primacy of the love of God, and showing little interest in the traditional care for the heavenly destiny of one's neighbor. Biblical charity had encouraged acts of benevolence toward our fellow humans, but not necessarily through the agency of mastery of nature, and certainly not as an end in itself. However, by knowingly altering the meaning of biblical charity, Bacon provides a biblical sanction for the humanitarian character of modern science, which it retains to the present day.

Since it was Bacon's reading of Genesis, and its story of the Fall, which appeared to lead him to his humanistic doctrine of charity, we must consider his biblical interpretation more closely. It is striking that he uses the same term "contemplation" to refer both to Greek philosophy and to the characters of the biblical narrative. Adam's activity in his original state prior to his fall from grace "could be no other than work of contemplation," because the end of that work was "for exercise and experiment, not for necessity." "For," Bacon continues, "there being then no resistance of the creature, nor sweat of the brow, man's employment must of consequence have been matter of delight in the experiment, and not matter of labor for use."[8] Adam's acts were to observe the creatures, and to impose names on them. Adam is a contemplative in the Greek sense mentioned above, insofar as his search for knowledge is not compelled by necessity; and he is free of necessity because his needs are supplied by God's institution, through the fertility of the Garden in which he has been placed. Accordingly, the term contemplative is also applied to Abel, but not to Cain; it is not restricted to Adam's original situation. Abel represents the contemplative life "because of his leisure, his rest in a place, and living in the view of heaven."[9] Why Abel also represents the contemplative state becomes more evident through the contrast with Cain, who represents "the active state." Abel is a passive beholder of heaven, inactive despite

---

8. Ibid., 296.
9. Ibid., 297.

his living after the Fall; Cain tills the ground, and thus anticipates the development of the arts, which led to the Tower of Babel, and God's punishment by means of the confusion of tongues, a punishment harmful to the advancement of learning, as Bacon observes. God's favor goes to Abel, whose contemplative life is like that of Greek philosophy, unrelated to the action required to remedy our human condition. It is the active life, by which man improves his condition through the arts, that is the root of mastery of nature; and in this life man relies exclusively on himself. Bacon is ostensibly talking about characters in the Genesis narrative. But his anachronistic use of "contemplative" shows that he is imputing trust in the divine order to Greek philosophy. Why Bacon makes no mention of Genesis 1 verses 26 and 28 now becomes intelligible. The command given there to dominate the creatures is not a command to rely exclusively on oneself, for prior to the Fall man remains reliant on God. Mastery of nature, then, is not for Bacon obedience to divine command, but man's self-reliant response to his human condition of neediness after the Fall. It is a response of entirely human origin.

The essence of "contemplation" in its original form is trust in the benevolence of the divine order. Adam before the Fall, Abel after the Fall, and Greek contemplative philosophy as Bacon understands it all exhibit this trust. Bacon provides an analysis of Greek contemplative philosophy in his doctrine of the Idols in the *New Organon*. Except for one mention of his contemporary, Gilbert, every philosopher referred to there is Greek. But the analysis in the *New Organon* does not confine itself to what it considers a Greek error. For the first of the Idols, the Idols of the Tribe, concern human nature generally. And while each of the four kinds of Idol is of philosophical moment, only the fourth, the Idols of the Theater, especially target Greek philosophy. With both the first and the last of the Idols, Bacon takes up the question of final causality. Putting together the relevant aphorisms, we see that for Bacon a philosopher's avowal of final causality is primary evidence that the philosopher avows divine purposiveness governing the whole.

Bacon's analysis of this belief, in its psychological form, turns on three points. In his discussion of the Idols of the Tribe he first asserts that the human mind has a restless striving for what is ultimate, a first cause. Second, when this striving fails to attain its object, Bacon claims that it "falls back upon that which is nearer at hand, namely on final causes, which have relation clearly to the nature of man rather than to the nature of the universe." Third, final causality is said to be a defilement of philosophy, originating in the human desire for a provident order of the universe.[10]

10. Bacon, *New Organon, Works* 1.167, 4.57.

In the course of this exposition, Bacon makes two assertions upon which his judgment about final causality depends. He says that the general principles discovered by philosophy cannot in truth be referred to as a first cause; and he adds that they should henceforth be regarded as merely "positive" (*positiva*). He is fully aware that this account of final causality must be strengthened by another argument, to which I shall return.

Already within the doctrine of the Idols, however, he brings to the foregoing psychological analysis the support of another Idol. The internal or innate account of the Idols of the Tribe is supplemented by an external cause, one he calls an Idol of the Theater. A strictly psychological cause is not itself sufficient to account for the idea of a final cause, which typically takes the form of a religious dogma, and is embedded in a body of theological dogma. So Bacon imputes the corruption of philosophy, as regards final causes in, for example, Plato, to "superstition and an admixture of theology."[11] The argument being advanced is not limited historically to Greek antiquity. Bacon is aware that during the entire period we call "medieval" the fate of philosophy was deeply intertwined with that of theology. In the context of the Idols of the Theater he says that some "have with extreme levity indulged so far as to attempt to found a system of natural philosophy on the first chapter of *Genesis*, on the book of *Job*, and other parts of the sacred writings, seeking for the dead among the living.... [F]rom this unwholesome mixture of things human and divine there arises not only fantastic philosophy, but also a heretical religion."[12] So much for the biblical inspiration of Baconian science.

Yet it is not religion but nature that Bacon identifies as the deepest source of belief in final causality. On the one side, it is the restless striving of human nature for ultimacy in the order of causes; and on the other, it is nature's inaccessible obscurity, which defeats that striving. Thus, it is nature in this dual sense that must be mastered; and the particular instrument of that mastery will be the experimental method, which corrects the naturally aberrant tendencies of the human mind, and which forces nature to answer man's questions.

Outside the doctrine of the Idols, Bacon returns to the restlessness of the human intellect, and gives it a methodological analysis. The explicit subject under scrutiny is "the form of inquiry and discovery that was in use among the ancients."[13] The order of inquiry of ancient philosophy was to begin with some examples and received opinions, and ascend to the most general conclusions or first principles; these first principles it

---

11. Ibid., 1.175, 4.65. Pythagoras and Aristotle are also identified here as having made this error.
12. Ibid., 1.175–76, 4.66.
13. Ibid., 1.219, 4.111.

took as fixed, and then descended by way of intermediate positions. But this is no genuine ascent; an ascent would seek out and adhere to intermediate steps on the way to the most general conclusions. Ancient inquiry is a flight or a leap. The famous ascent of Greek philosophy, which begins with what is "first to us" and culminates in what is "first in itself" is either a self-deception, as Bacon understands it, or a deception of others. We recall that Bacon has already told us in the section on the Idols that an ascent to a truly First Cause is not possible, and that the most general truths should be regarded as merely "positive." What would be required would be a "just scale of ascent" "by successive steps not interrupted or broken": Bacon's point is that we do not find such a just scale of ascent through all the intermediate steps when Plato or Aristotle claim to ascend to a first principle. Putting the two Baconian arguments together, the psychological and the methodological, the reason why we do not find a just scale of ascent is that the human mind, confronted with the extreme subtlety of nature, is of such a nature that rather than secure knowledge that it is not deceiving itself, it prefers to leap to the comfort of accepting a final cause as the truth about the universe.

The importance of final causes, in the judgment of Bacon, regarding the contemplative philosophy of Plato and Aristotle, is stated in a passage in the *De augmentis* (1623), written near the end of his life:

> The natural philosophy of Democritus and others, who removed God and Mind from the structure of things, and attributed form thereof . . . to Fate or Fortune . . . without any intermixture of final causes, seems to me . . . to have been, as regards physical causes, much more solid and to have penetrated further into nature than that of Aristotle and Plato; for this single reason, that the former never wasted time on final causes, while the latter were ever inculcating them.[14]

NATURAL PHILOSOPHY

We now consider the formal presentation of "natural philosophy," which, in the *Advancement of Learning*, is the second of the three great partitions of philosophy, the other two having God and man as their theme. It has always been acknowledged that the key to Bacon's natural philosophy is what he calls "form" initially, in the *Advancement*, and later, in the *New Organon*, a "law of nature."[15]

Bacon breaks with the Aristotelian tradition with unmistakable explicitness. "The forms of substances are not to be inquired. . . ." The Aristotelian substance was a compound of form and matter, in which the

---

14. Bacon, *De augmentis scientiarum*, in *Works*, 1.570–71, 4.363–64.
15. Bacon, *Advancement of Learning*, 3.355.

form was the end, that final cause for the sake of which the development of the substance to its maturity occurred. In place of compound substances, Bacon advocates the investigation of the forms of simples. This marks the introduction of the Baconian form. Initially, this form is the form of a simple property, which is called a "simple nature" since it is the element out of which a whole is to be constituted. To conceive a whole out of simples understood as elements is an enterprise often found in ancient philosophy. What is new with Bacon is that the simple is conceived as a property, not as some subsisting entity; and a collection of properties is that from which a whole is said to be constituted. Bacon then takes the radical step of positing a "form" of each property, and this form is the underlying movement of subsensible bodies that accounts for the property. The term property is replaced by "simple nature," and Bacon conceives that there is an "alphabet" of simple natures that includes all the constituent elements of all the beings there are.

From the start Bacon thus challenged Aristotle on the fundamental issue: How is a natural being to be understood? The difference is from the start a difference of standpoint: Bacon's seeks to understand a being in terms of how it initially came to be, in order that its production might be reproduced by man. The question of genesis is coupled with another: how to rejuvenate a living being as it becomes aged and undergoes senescence. He justifies the turn to simples as a taking notice of "what are the forms, the disclosures whereof are fruitful and important to the state of man."[16]

Bacon experienced great difficulty conceiving a whole that could be thus constituted out of simples. Three aspects had to be considered. There was, first, the simple nature; second, the form of the simple nature; and third, the matter or particulate material from which the form was inseparable. Among these three it was the form that was the intermediate between the simple nature and the underlying material particles. As regards the simple natures, clearly there was needed some bond that would make them into a unified whole, or, more precisely, what was needed was a coupling form that would unify the forms of the simple natures. This problem remained without a solution. It reminds us of Leibniz's need for a bond or chain, a *vinculum substantiale*, to bind into one whole the simple monads. The simple natures doctrine was not fruitful as a way of constituting beings. But Bacon realized that certain of the fundamental natures, such as heat, and light, and gravity, were constituent forces in the natural world, and as such, worthy of investigation apart from any role they might have in constituting wholes. Moreover, "heat" in

16. Ibid.

this sense of a force indifferent to the kind of being in which it was to be found was clearly something whose understanding could be of great importance in industrial processes, and perhaps also in explaining the heat of the human body. By the time of the *New Organon*, the forms of the simples as elements of compounds had been replaced by the new theme, the forms, or laws as they were now called, of heat and such like constituent, primordial forces in nature.

The problem now became: To what kind of material were the laws related? From the fifteen years between the *Advancement* and the *New Organon* we have several fragments, and one finished writing, the *Wisdom of the Ancients*, in which Bacon takes up the question of the nature of matter. Bacon was always a materialist, but never an atomist. Atomism was for him another example of the hubris of ancient Greek philosophy, which claimed to know what is ultimate in the universe. Like other Greeks, Democritus understood nature as that which is always and everywhere—in this case, the atoms. But the atoms, as eternal things, must not have the same properties as the compounds made out of them, which are perishable things. Still, the atoms had size and shape, as did the compounds made out of them; how then could the atoms be eternal or imperishable? So Baconian natural philosophy parts company with the natural philosophy of the Greeks: it wholly lacks first beings of any kind. Therefore "nature" in the sense common to all the Greek philosophers, the first things of the whole, ends with Bacon. Stated differently, what begins with Bacon is "naturalism." In naturalism, the truth of propositions about natural things is established not by reference to that which is always and everywhere, but by means of method, by a methodical verification, at a particular time and place: naturalism is inevitably historical.

The *Wisdom of the Ancients* (1609) is in great part an inquiry into the cosmologies of the Greeks, in which the theories of the philosophers are compared adversely with those of the poets and their myths. Having rejected eternal matter, he was forced to ask, What can be known about the successive forms that matter takes? Just as Proteus in the myth keeps taking different forms as he is bound and constrained, so matter under the constraint of experiment takes a succession of forms, each of which belongs to a different phase of a changing universe. Bacon posits a finite number of phases; these begin to repeat themselves once they have been run through; there is an eternal return,[17] which we can know provided

17. Bacon, *Wisdom of the Ancients*, in *Works*, no. 13: "Proteus, sive materia," 6.651–52, 725. See Howard B. White, *Antiquity Forgot: Essays on Shakespeare, Bacon, and Rembrandt* (The Hague: Martinus Nijhoff, 1978), 124, for a discussion of Proteus; and Jerry Weinberger, *Science, Faith, and Politics: Francis Bacon and the Utopian Roots of the Modern Age* (Ithaca, N.Y.: Cornell University Press, 1985), 241. For the connection between experimental method and

that experiment does in fact disclose to us in our phase of the universe all the other phases. Bacon knows, of course, that he is making a hyperbolic claim for the virtues of experiment: he hasn't a clue as to whether the sequence of phases is finite, and if finite, whether the number of phases is relatively small or extraordinarily large. Two things Bacon has discovered about the experimental: First, it discloses to us that which is not the case now, the counterfactual. And second, it shows us that the world we live in has to be regarded as the "ordinary course of nature" only, and not some appearance of the true world. The ordinary course of nature becomes the cave from which the experimental method may, or may not, provide us an escape.

In the "ordinary course of nature," which is the prescientific world or *Lebenswelt* in which we all live, a given "nature" in Bacon's sense, for example, heat, manifests itself in a variety of ways. He postulates that the form underlying this nature is one and the same in all its manifestations. The heat of the sun and the heat of a living body and also the heat of a cup of coffee are, in their underlying form, one and the same everywhere in the universe. We can then gather their instances, and examine their common properties, provided, of course, that we make the assumption of a limited variety in the universe. A Baconian law is a pattern of the movement of the underlying corpuscles that is uniquely correlatable with an observable simple nature. It is not necessary to know some one ultimate kind of matter, but only to attend to what the properties of matter are in this or that context. But the Baconian law is also related to other laws, and its peculiarities should enable us to rank it as subordinate or superordinate to those others, thus allowing us to place it within a system of laws.

Bacon uses the image of a pyramid to represent his natural philosophy as a whole. He did not give us a nature as a whole, that is, a cosmology to which he committed himself, although he did write expositions of a speculative cosmology.[18] The pyramid of natural philosophy has its unity from the connection Bacon has made between the different sciences represented. The basis of the pyramid is natural history, which is an experimental classification of the phenomena in the ordinary course of nature.

---

possibility, see Thomas S. Kuhn, "Mathematical versus Experimental Traditions," in *The Essential Tension: Selected Studies in Scientific Tradition and Change* (Chicago: University of Chicago Press, 1977).

18. G. Rees, "Francis Bacon's Semi-Paracelsian Cosmology," in *Ambix* 22, no.2 (July 1975): 81–101. Among Rees's many Baconian publications, see esp. the chapters on Bacon's speculative philosophy, in his edition (with Christopher Upton) *Francis Bacon's Natural Philosophy: A New Source* (London: British Society for the Advancement of Science, 1984).

The next higher level of the pyramid is called "physics," and is concerned with the ordinary beings in the ordinary course of nature, and with their efficient and material causes. The highest level of the pyramid is called "metaphysics," which is the science of the laws of nature, which are "eternal and immutable." Thus physics is a science of perishable beings, and metaphysics a science of eternal laws. As for the vertical point of the pyramid, it is the "summary law of nature," also called "the work which God worketh from the beginning to the end." The entire pyramid is meant to represent the ascent from the beings to the laws and their structure up to the supreme or most general law of nature, or as he once describes it, the supreme law of motion in the universe. The unit of the ascent, as it were, is the subordinate/superordinate relationship of one law to a still more general law. Bacon even stipulates that to know a law requires that we know its relationship to another law, and to know that other law, it is necessary to know a third law. The problem of continuous regress is present. And since the source of all laws, and especially the supreme law, is matter itself, beyond the supreme law lies the unknowable matter that cannot be represented in the image.

If we scrutinize the pyramid, we notice that physics and metaphysics are disjunctive of each other. The one is a science of beings of the ordinary course of nature, the other a science of the laws of the primordial simples like heat and gravity. Man must exist as an object of physics, but metaphysics, the true science of nature, has nothing to say about man as such. Man and Baconian "nature" are disjunctive of each other; the domain of human activity, as outside of nature in the strict sense, becomes the historical, as we suggest in our final section. As mentioned earlier, natural philosophy is the first part of the triad of Baconian philosophy, which is divided with reference to God, nature, and man. Only the whole triad would disclose to us what the investigation of natural philosophy does not, and cannot, show, namely, that the end for the sake of which natural philosophy is pursued is actually no single end; or rather, it is a general end, those human interests and passions of which there are no laws, and also no natural standards.

NATURE AND THE HISTORICAL PROCESS

Francis Bacon is a utopian. He is the author of one of the two perhaps most famous utopias, the *New Atlantis*. We might suppose that a utopian must necessarily think historically, must ponder the future of the race, or some part of it. But Plato's *Republic*, perhaps the greatest of utopias, is an utterly unhistorical regime. It is utterly unchanging, outside of time. By contrast, Bacon's utopia comes into being through the historical process and always remains within it. That is not true, however, of the *New Atlantis*, that utopia on an island, ruled by philosophers, which strongly reminds us of the Platonic republic, and which is, for the most part, outside of time. Yet the true utopia of Bacon is given its name in the title of his major book, the *New Organon; or, On the Interpretation of Nature and the Kingdom of Man*. This book is the *New Organon* because it is the replacement for the old "organon," Aristotle's theory of science. The new organon is the "interpretation of nature" because nature is much more subtle than our ancestors had ever dreamt; and the method for the interpretation of such a nature will take many centuries to overcome that subtlety. But the achievement of that overcoming will deservedly be called the "Kingdom of Man" because man will live freely for the first time in his own world, a world of his own making, a kingdom within the "Kingdom of Nature," a phrase Bacon also uses.

Let us begin from the beginning. Bacon is the greatest disciple of the greatest antiutopian, Machiavelli. Bacon says "we are much beholden to Machiavel and others, that write what men do, and not what they ought to do." He also says, virtually borrowing from the same famous Chapter 15 of Machiavelli's *Prince*, "As for the philosophers, they make imaginary laws for imaginary commonwealths: and their discourses are as the stars, which give little light, because they are so high."[19] But Bacon believed that it was precisely his Machiavellian beginning that compelled him to become a utopian.

Machiavelli's political science sought to master *fortuna* or chance, but limited itself to human affairs. The *fortuna* or chance most harmful to man comes, however, not from other men but from nature. The shortness of life, its vulnerability to disease, the weakness and misery of old age, have to be laid at the door of nature, not other human beings. Therefore Bacon embarked on the project of eliminating chance from the nature of things, a project that Machiavelli might well have regarded as mad. For one thing, Baconian technology means that a free republic depends no more on the military virtue of its citizens, but on military technology. Furthermore, Machiavelli's pursuit of wisdom was still the inquiry of one individual, of course with the comradeship of friends, whereas after Bacon the pursuit of wisdom becomes a function of a corporate endeavor, that of the body of scientific investigators.

At this point we glimpse the reason why Bacon's enterprise must be transformed into the attempt to master the historical process. The problem is two-sided. If mankind is ever to know the *summa lex*, the supreme law of the whole of nature, then we must reinterpret "tradition." Hitherto,

---

19. Bacon, *Advancement of Learning*, 3.430, 475.

although a philosopher was greater than even his best disciples, and so did not succeed in handing down his knowledge in all its fullness even to the next generation, that failure was not thought either to impugn the worth of a philosophical "school," or to be an impediment to the formation of new "schools" still somehow faithful to the original master. But once inquiry becomes a function of experiment, this handing down—*traditio* in its original sense—means stating precisely, in a manner fully intelligible to another, the hypothesis, procedure, and result of the experiment. The "experience" of the later generations means *experientia literata*, if I understand that Baconian phrase.[20] The scientific research report is certainly not literature in its older meaning, which seems to retain an abiding superiority to its readers, but it is the sort of writing that advances progress. Because it has done its job, we can read it and put it behind us, in this way carrying forward its intention with perfect fidelity.

On the other side, Bacon learned from Machiavelli that unarmed prophets, if armed with the right doctrines, can succeed. Bacon thus turned to Christian doctrine, and borrowed its teaching on charity, in order to consecrate the mastery of nature. Science became Christian humanitarianism, a garb it wears, although with some minor alterations, to the present day. Charity becomes the patriotism of the Kingdom of Man. The combination of the methodological guarantee of knowledge, the repeatable experiment, the reliable control of tradition, and the humanitarianism of the society that fosters the project of science, conspire to guarantee or virtually guarantee, the progress toward the Kingdom of Man.

20. "Now no course of invention can be satisfactory unless it be carried on in writing But when this is brought into use, and experience has been taught to read and write, better things may be hoped"; *New Organon*, I, §§ 101–3 convey the meaning of Bacon's "experientia literata." See *Works* 1.203–4, 4.96–97.

3 Method and Metaphysics: The Foundation of Philosophy in the *Discourse on Method*

PAMELA KRAUS

Interpretation of the *Discourse on Method*[1] usually takes its bearing from other Cartesian works rather than from the *Discourse* itself. This is due in some measure to its rhetoric, which has abetted its philosophical effacement in important ways. Because it is a popular writing, the *Discourse* does not attempt to argue for or to explicate its teachings thoroughly. The famous rules of Cartesian method are but briefly summarized, as is the cosmology of *Le monde*, and—with an important exception—the physiology of the *Treatise on Man*. As for two theses that have become virtually synonymous with Descartes's philosophy, one, the substantial distinction beween soul and body, is swiftly introduced in and just as swiftly dropped after a single paragraph; the other, the divine guarantee for rational certitude, is simply announced independently of the first principle of philosophy and without any preparation whatsoever.

If its popular character deprives the *Discourse* of the amount and level of argumentation we may desire or be accustomed to, the mode in which its thought is popularized has posed another sort of difficulty for interpretation of the work. That it contains an intellectual autobiography has led some who toil in the fields of historical accuracy to devalue the *Discourse*, at least implicitly, because it is not factual, that is, because it does not report the actual scientific practice of Descartes but is an artful account.[2] Yet Descartes unapologetically describes the *Discourse* as a fable or

---

1. *Oeuvres de Descartes*, ed. Charles Adam and Paul Tannery, 11 vols. (Paris: J. Vrin, 1964–1974). Hereafter abbreviated as AT. The *Discourse* is found in vol. 6. Citations in English, except where explicitly indicated, are from *The Philosophical Writings of Descartes*, trans. J. Cottingham, R. Stoothoff, and D. Murdoch (Cambridge: Cambridge University Press, 1985), vol. 1. Hereafter abbreviated C; vol. 2 is abbreviated C.v.2.

2. See, e.g., John Schuster, "Whatever Should We Do with Cartesian Method? Reclaiming Descartes for the History of Science," in *Essays in the Philosophy and Science of René Des-*

history, understanding both to be products of serious arts, and to be so appealing to the imagination that he even provides us with cautions for reading them.³ The problem that the autobiographical form raises is not how to adjust it to events as they happened, but how to interpret the story that the *Discourse* tells, including Descartes's reflection upon and rendering of those events.

That it is a coherent story some have doubted, since the parts of the writing, even as artful intellectual history, have proved difficult to fit together. For example, the path to rules of method and the subsequent application of them to mathematical problems described in Part 2 seem to have a tenuous connection to the provisional morality of Part 3. The Stoic moralism in Part 3 appears incompatible with the great designs upon the world hinted at in Part 1 and openly avowed in Part 6. Part 4, with its enforcement of doubt, has a controversial relation to the methodical considerations of Part 2, governed as they are by the rule of clarity and distinctness. And finally—though by no means is this the last of the problems—the assertion of the nonmateriality of the soul, whose nature is thinking, is followed in Part 5 by the claim that reason is a universal instrument. Thus some commentators conclude that the *Discourse* is a groping work, reflecting Descartes's state of transition to his mature thought,⁴ while a few others judge that it lacks literary integrity.⁵ But the

---

cartes, ed. Stephen Voss (New York and Oxford: Oxford University Press, 1993), 195–223. Schuster holds that Descartes had abandoned the idea of a single scientific procedure in the 1620s and that in the *Discourse* he "was cynically exploiting the method as a rhetorical device in the traditional pejorative sense" (219). Schuster does not think of Descartes primarily as a philosopher, but wants to reclaim Descartes for the history of science. He reads the *Rules for the Direction of the Mind* accordingly, and does not attend to philosophical considerations or attempt to interpret the *Discourse* in this article.

3. "But I am presenting my work only as a history, or if you prefer, a fable in which, among certain examples worthy of imitation, you will perhaps also find many others that it would be right not to follow" (AT 4/ C.112). Descartes's advice for interpreting such works is found in two places in part 1: " . . . the charm of fables awakens the mind, while the memorable deeds told in histories uplift it and help to shape one's judgment if they are read with discretion" (AT 5 l.22–25/C.113), and " . . . fables make us imagine many events as possible when they are not. And even the most accurate histories, while not altering or exaggerating the importance of matters to make them more worthy of being read, at any rate almost always omit the baser and less notable events; as a result, the other events appear in a false light, and those who regulate their conduct by examples drawn from these works are liable to fall into the excesses of the knights-errant in our tales of chivalry, and conceive plans beyond their powers" (AT 6 l.31–7 l.10/C.114).

4. Ferdinand Alquié, *La découverte métaphysique de l'homme chez Descartes* (Paris: Presses Universitaires de France, 1950). Alquié advised that we read the *Discourse* as an historical document, preceding and leading to Descartes's "metaphysical discovery of man." The work, according to him, reflects the "diversity of attitudes" Descartes takes toward the world prior to this discovery.

5. *Discourse de la méthode, Précédé d'une introduction historique suivi d'un commentaire critique*,

very problem of seeing its coherence is in great measure caused by the interpretive principle that imports positions from other writings—predominantly the early *Rules for the Direction of the Mind* and the *Meditations on First Philosophy*—in order either to show the inadequacy of the *Discourse* or to invest its statements with a philosophical weight and merit they otherwise would not possess.[6]

This strategy obviously undermines the *Discourse* in an effective way. When particular philosophical claims as they are understood from other writings with intentions, doctrines, and modes of presentation different from the *Discourse* are drawn upon to flesh out and highlight the *Discourse*, they but shadow over its peculiar teachings and difficulties, and efface its singular importance.[7] The *Discourse* is the only writing that treats

---

d'un glossaire et d'une chronologie, by Gilbert Gadoffre (Manchester, UK.: Manchester University Press, 1941). In his introduction, Gadoffre maintained that the work has too many inconsistencies to allow us to believe that it is "une brillante et rapide improvisation de 1636, contenant l'essentiel de la doctrine cartésienne à cette date." Recently, he has adjusted his view, in "La chronologie des six parties," in *Le Discours et sa méthode*, ed. Nicolas Grimaldi and Jean-Luc Marion (Paris: Presses Universitaires de France, 1987), 19–40. Edwin Curley defends the integrity of the work in the same volume, in "Cohérence ou incohérence du *Discours*," 41–64.

6. Gilson saw the *Discourse* as anticipating the later writings and summarizing some of the earlier. His commentary makes copious use of the *Meditations* as well as many other writings. See Etienne Gilson, ed., *Discours de la méthode* (Paris: J. Vrin, 1967).

7. Leon Roth is one of the few to acknowledge this. See his *Descartes' Discourse on Method* (Oxford: Clarendon Press, 1948), where he argues that the *Discourse*, rather than any other writing, is "the primary document for the understanding of Cartesianism" (v). Recently, two scholars claim to have found a metaphysics proper to the *Discourse*. J.-M. Beyssade, "Certitude et fondement: L'évidence de la raison et la véracité divine dans la métaphysique du *Discours de la méthode*," in *Le Discours et sa méthode*, 341–64, insists that the difference between method and metaphysics is marked by the Divine Guarantee, which, coming so late in Part 4, introduces "retrospectively" the doctrine of the *Meditations*. But this is exactly the problem. Since in the *Discourse* the guarantee enters as a fiat, without a hint that clear and distinct evidence is doubtful, the guarantee can only be interpreted as a metaphysical moment rather than a moment of divine revelation by reading into the *Discourse* an interpretation of the *Meditations*. J.-L. Marion, in "La situation métaphysique du *Discours de la méthode*," in *Le Discours et sa méthode*, 365–94, influenced by Heidegger's reading of the *Meditations*, detects an incipient metaphysics even in Descartes's earliest methodical writing, *Rules for the Direction of the Mind*. When considering the *Discourse*, then, Marion finds in the entirely undeveloped assertion of the substantiality of the soul, contained in a single paragraph of Part 4, an elaborate version of a metaphysics midway between the "grey ontology" he ascribes to the *Rules* and the ontotheology he ascribes to the later *Meditations*. See *L'ontologie grise de Descartes* (Paris: J. Vrin, 1975). In a more recent publication, Marion argues that the *Rules* contains the elements of metaphysics: "Instead of marking out an uncrossable frontier between the *Regulae* (and *Discourse*) and *Meditations*, . . . we should recognize that metaphysics is itself embedded in the theory of method, in the *Regulae*, but it is present as a possibility which the *Regulae* does not unfold." See "Cartesian Metaphysics and the Simple Natures," trans. John Cottingham, in *The Cambridge Companion to Descartes*, ed. John Cottingham (Cambridge: Cambridge University Press, 1992), 119–20.

the whole of Cartesian philosophy and shows the parts of that philosophy in relation to one another. But this can be seen only if the *Discourse* is allowed to tell its own story. The "history" or "fable" is the mode in which Descartes renders his philosophical thought.

It is the purpose of this essay to begin to retrieve the philosophy of the *Discourse*. To substantiate fully the claims that the *Discourse* has a philosophical integrity of its own and that it is of first importance in the study of Descartes would require a quite lengthy exposition. Here one central problem will be the subject, namely, the relation between Part 2 and Part 4, or, as it is customarily understood, between method and metaphysics. We shall discover the need to depart from that customary understanding, derived as it is from the *Meditations*. This discovery is one key to the integrity of the work. Section 1 treats the interpretive problem posed by the opening of Part 4, namely, how to understand the search for firm foundations. Section 2 turns to Part 2 of the *Discourse* to show that the four rules, usually regarded as a summation of Cartesian method, cannot be understood independently of the philosophical enterprise begun in Part 1 of the work. In the *Discourse* philosophy begins not with Part 4 but at the beginning of the text. Thus method is not science in distinction from or prior to philosophy, and the relation under investigation here is not at bottom between method or science and metaphysics, but between methodical philosophy and its foundation or first principle. In Section 3 we examine the opening paragraphs of Part 4 in light of the problem they are meant to address, the problem of the infirmities in methodical philosophy. We shall see how Part 4 provides a foundation for that philosophy. In the concluding Section 4 we briefly consider the issue of metaphysics in the *Discourse* as well as the role of the Divine Guarantee with respect to the foundation of philosophy.

1. THE PROBLEM OF FOUNDATIONS IN PART 4

The philosophical thought expressed in the *Meditations* is often judged to be found in Part 4, if anywhere in the *Discourse*. Subjects treated in this part are resonant of themes around which the *Meditations* as a whole is built: what comes to be called the "cogito," the assertion of the nonmateriality of the soul, and the consideration of the Divine Being. That these teachings of Part 4 are different from those in the *Meditations*, at least in amplitude and in purpose, has not posed an obstacle for many. The purpose of the *Discourse* is either ignored or slighted,[8] and

---

[8]. In Part 6 Descartes treats the purposes for which he wrote and published the *Discourse*. He

the sketchiness of its arguments precisely at points where it seems to anticipate the *Meditations* is treated as an open invitation to the doctrines of the *Meditations*, even when it comes to understanding the very turn away from method. In such views the *Discourse* is taken to reveal that method, or Descartes's early concern with a science that was certain, led directly to the turn to a different approach, to the metaphysical subjects alluded to or summarized in Part 4. As a consequence, the *Discourse* is reduced to the position of host to a more illustrious guest.

Such an interpretation must confront the difficulty posed by the reflections that open Part 4. At first sight, there seems to be little difficulty, since Part 4 begins by dramatically announcing and specifying its difference from earlier parts. Here there is to be something new, something "metaphysical" and "out of the ordinary." Even in its difference, however, Part 4 is tied to earlier parts, especially to Part 2, for Descartes reveals this extraordinary thought expressly so that one may judge if the "foundations already laid are firm enough." It is on the issue of the "foundations already laid" that the difficulty arises. If we are guided by the *Meditations*, we are likely to see certitude as the crux of the issue: the methodical perspective undergoes a confrontation with philosophical skepticism in Part 4 and becomes justified by the certitude of the first principle of philosophy, "I think, therefore I am," or perhaps ultimately by the Divine Guarantee. Viewed in this way, Part 4 presents the transformation from Cartesian method or science to Cartesian philosophy, a philosophy that comes to sight through doubt, is founded on certitude, and is developed as a metaphysics.

Part 4 of the *Discourse* calls such a view of itself into question, because in the first place the doubt of Part 4 is not "hyperbolic" as is that of the *Meditations*. Although demonstrations, that is to say, the results of the new reasoning process announced in Part 2, are doubted, the cornerstone of that process, clear and distinct evidence, escapes the series of doubts that lead to the first principle. Although it calls into question "all the arguments I had previously taken as demonstrative proofs," the argument supposedly leading to this conclusion is formulated so as to circumvent the issue whether clear and distinct evidence is intrinsically dubitable. We are asked to allow errors in reasoning committed by others to call our own reliability into question. Some explanations for errors in reasoning go unmentioned—carelessness and deficient abilities—as does the attentiveness to

---

cites as reasons not only the great advantages for human life of his practical philosophy, but also the need to safeguard his reputation and to encourage help from others in making scientific progress.

clear and distinct evidence by which they can be avoided. Clear and distinct evidence as such is not doubted.[9] As regards indubitable evidence, then, Parts 2 and 4 are continuous and thus the problem of evidence is not the problem to which Descartes alludes at the opening of Part 4, the problem whether the foundations are sufficiently firm.

Second, Descartes not only identifies the "first principle of the philosophy I was seeking," he also asserts that clear and distinct evidence underlies it. Descartes claims that he is assured of its truth because he sees "very clearly that, to think, it is necessary to be."[10] What is more, the "general rule" of truth that he immediately formulates is a virtual reaffirmation of the first rule of method: "[T]hings that we conceive very clearly and very distinctly are completely true." But this means that the relation between the two parts is the reverse of what is usually asserted. The meditations upon the foundations of philosophy show not that method is surpassed and grounded in certainty in Part 4, but that the cornerstone of method, clear and distinct evidence, is and has been all along the foundation of philosophy. The "turn" inaugurated in Part 4 no longer looks like a turn to philosophy, but the continuation of method and the derivation of the first principle of philosophy from it.

This difficulty explains why some deny that the *Discourse* ever advances beyond a scientific perspective. They may use as corroborating evidence Descartes's comprehensive claims about method made in Part 1: "I formed a method whereby . . . I can increase my knowledge gradually and raise it little by little to the highest point allowed by the mediocrity of my mind and the short duration of my life."[11] But this view has its own serious defect: it does not explain Descartes's claim to have provided a first principle of philosophy in Part 4, nor how that first principle secures foundations that seemed to be infirm.[12]

To extricate ourselves from these problems, let us first reconsider the question of foundations, for it is because the issue of firm foundations has been assumed by many to center on certitude or indubitability that the problems appear at their most perplexing. If, on the issue of certainty, Part 2 and Part 4 are continuous, then, rather than devising ways to circumvent the anomalies caused by this assumption in order to fit the *Discourse* with the *Meditations*, it is more reasonable to conclude that the

---

9. See Alquié's edition of the Discourse in *Oeuvres philosophiques* (Paris: Editions Garnier Frères, 1963), 1.602n2.
10. AT 33 l.16–19/C.127.
11. AT 3/C.113.
12. Such problems may account for why Beyssade calls on the Divine Guarantee to provide not only support for clear and distinct evidence, but also a reason, however retrospective, why such support is needed, in order to read into the *Discourse* the context of the *Meditations*.

problem of firm foundations lies elsewhere. We must ask what foundations are under examination, what infirmities they are liable to, and what is it that secures these foundations. We shall discover that the reason the relation between Part 2 and Part 4 has proved so troubling is that the character of those two parts has been misunderstood: Part 4 does not initiate the turn to philosophy; rather, it secures the first principle of the philosophical activity initiated at the beginning of the work. The *Discourse* itself forces us to abandon the equivalence between method and science, and the simple equivalence between philosophy and metaphysics in terms of which so many who begin with interpretations imported from other texts have attempted to understand the relation between these two parts. In order to see this, we turn to the sustained reflection which results in the positing of four rules in Part 2.

2. THE PHILOSOPHICAL CHARACTER OF METHOD

It is often taken for granted that the four rules sketched in Part 2 of the *Discourse* are a summary of Cartesian method,[13] but what the character of that method is and how it is to be used is difficult to determine. Numerous problems arise if we attempt to fill out these brief rules, perhaps using the *Rules for the Direction of the Mind*, or to detect their presence in Descartes's own scientific practice. However interesting and intricate these problems may be, in the *Discourse* they are overshadowed in importance by the necessity to understand their fundamental context. If we look to the context in which they are proposed, if we ask what is their purpose and what leads to their being posited, we discover that the four rules are a part of Cartesian philosophy. Then if we take into account Descartes's claims about method—its purpose, its character, its origin— we see that, far from being a procedure belonging to a scientific, nonphilosophical phase, it is in fact a component of Descartes's philosophical project, a project being described and partially executed from the beginning of the *Discourse*. Part 4 of the work is launched in order to give the philosophical project a firm foundation. The story that takes Descartes from dissatisfaction with the Schools and the world to success in solving numerous mathematical problems by means of a new procedure, and ultimately to foundation in a first principle, reveals the institution and character of Cartesian philosophy.

Consider the brief résumé in Part 2 recounting Descartes's reflections on logic, geometrical analysis, and algebra, reflections that issue in the four rules. We are told in this account that the four rules are meant

---

13. See Gilson, *Discours*, 96, for example.

to replace a barren logic overloaded with precepts as well as tedious and overly complex procedures in the mathematical sciences. As a corrective, the rule of indubitable evidence, combined with rules requiring orderly division of problems and sequentially certain steps, are both productive and reliable, as his success in solving mathematical problems attests. But notice how the story allows him to remove other philosophical theses and replace them with those of his own.

First of all, Descartes applies the procedure to mathematics but purposely disregards relevant philosophical issues. Confronted with the differences among the special mathematical sciences, Descartes treats the relations and proportions that obtain without considering the objects in which they obtain. But in the received tradition the mathematical sciences had been distinguished into special sciences for philosophical reasons, primarily because of the kind of object in which the mathematical properties and relations are present. Descartes knew these reasons, and had expressly repudiated them in the *Rules*.[14] In that work he replaced the philosophical underpinnings of the tradition with a different philosophical account. He claimed that one can treat relations and proportions without specifying the kind of quantities being so treated, by using the notion of "magnitudes in general."[15] He even described powers of the mind by which such magnitudes may be known and properly used. In the *Discourse* he does not argue this thesis; instead, he proposes it as if it were merely a matter pertaining to mathematics, and as if mathematics were not only in practice but also theoretically independent of philosophical claims. In such fashion, he circumvents philosophical controversies, relying instead on the story to persuade us of his view.

Second, the rules are proposed as directives for human inquiry. To stipulate that true knowledge must begin only with what is clear and certain; to propose that at each stage our learning must clearly follow from the preceding step; and to lay down rules for knowing without any consideration of beings, or, more cautiously, of what "objects" are under investigation, are philosophical claims.[16] And whether Descartes succeeded or failed in finding a rigorous procedure that he did or did not

---

14. J. Klein, *Greek Mathematical Thought and the Origin of Algebra*, trans. Eva Brann (Cambridge, Mass: MIT Press, 1968); David R. Lachterman, *The Ethics of Geometry* (London: Routledge, 1989).

15. AT 10.440–41/C.58.

16. The brief exposition of rules in Part 2 is utterly devoid of assertions about being or existence. The first rule simply states conditions under which "things" (*choses*) are accepted as true. But it does not tell us how to understand these "things." Later, in Part 4, and after the Divine Guarantee, Descartes asserts that "our ideas or notions, being real things (*choses réelles*), and coming from God, cannot be anything but true, in every respect in which they are clear and distinct" (AT 38/C.130). Nowhere does the *Discourse* explicate what "real things" means.

use in his practice, he never once faltered in his opinion that there must be a new order of reasoning, one that rejects the senses as a starting point for knowledge, begins with what is evident to the mind, and will perfect reasoning.

Finally, the strange sequence reveals the real order of his story. Descartes portrays himself as a young man who is in search of something both certain and useful, but fails to find it either in his studies or in the ways of the world. So he decides to examine all his opinions with his own reason as a guide and measure against which all his opinions will be judged: "I could not do better than to undertake, once for all, to remove them [his opinions] so that I could afterwards replace them either with better ones or even with the same ones, once I had adjusted them to the level of reason."[17] Given the buildup of Part 1 we expect him to begin to execute this urgent task, but he does not do it. Instead, he looks for "the true method for arriving at the knowledge of everything of which [his] mind is capable."[18] But if his opinions are so suspect, how can he be assured of finding a true method *before* he has purged them from himself? The method replaces and stands outside the very self-examination he had led us to think indispensable. Rather than a universal or unprejudiced examination of opinions, we have a positing of rules; and the positing of rules is overseen by a decision or "resolution" to adopt the models of architectural design and legislation, of particular kinds of human achievement, as the appropriate ones for the human mind. The story we are being told, then, is not of a series of intellectual steps taken out of a search for certitude, but of a series of resolutions made in order to establish a new kind of philosophy.

Part 2 begins with reflections on perfection in works and deeds, most notably the deed of legislation or founding. Three qualities of "perfection" are identified. First, in each case examined, a single individual is responsible for the achievement, obedient only to his own design. Let us call this "autonomy." It refers primarily to the source, the designer or legislator. Second, the design is simple and ordered, a sign of the work of reason. Let us call this "rational order." It refers to the characteristic of the design or law. Third, each case promotes an effective, praiseworthy, even magnificent result. This we shall call "effectiveness," related to the end or purpose of the design or law.

These qualities of perfection govern the positing of the four rules.[19] Descartes salvages what he can from the tradition in logic and mathematics, and incorporates it within rules of his own devising, rules character-

---

17. AT 13/ C.117.
18. AT 17/C.119.
19. For the list of rules, see AT 18/C.120.

ized by indubitability, by simplicity, and by order, so that each step is clearly linked to previous steps, and by effectiveness in solving problems, at least in mathematics at this point. The four rules are stipulations for the inquiring mind, rules for how it ought to proceed, laid down by their architect for the purpose of solving problems.

Whatever the efficacy of clear and distinct evidence, its position and importance is derivative from a larger, philosophical condition. The first rule of method is not the principle guiding the legislation of rules, but simply one, indeed, the chief rule issuing from the decision of their legislator. The legislation of the rules in no way meets the criteria established within the rules, nor does it attempt to do so. It is Descartes's decision, made in solitude, that reason's activity ought to imitate certain productive arts in their effective purposiveness, in their rationally designed, instrumental character, and in their origin in a single or autonomous maker. This unique act of intellect and will guides the legislation of the rules in Part 2. That is the real meaning of his decision to adjust all to the level of reason. The way to the perfection of reason, or its closest approximation, is the achievement of a human designer taking as his model the achievements of designers and legislators in the past, but looking to surpass them in the magnitude of his deed.[20]

The adoption of human achievement in works and founding deeds as the model of perfection for the human mind is a decision of great consequence, perhaps the defining step of Cartesian philosophy, for it is a rejection of and replacement for not only textbook philosophical thought, thought as it had been codified and presented in the Schools, but also speculative philosophical reflection altogether. The immediate aim of the decision is to transform philosophy into an art.[21] Once again Descartes achieves this revolutionary purpose without confronting the prior tradition directly. He had dismissed traditional philosophical thought in Part 1 by means of the attack on the teachings of the Schools. Instead of facing any tenet directly, he chose to present the whole body of

---

20. "... if among the occupations of men as men, there is one which has solid worth and importance, I dare think it is the one I have chosen" (AT 3/C.112, my translation). See Art. 156, *The Passions of the Soul* AT 11.447–48/C.385.

21. AT 31/C.126–27. In the Aristotelian and Platonic traditions "art" is only one and not the most noble among human activities. See *Nicomachean Ethics* 6, and *Republic* 10, for example. Epicurus rejected the way of prior education and mathematics, replacing it with the way of our senses in order that we attain the highest pleasure; see *Letter to Herodotus*. See also J. M. Rist, *Epicurus* (Cambridge: Cambridge University Press, 1972). And although virtue is an art according to prominent Stoics, the art must be ordered in accordance with nature, the natural whole. See the discussion of Zeno by F. E. Sparshott, "Zeno on Art: Anatomy of a Definition," in *The Stoics*, ed. John Rist. (Berkeley and Los Angeles: University of California Press, 1978), 273–91.

letters and thought in its institutional form, and to level skeptical criticisms against it in that derivative guise. The result is that he defeats the tradition without having to engage it directly in battle.[22] The opening paragraphs of Part 2 show just how radical is his achievement and his design. Descartes there singles out and adopts human achievement as a model of perfection for human inquiry without once considering the two most powerful standards for that activity in the tradition, nature and God.[23] Only *after* the true method is legislated does he turn, in Part 4, to consider these alternatives; but at that point he is not at all interested in considering them as possible guides for the mind. Instead, he reformulates our relationship to them in light of that with which he has decided to replace them.

As long as we take the story as recounting stages of an inquiry on the way to Cartesian philosophy, we do not sufficiently attend to the decision that establishes the rules with clear and distinct evidence in a primary position, and we accept too quickly the revision that is being carried out. Descartes hands over responsibility for the mind's conduct to human devising: look to a goal, and design a plan from one's own resources to achieve it. Only if some human being—namely, René Descartes—using his own reason independently of other authorities—whether the Schools, or nature, or God—devises a procedure for our minds to follow, can we ultimately succeed in knowing what we seek to know.

The decision to adopt such a model is taken for a purpose both comprehensive of human interests and addressed to the perfection of our natures. He seeks what he regards as the highest and most comprehensive goal, in continuation of that "extreme desire" of his youth for a "clear and certain knowledge of all that is useful for life": "I have formed a method whereby it seems to me that I can increase my knowledge by degrees and elevate it little by little to the highest point that the mediocrity of my mind and the short duration of my life allow."[24] The method is a component of the entire conception. This conception includes the formulation of the goal or purpose, a purpose that extends to morals as well as knowledge in the sciences, the means to the goal, and the source or initiation of the goal. The "rules" laid down in Part 2 belong to the second of these. They are a revision in the procedure of thinking with respect to truth in the mathematical sciences. But if we fail to consider

---

22. AT 6–9/C.113–15.
23. God is mentioned in the reflections on perfection as having made laws to govern religion. Note how restricted is God's lawmaking. He is not described here as maker of natural laws. Not until Part 5, that is to say, after the founding of philosophy, does Descartes assert that God has established "certain laws" in nature (AT 41/C.131).
24. AT 3/C.112.

their source, the resolution to model inquiry on human achievements, and their end, the successful explanation of perplexities with an ultimate view to perfection of mind, we then fail to assess their meaning correctly—we blind ourselves to their philosophical character, and to the philosophical character of the *Discourse* as a whole.

At this point it becomes clear in what respect these "foundations already laid" require further support. The reflections on perfection in works and deeds that opens Part 2 show us that the standard of clarity and distinctness belonging to the rules is not the standard belonging to the adoption of the rules, to the choice, or "resolution" that instituted them. We may acknowledge that evidence such as the first rule describes inevitably demands our assent; yet it is by no means clear that this kind of evidence is the only standard. Is there any reason why it should be the cornerstone of a way of inquiry, other than that Descartes has decided to put it there? This is a pressing problem, given that Descartes anticipates solving questions in physics,[25] while at this point he has made no connection between this kind of evidence and natural beings or their properties. In fact, no connection to beings has been appealed to or been made in fashioning the rules at all. These connections have been purposely avoided lest they compromise the autonomy as well as the strategy of their designer; they may even require alteration of the rules of method. Even so, some foundation other than the imitation of architects and legislators must be provided if the procedures are to be appropriate for inquiry into nature.

This points to a more radical problem of foundations. The adoption of an artisanal model for human inquiry looks like a limitation of rational powers. If Descartes simply uses standards of perfection taken from architecture and legislation in an art of human reasoning altogether, he relegates that art to the status of other arts. It becomes one among many. Yet a true art of human inquiry cannot be a mere imitation of characteristics found in other arts, it must be their basis. The characteristics of perfection must be founded on powers belonging to humans as such.

3. THE FOUNDATION OF METHOD

The philosophic enterprise that Descartes is founding arises out of a desire both for truth in the sciences and for a sure, commodious way to live. His claim is that satisfaction of this twofold desire requires human

---

25. "... since I did not restrict the method to any particular subject-matter, I hoped to apply it as usefully to the problems of the other sciences as I had to those of algebra" (AT 21/C.121). Descartes goes on to say that the principles of these sciences depend on philosophy, and that he had not yet discovered any certain principles in philosophy. But this does

devising at the outset in accordance with the model of legislation or founding. Part 2 of the *Discourse* brings this claim out into the open; but Part 2 prescribes rules that seem to advance, or promise to advance, only one portion of that goal, truth in the sciences. To treat the question of the moral aim would require that Part 3 also be examined in relation to Part 4. This merits its own study, but let us simply take note of two crucial considerations. First, discoveries in the sciences are of pressing importance to moral life, as Descartes will suggest in Part 5 and openly state in Part 6,[26] because they clarify the relation of our passions to bodiliness and thereby promise us some management of them through medicine. Second, the provisional morality of Part 3 must be considered as part of the revision of the tradition begun in Part 1, and that means with respect to human and nonhuman authorities, especially because of the decisive role of choice or resolution in Part 4, as we shall see.

In Part 4 Descartes brings his philosophical enterprise before two other, alternative guides for human endeavor, but he treats these separately and differently. Nature or the natural order is at issue from the opening of Part 4 through the discovery of the first principle of philosophy up to and including the assertion of the general rule of truth; he begins his consideration of God or a divine order only after that point, and continues it through the remainder of Part 4. The foundation of methodical philosophy requires that the meaning of nature be reformulated and incorporated into philosophy; God emerges as an issue once philosophy has received its foundation. Consequently, we turn now to the first of these.

The triad of perfections characteristic of human achievement singled out at the opening of Part 2 point to a triad of human resources: the autonomy or freedom to design; the intelligence by which that design is fashioned; and the power to execute or achieve the design. Adopting this artisanal model as the model for the most important, most satisfying human endeavor, might seem to be a limitation, however remarkable those resources. As we noted in the previous section, Descartes wants not

---

not say that he had not been engaged in philosophy himself, nor that he has not begun to carry out a revision in philosophy. At the end of Part 3, we are told that he put off the inquiry into a "foundation of philosophy more certain than the vulgar" (my translation) for some nine years. Again, this does not allow us to conclude that his own philosophical thought began only with the considerations of Part 4 (AT 30/C.126).

26. See the summary of the *Treatise on Man* in Part 5 (AT 55–56/C.139) for a mechanical account of the passions, to which Descartes adds the assertion at the end of Part 5 that the soul "must be more closely joined and united with the body in order to have, besides this power of movement, feelings and appetites like ours and so constitute a real man" (AT 59/C.141). In Part 6 he makes the connection explicit: medicine is essential for wisdom (AT 62/C.143).

to practice another allied art, but to establish the fundamental character of human reasoning, and thus provide a foundation for all arts. Part 4 moves to this deeper level. Through a radical exercise of freedom it rethinks the situation of the human mind with respect to knowledge—which simultaneously redefines the relation of the mind to the properties of natural beings—so as to support the legislation of rules. The three resources noted above shift into place as the most important considerations. In this way Part 4 provides the foundation for Cartesian philosophy.

As with Part 2, Part 4 virtually begins with a decision, the adoption of a governing resolution: "But since I now wished to devote myself solely to the search for truth, I thought it necessary to do the very opposite and reject as if absolutely false everything in which I could imagine the least doubt." This resolution marks a difference between this part of the *Discourse* and Part 2. The resolution here is not a mere application of the first rule asserted in Part 2; it is much more sweeping. The first rule was a rule for inclusion: accept only what is so clearly and distinctly present to mind that it is indubitable. It makes no pronouncement on what escapes this kind of evidence either because it is uncertain or because it does not present itself to the mind spontaneously in this fashion. What we cannot admit as true according to the first rule of Part 2 has a status that the rule itself cannot determine: such things may turn out to be false, but they may also turn out to reveal themselves clearly and openly; or they may also remain uncertain and yet have an important role to play in knowledge. The resolution of Part 4 makes the decisive step by pronouncing on those matters that lie outside the perimeter of rule 1, so that whatever can be imagined to have the least doubt is to be considered false. This rejects the claim any dubitable opinion or perception may have upon our knowledge, but it also, as we shall see, is a means for extending the domain of certain knowledge.

The resolution of Part 4 is a radical decision to explore and expand the boundaries of rational thought by removing limits already in place. The capacity for certitude is not adapted to rules in a simple imitation of an external model, artisanship, as it is in Part 2; instead, Descartes concentrates on what one's own mind can imagine as possible in thought. What one can doubt, one will doubt, as far as is possible. This resolution has at its core rational freedom or autonomy, since it purposely allows only one kind of constraint to affect it: indubitability. The autonomy of artisanship is derivative from this more fundamental freedom. It means that designers of buildings and lawgivers are not just models for us to imitate; by looking to them we do not look away from what is rational, provided we know how to look to our full powers. We are free to think what we may, allowing ourselves to be constrained in thought only by what is indubitable. Thus Descartes takes what had been regarded as a defining limitation of art, especially in the Aristotelian tradition, and transforms it into the mind's very virtue; that is to say, art had been regarded as of a lesser rank than speculative thought because art does not concern itself with what is necessarily, but rather what could be other than it is; and it brings about that which would not come to be by nature alone. The resolution at the start of Part 4 will allow these traits to be sources of advancement in knowledge and effectiveness. The mind opens itself to possibilities both in thought and in deed. Philosophy can concern itself with what comes about due to our intervention. The freedom or autonomy of mind is not thematized in the *Discourse*, it is exemplified and used: without it there could be no discovery of the first principle of philosophy. The foundation of this philosophy requires the exercise of a radical freedom of reason.[27]

The series of doubts that follow show that the reinterpretation of nature and natural properties of beings is the first effect of the resolution. The first doubt concludes with the falsity of what is often called the "similitude" thesis, namely, that the senses present us with true or real properties in things. The resolution requires us to equate sometime error with inevitable deception. Thus, because we are sometimes deceived by the senses, we reject them as false, thereby removing the possibility of a sensible correction of the senses, as, for example, when upon closer inspection an apparently round tower is discovered to be square. The result of the doubt is that we no longer take unreflectively the sensible presentation of things around us and the properties of those things. We are now ready to accept the view that the causes of our sensations and the sensations themselves are different. This means that sensible evidence plays no part in the knowledge of natural phenomena. Nature does not present itself for our knowledge through the senses. The opinion that it does so has been removed as an obstacle to our knowledge.

The second doubt, as we described in Section 1, includes demonstrations we have already received, but excludes clear and distinct evidence present before the mind. The character of evidence remains the same as it was in Part 2; now, however, the truths we may have discovered by using the rules are going to be included in the deeper foundation Part 4 provides. This becomes clear from the third doubt. This last doubt links the conclusions of the previous doubts and brings us to the most important effect of the resolution of Part 4. To the rejection of the senses, it adds a

---

27. There are other allusions to this in the *Discourse*, e.g., in the distinction between "strong" and "weak" minds. The doctrine of the will makes an appearance in *Meditations* Part 4; but a full account of the will would have to have recourse to *Passions of the Soul.*

rejection of any reference to external objects. Because we may dream what we also sense while awake, whatever we sense has the status of a dream. If we accept this equivalence between waking and dreaming, we regard them as mental episodes or mere thoughts, the causes of which are not determinable from those thoughts themselves. Thus mathematical demonstrations and propositions, even clear and distinct ones, are mental episodes or thoughts. The purpose of the third doubt is not so much to call into question our ability to make the distinction between waking and dreaming, to raise a theoretical problem for us to ponder, as to achieve the equivalence of thoughts. That thoughts can be rendered equivalent does not mean that there is no difference among them, nor that we cannot ourselves differentiate among them. It is a denial that thoughts, when considered in and of themselves, present us with any clear connection to existing things, with one exception, which we see in the first principle. In this respect, mathematical demonstrations and square towers are the same: they are mental episodes or thoughts.

Thus we see how, even before the first principle is enunciated, some of the problems we noted about Part 2 are being addressed. No such equivalence between sensible and mathematical thought could be made on the basis of the account in Part 2. To bring the standard of clear and distinct evidence directly to sensible evidence would illicitly extend it over domains it cannot pronounce upon and would immediately reflect on the legitimacy and adequacy of the rules. Even if one were willing to acknowledge the superior certitude of rational evidence over that achieved by or through the senses, that alone would not exclude the senses from a fundamental and irreplaceably original role in the acquisition of knowledge. The resolution of Part 4 and consequent doubts topple the insistence of sensible evidence while reformulating its meaning. The senses are no longer trustworthy as that in which or through which properties of beings, especially natural beings, are revealed. Henceforth, both the sensible and the intelligible are understood as mental episodes or thoughts.

As a result, clear and distinct evidence extends to nonmathematical and nonlogical problems, such as problems about natural phenomena. What stood in the way was not that clear and distinct evidence was doubtful or unreliable; quite the contrary. The problem was twofold. First, in Part 2 evidence is limited. Questions of existence and of the particular properties of existing things fall outside its scope. Second, sensible evidence, that is to say, the sensible presentation of the sensible, however varying and unreliable, had seemed to be and had been regarded as a standard or at least a starting point for thought about natural beings. The resolution made at the outset of Part 4 removes both the limitation of clear and distinct evidence and the claim of sensible evidence to be some kind of standard, since it does not emerge out of our own reason. One could put the matter another way. Just as Part 1 undermined the authority of tradition and the Schools, the opening paragraphs of Part 4 undermine that of nature as it is naturally available to us through our senses. What appears to us in nature is not naturally ordered to our minds; it is necessary to reexamine these appearances rationally and to order these things ourselves. Nature has been readied for the activity of reason.[28]

These several strands are united and deepened in the first principle, "I think, therefore I am."[29] We have indicated that the series of doubts leads to a stratum in which all thoughts are regarded as mental episodes, but they are connected in a more important way. All thoughts, whether mathematical propositions, sensible presentations, dreams, or illusions, whether dubitable or not, lead to the same thing, to the knowledge, and therefore to the assertion "I am." And to no other knowledge do they all invariably lead. This assertion is the indubitable core in every thought, therefore it is first.

It is first, but it is not first to us.[30] The way back to "I am" requires a resolution to make it appear. The ready certitude of some thoughts, such as that of some mathematical propositions, may encourage us to tease out other mathematical implications or to solve mathematical problems; sense experience in its vividness usually distracts us to supposedly external objects. Both lines of thought appear to lead us away from ourselves. But Descartes has shown that any of these thoughts can be the occasion to notice that one knows one's own existence. By bringing all thoughts into doubt, he clears away everything that might obscure the connection between "I think"—which we may regard as an abbreviation for any and all thoughts—and "I am," and at the same time he allows the primacy of this connection to show forth. Nevertheless, by so referring all thoughts to the single "I am," Descartes has not utterly homogenized them. He has left intact clear and distinct evidence, and he has baptized the unreliability of sensible experience. These ways of differentiating thoughts remain latent, and could be retrieved at any time, obscuring but not obliterating their similarity as mental episodes pointing to one's own existence.

Now we see that the unshakeable certitude of the first principle, although necessary, is by no means the most important qualification for its

---

28. The step to the foundation of philosophy, as well as the character of the foundation, is thus guided by the requirements of Descartes's conception of physics. The investigation of nature so reformulated may require that the procedure of inquiry outlined in Part 2 be altered.
29. The *cogito* of the *Meditations* differs in formulation: "I am, I exist," and is not called the first principle of philosophy.
30. See by contrast Aristotle *Physics* 1 1.

being first. Certainly it is not that which marks the difference between the methodological thought of Part 2 and the foundation for that thought in Part 4. Descartes believes his first principle provides the foundation in several ways. In the first place, the "I think" illustrates that there is a knowledge of existence that is implicit in every thought and yet is utterly independent of the world or of bodiliness, of sensing and of our customary way of taking sensing. One does not need knowledge of anything else as a condition of knowing that one exists. The knowledge is brought into sight by our own intervention, our own decision, but it relies on no other knowledge, hence its autonomy as knowledge. We stress this last point because in other respects it is not autonomous at all. One does need some mental episodes to be taking place in order to know "I am," and the account of the source of these episodes in most cases requires an appeal to the body, as we see in Part 5.[31]

Second, the first principle is the only clearly and distinctly known thing that delivers knowledge about existence. Other matters can be evident in a way that is undeniable, as in the case of mathematical propositions; sensible evidence purports to be evidence about existence, but it is not clear and distinct. Only the first principle combines evidence and knowledge of existence. It is linked to a thing that, in the capacity to experience its own thinking, knows itself to exist.

Third, the primary way this evidence of thinking and existing appears, once obstacles to it are removed, is intimately affective, rather than contemplated or posited.[32] The thinking is neither representational nor characterized by intentionality, as Marion has argued.[33] It is prior to other modes of knowing.

Fourth, as a consequence, the first principle is prior to mathematical and logical principles, especially the first rule. Rational certitude has a place; it is not simply free-floating, as in its independence of the world it might appear to be. We have shown that all thoughts, whether clear and distinct or not, lead, when properly guided, to this evidence of one's own existence. The thinking experience of an existent is prior to logic, to the ordering required in the service of knowledge. The first principle reveals the place where certitude appears as being first and foremost before an attentive human mind in its very thinking. The decision to adopt clear

---

31. AT 55–56/C.139.

32. This shows its difference from the assertion of existence in the ontological argument. Neither should we understand the "I" of Cartesian thinking as a transcendental ego since it is not a nonappearing necessary condition for all appearances.

33. Developing suggestions from M. Henry, Marion proposes that it is a case of "auto-affection," of the soul afffecting itself, and that it allows us to link the cogito to the notion of *générosité* from the *Passions of the Soul*; see J.-L. Marion, "Générosité et phénoménologie," *Les études philosophiques* (January–March 1988): 51–72.

and distinct evidence rests on what undeniably belongs to the human mind. Only someone or something thinking can be the foundation for knowledge. The first rule is now enunciated as a "general rule" discovered out of one's own knowing, rather than being merely legislated into position.

Knowledge, not just mathematical knowledge, but the knowledge of anything, begins with what is present to mind or thinking. The foundation for methodical thought and for legislating a way to knowledge lies in thinking, the thinking of an existent thing, and not in some external, nonhuman source. Descartes considers this thinking a firm terrain since it unifies the universe of thoughts by establishing them in one province and shows that in the fundamental sense of their appearing, our thoughts are not ordered to or shaped by some external criterion, at least one that bears on our knowledge. Surely we are right to want a more ample treatment of the foundation of philosophy than we have here in the *Discourse*, but we do not find elucidation of its deepest problems and ambiguities in the *Meditations*. Although it returns to the subject of the *cogito*, the *Meditations* focuses on certitude, but does little to clarify the fundamental role of the will in acquiring the first principle.[34]

Descartes proposed that philosophy be conceived of as a human institution. Through the inquiry in Part 4 he achieved two things essential to the realization of this conception. He removed obstructions to it and provided it with a foundation. The propensity to think that some natural order of things independent of the human mind guides our knowledge he relegated to the status of an insufficiently founded opinion. We have been languidly related to our world because we have not realized our powers. To other humans and to nonhuman nature we have granted an authority over our thoughts that they do not deserve. The very freedom of mind that has effected the removal of the obstruction lies at the deepest level of the foundation. The human mind is free not only to restrict itself to clear and distinct evidence, but also to think what needs to be thought and to do what needs to be done in order to solve problems. Descartes has founded his philosophy upon the power of the human mind.

4. METAPHYSICAL AND THEOLOGICAL CONSIDERATIONS

In the précis that begins the *Discourse* Descartes asserts that the existence of God and of the human soul "are the foundations of his metaphysics."[35] On these two issues the temptation to slight the *Discourse* and

---

34. We do not have a sustained treatment of the first principle of philosophy in any single Cartesian work.

35. AT 1/C.111.

to introduce doctrines from the *Meditations* is strongest.[36] On these metaphysical issues the difference between the *Meditations* and the *Discourse* ought keep us most on guard. The *Discourse* is a summary of Cartesian philosophy. It presents the methodical teaching and shows its foundation. It will be said that since the subject of the *Meditations* generally coincides with the two designated metaphysical subjects, its being used to understand those subjects in the *Discourse*, or even as a standard against which its teachings should be measured, is justified. But the introductory "Letter to the Sorbonne," besides revealing its wholly different, apologetic intention, tells us that the *Meditations* is itself an application of method, that is to say, of the philosophy given exposition in the *Discourse*.[37] We must learn the metaphysics of the *Discourse* before we evaluate it in light of that in any other text. These subjects, of course, require a further inquiry; yet we can indicate certain considerations that demand our attention.

The discovery of the first principle of philosophy is a discovery that there exists some thing with the power of thinking, able to know that it exists and to experience its own thinking. Descartes calls this "myself" or "soul." In Part 4, the soul first comes to sight having exempted itself from any claims the external world or anything else save rational necessity may make upon it. It knows itself to exist, but not yet what it is. It thinks; that is to say, it has mere thoughts, but how those thoughts may differ from one another, and what may be their cause, it does not know, and cannot know without shifting its attention away from itself exclusively. Then, before the assertion of the general rule, Descartes addresses the question what it is. He invites us to use the terminology of the metaphysics of substance and attribute, claiming that the mind is a substance, that its whole essence or nature is to think, that it does not depend on matter, and is entirely distinct from body.[38] This terminology, originally grounded in a

---

36. "Ces deux vérités, l'existence de Dieu et la nature de l'âme, forment le contenu essentiel de la métaphysique, tant par la connaissance qu'elles nous apportent de Dieu et de l'âme memes que par les conséquences de toutes sortes dont elles sont le fondement. L'existence de Dieu parfait constitue, en effet, la garantie de toutes nos certitudes scientifiques, et la connaissance de l'âme fonde la distinction réelle de l'âme et du corps, vers laquelle tendent les *Méditations métaphysiques* tout entières comme vers le fondement de la physique mécaniste" (Gilson, *Discours*, 355).

37. " ... I was strongly pressed to undertake this task by several people who knew that I had developed a method for resolving certain difficulties in the sciences—not a new method (for nothing is older than the truth), but one which they had seen me use with some success in other areas; and I therefore thought it my duty to make some attempt to apply it to the matter in hand" (AT 7. 3/C.v.2, 4).

38. Since he is unable to doubt without knowing that he exists, he asserts: "I knew I was a substance whose whole essence or nature is simply to think, and which does not require any place, or depend on any material thing, in order to exist. Accordingly this 'I'—that is,

well-articulated if difficult understanding of being and developed with many subtleties throughout the tradition, is given no clarification or amplification by Descartes, and he pays only sparse attention to it in later writings. Given that the Cartesian first principle of philosophy is a radically different one from anything in the tradition, sanctioning a new understanding of the mind and its powers, and that it is laid down for the purpose of founding a philosophy expressly different from that of the tradition, this is a remarkable moment. Heidegger, arguing from the *Meditations*, maintained that the metaphysics of substance is not what is required as a metaphysical foundation for Cartesian method. He faulted Descartes for not having seen his way to the needed metaphysics but tried to remedy Descartes's failure by using his own resources on the *Meditations* exclusively, in order to establish the sense Descartes "himself would have wanted."[39]

Before we charge Descartes with relying too much on the very tradition he sought to reform, we must consider the whole case in the *Discourse*. In Part 5 Descartes provides a mechanical explanation of activities once attributed to soul, waking, sleeping and dreaming, sensation, hunger, thirst, motion, and the like, and insists that the rational soul cannot be "derived from the power of matter."[40] It must be expressly created, he tells us, and "cannot be lodged in the human body like a pilot in his ship, except perhaps to move its members, but it is necessary that it be joined and united more closely with it in order to have sentiments and appetites like ours and thus to compose a true man."[41] The metaphysical

---

the soul by which I am what I am—is entirely distinct from the body"(AT 22–23/C.127). Later Descartes responds to the objection that from the fact that the mind does not perceive itself to be anything other than a thinking thing, it does not follow that its nature consists in being only a thinking thing: ". . . it was not my intention to make those exclusions [whatever else could belong to the soul] in an order corresponding to the truth of the matter (which I was not dealing with at that stage) but merely in an order corresponding to my own perception. So the sense of the passage was that I was aware of nothing at all that I knew belonged to my essence, except that I was a thinking thing, or a thing possessing within itself the faculty of thinking." See "Preface to the Reader," *Meditations on First Philosophy* AT 7.7–8/C.v.2, 7.

39. "Descartes himself offers a superficial and inadequate interpretation of *res cogitans*, inasmuch as he speaks the language of the doctrines of medieval scholasticism . . . [this is] . . . the most palpable example of earlier metaphysics impeding a new beginning for metaphysical thought. A historiological report on the meaning and nature of Descartes' doctrine is forced to establish such results. A historical meditation on the inquiry proper must strive to think Descartes' principles and concepts in the sense he himself wanted them to have, even if in so doing it should prove necessary to translate his assertions into a different 'language'" (M. Heidegger, *Nietzsche*, trans. Frank A. Capuzzi (San Francisco: Harper & Row, 1982), 4.115.

40. AT 59/C.141 (my translation).

41. Ibid.

view of the *Discourse* with respect to the human soul must take into account all these treatments. Descartes left us plentiful evidence that he thought deeply and complexly about the mind in the *Discourse*, more so than one could gauge from trying to replace its teaching with a metaphysics of substance from the *Meditations*.

On the issue of the Divine Being we must also take into account the specific differences between the treatment in the *Discourse* and that of the *Meditations*. The former is not merely a pale or partial version of the latter. The Divine Being enters the *Discourse* only after the foundation of Cartesian philosophy, a foundation not subject to doubt. In the *Meditations*, God enters as a possible source of deception that we must remove by recourse to arguments for his existence and goodness. The Divine Guarantee, then, differs in function in the two writings. Furthermore, arguments for the existence of God differ in the two works, as others have noted. A second reflection on perfection precedes God's entrance into the *Discourse*. This must be thought about with respect to the first reflection, in Part 2, especially given its strategic importance. Finally, even if the Divine Being is treated more amply in some respects in the *Meditations*, the *Discourse*, but not the *Meditations*, treats God in his cosmological role.

The *Discourse* is a work about the origin and character of Cartesian philosophy. The philosophy is not only Descartes's first principle and the teachings derived from it, but includes the very founding of the philosophy. We have tried to show the character of that philosophy, and the laying of its foundation in the powers of the human mind. We could not consider all parts of the *Discourse* or attempt to show how each part of the work contributes to the whole. We have concentrated on the problem of the relation of Part 2 to Part 4 because it has impeded us most from appreciating the work. As long as teachings taken out of the context and argumentation from other writings substitute for reading the *Discourse*, we cannot begin to discern its unity and philosophical importance.

4 Hobbes and the Dogmatism of the Enlightenment

ROBERT P. KRAYNAK

It would be hard to exaggerate the importance of the Enlightenment for modern civilization. Much of the pride and self-confidence of the modern age arises from the belief that it has overcome the prejudices of the past and replaced them with new modes of thought that are "enlightened"—open-minded rather than close-minded, tolerant rather than intolerant, skeptical and questioning rather than dogmatic and settled. To highlight the contrast between the old and new modes of thinking, the proponents of enlightenment refer to the past as the "Dark Ages"; and they rely on the powerful stigma of this phrase to discredit the older ways of thinking. Whether it be in the treatment of the Christian religion as an outmoded superstition, or of Greek and Latin as dead languages, or of divine right monarchy as an antiquated form of government, or of patriarchy as a relic of primitive societies, modern thinkers have advanced their cause by claiming that the dogmatism of the Dark Ages must give way to the enlightenment of modern civilization.

One of the most important philosophers in developing this rationale for modern civilization was Thomas Hobbes (1588–1679). Although Hobbes was not the first to make such arguments, he invented and popularized the vivid metaphor of the "kingdom of darkness" to stand for the ancient and medieval worlds (especially for Aristotelian and Scholastic philosophy); and he viewed his own philosophy as the best means for bringing light to the darkness of the past. Moreover, it is clear from Hobbes's historical writings that he conceived of his philosophy as a dramatic turning point in history—as the end of dogmatic thinking and the beginning of a new age of intellectual freedom in which science would produce indisputable knowledge and lasting civil peace. In these respects, Hobbes contributed to the founding of the Enlightenment and to its high expectations for the modern world.

It is particularly illuminating, therefore, to reexamine Hobbes's thought and to ask if it lives up to its bold and novel claims. Can it really be shown that the new mode of philosophy developed by Hobbes—his science of enlightenment, as I shall call it—is superior to the older ways because it is less dogmatic? Are the fundamental doctrines of his science, such as mechanistic materialism and the right to self-preservation, adequately grounded and rationally justified; or do they simply reflect Hobbes's idiosyncracies (his well-known diffidence and temperamental extremism)? If his doctrines are not well grounded, are they just another example of philosophical dogmatism—further evidence of Nietzsche's claim that all philosophy is merely the personal confession of the philosopher's deepest instincts?

The answers, I believe, are far more complicated than Nietzsche's sweeping assertion would imply. There *is* something dogmatic about Hobbes's philosophy; but the dogmatism is not simply due to Hobbes's idiosyncracies. Rather, it arises from a dilemma that is inherent in his science of enlightenment. What I hope to show is that Hobbes's attempt to abolish the kingdom of darkness leads him to embrace a view of reason that radically separates the mind from the external world of nature; but the success of his project also requires him to overcome the separation of mind and nature by an act of willful assertion. From this dilemma, a new form of dogmatism arises that is more insidious and dangerous than any kind alleged to spring from classical and medieval thought. To demonstrate my thesis, I shall first attempt to define the science of enlightenment and then explain the ways in which it gives new meaning to the word *dogmatism*.[1]

DEFINING THE ENLIGHTENMENT

It may be presumptuous to begin with a snap definition of the Enlightenment because so many philosophers and scientists have contributed to its origins and development. Yet I believe that a common definition can be derived from a few significant examples of seventeenth- and eighteenth-century thinkers, including Hobbes, and that this definition can serve as a beginning point for examining the underlying assumptions of the Enlightenment.

To arrive at a definition, it is easiest to start with Kant's famous essay, in which he gives a succinct and unforgettable answer to the question "What is enlightenment?" Enlightenment, Kant says, is "man's release

---

1. The argument presented here is an adaption of the last chapter of my book, Robert P. Kraynak, *History and Modernity in the Thought of Thomas Hobbes* (Ithaca, N.Y.: Cornell University Press, 1990), 187–216.

from self-incurred tutelage."[2] The main point of this statement is that enlightenment is the emancipation of the mind from the habit of deferring to authority and the use of one's reason without direction from another. Kant's definition is nicely captured in the slogan used so frequently in American schools and society today: "Think for yourself." In Kant's philosophy, thinking for one's self is part of the larger idea of autonomy, which literally means self-legislation and more generally refers to the development of a moral personality. The Kantian formulation for the Enlightenment can thus be summed up in the notion of autonomous reason.[3]

To sharpen the definition, we might consider another figure who is indisputably a founder of the Enlightenment, Descartes. For Descartes, the Enlightenment is a new method of thinking: the method of radical doubt. It is the resolve to question and doubt all received opinions, and especially to doubt the trustworthiness of the senses as a reflection of the external world. Enlightened thinking prevents one from extending the will to believe to anything that merely *appears* to exist outside the mind without proving that it exists from indubitable premises.[4]

Withough pausing to elaborate these formulations, let us consider the case of Hobbes and make some comparisons. Like Descartes, Hobbes views enlightened thinking as distrust of the senses and of the imagination, as illustrated in the opening chapters of *Leviathan*. In addition to teaching distrust of the senses, Hobbes also teaches, like Kant, distrust of other men—distrust of those who pose as intellectual authorities and who seek to reduce the common people to a condition of tutelage or dependence on their wisdom. In fact, Hobbes gives greater emphasis to the distrust of men than to distrust of the senses; for language (words, speech, logos) is a more deceptive faculty than sensation, and language depends on other men. The deceptions of language are also more dangerous. For those who claim to speak for higher powers, such as God or Nature, seek to impose their opinions and doctrines on others; the result, most often, is sedition, civil war, and the ruin of civilization.

From these remarks, we can see that Hobbes's understanding of en-

---

2. From the essay, "What Is Enlightenment?" in Immanuel Kant, *On History*, trans. and ed. Lewis White Beck (Indianapolis, Ind.: Bobbs-Merrill, 1963), 3.

3. For this formulation, see Ernst Cassirer, *The Philosophy of the Enlightenment* (Boston: Beacon Press, 1955), xi, 3–36. Cassirer basically sees the Enlightenment as the march toward Kant: the progressive development of "the autonomy of reason" that reaches full maturity in the philosophy of Kant.

4. See esp. Part 2 of the *Discourse on Method* and the First and Fourth Meditations of the *Meditations on First Philosophy*, in *The Philosophical Works of Descartes*, 2 vols., trans. Elizabeth S. Haldane and G. R. T. Ross (Cambridge: Cambridge University Press, 1969), 1.87–94, 144–49, 171–79.

lightenment has two sides to it. The first is distrust of the wisdom of authorities—distrust especially of the speech of authorities out of fear of persecution and death over disagreements of opinion. Such distrust is rooted in the "fear of violent death" that Hobbes describes in his political treatises. The other side of enlightenment, which is simply the flip side of fear and distrust, is thinking for one's self or intellectual self-reliance; it requires using only those words that refer to clear thoughts in one's own mind.[5] These simple formulations—distrust of authorities and thinking for one's self—which are developed by Hobbes are very useful as preliminary guides to the Enlightenment.

But they need further clarification. For the older kind of philosophy, classical philosophy as practiced by Socrates, Plato, and Aristotle, also claims to question authorities and to submit received opinions to rational examination. What, then, is new and different about the science of enlightenment?

In the first place, enlightenment science is different from classical philosophy in its attitude toward *opinion*—by which I mean all forms of prescientific knowledge, such as common sense, ordinary language, trust in tradition, received wisdom, and religious faith. Opinion is the beginning point for classical philosophy because its method of reasoning is dialectical (this is also true of medieval philosophy whose disputative method is an adaption of classical dialectics).[6] But it is not true for the philosophers of the Enlightenment, who emphatically reject opinion as the beginning point for reasoning. This important difference may be understood in the following way.

In classical and medieval philosophy, the claim is made that one cannot begin reasoning without already knowing something. For the first act of reason is to question—to ask what something is and why it is so—and one must already possess some knowledge of the phenomenon (if only to identify it) in order to ask such questions. Hence, one must begin with an opinion, which means an untested belief derived from sensations and speech about something, such as the opinion of common sense that the earth is at rest at the center of the universe or the opinion of democratic citizens that justice is equality. The task of reason is to critically examine such opinions, especially when they conflict with other opinions, by treating them as "hypotheses" and testing them, sorting out truth from

---

5. See *Leviathan*, ed. Michael Oakeshott, introduction by Richard Peters (New York: Collier-Macmillan, 1962), chap. 4, p. 7; chap. 5, pp. 41–45; chap. 13, p. 100; chap. 36, pp. 314–17.

6. On the connections between classical dialectics and medieval disputation, see, e.g., Josef Pieper, *Guide to Thomas Aquinas*, trans. Richard Wilson and Clara Wilson (San Francisco: Ignatius Press, 1991), 75–89.

falsehood and eventually arriving at true knowledge of the thing in question. This process of ascending from opinion to knowledge is the heart of dialectics.[7]

Underlying the dialectical method, of course, is the assumption that opinions provide some kind of intuition or divination of the way things really are. In other words, it is assumed that received opinions, however strange, are not wholly arbitrary; they are merely partial, incomplete, or distorted images of reality. All serious opinions make some contact with reality because they are mental responses to something "given" from the world; they even contain embryonic explanations of the phenomenon—of what it is and why it so—however fanciful or mythical those explantions might be. Stated more broadly, the premise of pre-Enlightenment philosophy is that one can begin from opinions because there is some kind of harmony between the mind and reality.

By contrast, Hobbes rejects all trust in opinion as an intuition of reality and as a beginning point for science. He rejects such trust as a vain illusion—as a kind of self-love or vanity in which the human mind insists on believing that there is a harmony between itself and reality. This naive belief, which Hobbes emphatically rejects, might be summarized in one word: *Providence*, the belief that Nature or Nature's God in some fashion cares about the human mind, and wishes to be understood, and actually provides for such understanding with the gifts of sensation and speech.

Because Hobbes rejects the belief in Providence as vanity, he rejects the dialectical method of trying to ascend from opinion to knowledge. Instead, he seeks to abolish opinion altogether and to relegate it to the past, to the dustbin of history. In other words, Hobbes treats opinion as an *historical category*—as something that will disappear over time and be forgotten or that will be remembered only as a relic of a more naive era called the Dark Ages.[8]

This is a new attitude toward opinion. Before the Enlightenment, it was held that opinion (its use as a basis for reasoning) was a permanent feature of the human condition, that error would always coexist alongside of truth, and that conflicts of opinion, including deadly wars and civil wars, would always exist. Because Hobbes rejects the pessimistic implications of the traditional view, his position actually raises a utopian

---

7. See Plato, *Republic*, 531e–539c; and Aristotle, *Topics*, 1.1 and 1.10–11, 8.11.
8. As Strauss says in the context of discussing Spinoza: "The struggle of the Enlightenment against prejudice has an absolute meaning ... [in which] the age of prejudice and the age of freedom stand in opposition to each other.... *'Prejudice' is an historical category*. This precisely constitutes the difference between the struggle of the Enlightenment against prejudice and the struggle against appearance and opinion with which philosophy began its secular journey [in classical philosophy]"; see Leo Strauss, *Spinoza's Critique of Religion*, trans. E. M. Sinclair (New York: Schocken Books, 1965), 181, emphasis added.

claim: that at some point in history—namely, the seventeenth century—opinion and the whole idea of received wisdom will be finally and irrevocably overcome. The utopian claim of relegating opinion and conflicts of opinion to the dustbin of history is a decisive difference between enlightenment science and the classical or medieval versions of dialectical philosophy that it sought to replace.

A second difference may be inferred from the first. The subject matter and method of philosophy are radically changed. If Hobbes rejects trust in opinion and its ultimate assumption of harmony between mind and reality, what remains as a basis for reason? Hobbes's answer is the Mind itself, separated from contact with the external world. In other words, the subject matter of philosophy is no longer Nature or Nature's God, but the human Mind or Understanding. As a result, the Enlightenment *replaces dialectics with introspection* as the method of philosophy. Introspection means looking into the thoughts and passions of the mind, deliberately purged of trust in the external world. The introspective method that Hobbes advocates is to read over the thoughts or ideas of the mind, and to study their operations and discard their illusions. Introspection may also be used in the study of natural phenomena—that is, in physics—but Hobbes treats the ideas in the mind as nothing more than appearances of the external world and only speculates about how they might have been produced in the mind, without ever knowing their ultimate causes.[9]

This view of the Mind standing alone, reflecting on its own operations and appearances, is commonly called autonomous reason or the self-reliant mind of the Enlightenment; and its premise is the disharmony of mind and reality.

THE HIDDEN PRESUPPOSITIONS OF THE ENLIGHTENMENT

If this analysis is correct, we must acknowledge that the basis of the Enlightenment will be unusually hard to find and may even be deliberately obscured or hidden. For the science of enlightenment must claim to stand on its own foundations—on mental ideas purged of every form of trust that connects them to the external world. These mental ideas must then be used for self-evident or arbitrary definitions, the axioms of a deductive science. By building in this fashion, enlightenment science can claim to possess the intellectual certainty of a self-contained system.

But does Hobbes actually build his system in this fashion? Does he

---

9. See *Leviathan*, "Author's Introduction," and *De Corpore*, 4.29.

begin simply by positing self-evident definitions, as his treatises seem to suggest, or does he begin with some prior knowledge of the world? I contend that his definitions are derived in response to a concrete problem in the real world; and his understanding of the problem precedes the science proper. In other words, Hobbes's definitions may appear to be self-generated; but they have presuppositions that come from historical experience. Historical knowledge precedes science in Hobbes's thought, although he cannot admit this fact in his scientific treatises. To uncover the historical presuppositions, we need to consult Hobbes's historical works, particularly his history of the English Civil War, *The Behemoth*.

These works reveal that Hobbes was a serious student of what he called "civil history"—the history of civilization—and developed his own historical theory focusing on the development of the human mind. Stated briefly, Hobbes's theory of history is as follows. Civilization emerges from barbarism when men have the peace and leisure to cultivate the arts and sciences and to refine language and reason. Gradually, the rule of brute force in barbaric conditions, where military conquerors and tribal patriarchs were the supreme powers, was replaced by a more civilized kind of rule: the rule of opinion about law, justice, and right. These opinions were refined into doctrines by learned men, such as priests, philosophers, and scholars. Hence, civilization seems like an advance over barbarism because the rule of brute force is replaced by a more gentle kind of rule, by intellectual persuasion or by opinions and doctrines of right.

But Hobbes does not think that this development makes civilized men more happy than savages or barbarians. Somewhat like Rousseau, he thinks it makes civilized life more miserable. For the learned scholars who preside over the opinions and doctrines of civilization are vain and ambitious. With naive vanity, they place their trust in appeals to higher authorities, such as God, Nature, or custom; and with ruthless ambition, each one seeks to have his own view recognized as the authoritative wisdom of society. But everyone stakes his claim of superiority on an appeal to authority, which leaves the parties no recourse but violence to settle their disagreements. Hence, they gather followers and fight over doctrines, and *doctrinal warfare* becomes the plague of civilization.

This was true, Hobbes argues, in ancient Israel when Moses claimed to be the chief prophet and was challenged by Aaron and Korah, as well as in the days of Israelite kingship when the latter prophets criticized royal rule. It was also true in the time of Socrates, when dialectical philosophy unsettled the Greek city-states; and true again in the Middle Ages when Scholastic disputation rocked the universities; and still true in Hobbes's own time when the doctrinal conflicts of the Protestant Reformation and the democratic Levellers produced the English Civil War. In fact, Hobbes sees the English Civil War as the inevitable outcome of the doctrinal politics built into Western civilization, implying that the very activity of civilization—its cultivation of the arts and sciences—is the cause of its own destruction.[10]

This historical analysis, of course, leaves Hobbes with a profound dilemma. On the one hand, he could abandon civilization and try to return to the ignorance of barbarism. But Hobbes rejects this option because he saw (unlike Rousseau) that savages were killers too, although Hobbes concedes that they were less cruel and vindictive than civilized intellectuals. On the other hand, if a return to prescientific life is undesireable, how could Hobbes be assured that the philosophy and science of civilization would be more effective in ending doctrinal warfare? Would not any new *doctrine* simply create another round of doctrinal warfare? Hobbes's only hope lies in a doctrine that is somehow qualitatively different from all those of the past, a doctrine that could actually produce indisputable knowledge.

The foremost characteristic of such a doctrine would have to be a new beginning point for reason. It could not start from received opinions and, by dialectical analysis, test and revise those opinions, gradually moving to greater clarity and certainty. To proceed in this way would cause another doctrinal conflict, and Hobbes would be ensnared in the historic problem of civilization.

Hobbes's alternative is to propose a kind of historical leap, from the realm of opinion into the realm of enlightenment science. This is achieved by rejecting the habitual trust in sensation and speech and by starting with definitions that refer only to the mind—to self-evident mental ideas or arbitrary constructs. Hobbes's proposal, in other words, is to assert the autonomy of reason: to make the enlightened mind stand alone, separated from the external world. Beginning here, with the separation of mind and reality, self-evident mental ideas of natural bodies can be conceived and a theory of human nature and sovereignty deduced.

The result, supposedly, is an indisputable doctrine that makes an absolute break from the past, a quantam leap to a new foundation for civilization. One could say that there is an implicit "end-of-history" argument in Hobbes's position (a forerunner of the view recently popularized by Francis Fukuyama with reference to Hegel but without acknowledgment of Hobbes).[11] Hobbes's end-of-history argument is found in the "Preface"

10. A more detailed account of Hobbes's historical critique of civilization can be found in Kraynak, *History and Modernity in the Thought of Thomas Hobbes*, chaps. 1–2, pp. 7–68.

11. Fukuyama relies mostly on Hegel (as modified by Kojève) and finds forerunners of the Hegelian end-of-history argument in Saint Augustine, Kant, and Condorcet, but not in Hobbes; he cites Hobbes for contributing to the theory of liberal-bourgeois civilization and

to *De Cive*, where he says that his political science will inaugurate an era of "immortal peace"—a permanent end to all doctrinal disputes and the public recognition of certain knowledge.

THE NEW DOGMATISM

If this interpretation is correct, then we can identify precisely where Hobbes's thought turns dogmatic, and a new kind of dogmatism enters into the Enlightenment.

In order to make a radical break with the past, Hobbes must purge the mind for the first time in history of its vain trust in providential support and make the mind stand on its own foundations. The enlightened mind will then be self-grounding and can claim to achieve intellectual certainty within a self-contained system. Yet this historic move creates a huge problem: the enlightened mind cannot simply stand alone. It must reconnect itself with the external world of Nature, otherwise it is merely subjective certainty, merely an artificial construct, and lacks the power to expel the kingdom of darkness. *The dilemma of the enlightened mind is that it rejects a grounding in Nature, yet it needs a grounding in Nature.* Hence, the greatest question for modern philosophers like Hobbes is the following: How can the enlightened mind, which from the outset is separated from reality by radical distrust of language and the senses, reconnect itself to the external world of Nature?

That Hobbes does separate and then reconnect the mind to the external world of Nature is undeniable. It is evident from the way he describes his system. For he claims, on the one hand, that his system is an artifical construct, made from names arbitrarily imposed; but, on the other hand, he also calls it a "science of *natural* justice," a teaching about *natural* right, and a science of real material bodies.[12]

This paradox runs throughout his system. In politics, Hobbes combines in seemingly contradictory fashion a teaching about positive law and natural law: he maintains that the command of the sovereign is just, even though it is arbitrary; but the arbitrary will of the sovereign must be obeyed because it secures civil peace which is naturally right. Likewise, in physics and metaphysics, Hobbes combines positivism and metaphysical "realism": he says that knowledge of natural phenomena is purely hypothetical but the ultimate nature of reality is known to be material.

---

to the master-slave dialectic but not to the theory of history. See Francis Fukuyama, *The End of History and the Last Man* (New York: Free Press, 1992), 56–64, 153–61, 193.

12. *Leviathan*, chap. 31, p. 270; chap. 14, p. 103.

To state the paradox more broadly, Hobbes's doctrine is both artificial and natural, both positivist and realist.

The reason for this paradox is now apparent. After separating the mind from reality, Hobbes feels the need to reconnect the two; but he is able to so by one means alone: by dogmatic assertion, which means by an act of will rather than by rational demonstration. For the two realms of mind and reality—of thinking and being—have been separated at the outset and would seem to have no right of ever being joined again—like a couple that has been divorced and swears to remain apart forever. And yet they always find a way of getting back together (rather like the behavior of Elizabeth Taylor and the late Richard Burton). Likewise, Hobbes and every Enlightenment philosopher does rejoin or remarry the two realms of thinking and being at some point. And we can see why the remarriage must occur: because the enlightened mind must wage a war to defeat the historical kingdom of darkness, and can only do so by having a grounding in Nature or the divinely created natural order.

The enlightened mind comes into being, then, not by self-generation from its own concepts, but by a willful act of rebellion and transformation. In the process, mere mental concepts are turned into claims about reality or the natural order of things. But the transformation is done dogmatically, without rational justification.

In the case of Hobbes, the dogmatism is so flagrant that scholars have rarely bothered to discuss it. His two most fundamental principles are the natural right to self-preservation and the metaphysical claim that body alone is real. Yet as countless critics have pointed out, there is really no proof, nor even an attempted proof, of either of these principles in Hobbes's entire corpus. And since Hobbes himself says that science begins with definitions, which are either arbitrary or self-evident, it seems that he is simply following his own method.

Now if Hobbes merely claimed that these two principles were mental concepts, then no charge of dogmatism could be leveled at him. And actually, he seems to say this in certain places. For example, concerning the doctrine of material bodies, Hobbes says in *Leviathan* that metaphysics or First Philosophy is the definition of those names that are "the most universal ... and necessary to the explaining of a man's *conceptions* of bodies" (chap. 46, p. 483, emphasis added). This statement is echoed in Hobbes's treatise on natural science, *De Corpore*, where he says that all scientific knowledge is about "internal accidents of our mind ... or [of] species of external things, not as really existing, but only appearing to exist, or to have a being outside us" (7.1). The meaning of these passages is that the doctrine of bodies in motion or mechanistic materialism is merely a conceptual model, a necessary mental idea of how we conceive of change or causality. Accordingly, Hobbes's only argument in defense of mechanical causation is a kind of mental deduction from the concept of inertia (as it was later called): imagining a change in the rest or motion of a body requires an image of bodies touching or pushing; action at a distance through an empty space is inconceivable.[13]

But Hobbes does not use mechanical causation as a mere conceptual model; he is not so modest or so consistent. Without additional arguments, he also asserts that body alone is real or that "every part of the universe is body, and that which is not body, is no part of the universe" (*Leviathan*, chap. 46, p. 483; *De Corpore*, 8.1). Clearly, Hobbes wants to have it both ways. He wants to say that materialism is a self-evident concept, known simply by introspection of mental ideas; *and* that materialism is the truth about the way things really are in the external world of Nature.

The only explanation that I can think of to account for Hobbes's unwarranted leap or flagrant inconsistency in turning a mental concept into a metaphysical truth is his overwhelming drive to defeat the traditional doctrine of immaterial substances or incorporeal bodies. This is a new kind of dogmatism. For the old kind of dogmatism—the kind alleged to have been committed by the classical philosopers and medieval Scholastics—is the assumption of a harmony of mind and reality and the unfounded trust in receieved opinion. Their alleged dogmatism was to require thinking to conform to being. But Hobbes's enlightenment science, by assuming a disharmony of mind and reality, actually creates reality by an act of will. A mental concept, which has no grounding of its own, is imposed on the world. In this new kind of dogmatism, *thinking creates being*, which is a kind of metaphysical magic unknown to the ancients and medievalists.

A similar pattern can be observed in Hobbes's treatment of the moral question of the greatest good. Hobbes denies that there is a greatest good because nothing really satisfies man's restless desire for power and every attainment of goals produces a new craving and every person has different tastes; hence, he concludes, there is no objective good.[14] But

---

13. Contrast Hobbes's brief conceptual argument for mechanical causality in *De Corpore* 9.7 and 8.19 and his completely a priori mechanical model of cosmology and the solar system in *De Corpore*, chaps. 21–22 (in *The English Works of Thomas Hobbes of Malmebury*, vol. 1, ed. Sir William Molesworthy [London: John Bohr, 1839–1845]) with the argument of his more empirically minded contemporary Robert Boyle, in "The Excellency and Grounds of the Corpuscular or Mechanical Philosophy" (published 1674). Boyle defends the mechanical hypothesis for its ability to explain the experimental results of chemical changes or the carefully observed qualities of things. See Marie Boas Hall, *Robert Boyle on Natural Philosophy: An Essay with Selections of His Writings* (Bloomington: Indiana University Press, 1965), 187–210, 231–73.

14. These arguments are found in *Leviathan*, chap. 6, p. 48, and chap. 11, p. 80.

there is a greatest evil, death, especially violent death at the hands of other men. The most astonishing feature of Hobbes's view, as Strauss so forcefully points out, is that Hobbes never *proves* that violent death is the greatest evil. There is no dialectical weighing of different opinions about the good—whether it is pleasure, wealth, honor, virtue, wisdom, or salvation—to show that self-preservation is the only morally justifiable end of human striving.[15] And, of course, there is hardly a reader of Hobbes who does not find this behavior a little strange.

Instead of giving arguments or proofs, Hobbes treats the primacy of self-preservation as a self-evident truth. Hence, in *De Cive* he says: "[E]very man desires what is good and shuns what is evil, but chiefly the chiefest of natural evils which is death; and this he does by a certain impulsion of nature, no less [than] a stone moves downward" (1.7). Or he makes bold assertions: "Inasmuch as a necessity of nature makes men desire what is good for themselves and avoid what is hurtful; but most of all the terrible enemy of Nature, death, from whom we expect the loss of all power and the greatest bodily pains, it is not against reason that a man does all he can to preserve his own body from death and pain" (*Elements of Law*, 1.14.6). In these passages, Hobbes asserts without proof that the aim of all life and of Nature itself is to avoid violent death and to preserve itself.

But does he really think that self-preservation is the strongest and most powerful urge of all mankind and even of all natural beings? Not really. In fact, Hobbes denies it in other passages. He says explicitly in *De Cive* (3.12) that "most men would rather lose their lives . . . than suffer slander"—a clear admission that a sense of *honor* is often more powerful than the desire to preserve one's life. Hobbes also acknowledges the common temptation to commit suicide in order to escape a wretched life; hence, he says, "though death is the greatest of all evils . . . the pains of life can be so great that . . . [men] may number death among the goods" (*De Homine*, 11.6). In other words, the claim that self-preservation is the most powerful passion is not an empirical truth about the way men really are. Rather, it describes the way they will become after they have been reeducated by Hobbes. It is merely a hypothetical or conceptual truth that Hobbes willfully asserts to be natural or naturally right in order to change human behavior—in order to transform human nature according to his abstract idea of what men should be, namely, peaceful Hobbesian citizens who will obey the established powers.

In sum, we can say that the dogmatism of Hobbes's science of enlightenment is to take mental concepts about material bodies and self-

---

15. Leo Strauss, *The Political Philosophy of Hobbes*, trans. E. M. Sinclair (Chicago: University of Chicago Press, 1936), 152–53.

preservation and to treat them as metaphysical truths about Nature and human nature. His motive, then, is not to understand the world but to change the world—to rebel against the existing world and transform it according to abstract ideas. In this way, the mind and reality, which have been separated at the outset by radical skepticism, are reconnected in the willful act of making reality conform to ideas of the mind.

CONCLUSION: THE DOGMATIC TURN IN ENLIGHTENMENT SCIENCE

In this analysis, I have tried to uncover a new kind of dogmatism in the thinking of Hobbes and the Enlightenment—namely, the creation of reality from mental concepts by willful assertion, which might be summed up in the phrase "thinking creates being." Because of this dogmatism, the Enlightenment introduces a strange dynamic into the modern world which can be seen in the behavior of many modern philosophers.

One aspect of that dynamic is the need of modern philosophers to live parasitically off the tradition they are trying to destroy. Because such thinkers cannot generate from their own autonomous reason the metaphysical truth or moral authority needed for their doctrines, they must actually borrow it from the tradition. Hence, the notion of Nature or Being as an intelligible moral order and the idea of Higher Law or Natural Law are carried over (often covertly) in the very act of subverting and transforming the tradition. So far from generating itself, then, the enlightened mind is the ungrateful child of the tradition.

At the same time, the Enlightenment is necessarily driven to a kind of ideological utopianism: taking mental concepts and trying to impose them on the world, willfully, even violently. It is precisely this tendency that called forth the protests of Edmund Burke and other conservative critics of the Enlightenment. Burke saw a new and more dangerous kind of doctrinal politics emerging from the Enlightenment, one that sought to remake human nature. Burke's advice was to return to the older view, that the mind cannot reason without trust in the authoritative wisdom of tradition and without trust in supernatural Providence.

Yet, it might be objected to Burke, that the Enlightenment is not *necessarily* dogmatic. It may have a powerful temptation to reconnect the autonomous mind to the external world by dogmatic assertion; but, strictly speaking, this does not have to happen. The enlightened mind could exercise self-restraint and remain in a strictly neutral posture toward the character of the external world. It could be metaphysically and theologically neutral and take no stand on the existence or nonexistence of God, on the material or immaterial character of Nature, or on the ultimate attributes of Being. Following this line of thought, the only consistent doctrine of the fully emancipated enlightened mind would be positivism—the renunciation of all rights to metaphysics or theology. And it may be the case that this strand of the Enlightenment is the most productive one when applied to certain spheres of natural science. For who can deny the success of modern natural science in providing mathematical models that explain empirical data but cannot claim to explain the ultimate nature of reality? [16]

The question then arises as to whether there has ever been a thoroughly consistent or honest positivist—either in thought or in action.[17] In the case of someone like Descartes, it is extremely difficult to determine if he follows his own advice in his *Meditations on First Philosophy* (Fourth Meditation) about making unwarranted metaphysical leaps. Descartes's advice is that the philosopher should exercise stoical self-restraint and never permit the "will to believe" to exceed the understanding. If Descartes has violated his own stoical rule, then he makes an unwarranted leap of faith in asserting that God guarantees some kind of correspondence between a clear idea and some being in the external world.

While finding it difficult to pass judgment on the honesty or dishonesty of such philosophers, I would nevertheless like to point to a recurring pattern of behavior among many modern thinkers: a pattern of combining in some fashion an attitude of radical skepticism with dogmatic assertions in metaphysics and morality. I am thinking of someone like Locke and his movement from doubt about innate ideas to his belief in a *natural* law of self-preservation, and his movement from doubt about knowing the nature of reality to his belief in "real essences." I am thinking of Kant and his movement from critical thinking to the positing of the mysterious thing-in-itself and to his postulates of practical reason,

---

16. While recognizing the successes of positivistic models in mathematical physics, one should not forget the insistent claims of Stanley Jaki that most of the great modern scientists, like Newton and Einstein, thought they were explaining the way nature really worked; most were not positivists like Mach but were driven by a passion for discovering true knowledge of the nature of things and were engaged in what used to be called "natural philosophy" (and unwittingly may even have been engaging in "natural theology," as Jaki would like to believe). See Stanley L. Jaki, *The Road of Science and the Ways to God* (Chicago: University of Chicago Press, 1978), 145–61.

17. In an excellent little study, Edwin Burtt shows that no theory of modern science can remain positivistic but always, explicity or implicity, contains a metaphysical view of nature. In particular, he shows that the positivistic interpretation of Newton's mechanics is untenable, although the awesome explanatory power of Newtonian mechanics gave authority to the mechanistic worldview that was at odds with Newton's real metaphysics—his deism or natural theology. See Edwin A. Burtt, *The Metaphysical Foundations of Modern Physical Science* (Garden City, N.Y.: Doubleday, 1954; originally published in 1924), esp. 227–302.

which are supposed to be merely the *logical* necessities of an unconditional morality—permitting us to act "*as if*" God, immortality, and freedom were real—while making it impossible to treat freedom of the will and hence human dignity as a mere possibility. I am also thinking about scientific positivists who move from strict neutrality about the existence of God and spiritual beings to crusading and militant atheism. I am also thinking about "deconstructionists" and their missionary moralism of teaching rebellion, as well as their godfather Nietzsche, who moves from rejecting all metaphsyical and moral truths to assertions of human nobility and the doctrine of the will to power. And I am also thinking of Hobbes, who may be the founder and prototype of this kind of dogmatic turn in modern philosophy.

From these disturbing observations, we are led to a fundamental question: Does the kind of dogmatism and apparent dishonesty that modern philosophers repeatedly exhibit provide sufficient justification for rejecting the Enlightenment project of separating thinking and being? The answer, I think, is Yes, which may not sound like a very bold conclusion today, when rejection of the Enlightenment is commonplace among so many "postmodern" intellectuals. But the number who really understand the implications of this rejection are few. Among those who do, I would say that Etienne Gilson in his Neo-Thomist realism, along with Leo Strauss in his recovery of Platonism, provide the clearest guidance. What Gilson and Strauss suggest is that the inconsistency of modern philosophers in continuously divorcing the mind from reality and then remarrying them, is unnatural and, in a way, impious: a sin of pride.[18]

Thus, it makes more sense to return to the pre-Enlightenment position and to begin again from opinion, and then to follow the slow path of dialectical ascent from the cave. In other words, it is wiser to begin with the mind and reality joined together as they were intended, than to rudely divorce and then to remarry them. And so we may conclude that in philosophy as well as in marriage the words of the Gospel provide the best advice: "What God has joined together, let no man put asunder" (Matthew 19.6).

18. As Gilson puts it so simply: "You must either begin as a realist with being, in which case you will have knowledge of being, or begin ... with knowledge, in which case you will never come into contact with being"; see Etienne Gilson, *Thomist Realism and The Critique of Knowledge* (San Francisco: Ignatius Press, 1986), 149. For a succinct overview of the criticisms of modern philosophy, see Etienne Gilson, *Methodical Realism*, trans. Philip Tower (Front Royal, Va.: Christiandom Press, 1990), and Leo Strauss, *What Is Political Philosophy?* (Glencoe, Ill.: Free Press, 1959), 9–55.

5   Pascal on Certainty and Utility[1]

JOHN C. MCCARTHY

In what was to have been *An Apology for the Christian Religion*, but has come down to us as the *Pensées*, Pascal writes "Descartes: useless and uncertain."[2] This mordant dismissal of the father of modern philosophy is reminiscent of Descartes's treatment of his predecessors. Just as the teacher of the *cogito* rarely mentions the ancient and medieval traditions he openly seeks to replace, so Pascal leaves largely unstated the substance of his quarrel with Descartes: there are perhaps a dozen explicit references to his opponent in the entire oeuvre of Pascal. Little wonder, then, that Pascal's relation to Descartes should so frequently have been a subject of scholarly concern.

The principal reason for Descartes's hesitation to speak at length against his foes was his desire to avoid controversy, which would have impeded both his inauguration of his project and the public's acceptance and execution of it.[3] The relative absence of philosophic disputation in

---

1. This essay is a revised version of "Pascal on Uncertainty and Utility," originally published in *Interpretation* 22 (1994–1995): 247–69.

2. *Pensées sur la religion et sur quelques autres sujets*, ed. Louis Lafuma (Paris: Editions du Luxembourg, 1951), vol. 1, *Textes*, fragment 887. All further references to the *Pensées* will employ Lafuma's enumeration, together with the corresponding fragment number in the Brunschvicg edition (in the present instance, 78). Translations of Pascal are my own.

3. See *Discours de la méthode*, 5th ed., ed. Etienne Gilson (Paris: J. Vrin, 1976), 23, 41, 60, 66, 68, and 75. For an English translation, see *The Philosophical Writings of Descartes* (henceforth PW), 2 vols., trans. J. Cottingham, R. Stoothoff, and D. Murdoch (Cambridge and New York: Cambridge University Press, 1985), 1.123, 131–32, 141–42, 144–45, 146, and 149. That Descartes adopted Ovid's motto, *Bene vixit bene qui latuit*, is sometimes noticed, but seldom brought to bear on Cartesian studies. Also suggestive is the letter to Mersenne of April 1634, in *Oeuvres* (henceforth AT), ed. C. Adam and P. Tannery (Paris: Cerf, 1897–1913), 1.286, and the letter to Regius of 1642, AT 3.491–510. For English translations, see *The Philosophical Writings of Descartes*, vol. 3, *The Correspondence* (henceforth PWC), trans. J. Cottingham, R. Stoothoff, D. Murdoch, and A. Kenny (Cambridge and New York: Cambridge University Press, 1981), 42–44, 205–9. For an iconoclastic presentation of Descartes's art of writing, consider Hiram Caton's "Analytic History of Philosophy: The Case of Descartes," *Philosophical Forum* 12 (1981): 273–94. A more scholarly assessment is provided by Louis E. Loeb's "Is There Radical Dissimulation in Descartes' *Meditations*?," in *Essays on Descartes' "Meditations,"* ed. A. O. Rorty (Berkeley and Los Angeles: University of

the *Pensées* would appear to be due to more accidental considerations. As is well known, chronic illness and an untimely death prevented Pascal from realizing his designs for that work. On the other hand, we learn from his sister, Gilberte Périer, that Pascal came to distrust eristic. Despite his youthful delight in polemics, so evident in *Les provinciales*, he seems to have concluded that his talent for the art could not be made to serve his most serious dialectical intentions.[4] There is, moreover, ample evidence from the *Pensées* itself that Pascal thought it necessary to make his case to the nonbelievers by indirection. The orderless order that has resulted (532/373) suggests the following methodological principle. The fragments he bequeathed to posterity must not be read in a fragmentary way; so far as is possible, each is to be interpreted in the light of all the rest.[5] Accordingly, we are compelled to consult a wide range of texts should we desire to make sense of those few explicitly devoted to Descartes. A reconstruction of Pascal's brief against Cartesian philosophy is unavoidable.

No competent reader would question the necessity of approaching the various parts of the *Pensées* with an eye to the whole they mean to serve. Still, opinion is far from unanimous as to how Pascal's case against Descartes is to be understood. In the main, scholars agree that Pascal's intention was fundamentally anti-Cartesian. Some have argued, however, that Pascal was closer to Descartes than he, Pascal, may have realized; and this argument has engendered a variety of claims about the degree of their kinship. The scholarly debate, which has gone on for the better part of a century, has yielded numerous helpful precisions, but shows scant signs of resolution. One might be tempted to blame this lack of accord on the indeterminate character of the "thoughts" Pascal bequeathed to us, which would be to say that the matter is irresolvable. A safer explanation (cf. 257/684) is at hand, however: students of Pascal have often been too quick to assume familiarity with Descartes's philosophic intentions, such that the range and depth of Pascal's dispute with him could

---

California Press, 1986), 243–70. David R. Lachterman, *The Ethics of Geometry: A Genealogy of Modernity* (New York: Routledge, 1989), 1–7, conjectures that the reasons for Descartes's reticence about his predecessors are not prudential or tactical merely, but concern the very substance of his teaching: what purports to be radically new cannot appear to constitute itself through a rejection of that which it claims to have superseded.

4. For his sister's witness, see "La vie de Monsieur Pascal," in Blaise Pascal, *Oeuvres complètes*, ed. Jacques Chevalier (Paris: Bibliothèque de la Pléiade, 1954), 19; cf. 773/135. All references to writings of Pascal other than the *Pensées* will be to this edition, and will be cited by page number.

5. See 199/72, 784/23. For further clues to Pascal's art of writing, see *Pensées* 55/111, 91/336, 308/793, 529/105, 542/370, 584/15, 696/22, 701/9, 737/10, 798/41, 927/505, and 933/460; also see "Fragment d'une lettre," 525–26, and "De l'art de persuader," 594–602.

not help but be obscured. Neglect of Descartes's reflections concerning the end of his philosophy ensured that many readers of Pascal would miss much of his indictment against Cartesian "utility." Similarly, when commentators failed fully to grasp the revolutionary character of Descartes's "method," loss of precision regarding Cartesian "certainty" was inevitable, such that Pascal's objections to it would not be thoroughly considered. In short, comparisons of Pascal and Descartes have, typically, understated Descartes's disagreement with his opponents, which has meant that many fragments of the *Pensées* relevant to Pascal's stance toward his compatriot have been overlooked. In sum, the extent to which Pascal calls Descartes's philosophic revolution into question has not been sufficiently appreciated.[6]

There should never have been the least doubt about the sweep of Pascal's wry remark. "Utility" and "certainty" are the two watchwords of Descartes's most programmatic writing, the *Discourse on the Method*. Indeed, if Hegel is correct, they stamp the whole of the "Enlightenment" Descartes helps inaugurate.[7] Surely Pascal means to condemn Cartesianism root and branch. But in order to evaluate that condemnation we must confront yet a third difficulty, one rarely broached, besides the fragmentary and indirect style of the *Pensées*, and the need for an accurate understanding of the position Pascal opposes. From first to last, the *Pensées* is stamped by Pascal's experience of Christianity, which is to say that

---

6. The literature on this question is too extensive to list here. Michel Le Guern, *Pascal et Descartes* (Paris: A.G. Nizet, 1971), provides a useful, albeit partial summary of the debate. Both he and E. Baudin, *Études historiques et critiques sur la philosophie de Pascal*, vol. 1, *Pascal et Descartes* (Neuchâtel, Switzerland: Editions de la Baconnière, 1946), argue that Pascal was heavily indebted to the philosophy he so openly rejects. Earlier Léon Brunschvicg had suggested that the disagreement between the two could be traced to their common debt to Montaigne; see *Descartes et Pascal: Lecteurs de Montaigne* (New York: Brentano, 1944). More recently, and in defense of the view that the two figures were antithetical, is Pierre Magnard's. "Descartes inutile et incertain," *Revue des sciences philosophiques et théologiques* 75 (1991): 63–80. Magnard represents many others when he claims that "inutile" means essentially "inutile pour le salut." Descartes's "uncertainty" is generally thought to concern either particular errors Pascal locates in Descartes's physics, or the inability of Cartesian science to deliver the certainty, once again, of "salvation." See also Geneviève Rodis-Lewis, "Doute et certitude chez Descartes et Pascal," *Europe* 59, no. 594 (October 1978): 5–14. The failure to appreciate the scope of Descartes's revolution is not a new phenomenon. Antoine Arnauld, a colleague of Pascal's at Port Royal, and subsequently one of his editors, believed, despite Pascal's express warnings to the contrary, that Descartes's writings were "a singular effect of God's providence" serving to "stop the dreadful inclination shown by many persons of late towards irreligion and libertinage." The remark is cited by Stephen Nadler in *Arnauld and the Cartesian Philosophy of Ideas* (Princeton, N.J.: Princeton University Press, 1989), 30 n. 24.

7. *Phenomenology of Spirit*, trans. A. V. Miller (Oxford: Oxford University Press, 1977), 349–55. For the backhanded compliment that is Hegel's assessment of Pascal, see *Introduction to the Lectures on the History of Philosophy*, trans. T. M. Knox and A. V. Miller (Oxford: Oxford University Press, 1985), 162–63.

the *Apology* of this modern Socrates (as he is sometimes called) is not perfectly Socratic. Since Descartes, on the other hand, is remarkably candid about his unwillingness to pursue properly theological investigations—they would require, he says, that he "be more than a man"[8]—it would seem obvious why Pascal should have been so hostile. As commentators could not fail to notice, the God of Abraham, Isaac, and Jacob provides for him the only adequate measure of "certainty" and "utility"; what does not fully conform to God's measure is either "figure" or "folly" (cf. 267/680). But for just this reason one is led to wonder whether Pascal meets his adamantly philosophical adversary on common ground. If the quarrel between the two thinkers turns in effect upon a common confession of fideism, if their disagreement derives from agreement that "Athens" has nothing to do with "Jerusalem," can their logomachy be of anything more than doxographical interest?

It is clear that the *Pensées* abjures any rational articulation of the traditional *praeambula fidei*. "Philosophy" so conceived has ceased to be protreptic to theology, as it had been for the great medieval theologians. Thus the nearest literary precursor to the *Pensées* is not the *disputatio*, still less the *summa*; it is the Augustinian form of "confession."[9] In keeping with this form, Pascal posits his own life as a clue to the whole, and so does not hesitate to lay bare his heart (418/233, 689/64); but with Augustine, he also insists that his own person be forgotten (396/471), urging instead a paradoxical esteem for hidden virtue (643/159, 719/788). Like the *Confessions*, the *Pensées* is written in and from an awareness of God's abiding presence (99/536, 931/950), and even presumes at times to speak on God's behalf (149/430, 919/553); but true to form, it also addresses itself to those who do not acknowledge his presence, much less his words. In sympathy with such readers, Pascal searches tirelessly for reasons that will make his faith more accessible to them; and yet, student of Augustine that he is, he must admit that this faith lies beyond what his or any human reason can adequately convey (308/793, 380/284, 588/279, 808/245). Precisely as confession, however, the *Pensées* speaks

---

8. *Discours*, 8 (PW 1.114); "Preface to the French Edition," in *Principia philosophiae*, AT 9B, 3–6, 10 (PW 1.180–81).

9. On the meaning of "confession," see Joseph Ratzinger, "Originalität und Überlieferung in Augustins Begriff der *confessio*," *Revue des études augustiniennes* 3 (1957): 375–92; Ann Hartle, *Death and the Disinterested Spectator* (Albany: State University of New York Press, 1986), 85–87; John C. McCarthy, "Desire, Recollection, and Thought: On Augustine's *Confessions* I, 1," *Communio: International Catholic Review* 14 (1987): 146–57; Frederick J. Crosson, "Structure and Meaning in St. Augustine's *Confessions*," *Proceedings of the American Catholic Philosophical Association*, vol. 63 (Washington, D.C.: American Catholic Philosophical Association, 1990), 84–97; and especially Thomas Prufer, "Notes for a Reading of Augustine, *Confessions*, Book X," in *Recapitulations: Essays in Philosophy* (Washington, D.C.: The Catholic University of America Press, 1993), 27–32.

to all men about "the whole of man" (848/806; cf. 12/187). Because "man is obviously made to think" (620/146), and because "the science of man" should be man's proper study (687/144), Pascal invites believer and unbeliever alike to reflect upon the human experience of the human. And because the human being experiences himself as positioned between what is above him and what lies beneath, any science of the human things necessarily implicates the sub- and the superhuman as well. From the standpoint of unaided reason, then, what unifies this *Apology* is an old question, a question of intense interest to Athens and Jerusalem alike: What is man? As an astute commentator has observed, the fragments Pascal left to us provide an *anthropologia ancilla theologiae*.[10] We can safely conclude, then, that Pascal does continue the line of inquiry initiated by Socrates after all.[11] That said, we must not permit Descartes's apparent disdain for the legacy of Socrates to blind us to the fact that the Cartesian teaching on utility and certainty also depends, finally, on a sustained meditation upon the human things. As the peculiarly autobiographical form of the *Discourse on the Method* means to indicate, Cartesian "method" derives from a comprehensive, premethodological examination of the human situation. In sum, Pascal's theological dispute with the rationalist Descartes can and indeed must be interpreted in light of a common concern.

The present essay falls into two parts. The first proposes that Descartes's doctrine of utility issues from a revision of the traditional view of the human good. Loosely speaking, that revision involves a reconsideration of the relation between mind and body, with the result that a nonteleological physics becomes the most effective instrument of human completion. Although echoes of Descartes's opposition to the tradition regarding the hendiadys of body and soul are to be found in the *Pensées*, Pascal flatly rejects the "dualism" implicit in Descartes's account of the good. As he views the matter, Cartesian utility fails to address the real split in human being, which occurs deep within "soul," and is the source of an unease without any human remedy. The second part of the essay begins by noting that Descartes's method presupposes a novel understanding of the relation between mind and world. Human intelligence as traditionally conceived is summarily displaced once Descartes casts the availability of "first principles and causes" into methodical doubt. However, method quickly recovers from this crisis of its own making by establishing "foundations," which, as the word suggests, are independent of any natural access

---

10. Hans Urs von Balthasar, "Pascal," in *Studies in Theological Style: Lay Styles*, vol. 3 of *The Glory of the Lord: A Theological Aesthetics*, trans. Andrew Louth et al. (San Francisco: Ignatius Press, 1986), 190.

11. Cf., e.g., *Phaedrus* 230a with 130/420, 477/406.

to the being of beings. Pascal, although keenly aware of the difficulty we face in coming to know the things themselves, disavows any methodical solution to the problem of knowledge. His teaching on the "heart" is meant to indicate the way to such certainty as is humanly available. Yet the heart's prompting can only be taken seriously if the human soul is, for all its divisions, disclosive of the wholeness of the whole. In effect, Pascal offers the "heart" as refutation of the Cartesian separation of mind and nature, and therewith of the true and the good.

To sum up, the essay seeks to demonstrate that in Pascal's estimation, Descartes is useless because his conception of the good is uncertain, and uncertain because his appraisal of the true is useless.

BODY AND SOUL

No reader of Descartes could fail to observe that he proposes to replace "the speculative philosophy taught in the Schools" with a "practical one" promising to make its adherents "masters and possessors of nature." Cartesian science pledges to be useful in the highest degree, useful like no other teaching, by enabling us to put all of nature to use. This is only possible because, as Part 5 of the *Discourse* asserts, nature has no real uses of its own: as everyone knows, Cartesian physics dispenses with formal and final causality. "Utility" is ordered in turn to "the general good of all men," and this good common to all is said to be the private interest of each in a healthy, pleasant, and lengthy life.[12] At a stroke, the "common good" has ceased to be common in the old sense. This is not to say that the interest that moved Descartes to think and to publish is identical to the interest the public has or ought to have in reading him. Although he boasts that his method will relieve man's estate more quickly and effectively than Baconian method ever could, he does not think his own health will benefit much from the innovations of his science.[13] Conversely, in announcing that the public and the philosophical uses of reason can be made mutually beneficial, Part 6 of the *Discourse* takes pains to steer the bulk of its intended readers clear of the rigors of scientific research. All the same, theory and practice also converge for Descartes. Hence, for example, the charter statement of Cartesian philosophy describes the "laws of mechanics" as the most "important" truths discovered by method, which would suggest that the very substance of Descartes's science of nature has "applications," as we would call them, ever in view.

12. *Discours*, 61–63 (PW 1.142–43). The health of the body is there said expressly to be "the first good and the foundation of all the other goods of this life."
13. *Les passions de l'âme*, AT 11.320–22, together with "Preface to the French Edition," *Principia philosophiae*, AT 9B, 20 (PW 1.189–90).

However that may be, mechanistic physics surely does not elevate the knower in the way that traditional "speculative" philosophy had claimed to do, namely, by enabling him to contemplate the first and highest things, the divine things. Quite consistently, therefore, the *Discourse* characterizes reason as a "universal instrument."[14]

Pascal agrees with Descartes that the Scholastic approach to nature is gravely flawed. His own scientific writings often betray his impatience with the tendency found in the Schools to substitute speculative dicta for careful observation of the phenomena. Witness his involvement in the controversy over the vacuum.[15] Nevertheless, he says little about the practical potential of his own mathematical and physical pursuits. Once in passing he refers to a particular discovery as "useful," but its utility is obviously only heuristic.[16] However modern his doubts about Schoolbook physics, he nowhere associates his own contributions to science with the universal benevolence of "practical philosophy." Yet one looks in vain in Pascal for a blanket condemnation of Descartes's utilitarian turn. Indeed, he clearly approved of the application of theoretical principles to practical problems. Over the course of his short life he devoted considerable time and energy to the easing of the human estate, with his celebrated calculating machine being only the first of several practical innovations.[17] In order to gain an accurate understanding of Pascal's argument against Cartesian utility, it is therefore necessary to join the issue at a deeper level. That will require in turn that we consider an important point of agreement between the two thinkers. As we shall see, Pascal accepts in large measure Descartes's rethinking of the "common good."

The mastery of nature teaching, addressed as it is to scientists and nonscientists alike, involves a two-pronged critique of the good as it had hitherto been conceived: a critique of conventional morality and a critique of the philosophers. Against the philosophers, the *Discourse* argues that they have never known a truly common good, because they have never been able to hold anything in common. The history of philosophy

---

14. *Discours*, 41, 57 (PW 1.131–32, 140); also "Conversation with Berman," AT 5.165. My argument here relies considerably upon Richard Kennington's "Descartes and Mastery of Nature," in *Organism, Medicine, and Metaphysics*, ed. S. F. Spicker (Dordrecht, Holland: D. Reidel, 1978), 201–23.

15. "Préface pour le traité du vide," 529–32; "Lettre à M le Pailleur," 400. Notably, Pascal regards Descartes's defense of the plenum as one more Scholastic error.

16. As A.W. S. Baird notes in his *Studies in Pascal's Ethics* (The Hague: Martinus Nijhoff, 1975), 13. See also *De l'esprit géométrique*, 577.

17. On Pascal's interest in "practice," see 931/550 For a list of Pascal's inventions, see Pierre Humbert, *L'oeuvre scientifique de Pascal* (Paris: Albin Michel, 1947). René Taton, "Sur l'invention de la machine arithmetique," in *L'oeuvre scientifique de Pascal*, ed. P. Costabel et al. (Paris: Presses universitaires de France, 1964), 207–28, offers a more cautious assessment of Pascal's practical accomplishments.

is a history of endless disputation. Should one inquire into the ground of the philosophers' differences, one would find "insensibility, pride, despair, or parricide." Obviously, Descartes means this allegation to call into question the possibility of philosophic detachment, of an interest in truth for its own sake. But does not such suspicion poison the well for his own philosophizing? Not necessarily. The scientific pursuit of utility suggests, if not the coincidence, then at least the intersection of the Cartesian philosopher's self-interest and his interest in the "truth." By the same token, "what works" promises to overcome the contention attending the old speculative claims by providing an indisputable measure of scientific "success."[18]

Descartes's argument against common life proceeds along similar lines. According to the self-understanding of all premodern regimes, not narrow self-interest, the pursuit of honor or external goods, say, but some understanding of justice is the proper judge of a city and its citizens. Even if a given polity were never altogether just, its origin and continuance were acknowledged by all but the most wicked and self-indulgent citizens to depend upon some divination of and commitment to a good beyond individual self-assertion. The philosophically minded within a city's walls certainly have had reason to doubt the impartiality of its civic justice, but at least for those of the Socratic school, the city's openness to, and limited apprehension of, the just "in itself" meant that the city could never be wholly reduced to its subcivic parts.[19] The effect of Descartes's hyperbolic doubts, which fix upon the variety of existing moral and political arrangements, is to intimate that such differing conceptions of the good are purely arbitrary, having no real relation to anything true or just. Hence he particularly esteems Sparta, not because it more closely approximates a just civic arrangement than any other regime, but because it enjoyed the greatest unity of purpose, thanks to the unity of its origin in the will of the founder. On the basis of his unmasking of received opinion, Descartes believes himself free to set aside the old Socratic question about justice, and to ignore all common talk about morality. As already the opening sentence of the *Discourse* wryly insinuates, the natural equality of human egoism entails that men by nature show scant desire to know.[20] Yet the outcome of this argument is not, as may appear, Descartes's complete withdrawal from public life. To the contrary, having dispatched prescientific opinion about the good, he goes on to announce, if only in barest detail, his ideal republic, the polity informed by,

---

18. *Discours*, 8–10 (PW 1.114–15).
19. See, e.g., *Politics* 1280a10, 1283a24.
20. *Discours*, 1–2, with 15, 59, 61 (PW 1.111 with 1.118, 141, 142).

and supportive of, his science. In short, Cartesian science will be useful to the ordinary citizen not despite but precisely because of its rejection of the ordinary citizen's understanding of the good.[21]

Pascal is close to Descartes on both counts. As regards ordinary morality, he professes, like Descartes, to be struck by the sheer number of moral codes found in the world; and like Descartes, he takes this variety to be a sign of the arbitrariness of political authority. "[W]e see nothing just or unjust that does not change in character with a change in climate. Three degrees of latitude reverses all jurisprudence; a meridian decides the truth." He mentions the view that common or natural laws underlie such differences only to reject it: the range of actions deemed just by the world is too extreme (60/294). With a candor his Port Royal editors found shocking, he concludes that the sole warrant for obedience to the law is, paradoxically, its customary origin, and "not because it is reasonable or just."[22] He hereby announces for all to hear what Descartes utters only guardedly. And this difference is instructive. For while Descartes is

21. *Discours*, 2, 10, 13, 16, 23 (PW 1.112, 115–16, 117, 122–23).
22. 60/294, 525/325; cf. 9/29, 25/308, 51/293, 61/309, 828/304. See Mara Vamos, "Pascal's *Pensées* and the Enlightenment: The Roots of a Misunderstanding," *Studies on Voltaire and the Eighteenth Century* 97 (1972): 7–145, for a valuable study of the editorial work done on the first edition by Pascal's friends at Port Royal, of the deficiencies of their edition, and of the influence of its defects on the Enlightenment reading of Pascal. Notwithstanding his seeming indiscretion about the conventional basis of political life, Pascal certainly does not intend to preach subversion. He admits that if the truth about politics were made widely known, the existence of all regimes would be imperiled (60/294, 66/326). Drawing a conclusion reminiscent of Hobbes, he claims that precisely because convention, sustained by force, is the sole source of law, we can have no *reason* either to contest the laws or to incite the many to disobedience (103/298, 525/325). But even if reason's relation to the law has been simplified in this way, it is unlikely to prevail over subrational inclinations to violate the law, which is why force, fortified by the imagination (25/308, 60/294, 87/307), must lend support to the law (81/290, 85/878, 828/304). Yet Pascal also avows that a merely conventional grounding of law is manifestly *faute de mieux* (103/298), and that no amount of force suffices to shore up conventions if men do not somehow believe those conventions to be in some way reasonable or just (525/325), which is to say that the irrational foundations of political life are not indifferent to the demands of reason after all. For Pascal, the hard truth about politics needs the flimsy protection of a lie, the ghostly shade of the truth (60/294). It is therefore hard to escape the conclusion that Pascal himself would have been forced to trim the sheets of his *Apology* had he seen it into print. How he would have done so is unclear, however. For while he acknowledges the necessity of political lies, and is aware of the uses made of irony in other contexts (265/677, 276/671, 279/690, 533/331), his censure of the Jesuit practice of equivocation is severe (cf. *Lettres provinçiales*, no. 9, 760–61). The squeamishness of Pascal's Port-Royal editors was surely not unreasonable. We hasten to add that the rhetorical or political problem Pascal managed accidently to avoid need not point to an inconsistency in his understanding of moral and political life. Even granted that his observations about the inconsistencies of existing conventions are unguarded, he might well argue that prudent reserve would not alter the fundamental truth about politics, namely, that it is not fully rational. In addition, he does advert to a positive reason for deferring to the moral and political authorities of one's age. This argument for obedience, which is perfectly traditional, i.e., quite un-Hobbesian, does

prepared provisionally to accept the strictures of conventional morality until his scientific reform is fully in place,[23] Pascal appears unwilling to see in any customary human practice even an instrumental value in the realization of the human good.[24]

Pascal is also more forthcoming than Descartes about the failure of philosophy to identify the good, although his argument is, again, much the same. He repeatedly observes that "the philosophers split themselves

---

after all look for reasons within political life that are not wholly visible in, but still underlie, the conventionalistism of ordinary politics (cf. 14/138, 90/337 with Romans 13.2).

23. *Discours*, 22–28, 60 (PW 1.122–26).

24. A. J. Beitzinger, "Pascal on Justice, Force, and Law," *Review of Politics* 46 (1984): 212–43, provides a summary of Pascal's political thought that negotiates fairly successfully through many of its perplexing features. Among other things, he answers the charge made by Jacques Maritain, in "The Political Ideas of Pascal," in *Ransoming the Time*, trans. H. L. Binsse (New York: Charles Scribner's Sons, 1948), that Pascal was a "Christian cynic." A more serious difficulty is raised by Leo Strauss, in *The City and Man* (Chicago: Rand McNally, 1964), 18, when, in light of such fragments as 60/294, he claims that Pascal "while admitting that there are things which are by nature just ... denies that they can be known to unassisted man owing to original sin." By directing our attention in a footnote to *Laws* 804b3–c1, Strauss effectively restates Nietzsche's judgment of Pascal, as outlined, e.g., in *The Antichrist*, §5 (*The Portable Nietzsche*, trans. and ed. W. Kaufmann [New York: Viking Press, 1978], 571–72). While it is not to our purpose to explore Pascal's political science in detail, reasons can be offered for doubting the adequacy of Strauss's (and Nietzsche's) reading. It can safely be said that Pascal's leading political thesis derives from the precept of Saint Paul: "here we have no lasting city" (Hebrews 13.14). Nevertheless, Pascal defends that thesis in a way congruent with Aristotle's political analysis. According to his argument, there is indeed no single just principle of political rule available to "unassisted man." Reason would be the most likely candidate for principled rule, were the rule of reason not faced by insurmountable obstacles. The impediments to the direct rule of reason derive not only, or even primarily, from its fallibility and its allegiance to a suprapolitical order; they are owing especially to the inability of the unwise to recognize wise rule, and to their unwillingness to submit to it (60/294, 85/878, 360/482, 530/274, 533/331). A second best, or rather a better, principle of rule would be the ordering of all possible principles of rule, rational and subrational, i.e., the giving to each its due. However, just as the imputation of any one partial principle as the single true, or just title to rule would be indistinguishable from tyranny (21/381, 540/380; cf. 58/332, 569/872, 905/385, 977/320), so a political harmonization of all politically relevant natural principles is not presently conceivable because they are, on their own understanding, heterogeneous, at odds with one another (44/82, 372/483, 374/475, 421/477). Hence the inevitability of the distortion of the political truth (60/294) considered in the preceding note. Pascal avers that partial knowledge of what is just by nature is available, and not merely to the prudent few (81/299, 148/425, 421/477, 797/316). Indeed, only such partial knowledge can explain our present political confusion and dissatisfaction. Furthermore, or to state the same thought in positive terms, Pascal's rational apology for the Christian religion depends in part on the claim that a sense of the naturally just allows men to glimpse both in the Old Testament and in the New a fulfillment of the universal human longing for justice (cf. 85/878, 149/430, 280/614, 402/290, 421/606, 454/619, 482/289, 925/520). To conclude, while Strauss may be correct in claiming that Pascal's political reflections go "much beyond Aristotle," his belief in "original sin" cannot justly be imputed as the cause of political obscurantism or as an enfeebling disdain for the conditions of decent politics. For further indications about Pascal's politics, see Philippe Sellier, *Pascal et Saint Augustin* (Paris: Librairie Armand Colin, 1970), 98–103.

into a thousand different sects" (281/613; cf. 76/73, 456/618, 479/746, 507/363). Unlike Descartes, he sometimes attributes the philosophers' inability to reach accord to the tendency of every "sect" to emphasize some aspect of reality at the expense of others (127/415, 131/434, 398/525, 449/556), a second point of divergence, having the same root as the first, as we shall see. In the end, however, Pascal appears to accept the Cartesian reduction of philosophical differences to the "vanity" of the philosophers (142/463, 627/150). Those who profess a noble love for wisdom are as driven by base interests as is the most ordinary human being (145/461).

Still more striking is another point of convergence between the two thinkers. Cartesian utility means, to repeat, the pledge made by Cartesian science to promote bodily well-being rather than disinterested theorizing or civic virtue. Hence in the good it means to serve, as in the moral critique that prepares the way for its public service, the *Discourse* encourages a liberation of self-interest from traditional self-restraints. For according to Descartes's predecessors, the "common good" requires that human beings be educated in a kind of self-forgetting, so that we might learn to take an interest in both the political and the suprapolitical whole of which we are members, even or especially when such interest is at the expense of our private or bodily well-being. What is novel about the Cartesian doctrine of the good, therefore, is not so much its hedonism (to invoke an older and here somewhat inaccurate vocabulary), but that Descartes should identify the body's good both as "common" and as amenable to rational ordering: underlying Cartesian utility is the hypothesis that the interest of the human whole can be furthered by advancing precisely those interests of the human parts indifferent to the whole. As Leo Strauss describes this dramatic peripety in the career of self-interest, the good or rational political order is now to be brought about by forces that do not themselves tend toward the good or the rational.[25]

Remarkably, Pascal seems to endorse this novel idea. "All men naturally hate one another," he observes quite serenely. He then adds, apparently accepting the leading principle of Cartesian utility as an accomplished fact, "[w]e have used concupiscence as best we could to make it serve the public good." The effect of this "use" of concupiscence is not, as the ancients may have supposed, political fragmentation and intellectual degeneration, but rather "an image of charity."[26] Indeed, Pascal is so far

25. *Natural Right and History* (Chicago: University of Chicago Press, 1953), 315. Strauss calls this idea "the principle of modern political economy."
26. 210/451; cf. 106/403, 118/402, 211/453, 674/359. The *Discourse* does not quite arrogate *the* Christian virtue to itself, but it comes remarkably close: see *Discours*, 61, 66 (PW 1.142, 145).

from being scandalized by such arrant Machiavellianism that he points calmly to its workings in the Jansenist community at Port Royal (63/151). Nowhere else does the *Pensées* come so close to approving the core of Descartes's doctrine of the good, and therewith Cartesian utility. Yet it is precisely at this juncture that Pascal's opposition to Descartes comes into sight. Enlightened concupiscence may well be an image of charity, but it is, manifestly, a "false image" (210/451). We must now begin to consider why Pascal should have thought it false, and why he thought that mattered.

As the textbooks instruct us, Cartesian mind is strangely disembodied, not other-worldly certainly, but still somehow "above" the world. On closer inspection, the separation of mind from body, never satisfactorily defended by Descartes in metaphysical terms,[27] proves to be exactly what is required by mathematical physics, which can explain body or nature only apart from soul and its purposiveness (the dismissal of formal and final cause is thus a presupposition, not a fruit, of Cartesian science). By virtue of its rational conquest of nature, the new physics is able to effect in turn a reunion of sorts between human body and mind through its service to our bodily needs and desires (which could never be persuaded to abandon their teleological viewpoint). Prompted by what the *Meditations on First Philosophy* will call the "teaching of nature," set forth in the language of pleasures and pains, Cartesian physics thus dissects the human whole in order to benefit the human composite. Soul takes leave of body so as to manipulate the order of bodies, thereby bringing body and soul more closely into line.[28] To speak somewhat hyperbolically, then, Descartes radicalizes the duality of body and soul in order to overcome it. It is this understanding of the "mind-body problem" that may be said to be the crux of his teaching on utility.

The *Pensées* here moves in precisely the opposite direction. It goes without saying that Pascal never confuses soul and body (108/339, 115/349, 161/221, 418/233, 809/230). But he is also emphatic about their inseparability. There is for him no escaping our embodiment, not even conceptually. "The nature of man is entirely natural, *omne animal*" (630/94, 664/94b; cf. 795/160). Even at its purest, reason should defer to the "body [*corps*]" (cf. 372/483). This does not mean, however, that human rationality is simply subjugated to bodily necessities. To the

---

27. See Pamela A Kraus, "*Mens humana: res cogitans* and the Doctrine of Faculties in Descartes' *Meditationes*," *International Studies in Philosophy* 18 (1986): 1–18.

28. See Jacob Klein, "Modern Rationalism," in *Lectures and Essays*, ed. Robert B. Williamson and Elliot Zuckermann (Annapolis, Md.: St. John's College Press, 1985), 58–59; and Richard Kennington, "The 'Teaching of Nature' in Descartes' Soul Doctrine," *Review of Metaphysics* 26 (1972): 86–117.

contrary, incarnate reason elevates bodiliness, according it an unprecedented dignity. Hence the memorable remarks about the "thinking reed" (200/347). The human being is a being between, a worldly being not explicable in worldly terms. "Man must not believe that he is equal to the brutes or to the angels, nor be ignorant of either, but he must know both" (121/498; cf. 522/140). A properly human life is to be lived in tension, in the stretch between what lies above us and what lies beneath (678/358). Any attempt to overcome or even reduce this tension will result in the distortion or destruction of the human: "To depart from the middle is to depart from humanity" (518/378; cf. 678/358). Descartes's supremely pragmatic reconfiguration of the goal of science must, for Pascal, be just such a departure, aiming at once too high and too low. It is on this basis, and not owing to ad hoc theologizing, that he judges Descartes's best efforts as "useless."

Not that Pascal advocates a full-scale restoration of the theoretical life. For reasons we have already indicated, he doubts whether philosophy in the ancient sense can do much to improve our situation (cf. 926/582, 545/458). Still, what he sees to be the limits of human rationality never prompt him to reduce reason to something merely instrumental. As he says repeatedly, it is reason that "constitutes man's greatness" (759/346; cf. 111/339, 756/365). Indeed, not even the most unseemly possibilities of our nature compromise that greatness. Because it is only in the light of the high that the low can be understood as such, awareness of how low we can sink only underscores our inherent grandeur (53/429, 117/409, 470/404, 526/408). Against both "angelism" and "bestialism," Pascal insists that every human deed, no matter how base or sublime, expresses the essential unity of soul and body. But this is to say that soul, and not bodily appetite or the pineal gland, not the scientific domination of nature or mathematical transcendence of body, is the principle of human "health" or wholeness (cf. 686/336, 957/512, 958/75).

Consequently, Pascal, following his master Augustine, refuses to blame body for our woes. Again contrary to Descartes, it is for him a division within soul that is the origin of the human problem.[29] When he asserts that human nature is irreducibly dual, he is not referring to a split between soul and body. He has in view the ambiguity between "nature" in the sense of the end or perfection of the human being, and "nature" as that which holds true for human beings always and everywhere, the lowest common denominator. Unlike any other "nature" known to us (117/409, 149/430, 685/401), there is in us a terrible gap between what we are and what we ought to be (127/415, 131/434, 616/660).

---

29. Cf. *Les passions de l'âme* a.47, AT 11.364–66 (PW 1.345–47).

Some have attempted to explain this division within us by alleging that the exceptional nature simply proves the common rule: "This duplicity of the human being is so visible that there are those who have thought we have two souls" (629/417). Pascal, immune to the opposing charms of Platonism and nominalism, agrees with a long-standing tradition in supposing that the fissure within human being is as manifest in the few as it is in the many. By nature, we are all of us at odds with our nature, both drawn to and repulsed by the human good.

Of course, Descartes does not for a minute believe that his "common good" can be attained by physics alone, as though the problem were merely technological. Arguably no philosopher before him has offered so little in the way of an "ethics," but as we have seen, a primary purpose of his first publication is to teach readers not to blush in identifying the "first good" with the privacy of bodily health. The methodological mastery of nonhuman nature depends therefore upon premethodological self-mastery of a sort: those passions that naturally favor Descartes's project must be taught to prevail over any that are ill-disposed to it. The abiding duality of the human being leads Pascal to doubt whether appetites most amenable to Descartes's philosophic polity could ever truly dominate our more volatile urges. "The sweetness of fame is so great that, to whatever object we join it, even death, we love it" (37/158; cf. 44/82). In fact, "[a]ny opinion may be preferable to life, the love of which appears so strong and so natural" (29/156). Observations such as these do not entitle us to conclude that Descartes was naive about the obstacles posed by the passions to the indirect rule of his reason. Not for nothing does his final publication, *The Passions of the Soul*, takes up at length the possibility of a sentimental education, of the correction of passion by passion, posed implicitly in his first published work.[30] Nevertheless, Pascal remains far less sanguine about the chances for a long-term reform of our more truculent impulses. Having conceded that society may well be founded upon asocial "concupiscence," he insists that human life both individually and communally will always be feverish, alternating between sweats and chills (27/354; cf. 56/181, 621/412, 805/106). As regards our natural inclinations, the only thing one may rely upon is that they are not reliable.

The "reason for this effect" surfaces with Pascal's remarks on "distraction" or "diversion." Descartes's rejection of Scholastic "speculative phi-

---

30. Cf. *Les passions de l'âme*, §§ 48–50, AT 11.366–70; §§144–48, AT 11.436–42; §§153–61, AT 11.445–47 (PW 1.347–48, 379–82, 384–88, respectively), with the seemingly coincidental foreshadowing of themes in the anonymous first letter introducing the work, AT 11.301–23: passionate self-mastery is both the cause and effect of Cartesian science in the full sense.

losophy" for the sake of utilitarian "practice" echoes Machiavelli's "realistic" correction to the "idealism" of ancient and medieval thought, which Machiavelli had faulted for what he took to be its exaggerated and impotent esteem for the highest human possibilities. In a like manner, Descartes claims that the ancient writings on morals are like "proud and magnificent palaces built upon sand and mud."[31] Indeed, he outdoes Machiavelli in this regard insofar as the self-interested pursuit of health, when directed and abetted by Cartesian reason, looks as though it anchors thinking in something still lower, but even more solid, than the Machiavellian quest for "glory," to say nothing of ancient and medieval highmindedness. What Pascal's account of "diversion" may be said to show is that it is modern "realism" that suffers from "idealism." Precisely because they are so low, the human foundations of Descartes's scientific polity lack human solidity.

The teaching on diversion begins by reminding us that human desire is restless or insatiable. "[A]ll the unhappiness of men stems from a single thing, namely, not to know how to remain quietly in one's room" (136/139; cf. 362/472). One might counter that Descartes was also aware of the stubbornly indeterminate and restless character of human willing. After all, he promises not only cures for an "infinity of maladies," but also an "infinity of contrivances" to generate pleasures sufficient to occupy our increasingly long lives.[32] To this Pascal would reply that human restlessness is only aggravated by subordinating science to desire in this way: because our passions are passions of rational soul, any bid to satisfy them in the terms they themselves dictate must abstract from their real significance.[33] What they ultimately seek, or avoid, is not some thing or other. At bottom they are all driven by an unsettling emptiness no worldly object could ever fill. Whatever the object of a given passion, that passion is, as in some way rational, haunted by the awareness of the inadequacy of its object. "[R]emove [men's] distraction and you will see them dry up with boredom. They will then feel their nothingness without knowing it" (36/164; cf. 70/165b, 136/139, 137/142, 139/143, 414/171, 622/131). It is just this awareness of our nothingness that lends to human passions their peculiarly evanescent urgency. Catching a glimpse of man's radical inability to make himself whole, and divining the horror of this

---

31. *Discours*, 7–8 (PW 1.114).

32. *Meditationes de prima philosophia*, 4, AT 756–62 (PW 2.39–43); *Discours*, 62, together with 25–28 (PW 1.142–43 with 1.123–25).

33. Cf. 470/404. Descartes does caution against allowing the passions free reign to determine their proper objects, but Cartesian reason only corrects the course of the passions, it does not call their fundamental orientation into question. See *Meditationes* 6, AT 7.84–90 (PW 2.58–62); *Les passions de l'âme* §§ 138–48, AT 11.430–43 (PW 1.376–78).

(our "nothingness"), the passions steer us madly toward one temporary refuge after another.

But might it not be that Descartes's "contrivances" were intended, at least in part, precisely as distractions in Pascal's sense? It is a historical commonplace that the Enlightenment that looked back to Descartes actively sought to keep at bay all theological questions, and the bloody controversies that seemed to ensue from them. If the overcoming of distraction was a central aim of Pascal's religious apology, then surely his foes might wish to heap ever more of them upon us. Certainly there is nothing to stop Cartesian philosophy from being "useful" to us in ways that it would not be useful to discuss openly.[34] On Pascal's view, however, enlightened hedonism might win a battle or two, but it could never win the war. Even the most consuming diversions become tiresome, and unease breaks in upon us once again. Worse still, it is by no means clear that peaceful distractions can always successfully compete with the diversionary charms of violent combat, for example, as Nietzsche, here in sympathy with Pascal, would observe retrospectively of the Enlightenment's hope for nonsectarian peace. "Careless we run to the brink, having put something before us to prevent our seeing it," and by "something" Pascal means almost anything whatsoever.[35] Descartes was wrong to suppose bodily health to be the "first" because the most basic or indisputable human good. Good though it is, it cannot be counted upon to keep other candidates for "first" out of mind (21/381, 138/166, 638/109).

That said, the argument still leaves untouched the most recondite meaning of "utility" in Descartes's philosophy. It was observed above that the practical benefits of his public works project can provide no satisfactory explanation for his personal commitment to "do good to others." For that we must look to *The Passions of the Soul*, wherein Descartes announces his doctrine of *generosité*, foreshadowed in the *Discourse* and elsewhere, but set forth in detail only there.[36] The passion of *generosité* is the

---

34. *Discours*, 8, 11–12, 31, 39 (PW 1.114, 116–17, 126–27, 141); "Conversations with Berman," AT 5.176; "Preface to the French Edition," *Principia philosophiae*, AT 9B.18 (PW 1.204–5); *Passions de l'âme*, §§ 76–78, 83, 145, together with §§ 48–50, AT 11.385–86, 390–91, 437–39, 366–70 (cf. PW 1.355–56, 357–58, 379–80, with 347–48). The political theology of the Enlightenment has been treated at length by Robert P. Kraynak in *History and Modernity in the Thought of Thomas Hobbes* (Ithaca, N.Y.: Cornell University Press, 1990).

35. 166/183; cf. 36/139, 414/171, 622/131. Pascal's analysis of the human confrontation with nothingness does much to garner Nietzsche's respect. See, e.g., *Unmodern Observations*, part 1, *David Strauss: Writer and Confessor*, ed. William Smith (New Haven, Conn.: Yale University Press, 1990), 46.

36. For the *Discourse*'s suggestions as to how Descartes himself regards the good of the method, see his discussion of the relative perfection of human "works," *Discours* 11–13, with the correction he provides of the culminating work at 72 (PW 1.116–17, 148). See also

real origin of Descartes's rational conquest of nature. Combining Aristotelian, Stoic, and Epicurean elements in an audacious new whole, this distinctively Cartesian virtue names the self-regarding, self-controlled, and self-gratifying excellence of one who esteems the freedom, resolution, and power of his "will," whether in action or at rest. Viewed from its heights, Cartesian method may be said to be a manifestation of Descartes's self-satisfaction in being "beyond the power of fortune." As the most radical and far-reaching expression of rational human autonomy, *generosité* is both the sign and the seal of the attempt to master nonthinking nature. It is the most powerful embodiment of Cartesian "wisdom," whose principal "use" is said in *The Passions of the Soul* to be "that it teaches us to render ourselves master of our passions to such a degree, and to manage them with such adroitness, that the evils they cause are quite bearable, and even that we derive joy from them all."[37] So sublime is the passion or virtue of *generosité* that it "renders us in a way like God." Here lies the deepest and most provocative stratum of Cartesian "utility."

What reasons might the *Pensées* offer for applying the tag "useless" even here? Pascal readily acknowledges the pleasure to be had from overcoming this or that aspect of our "fortune" (552/107): despite his esteem for Epictetus, he was no Stoic. He even professes admiration for the "extraordinary greatness of soul" necessary to perform rare deeds of good *and* evil (526/408; cf. 157/225). Yet he cannot approve of the magnanimous bid to put all of nature to use (788/486). Such ambition does not reckon sufficiently with the contingency of the human being. But while Pascal often points to the body as proof of our lack of real autonomy, the core of his argument again concerns the limits of human soul.[38] Hence, in the first place, his insistence that "it is not in our power to control our heart" (100/467). The primary thrust of this remark is not that our desires take us places we would not go (149/430). More fundamentally, he means that human beings are born into, or constituted by, an

---

Richard Kennington, "Descartes," *History of Political Philosophy*, 3d ed., eds. Leo Strauss and Joseph Cropsey (Chicago: Rand McNally, 1987), 421–39.

37. *Les passions de l'âme*, §§ 152, 187, 212, AT 11445, 470, 488 (PW 1.384, 395, 404). On *generosité*, see G. Krüger, "Die Herkunft des philosophischen Selbstbewusstseins," *Logos: Internationale Zeitschrift für Philosophie der Kultur* 22 (1933): 225–72, and esp. 251–61; reprint, Darmstadt:Wissenschaftliche Buchgesellschaft, 1962. See aslso Kennington, "Descartes," 432–35.

38. His restatement of the doctrine of a cyclical fortune (27/354, 705/180) is not enough to command acquiescence, of course, because as Descartes had observed, it is surely unwise to submit to unhappy circumstances before we have made a rational determination of what is in our power (*Discours*, 27–28; PW 1.124–25). Similarly, Cromwell's kidney stones (750/176) and Cleopatra's nose (413/162) prove only that traditional political action is particularly susceptible to accidental reversal; they do not prove the fragility of the new, practical philosophy.

unalterable longing: the heart we have we did not choose. This longing would lead us beyond ourselves, to transcend ourselves, to leave the "hateful me" behind (597/455). And although its existence will prove to be a sign or trace of that which would satisfy us, the heart cannot on its own quite know what it wants, much less can it assure our satisfaction. In short, the "heart" spells our essential dependence upon something "outside" of us to complete us (136/139, 143/464, 407/465, 564/485).

A second reason for supposing that the bid for rational self-mastery is a delusion is this: even our thoughts are more adventitious than is acknowledged by Descartes. "What an absurd god," he says of the creature whose thinking may be disturbed by a fly buzzing round his ears (48/366; cf. 829/351). Less egregious but no less indicative of our humble state is the fact that even our best thoughts come to us largely unbidden, and, owing to the fallibility of memory, are likely so to depart, our artful efforts notwithstanding (542/370, 656/372). Pascal surely would not dismiss out of hand Descartes's distinction between "weak" and "strong" minds,[39] but the distinction is here immaterial. Strong or weak, reason is ineluctably discursive, which is to say that the human mind can never come fully into possession of its thoughts, and so of itself, or of its substance (cf. 821/252).

Finally, and most decisively, Pascal would have us ponder the radically contingent character of our very existence. The rhetoric of his argument can be misleading, however. Consider Fragment 135 (206): "The eternal silence of these infinite spaces unnerves me." One might be forgiven for regarding this celebrated phrase, and others akin to it (cf. 68/205, 135/469, 154/237, 194/208, 198/693), as a neurotic's *cri de coeur*. On closer inspection it becomes clear that Pascal's intention here is dialectical: he seeks to awaken in distracted readers questions that follow naturally from a confrontation with their finitude.[40] Here we would do well to recall Descartes's most memorable lesson. Thought's availability to itself, the evidence of my being a thinking being, is so manifest or indisputable that mind almost appears to itself as existing necessarily. From this commonplace of the philosophical tradition, Descartes derives an entirely new sort of "first principle," the "I think."[41] Pascal's most

---

39. *Discours*, 24, 59; cf. 510/7, 512/1 (PW 1.123, 141).

40. Thus the long fragment 427/194 puts similar words in the mouth of an interlocutor. See also 958/75: "What is there about the vacuum that could make them fear? What could be baser and more ridiculous?" On the histrionic character of Pascal's argument, consider P. Topliss, *The Rhetoric of Pascal: A Study of His Art of Persuasion in the "Provinciales" and the "Pensées"* (Leicester, U.K.: Leicester University Press, 1966), esp. 274–304. Balthasar, in *The Glory of the Lord*, 2.94–95, observes that "[t]he spatially infinite is for him a pointer (which even the dim-witted can grasp)."

41. *Discours*, 32 (PW 1.127); *Meditationes* 2, AT 7.25 (PW 2.17); *Principia philosophiae* 1 §§ 7–13, AT 8A.6–11 (PW 1.194–96).

poignant formulations mean to stress, contrarily, the uncanniness of the "I" who thinks, the strange incongruity between our spatial and temporal situation, and the mind's self-givenness. Cartesian mastery of self and world, no matter how successful in the short term, simply cannot overcome the obscurities attending reason's self-discovery, which always occurs in a particular place at a particular time. The "thinking reed" knows himself to be superior to, and in that sense prior to, the whole of the visible universe; but "reed" that he is, he is also aware that he did not make himself, and so can never fully recoup his origins or fend off his expiration. To sum up, the *Pensées* suggests that by virtue of its directedness, its operation, and its situation, human reason, no matter how exemplary, is unable to achieve autonomous or fully rational rule over itself and its circumstances. From Pascal's perspective, there can be little to admire about Cartesian *generosité*.

Why is Descartes useless? Pascal does not oppose the Cartesian teaching on the good with an alternate theory. He simply insists that while an adequate understanding of the good is the one thing needful, we lack such an understanding. The problem is twofold, involving a failure both of intellect and of will. We do not know what is truly in our interest, and we do not make much of an effort to find out.[42] Thus the difficulty is not, as the moralist mistakenly interprets Pascal's "hateful me" (597/455), that human beings are excessively self-interested. To the contrary, we are obstinately deficient in self-interest (119/423, 383/147, 418/233, 427/194, 428/195, 450/494, 823/217). Should it be objected that some human beings at least have caught a glimmer of the good, and do strive to attain it, Pascal would reply that it is still not in their power to secure it for themselves (141/509, 148/425, 269/692). The evidence he adduces for his claim that we cannot secure our own happiness falls under the rubric of "misery," aspects of which we have already discussed. Human misery provides in turn a *ratio dubitandi* for the goodness of the Cartesian project. For if Pascal's analysis of the human condition is plausible, then Descartes's doctrine of utility, which was never shown to be "certain" in strictly mathematical terms, imperils Cartesian philosophy as a whole: a science whose purpose is uncertain is unscientific in a decisive sense.

To conclude, Pascal would seem to have shown that the mastery of na-

---

42. 2/227, 28/436, 75/389, 76/73, 119/423, 149/430, 401/437, 905/385. Cf. J. H. Broome, *Pascal* (New York: Barnes and Noble, 1965), 76–77. Descartes seems to agree with Pascal when he writes, concerning desire, that "the error that one is accustomed to commit here, is never that one desires too much, it is only that one too little desires." The essential point of difference is that Descartes, as opposed to Pascal, has in mind desire "whose outcome depends only on us"; see *Les passions de l'âme* § 144, AT 11.436–37; cf. §§ 139, 145, 146, AT 11.432, 437–40 (PW 1.379; cf. 1.377, 379–81).

ture is useless because it is uncertain.[43] "Useless" is hardly a neutral epithet, however. In the guise of furthering our well-being, Descartes's science diverts us from the urgent task of discovering and pursuing the good. We begin to see that Pascal's resolution "to write against those who deepen the sciences unduly" was anything but obscurantist (553/76; cf. 23/67, 164/218, 496/714, 687/144).

HEART AND MIND

Pascal provides reasons for doubting whether Cartesian science truly serves man as he is, to say nothing of man as he ought to be. But the charge of uncertainty is meant not only to impugn the goal or goals of Descartes's project; it also expresses Pascal's dissatisfaction with his means. In a word, Pascal questions the worth of Cartesian "method." What is at stake here, however, is much greater than the proper technique to be employed by the sciences: for neither Pascal nor Descartes is method itself to be understood methodologically. Because Descartes's doctrine of method, and the certainly it is to provide, issues from a sustained meditation on the relation between the knower and the world, Pascal's disagreement with him proves once again to concern the Socratic question of the nature and place of the human being.

It is in Descartes's *Regulae ad directionem ingenii*, unpublished during his lifetime, that we find some of his most suggestive remarks about the meaning of his new method. The first several of the "rules" explain why methodical direction of the mind should be required at all. Descartes proposes that while the "natural light" of the mind is able to attain simple and certain truths, as is shown paradigmatically by mathematics, nevertheless the "intuitive" power of the mind is naturally hobbled by our manner of proceeding. Instead of moving patiently and assuredly from truth to truth, "blind curiosity" prompts us to venture too quickly into obscure matters; in the absence of methodical discipline, we set our course by vague "experience" and hasty "conjectures"; such is our respect for authority that we rely excessively on "the writings of the ancients" despite their manifest failure to advance systematically. For these and other reasons such discoveries as have been made to date must be deemed a matter of dumb luck. Method will therefore take command of the mind's native ability to grasp truth, chasten its naive trust in its powers and in the world's self-display, and impose its own order upon mind. In this way, it aims to eliminate science's regrettable dependence upon fortune. As we

---

43. Kennington "The 'Teaching of Nature' in Descartes' Soul Doctrine," 116; "Descartes and Mastery of Nature," 212.

have already indicated, the mastery of nature doctrine looks both outward and inward.[44]

The most startling premise of Cartesian method is the claim, evident already in the first "rule," and operative ever thereafter, that thinking may rightly be ordered independently of its objects. In likening the mind to the sun, the *Regulae* upends the traditional solar metaphor for knowledge: not being or the good beyond being, but human intelligence alone lights up the way to the truth of the things known. By supposing that the mind can lay siege to what is without recourse to the world's self-disclosure, the method may bypass what had hitherto seemed the world's self-evident self-articulation into kinds. This means in turn that method can claim to be universal, the same for all "objects" of study: the interest in "certainty" coincides with the interest in "utility" in favoring the mathematical reductionism of Cartesian physics. Descartes is thus able, almost miraculously it must have appeared, to establish method on a scientific footing wholly in advance of any scientific encounter with the world; self-certifying method is to certify all future claims about the world even as it decertifies all prior convictions about it.[45] Not for nothing will the *Discourse* propose Descartes himself initially in the guise of an anonymous "I," as "the first principle of philosophy."[46]

A reader of Pascal who confined himself to *De l'esprit géométrique* might be pardoned for believing that Pascal accepted the notion of a universal method modeled upon the protocols of mathematical demonstration, what the *Regulae* calls "mathesis universalis."[47] The *Pensées* compels a different conclusion, however. To the extent that the literary character of that work embodies Pascal's intentions, a more anti-Cartesian style of writing could not be imagined (532/372). Specific fragments confirm the point. Consider the claim that there is no "art" available either to acquire or to conserve our thoughts (542/370); or note that the "ethics [*morale*] of the mind" is "without rules."[48] Still more emphatic is Pascal's insistence that an act of intellectual "submission," far from being a sign of weakness, may well be required by reason: submissiveness, needless to

---

44. *Regulae ad directionem ingenii*, AT 10.359–71 (PW 1.9–10); also *Discours*, 18–22 (PW 1.183–84); and see Pamela A. Kraus, "'Whole Method': The Thematic Unity of Descartes' *Regulae*," *Modern Schoolman* 63 (1986): 83–109.

45. AT 10.359–61 (PW 1.9–10).

46. *Discours*, 31–32 (PW 1.127); "Preface to the French Edition," *Principia philosophiae* AT 9B.9–10 (PW 1.183–84).

47. *Regulae ad directionem ingenii*, AT 10.378 (PW 1.19).

48. 513/4. On this fragment, see Buford Norman, "L'idée de règle chez Pascal," in *Méthodes chez Pascal: Actes du colloque tenu à Clermont-Ferrand 10–13 juin 1976* (Paris: Presses universitaires de France, 1979), 87–99; also see Thomas More Harrington, *Verité et methode dans le "Pensées" de Pascal* (Paris: J. Vrin, 1972), 82.

say, is not prominent among Cartesian virtues.[49] It comes as no surprise, then, that the *Pensées* flatly rejects the conceit of a single method suited to each and every object of study (511/2, 512/1), and advises us "not judge nature in accordance with us but in accordance with it" (668/457).

Pascal's willingness to be guided by nature's self-presentation by no means heralds a return to prescientific naïveté. He himself warns that "nature often deceives us and does not obey its own rules" (660/91). Or, as he puts it in the *Préface pour le traité du vide*, "the secrets of nature are hidden" (532). Moreover, he so frequently asserts that human nature itself impedes discovery of the nature of things that one cannot read the *Pensées* without thinking of the critiques of natural consciousness advanced not only by Descartes but by all the great early modern philosophers. Not the least of our troubles, Pascal notes, is our blindness to our deficiencies. As he writes in *De l'esprit géométrique*, "It is a natural malady of man to believe that he possesses the truth directly" (585). What, then, can he mean by "judging in accordance with nature"? And how would such a judgment be possible?

Among the most important of the statements on "nature" in the *Pensées* is Fragment 199 (72), entitled "Disproportion of Man." In that fragment Pascal effectively opposes Cartesian method for the very reason that could be said to have motivated it, namely, the fact that we do not possess knowledge of the whole, or more precisely, knowledge of the principles of the whole, and indeed that such knowledge scarcely even seems within our power. Pascal puts the difficulty in the following way:

Since all things are caused and causing, supported and supporting, mediate and immediate, and since everything is mutually sustaining by a natural and imperceptible chain that joins the most distant and the most different things, I hold it impossible to know the parts without knowing the whole, or to know the whole without knowing the parts in detail. (199/72; cf. 927/505)

He is scarcely the first to have stated the problem in these terms, of course. As it happens, an analogous statement is to be found in Descartes, although he puts it to a very different purpose.[50] Fragment 199, in any case, goes a long way toward explaining Pascal's doubts about Cartesian "certainty."

As is clear from the context in which the *aporia* appears, Pascal's purpose is not skeptical in the strict sense. He uses the *aporia* to awaken self-

---

49. 167/269, 170/268, 173/273, 174/270, 182/272, 188/267. Pascal is careful to distinguish "submission" from that bane of the Enlightenment, "superstition," which is for him as much as for any of the philosophes a serious not to say sinful corruption of reason (187/254). Hence his insistence that one demand reasons for one's submission (149/430, 184/811).

50. See *Regulae* 1, AT 10.361 (PW 1.10).

knowledge. More specifically, he would have us see the paradoxical limits of our ability to know. Those limits are paradoxical, of course, because they come into view only to the extent that we have in some measure overcome them. We can know that our knowledge of the whole is fragmentary only because, part though we are, knowledge of the whole is in some way available to us. And since nature is "an infinite sphere whose center is everywhere, and circumference nowhere," the human being must be said to be "disproportionate," a finite being aware of, and so desirous of completion by, the infinite, even though the infinite as such cannot ever complete anything finite, as we in our finite awareness are also aware. The uncanniness of mind is its unsteady grasp of its excessive reach.

Easily overlooked in Pascal's analysis of the problem of knowledge is the conception of the universe correlative to it. In the *Pensées* nature is neither monolithic, nor is it a heap of shards, a "bad tragedy." One might say that the work depends upon a divination of the wholeness of the whole, were it not clear that Pascal is writing as a scientist, for whom it is necessary to suppose that diverse beings exist in their diversity as constitutive of a causally unified world order (65/115, 541/120, 698/119). But precisely because our grasp of nature's wholeness is tenuous, Pascal also takes seriously the self-presentation of the parts, namely, the fact that particular beings themselves show up as relative wholes not reducible to a vaguely perceived whole beyond them.

Consequently, the way a part appears can on inspection be reason for revising one's initial formulation of the wholeness of the whole. Yet just because each part must be understood in terms of every other part, and of the whole that subsumes them all, one's apprehension of the whole must both guide and correct one's initial formulation of the wholeness of any whole part. Pascal's *aporia* in Fragment 199 thereby leads to a vindication of "experience," where "experience" signifies both the determining and the determined ground of all understanding.[51]

One aspect of this defense of experience, rarely discussed, is his assessment of opinion. Earlier we noted Pascal's affinity to Descartes in his

---

51. On "experience," see 111/339, 125/92, 128/396, 365/496, 403/174, 427/194, and esp. "Préface pour le traité du vide," 530, 535. Baird, who provides an otherwise excellent discussion of Pascal's views on nature, overstates the tension between Pascal's experimentalism and his desire for demonstrative arguments. Consider his "Inconsistencies in Pascal's Conception of Scientific Knowledge," *Aumla* 24 (1965): 220–38; and "Pascal's Idea of Nature," *Isis* 61 (1970): 297–320. In fact, it is clear even from *De l'esprit géométrique* that Pascal's science is hypothetical through and through (cf., e.g., 578). For an invaluable treatment of this and related themes, see Balthasar, *The Glory of the Lord*, 3.188–95. See also Strauss, *Natural Right and History*, 122–26, for a discussion of the Socratic approach to parts and wholes, the approach Pascal here emulates.

repudiation of both conventional morality and the moral ambitions of the philosophers. We must now call attention, contrarily, to Pascal's conviction that prephilosophic opinion, faulty though it is, does express a genuine apprehension of the truth, a conviction that leads him to mount a qualified rescue of it. Similarly, although he venerates no philosopher as wise, he is much more willing than Descartes to give the philosophers their due, appealing as he does now to one, now to another, in support of his position.[52] Whereas Cartesian method proposes to set aside all received opinion in order to proceed in a quasi-linear manner, building certainty upon certainty, Pascal holds that understanding can only advance in a "zigzag" fashion, moving dialectically from simplicity to sophistication to knowing simplicity, as partial truths are embraced, subsequently abandoned in light of a fuller understanding, and then appreciated anew in their partial truthfulness (90/337, 91/336, 92/335, 93/328). It is in such terms that we should interpret his by no means Pyrrhonian aphorism, "To mock philosophy is truly to philosophize" (513/4).

The preceding contrast could be put in another way. As is generally accepted, Descartes's method involves a curious amalgamation of skepticism and dogmatism. Experience is subjected to the severest skeptical scruples; what emerges unscathed from even "extravagant doubts," namely, "clear and distinct ideas," are to provide the "foundations" for a true or certain advancement in learning. According to Pascal, this procedure does both too much and too little. Too much, because we know enough to realize that hyperbolic skepticism is unreasonable; too little, because we know that nothing we know can be stated with dogmatic assurance (109/392, 131/434, 170/268, 406/395, 655/377). In his view there are no "simple" certainties, only innumerable partial truths. "Here each thing is true in part and false in part," which entails that all demonstrations involve some degree of circularity.[53] It is Pascal's unswerving adherence to the twilight state between dogmatism and skepticism that explains his derisive tone when adverting explicitly to Descartes. The title of Descartes's 1644 manual, *The Principles of Philosophy*, is called "ostentatious"; Descartes's opinions on matter and space are a "reverie . . . approved by pigheadedness [*entêtement*]"; the Cartesian philosophy as a

---

52. 94/313, 101/324, 520/375; 100/467, 109/392, 131/434, 140/466, 142/463, 449/556, 507/363, 533/331, 649/65, 691/432, and "L'entretien avec M. de Saci," 573–74.
53. 905/385; 527/40. On Pascal's reckoning, the mitigation of our certainties perdures even in the life of faith; cf. 926/582. Had Erich Przywara considered that fragment, he might not have described Pascal's theological position as "epistemological [i.e., Cartesian] Jansenism" in his otherwise suggestive "St. Augustine and the Modern World," in M. C. D'Arcy et al., *A Monument to Saint Augustine* (London: Sheed and Ward, 1945), 249–58.

whole is a "romance of nature, quite like the story of Don Quixote."[54] As these fragments indicate, it is not particular errors in Descartes's physics that vex him most. What chiefly perturbs him is the imperiousness of the method. That nature supplies reasons to question elements of Cartesian science is damning only upon the supposition of hyperbolic certainty, and the categorical dismissal of all that preceded it.[55]

But is it not true that Pascal accepts the notion of a mathematicized physics? Although he distinguishes physics from geometry (376), he clearly joins with Descartes in treating space as something homogeneous or absolute, indifferent to the kind of being moving through it (603ff.). And when he writes "Our soul is cast into a body where it finds number, time, dimensions; it reasons thereupon and calls this nature, necessity, and can believe nothing else" (418/233; cf. 420/419, 110/282, 583), it is impossible not to think of his opponent. He also seems to have entertained Descartes's notorious animal-machine hypothesis (105/342, 107/343, 738/341). Nevertheless, the evidence that Pascal rejected mechanistic physics is in plain view: the most apt contemporary example of an automaton available to Pascal was his own calculating machine, but the only time the *Pensées* mentions it, it is by way of contrasting animal volition with the performance of machines.[56] Of course, the logic of parts and wholes highlighted by Pascal in Fragment 199 alone suffices to show that he could never have accepted the science fiction Descartes advances in *Discourse* 5. While Pascal agreed with Descartes that Scholasticism had overlooked the promise mathematics held for the investigation of nature, he did not believe that Descartes's mathematicized physics would succeed in saving the appearances (cf. 84/79, 686/368, 958/75).

Although he does not say as much on the subject as one might wish, Pascal's own application of mathematics to the domain of nature would have proceeded along rather classical lines, as is suggested by a remark made in a short mathematical treatise entitled *Potestatum numericarum summa*. At the conclusion of that work he writes:

[I]n a continuous quantity, whatever quantities of some kind are added to a quantity of a higher kind add nothing to it. Thus points add nothing to lines, lines nothing to surfaces, surfaces nothing to solids; nor in the case of numbers

---

54. 199/72; 1005l; 1008. Regarding the last comment, and as scholars have occasionally noticed, Descartes himself advises his readers to read his work, at least on one level, as a piece of fiction. See *Discours*, 4, 7, 42 (PW 1.112, 114, 132); and "Preface to the French Edition," *Principia philosophiae*, AT 9B.12 (PW 1.185).

55. See the "Réponse au très bon révérend père Noël," 373–76; "Lettre à M. Le Pailleur," 387; also 161/221.

56. 741/340. On Pascal's objections to mechanism, see Baird, "Pascal's Idea of Nature," 313–16; also see Balthasar, *The Glory of the Lord*, 3.190n55.

... are roots commensurate with squares, squares with cubes, cubes with numbers of the fourth power, etc. Hence, inferior grades are not to be considered, since they are beings of no significance.

A lesser order of mathematical "being" prefigures but never itself yields, and so explains, the greater order, which may be said to contain it. Pascal goes on to say that he has subjoined this remark, which should be "familiar to those who are students of indivisibles," in order that "the connection never sufficiently admired, by which nature, lover of unity, assigns to a one those things that seem most remote" be better appreciated.[57] The reference to "nature" is crucial, for it suggests that Pascal's understanding of number points in the direction of what has been called the "arithmos structure of being," and away from mechanism.[58] According to such an understanding, it is impossible to investigate what is distinctive about a given being merely through analysis into its elements, as Cartesian method would have it. Once again, and as Pascal's mathematical inclinations are now seen to confirm, the lower must be read in the light of the higher. In opposition to the homogeneous universe of Descartes's physics, Pascal believes that even that most analytical domain, the domain of number, supports the view that nature is a hierarchically ordered unity of diverse kinds, or that the being of beings is "analogical," to invoke standard Scholastic usage. Consistent with this orientation, whereas Descartes is most impressed by the mutability of nature, its plasticity or power,[59] the *Pensées* calls attention to the astonishing variety of forms found in nature (65/115, 558/114, 782/266), a variety that is not a random multiplicity because, as Pascal insists, "nature imitates itself."[60]

That nature is drawn together into an analogical unity is, for Pascal, most evident in one being, the human being. The human being manifestly contains in his bodiliness what lies beneath him and prefigures in his thoughts what lies above. As a paradoxical union of apparent opposites, this being provides for Pascal an emblematic display of the wholeness of the whole. At the same time, the fact that human beings are di-

---

57. 171. Cf. 698/119. *De l'esprit géométrique*, 587–92, also advances some suggestive remarks on how mathematical kinds are to be conceived as both discrete and continuous.
58. See Jacob Klein, "The Concept of Number in Greek Mathematics and Philosophy," in *Lectures and Essays*, 43–52, for a brief statement on "eidetic numbers."
59. *Discours*, 44–45 (PW 1.133).
60. 698/119; cf. 541/120, 663/121. Passages such as these suggest that whatever Pascal means by the "infinity" of nature, he does not suppose it to be merely numerically without limit, or that it is abyssmally unintelligible. It looks, rather, as though Pascal's nature is in itself thoroughly intelligible, but in a way that for us must always remain somewhat elusive or mysterious; cf. 199/72. In any case, the imitative ordering Pascal admires is at some distance from the "chaos" at the origin of Descartes's universe, and its intelligible "matter" (*Discours*, 42–43 [PW 1.132]).

vided or fragmentary suggests to him that the natural whole is not ultimate or self-contained (199/72). Given the logic of parts and wholes, however, it is not only true that the being of the human being has implications for our sense of the whole; the being of the whole must also be brought to bear on our sense of ourselves. On this basis, Pascal wonders whether it is possible for us to attain an adequate "perspective" from which to judge who or what we are. The grandeur of the visible universe, and the prodigious minuteness of its smallest known parts, leads him to suspect that we are situated both too near to and too far from ourselves to be able to size ourselves up correctly. Furthermore, what we have divined about the nature of the whole sends an ambiguous message about our place within it: we see enough order within nature to lead us to think that we belong where we are, and enough disorder that we cannot be certain that our placement within nature is anything more than happenstance.[61]

Accordingly, the *Pensées* would seem to discredit what the *Discourse on Method* offers as the two paradigmatic instances of "certainty," mathematical reasoning and the author's indubitable awareness of his existence. Both sorts of certainty are empty, Pascal appears to say, too removed from the aporetic being of things to afford a reliable starting point for science. These same considerations suffice to show that Pascal's preoccupation with the human things is not a matter of narrow "anthropocentrism." The *Pensées* does not amount to a renunciation of Pascal's earlier scientific ambitions. To the contrary, this *Apology* issues from the discovery that human life in all its ambiguity affords us the most reliable point of departure, not to say foundation, for a genuine science of the whole. Although an investigation of the human things cannot help but involve some narrowing of focus, in no other part of the whole does pursuit of depth involve so little loss of breadth (cf. 195/37). And at the center of Pascal's investigation of the human things is, again, his teaching on the "heart."

What the *Pensées* announces about the heart constitutes Pascal's real alternative to Cartesian method. For it is the human heart that is, in his opinion, both the principal obstacle to, and the safest path to the truth about things. Now, although the romanticist reading of Pascal has long since been abandoned, it bears repeating that by "heart" he does not mean the seat of mere sentiment: "The heart has its *reasons* . . ." (423/277). The term is plainly of biblical provenance, as numerous scriptural

---

61. Among the many fragments relevant to the problem of an adequate "perspective" for self-knowledge, see 21/381, 54/112, 65/115, 199/72, 200/347, 558/114, 574/263, 701/9, and 113/348. On nature's ambiguous significance for our self-understanding, see 199/208, 427/194, 449/556, and 934/580. To my knowledge, no one has treated the cosmology of the *Pensées* better than Hans Urs von Balthasar, in "Pascal," *The Glory of the Lord*, vol. 3, passim.

citations in the *Pensées* attests, but Pascal's use of the term is not exclusively or even primarily theological. A survey of its appearances indicates that it names a *hendiadys*. In Thomistic vocabulary, "heart" designates both *intellectus* or "understanding" (as opposed to *ratio* or "reason") and *voluntas* or "will." The *Pensées*'s general refusal to employ two terms for what are, after all, two distinct powers of the soul surely involves some loss of precision, but it does have the advantage of maintaining their dramatic unity in view. Taken singly and in their being together these two moments of Pascal's teaching on "heart" offer a powerful challenge to Cartesian certainty.

When Pascal writes of the heart's possession of reasons "of which reason knows nothing," he has foremost in mind the fact that much of what we know we know nondiscursively, that a good portion of what we count as knowledge is given "all at once," "at a glance." In keeping with the tradition, he invokes the metaphor of sight to describe this noetic capacity. The proper objects of this power are what he calls "principles," which undergird the wholeness of the whole, and of its parts. Such principles mark the most subtle differences between things, which is to say that they are almost innumerable. Nor are they always easily communicated, especially if one's interlocutor does not have the "eyes" to see them (512/1, 751/3). Notwithstanding certain formulations, however, the author of the *Pensées* does not simply oppose the heart's easy insights to reason's hard labor. For he allows that owing to the limits of our noetic capacities, we must often work toward some truths discursively that are in principle available intuitively (110/282), even if it is "only to a certain degree" that reason can bring us to know things known or knowable through the heart (512/1). So, too, noetic apprehension of a principle does not eliminate the need for further investigation through both discursive and nondiscursive means, as a glance at *De l'esprit géométrique* makes plain (cf. 580–82). And while the directness of the heart's hold on what it knows does suggest a certain superiority to the more roundabout achievements of reasoning, Pascal never claims that the heart is infallible. To the contrary, he thinks it all too prone to err; indeed, its very superiority to reason's struggle to attain to what it knows is among the heart's greatest weakness, for of itself it is unable to distinguish genuine insight from woeful delusion (131/434, 530/274). Nevertheless, were reason skeptically to impugn the heart on the basis of the heart's inability to justify what it sees, reason would only betray its own stupidity, because human life, and indeed reason itself, cannot subsist without the acceptance of many indemonstrable principles (131/434, 512/1, 513/4, 514/356).

What may be said to be the subjective limitations of Pascal's "heart" do not entirely explain its scope, however, for its operation finally depends upon the givenness of the thing known, and not on its acuity. There are obscurities in things that cannot be cleared up, no matter how sharp the mind's eye (449/556). Or rather, the inability of the human heart to grasp all existing "principles" does not ultimately point either to its own intrinsic limitations or to the twilight intelligibility of nature's more recondite principles: what it really signifies is a superabundant intelligibility suffusing all that exists. That which most impresses itself upon Pascal's heart is that there is ever more to be seen than ever meets the mind's eye (512/1; cf. 931/550).

It should be clear why Pascal must think Descartes, and his methodically disciplined reasoning, so "uncertain." For Pascal, it is the thing known that provides the evidence sustaining the heart's knowing grasp of it.[62] Admittedly, thinking is not for the rationalist Descartes an entirely "rational" process either. If the frequent use of "intuition" in the *Regulae* is not an entirely accurate gauge of his subsequent intentions, still, later appeals to the "clear and distinct" do suggest something like an immediate apprehension of certain truths.[63] Still, Pascal obviously accords greater authority to the "heart" than Descartes ever would. The upshot of his account is that much of what the heart knows for certain, indeed among the most important and most "scientific" things it grasps, simply cannot meet the demands of methodical rigor. As we have indicated, the heart's knowledge is always subject to refinement and even correction. Thus what appears in Descartes as a "realistic" distrust of normal human attachments, and of premethodical opinion above all, proves for Pascal to be wedded to "idealistic" suppositions of a most suspect sort.[64] Pascal's teaching on the heart could be said to show, once again, that philosophy cannot exercise fully rational rule over itself.

Now, although the intuitive powers of "heart" are readily visible in the *Pensées*, Pascal's treatment of heart as the seat of volition obviously constitutes the dominant theme of his analysis. Even here, however, the issue is again primarily noetic, concerning as it does the ways human desire both

62. Cf. 255/.758, 7/248. This summary sketch does not mean to imply that the *Pensées*'s teaching on the heart fully restores the ancient theory of noetic intuition. Like so much else Pascal has left us, the argument here is undeveloped. Nor am I claiming that his vocabulary is entirely consistent. In *De l'esprit géométrique*, e.g., "heart" appears to have a somewhat more restricted meaning than in the *Pensées*; cf. 592–94.

63. *Regulae*, AT 10.361, 368–70, 379 (PW 1.10, 14–15, 20); *Discours de la méthode*, 32–33, 36, 39 (PW 1.127, 128, 130); *Meditationes*, 4, AT 7.58–59; *Principia philosophiae*, AT 8A.8, 21–24 (PW 1.206–9).

64. Baird points out a further difference between Pascal and Descartes on the question of "intuitive" knowledge especially relevant in this regard. Whereas Descartes argues for the separation of intuition from sensation and especially imagination, Pascal "expressly affirms that self-evident principles or axioms can derive from either the senses or the reason" ("Inconsistencies in Pascal's Conception of Scientific Knowledge," 223).

impedes and promotes our search for the truth. At the forefront of his analysis of the heart as an appetitive organ is his observation that "the eyes of the heart" (308/793) are often clouded by spurious interests, that our ability to lay hold of the proper starting points for understanding may be "poisoned" by corrupt inclinations. "How the heart of man is hollow and filled with dung," he laments (139/143; cf. 136/139, 310/801, 427/194, 470/404, 821/252, 978/100). Let us not allow this impassioned utterance to obscure his intentions, however. For he also insists that it possible for men to desire the truth, and even to do so wholeheartedly (149/430, 150/226, 427/194). The human being is not in his book utterly depraved; it would be more accurate to say that our hearts are "torn" (924/498). Hence two different men can construe the same experience in two different ways, the one's heart disposing him to see the thing as it is, the other's misdirecting him—the division between two hearts being a function of the division possible within any single one (503/675; cf. 539/99). Pascal's principal point is, therefore, that there is a deeply moral basis to all cognition. And this becomes especially significant when we are confronted by truths the evidence for which is equivocal (835/564). Indeed, if it is true that "everything here is partly true, partly false," that all knowledge is provisional or partial, it follows that all genuine science is and must be moral science. Again, the Cartesian method would seem not to confront the most serious obstacles to the advancement of learning.

One might object, however, that equally for Descartes the will plays an integral role in the attainment of truth. As it is introduced in the *Discourse*, the method depends at crucial junctures on its author's "resolve." And in the Fourth of his *Meditations* he explains that error has its origin in the fact that "the will extends further than the intellect," from which it follows that a willful disciplining of will is needed in order to limit our affirmations to what is really clear and distinct.[65] Pascal, however, could counter that precisely because thought always finds itself in the context of obscurity, restraint and resolve will never suffice. The burden of numerous fragments of the *Pensées* is to show that the only guarantor of our moving in the right direction is that our heart be in the right place; where certainties are not available (but also when they are), the best we can do is to dispose ourselves to be drawn to and to receive what truth there is to be known; and this means, in the final analysis, that we are again dependent upon something "outside" us, upon that which would

---

65. 12, 14, 16–17, 18, 22–24, 41, 60 (PW 1.116, 118–19, 120, 122–23, 131, 142); *Meditationes*, 4, AT 7.58–62 (PW 2.240–42). See Hiram Caton, "Will and Reason in Descartes' Theory of Error," *Journal of Philosophy* 72 (1975): 87–104.

rightly "incline our heart." In short, there can be for Pascal no permanent overcoming of the circle of intellect and will; what is left to us is the perpetual reconsideration of our own stance in every attempt to discern how things stand with the world.[66]

Both the noetic and the moral aspects of Pascal's teaching on the heart are implicit in his censure of Cartesian "theology."[67] "I cannot forgive Descartes: he would like, in all his philosophy, to do without God; but he could not prevent himself from granting to him a flick of the finger in order to set the world in motion; beyond this he had no use for God" (1001). Pascal here appears to overlook the fact that Descartes does not restrict God's role to filling in an explanatory gap in his physics. God's existence also functions in Descartes's philosophy as the third paradigm of certainty, after the indubitable "I think," and correct mathematical reasoning; in fact, it purports to be the rationally validated guarantor of the first two forms of certainty, albeit never as "first principle" of the method. But whatever one makes of the appropriateness of Descartes's use of the divine, the Deism his publications helped decisively to launch is, according to Pascal, not at all a sure thing. Worse still, it is almost as far removed from Christianity as is atheism (449/556; cf. 191/549, 463/243). Pascal's complaint is anything but sectarian. Quite apart from his concern to defend the specific claims of biblical revelation, he is troubled by a science which, under the banner of methodical certainty, would obscure the genuine traces of God's wisdom and goodness present in the world.[68] To be sure, the *Pensées* must itself seem curiously deficient, not to say insouciant, when viewed from a Scholastic perspective, given its inability or unwillingness to marshal an argument for God's existence drawn from the order of nature. Yet there is no disputing that Pascal understood the world and everything in it to be an image of God.[69] If he did not supply a natural theology of his own, this must have been in part because Descartes had helped him to see that formal and

---

66. Cf. 21/381, 558/114. Even the definitive correction of the heart's wayward tendencies, which comes from "above," and which Pascal, following Saint Paul, following Jeremiah, following Deuteronomy, calls "circumcision of the heart" (268/683, 270/670, 288/689, 453/610), does not eliminate all obscurities.

67. The theme has recently been treated in Vincent Carraud, "Le refus Pascalien des preuves métaphysiques de l'existence de Dieu," *Revue des sciences philosophiques et théologiques* 75 (1991): 19–45; and Francis Kaplan, "Deux attitudes face au problème philosophique de l'existence de Dieu," in the same source, 81–95. See notes 8, 26, and 34 above.

68. Note that Descartes's various "proofs," whatever other merits they may have, never proceed from some order perceived within the world. The turn to mechanism and away from teleology implies that nature expresses no divine "intentions," such that the only things Descartes offers as evidence for God's existence are his "ideas."

69. See 429/229, 471/441, 698/119, 934/580. Also "Lettre III à Mme. Périer," 484; "Lettre V à Mlle. de Roannez," 51; "Entretien avec M. de Saci," 571.

impersonal arguments do not necessarily serve Christianity. In general, he seems to have thought that ordinary Scholastic arguments failed to do justice to the obscurity of the subject, and that they did not attend sufficiently to the circumstances in which such efforts would be most useful. Especially in light of recent developments in physics, but even apart from them, Pascal expressed hesitations about the properly theological worth of ordinary natural theology: it is impossible thereby to "see" the biblical God, who reveals to man that he hides himself (242/585, 427/194, 449/556, 463/243). He was also convinced that those most in need of a proof for God's existence are least disposed to appreciate its force. "I see by reason and experience that nothing is more suited to arouse [the unbeliever's] contempt than the usual proofs for religion" (781/242; cf. 3/244, 190/543, 449/556). As for Descartes, to the limited extent that he does engage in "theology," he must truly be "more than a man," for the god in whom he would have us entrust all our certainties is introduced with little or no regard for human experience as such, and so can have little or nothing to teach us about our humanity. Here as elsewhere, the thrust of Pascal's interrogation of Descartes's method is that we cannot possibly make use of the certainty it professes to provide.

Pascal's teaching on the heart restores us to our point of departure. For if Cartesian utility is useless because it is humanly uncertain, Cartesian certainty is dubious because it is not humanly useful. Just as the problematic character of the good or goods Descartes's science means to foster calls the utility of that science into question, so, Pascal seems to argue, Descartes's method must fail to reach genuine certainty because it does not properly confront the disproportion of the human being, and therewith the divided heart, that which makes all knowledge both possible and problematic. Just as we cannot gain scientific access to the good apart from a sustained reflection on the true, so the true only comes into sight through a continuous meditation on the good. The *Pensées* would have us see that a science that departs from the human experience of the human will divert us from both the good and the true.

6   Spinoza, Biblical Criticism, and the Enlightenment

PAUL J. BAGLEY

For modern philosophers and Enlightenment thinkers, hopes for the improvement of the human condition rested largely upon a promise of unlimited progress through the attainment of what became interrelated goals. They included the eradication of theological prejudices and superstitions; the promotion of religious tolerance; the advocacy of personal civil liberties; the advancement of science through the development of technology; and an appeal to history as the criterion that would demonstrate the superiority of modernity over antiquity. Hence "the Enlightenment" is identified with the salient features of philosophizing in the seventeenth and eighteenth centuries, that is, a criticism of the dogmatic elements of religion, a defense of freedom of expression, the rise of political liberalism, and the acceptance of the "new science" with its promise of benefits to man through the improvement of the mechanical arts and medicine. But there is also another philosophic tradition of enlightenment, which differs from the modern project. This enlightenment owes its origin at least to the account of "an image of our nature in respect to its education and lack of education" offered by Plato in *The Republic*.[1] In the Myth of the Cave, the overcoming of darkness and shadows is made possible only by an ascent that involves the purification and correction of one's vision—although Plato is careful to warn his readers that such a transition from darkness to light is not accomplished with ease.[2]

Crudely stated, then, the very act of philosophizing may be inseparable from the act of enlightening. But the kind of enlightenment that applies to the ancients is quite different from that typically practiced by the moderns. In this essay, we are to consider Baruch Spinoza's relation to the modern phenomenon called "the Enlightenment." But in examining

1. 514ff.
2. 515c–516b.

that relation I also wish to question whether Spinoza's enlightenment tendencies were exclusively identified with those of his modern colleagues or successors.

SPINOZA AND MODERN ENLIGHTENMENT

If modernity, and hence the Enlightenment, invokes a radical and new orientation of philosophy toward science, politics, and theology, then we may locate the origins of the "new science" with thinkers such as Bacon, Descartes, Newton, and Leibniz, and of the "new politics" with Hobbes, Locke, and others. But in regard to what may be termed the "new theology," its Enlightenment progenitor was Spinoza.[3] For as the "new science" and the "new politics" evolved from the critiques of the prejudices of the established teachings about science and politics, so too the "new theology" emerged out of the critiques of theological prejudices; and Spinoza's *Tractatus theologico-politicus* was perhaps the first work to contain an overt methodical criticism of them.[4]

3. An important study of the significance and influence of Spinoza's teaching in the *Tractatus theologico-politicus* is Leo Strauss's *Spinoza's Critique of Religion*, trans E. M. Sinclair (New York: Schocken Books, 1965); for the relation between Spinoza's teaching and the Enlightenment, see esp.178–82. Spinoza's treatise is noted for its analysis of the foundations of Scripture, its attack upon theological prejudices, and its formulation of an historico-literary method of biblical interpretation. In addition, of course, the work contains a defense of democratic liberalism.
  The identification of Spinoza's *Tractatus theologico-politicus* more with theological issues than with political issues is warranted in part by the preponderance of the theological subject matter of the book. But it is worth recalling that both Hobbes and Locke also devoted much consideration to religious or theological matters in their political teachings. In *Leviathan*, Parts 3 and 4 of the work respectively address "The Christian Commonwealth" and "The Kingdom of Darkness." And in *The First Treatise of Government*, Locke contests the "scripture-proofs" adduced by Sir Robert Filmer in defense of "the original of political power" as somehow grounded in a divine right to kingship based upon the "natural slavery of mankind."
  4. All passages cited from the *Tractatus theologico-politicus* will be taken from the standard Heidelberg Latin edition and from the English translation of it by Samuel Shirley. See *Spinoza Opera*, 4 vols., ed. Carl Gebhardt (Heidelberg: Carl Winters Universitaetsbuchhandlung, 1925); and *Tractatus theologico-politicus*, trans. Samuel Shirley (Leiden: E. J. Brill, 1989). In the notes, the *Tractatus theologico-politicus* will be abbreviated *TTP*; page references will be to the Heidelberg edition and the Shirley translation, respectively. In the text, the *Tractatus theologico-politicus* will also be referred to as the *Tractatus* or the treatise, wherever appropriate.
  Spinoza's overt criticism in *TTP* of theological prejudice is frequent. For example, on the basis of the application of his historico-literary method of interpreting the Bible, Spinoza begins the final chapter of the theological part of *TTP* proper (i.e., Chapter 15) with the declarations that "*Scripturam non res philosophicas, sed solam pietatem docere, & omnia, quae in eadem continentur, ad captum & praeconceptas opiniones vulgi fuisse accommodata*"; and "*Qui autem contra rationem & Philosophiam Theologiae ancillam facit, is antiqui vulgi praejudicia tanquam res divinas tenetur admittere, & iisdem mentem occupare & obcaecare; adeoque uterque, hic sci-*

Spinoza's *Tractatus theologico-politicus* was published anonymously in 1670 or in the latter months of 1669. The title page of the first edition of the work indicated that it had been published in Hamburg by Henry Künrath, but in fact the work had been printed in Amsterdam. Only months after its publication, Jacob Thomasius and Friedrich Rappolt published works in Germany decrying the *Tractatus* as "blasphemous"; and by 1675 printing and circulation of the treatise had been banned by virtually every synod in The Netherlands. Still, at the beginning of the decade, three impressions of the *Tractatus* were made, all bearing the publication date of 1670; and from 1673 and 1674 there were four new editions of the treatise from Amsterdam and Leiden. Only one of the later editions bore the original name of the treatise; the other three were published under different titles.[5] In 1671, even after Spinoza asked his friend, Jarig Jelles, to prevent it, the publication of a Dutch translation of the *Tractatus* appeared from the hand of Jan Glazenmaker.[6]

With the increased availability of the treatise came more denunciations of it as an atheistical work.[7] In 1674 alone there appeared several refutations of the *Tractatus*. Their authors included Jacob Veteler, a Remonstrant preacher; Regner van Mansvelt, a professor of theology at Utrecht; Spitzelius, a Lutheran preacher; Musaeus, a professor of theology at Jena;

---

licet sine ratione, ille vero cum ratione insaniet"; see *TTP* 3.180/228. Also consider that in Epistle 30 to Henry Oldenburg, written in September or October 1665, Spinoza explicitly acknowledged that his composition of *TTP* was compelled by the "prejudices of the Theologians" inasmuch as they were an impediment to philosophizing: "*Compono iam tractatum de meo circa scripturam sensu; ad id vero faciendum me movent, Praejudicia theologorum; scio enim, ea maxime impedire, quo minus homines animum ad philosophiam applicare possint: ea igitur patefacere atque amoliri a mentibus prudentiorum satago.*"

5. See Jacob Freudenthal, "On the History of Spinozism," *Jewish Quarterly Review* 8 (1895–1896): 30–31. Detailed documentation concerning Spinoza's life and circumstances is contained in Freudenthal's *Die Lebensgeschichte Spinozas* (Leipzig Veit, 1899).

6. See Epistle 40 to Jarig Jelles. In that letter, Spinoza pleads that every means possible be exercised to prevent publication of a Dutch translation of *TTP*. Also see Brad Gregory's "Introduction" to Samuel Shirley's translation of *TTP*, 27.

7. It is worth recalling that the early reception of Spinoza's *TTP*, as well as his *Ethica ordine qeometrico demonstrata*, earned him a reputation as a proponent of atheism. In correspondence between Jacob Oostens and Lambert van Velthuysen, extant since the publication of the *Opera Posthuma* (Epistles 48 & 49 [Eps. 42 & 43 in the Wolf edition of *The Correspondence of Spinoza*]), the latter correspondent criticized Spinoza for teaching atheism in *TTP* and for doing so with "colored and disguised arguments." Bayle, in his famous *Dictionary* article on Spinoza, asserted that Spinoza was "a systematical atheist" who "brought his atheism into a new method" (a reference to the *Ethica* and its geometrical method of presentation). Moreover, Bayle accused Spinoza of trying to "disguise and conceal" his atheism. Only with the "Pantheismusstreit" of 1785 was Spinoza's name dissociated from atheism and increasingly a regard for him as the "Gottvertrunkenermensch" (the phrase coined by Novalis) became common. It could be suggested that one casualty of the Enlightenment was a serious regard for the "art of reading."

Willem van Blijenbergh, a merchant and correspondent of Spinoza; and Lambert van Velthuysen, an Utrecht physician.

Notwithstanding the ban on the circulation of the work, and the numerous tracts written in opposition to it, the *Tractatus* continued to be studied and distributed, albeit clandestinely or under some disguise. Between 1681 and the end of the seventeenth century, the *Tractatus theologico-politicus* was translated into French either two or three times; and, according to Pierre Bayle, it was printed under three different titles: *Traité des cérémonies superstitieuses des Juifs*, *La clef du sanctuaire*, and *Réflexions curieuses d'un esprit désintéressé*.[8] The first complete English translation of the treatise appeared anonymously from a London publisher in 1689 under the title *A Treatise Partly Theological and Partly Political, Containing Some Few Discourses*. But already in 1683, one of the principal figures in the Deist controversy in England and putatively one of the movement's founders, Charles Blount, had incorporated an English translation of Chapter 6 of the *Tractatus* ("Of Miracles") into his own book, *Miracles No Violations of the Laws of Nature*.[9]

Owing to its rapid and extensive circulation, the teachings contained in Spinoza's treatise exerted considerable influence on contributors to the French Enlightenment, as well as those responsible for "freethinking" in England, the Deists. In examining Spinoza's relation to the French Enlightenment, Ira Wade concluded that the *Tractatus theologico-politicus* "was destined to be the fountain-head of the whole deistic movement in the Enlightenment in France."[10] As is plainly indicated in manuscripts attributed to Boulanvilliers, Fréret, Dumarsais, Lévesque de Burigny, and Mirabaud, those thinkers of the French Enlightenment had a common aim; Boulainvilliers, the "leading spirit of the group," was avowedly attracted to the philosophy of Spinoza, and communicated that interest to the others.[11] One could observe in the body of works attributed to those thinkers "a community of interests, a conformity of religious and philosophic views, and a sharing of mutual ideas, all of which occur in one way or another in Spinoza, Bayle, or Fontenelle, which are more or less connected with Biblical criticism and lead to critical deism."[12] Furthermore, because Spinoza "was the force who almost single-handedly

---

8. Pierre Bayle, *An Historical and Critical Dictionary*, 4 vols. (London, 1710), 4.2789; also see Ira O. Wade, *The Structure and Form of the French Enlightenment*, 2 vols. (Princeton, N.J.: Princeton University Press, 1977), 1.183.

9. Blount's interpolation of Chapter 6 of *TTP* into his own work was quickly denounced in Thomas Browne's *Miracles Works Above and Contrary to Nature* (London, 1683), 2.

10. Wade, *The Structure and Form of the French Enlightenment*, 1.180.

11. Ibid., 1.185.

12. Ibid. On the connection between "critical deism" and the French Enlightenment, see Ira. O. Wade, *The Intellectual Development of Voltaire* (Princeton, N.J.: Princeton University

among the philosophers (though he had a massive following among the encyclopedists) questioned the historical tradition of the Bible," Wade asserted that "the long line of English and French Deists were for the most part followers of Spinoza's biblical criticism in the *Tractatus*."[13] The centrality of Spinoza's treatise to the program of Deism in England, and hence the development of an English Enlightenment,[14] was also affirmed by Leslie Stephen. In his *History of English Thought in the Eighteenth Century*, Stephen averred that "it is enough to remark that the whole essence of the deist position may be found in Spinoza's *Tractatus Theologico-Politicus*. A few of the philosopher's passages have expanded into volumes and libraries of discussions; but the germs of the whole discussion are present" in that work.[15]

In terms of Enlightenment thinking, Spinoza's connection with that movement seems reasonably clear. His open criticism of religious or theological prejudices resulted from a close examination of the Bible, which led him to conclude that extreme views dogmatically attributed to Scripture were the products of human ignorance or vanity rather than

---

Press, 1969), 511–13. There Wade discusses the importance of Spinoza's biblical criticism for the "school at Cirey" and its influence upon Voltaire's critical deism. Though Voltaire was no advocate of Spinoza's philosophy, the biblical criticism articulated in *TTP* was a chief source of inspiration for French Bible critics generally during the seventeenth and eighteenth centuries; see, e.g., 694: "The one incontrovertible fact is that the *Tractatus* was the source of all critical deism in the Cirey period."

13. Wade, *The Structure and Form of the French Enlightenment*, 2.238.

14. On the connection between "English Deism" and the "English Enlightenment," see Rosalie L. Colie, "Spinoza and the Early English Deists," *Journal of the History of Ideas* 20 (1959): 23–46, esp. 28–29 and 33: "In the period after the 1688 Revolution, Spinoza's sharply reasoned argument for toleration supported Englishmen like Blount, Gildon, and Toland, who sought precedents for their views wherever they could find any, whether among the theorists of the Commonwealth or of the continent. Spinoza, so thoroughly secular, criticized the theological schisms provoked whenever liberty of thought was restricted by law, and condemned the brutality involved in administering such legislation."

15. Leslie Stephen, *The History of English Thought in the Eighteenth Century*, 2 vols. (London: Smith, Elder, 1876), 1.33. On Spinoza's influence with respect to the Enlightenment in England, see Margaret C. Jacob, *The Radical Enlightenment: Pantheists, Freemasons, and Republicans* (London: George Allen & Unwin, 1981).

The use of Spinoza's biblical criticism was not limited to those who intended to contest the authority of theologians or to those who wished to restrict the influence of ecclesiastical power in scientific or political affairs. In a sermon delivered on 23 February 1682/83, Edward Stillingfleet considered Richard Simon's *Critical History of the Old Testament* and Spinoza's *TTP* with respect to the matter of prophecy. See Gerard Reedy, S.J., "Spinoza, Stillingfleet, Prophecy, and 'Enlightenment,'" in *Deism, Masonry, and the Enlightenment*, ed. J. A. Leo Lemay (Newark: University of Delaware Press, 1987), 49–60. On the points of agreement between Stillingfleet and Spinoza, see, e.g., 56: "Although Spinoza and Stillingfleet clearly mean different things when they invoke reason and rational proof in matters of divinity, both attempt to liberate divinity from superstition and from reliance on inner light as a means of verification."

divine inspiration.[16] Where darkness had prevailed, Spinoza would bring light; and to demonstrate the superstitious character of certain accepted theological doctrines, Spinoza actually appealed from traditional theology to the Bible itself.[17] In other words, Spinoza's success in exposing theological prejudices and superstitions was achieved by his having recourse to the very source from which those prejudices and superstitions themselves had been derived. To ascertain the authentic meaning of the Bible and separate it from human inventions, Spinoza required that one distinguish the shadows attached to the doctrines from the doctrines themselves. The lamp used to supply the light necessary for that task was a new method of scriptural interpretation.

SPINOZA AND BIBLICAL CRITICISM

In the Preface to the *Tractatus theologico-politicus* Spinoza asserts that the principal aim of the work is to demonstrate not only that freedom of judgment could be granted to individual citizens without endangering piety or the public peace, but indeed that piety and the public peace depend upon such freedom.[18] For Spinoza, men are prevented from the attainment and exercise of such freedom because they suffer from servitude to "religious prejudices" and they have come to despise the "natural light" in itself or to condemn it as a source of impiety.[19] To defend freedom of judgment in religious and civil matters, Spinoza seeks to establish that reason or philosophy and Scripture or theology are not essentially antagonistic to one another. Rather, Spinoza argues, they stand "on totally different footings"—though he also professes to have found "nothing expressly taught in Scripture that was not in agreement with the intellect or that contradicted it."[20] To demonstrate his conviction that Scripture does not

---

16. In the Preface to *TTP*, especially the first three paragraphs, Spinoza establishes the connection between ignorance of the operations of nature, the fear that ensues from such ignorance, and the resultant prejudices and superstitions that emerge.

17. See Leo Strauss, "How to Study Spinoza's *Theologico-Political Treatise*," in *Persecution and the Art of Writing* (Westport, Conn.: Greenwood Press, 1973), 193.

18. *TTP*, 3.7/51.

19. *TTP*, 3.7–9/52–53.

20. *TTP*, 3.10/54. The problematical nature of Spinoza's declaration is evident in respect to the question of miracles. The Bible relates events that are allegedly supernatural in origin. But Spinoza argues in Chapter 6 of *TTP* that miracles or events contravening the laws of nature are impossible. Only the recasting of the term "miracle" by Spinoza to mean "an event for which the natural causes are not yet known or indicated" can allow him to hold that there is no disagreement or contradiction between what is "taught in Scripture" and "the intellect" on the issue of miracles. It is thus evident that Spinoza retains the name "miracle" but strips it of any orthodox religious significance; only on that account can he profess that there is no disagreement to be found between reason and revelation.

inhibit the use of reason, and hence does not prohibit the exercise of free judgment, Spinoza proposes to proceed in "logical order and to settle the whole question conclusively" by "showing in what way Scripture should be interpreted," that is, by seeking an understanding of Scripture and spiritual matters from Scripture alone.[21] Such a procedure would involve the development of a biblical hermeneutic, or the application of some existing interpretative method. For Spinoza, "the method of interpreting Scripture is no different from the method of interpreting Nature, and is in fact in complete accord with it."

According to Spinoza, there is need for an assured method of scriptural interpretation because men frequently twist the meaning of biblical passages to "parade their own ideas as God's Word" in an effort to compel others to think as they do.[22] Even "the chief concern of theologians on the whole had been to extort from Scripture their own arbitrarily invented ideas,"[23] in Spinoza's view. Adopting a method of scriptural interpretation based upon the model of an interpretation of Nature would make it possible "to escape from this scene of confusion, to free our minds from the prejudices of the theologians, and to avoid the hasty acceptance of human fabrications as divine teachings."[24] The method proposed by Spinoza would enable one to examine the Bible "as the source of our fixed data and principles" and from them one could "deduce by logical inference the meaning of the authors of Scripture."[25] Essential and decisive to the method of scriptural interpretation advocated by Spinoza is its reliance upon reason as the single standard for determining the correct understanding of the meaning of the Bible.[26]

Spinoza's rationale for appealing to an objective method of scriptural interpretation is to prevent believers from accepting the meaning imputed to certain biblical passages by zealots, fanatics, and sectarians. Nevertheless, the method itself had limitations inasmuch as Scripture was problematical in respect to its form or content. A peculiar style of writing,

21. Ibid.; cf. the beginning of Chapter 7: *TTP*, 3.97–99/140–42.
22. *TTP*, 3.97/140.   23. Ibid.
24. *TTP*, 3.98/141.   25. Ibid.
26. *TTP*, 3.112/154–55: "I consider that I have now displayed the true method of Scriptural interpretation and sufficiently have set forth my opinion on this matter. Furthermore, I have no doubt that it is now obvious to all that this method demands no other light than the natural light of reason. For the nature and virtue of that light consists essentially in this, that by a process of logical deduction that which is hidden is inferred and concluded from what is known, or given as known. This is exactly what our method requires. And although we grant that our method does not suffice to explain with certainty everything that is found in the Bible, this is the consequence not of the defectiveness of the method but of the fact that the path which it tells us is the true and correct one has never been pursued or trodden by men, and so with the passage of time has become exceedingly difficult and almost impassable."

an ambiguous word, or an odd event contained in Scripture might not readily admit of a simple rational explanation or understanding. Yet in all such cases, according to Spinoza, the method was to employ the "natural light" as a touchstone. Thus, rather than purporting to give an account of the whole of the Bible, the method basically demanded that plain contradictions or inconsistencies among various biblical passages be rejected as untrustworthy. As a result, the teachings of revelation ultimately would be validated by reason (and hence the prospect of secularization was advanced).

Through use of the method, Spinoza reaches conclusions about scriptural matters that were quite heterodox, but nonetheless not entirely novel. For example, after considering passages from Genesis and Deuteronomy, Spinoza deduces in Chapter 8 of the *Tractatus* that it would be "contrary to reason" to affirm that Moses was the author of the Pentateuch.[27] And though that verdict follows from the methodological premise that the interpretation of Scripture must be conducted through the examination of Scripture alone, Spinoza also takes a cue from the arguments in the commentaries on Genesis and Deuteronomy composed by Abraham Ibn Ezra, which were also cited in Chapter 8.[28] There can be no doubt that Spinoza's open rejection of the Mosaic authorship of the Pentateuch was quite alarming. In fact, Ibn Ezra, as Spinoza himself acknowledges, had only hinted at such a conclusion and he urged those who understood his hints to observe silence regarding the matter.[29] Still, Spinoza was not the first among modern writers to contest the orthodox view that the first five books of the Bible issued from Moses' hand. In 1655 Isaac La Peyrère had announced the same conclusion in his *Praea-*

27. *TTP,* 3.124/167.
28. *TTP,* 3.118–19/162–63.
29. Ibid. To remove any doubt, it should be noted that the consequences of the denial of the Mosaic authorship of the Pentateuch bore implications that exceeded the scope of historico-literary criticism. The suggestion that the Pentateuch was not a single whole written by Moses brings into question the divinely inspired character of those books and the doctrines that they contain. In particular, the denial of the Mosaic authorship could occasion doubt about the authenticity of the Mosaic Law (and perhaps that was the "mystery" concerning which Ibn Ezra had recommended silence). As a matter of fact, Spinoza's teaching on that matter is at best equivocal. For while he says that the "book of the Law" was probably written by Moses as a short document to be read aloud to the people by the priests, Spinoza also asserts that the present form of the Law as it appears in the Pentateuch may have been edited by a later historian who "inserted them in due order in the life of Moses"; see *TTP,* 3.124/167. Perhaps, then, the Law as expressed in the Pentateuch is more than once or twice removed from the original composition of the Law. One should recall that in Chapters 9 and 10 Spinoza emphasizes the degree to which many emendations or adjustments have been made to early editions of the Scriptures by scribes and scholars. Such considerations do not enhance the authority of the Pentateuch nor the demand that the faithful be obedient to the law that it inculcates.

damitae.[30] And earlier still, Thomas Hobbes had declared the same in *Leviathan* (1651); though Hobbes was quick to affirm that Moses "wrote all that which he is there said to have written: as for example, the Volume of the Law."[31] But although at least some of Spinoza's unconventional verdicts about the Bible were also espoused by his contemporaries or recent predecessors, Spinoza is still distinguishable from them for the reason that he employs and openly instructs others about a method of biblical criticism.

In Chapter 7 of the *Tractatus*, Spinoza enunciates his rule for the interpretation of Scripture. The fundamental premise adopted by Spinoza is that "the method of interpreting Scripture is no different from the method of interpreting Nature." That is to say, just as we deduce the definitions of things from a detailed study of Nature, so too scriptural interpretation will proceed by a "straightforward study of Scripture" so as "to deduce by logical inference the meaning of the authors of Scripture."[32] The "universal rule" of the method is "to ascribe no teaching to Scripture that was not clearly established from studying it closely."[33] To succeed in

30. Isaac La Peyrère, *Men before Adam* (London, 1656), 208: "I need not trouble the Reader much further to prove a thing in itself sufficiently evident, that the first five books of the Bible were not written by *Moses* as is thought. Nor need anyone wonder after this, when he reads many things confus'd and out of order, obscure, deficient, many things omitted and misplaced, when they shall consider with themselves that they are a heap of Copie confusedly taken." La Peyrère's verdict on the Pentateuch was based largely on internal textual discrepancies within the first five books: e.g., the fact that Moses, the putative author of the books, discusses events occurring after his own death in a historical rather than a prophetical manner. The publication of *Praeadamitae* in The Netherlands in 1655 has been described by Richard Popkin as "the most shocking event in the intellectual world" at that time; see Richard Popkin, "Spinoza and La Peyrère," in *Spinoza: New Perspectives*, eds. J. I. Biro and R. W. Shahan (Norman: University of Oklahoma Press, 1978),177–95, 182. It is worth remarking that in the year following the publication of *Praeadamitae*, 1656, the Jewish Synagogue in Amsterdam excommunicated Spinoza together with Juan de Prado and Daniel Ribera. The accusations brought against the three men included their regarding the Pentateuch as being merely a "human text"; see I. S. Révah, *Spinoza et le Dr. Juan de Prado* (Paris: Mouton, 1959), 40–41. It is also known that the 1655 edition of La Peyrère's *Praeadamitae* was owned by Spinoza and still contained in his personal library at the time of his death. For a catalogue of Spinoza's library, see J. Freudenthal, *Die Lebensgeschichte Spinozas*, 160–64. Finally, the affinities between the views expressed by Spinoza in *TTP* and those enunciated by La Peyrère in *Praeadamitae* prompted Leo Strauss to conclude that La Peyrère was a principal influence on the form of biblical criticism adopted by Spinoza; see *Spinoza's Critique of Religion*, 64–85.

31. Thomas Hobbes, *Leviathan; or, The Matter, Forme and Power of a Commonwealth Ecclesiastical and Civil*, ed. Michael Oakeshott (New York: Collier Books, 1962), 278. It is worth noting that both Hobbes and Spinoza cite Genesis 12, verse 6, as evidence that Moses could not have written all the passages contained in the Pentateuch. In fact, the analysis of Genesis 12.6 was also the focus for Ibn Ezra's suspicion about the authenticity of Moses having written that portion of the Pentateuch. Compare *Leviathan*, 277–78, with *TTP*, 3.119/162–63.

32. *TTP*, 3.98/141.

33. *TTP*, 3.99/142.

applying that universal rule, three ancillary procedures are to be followed. In order to grasp the authentic meaning of a scriptural statement, the interpreter must (1) attend to the nature and properties of the books of the Bible, that is, the languages or idioms in which they were written; (2) offer an analysis of each book that reflects the arrangement of its contents and notes all passages deemed to be obscure, ambiguous, or mutually contradictory; and (3) provide a history of each book of the Bible, which relates the life, conduct, and studies of its author, indicates who he was, when he wrote as well as for whom he wrote, accounts for the fate of each book, and explains how it came to be that the books universally accepted as canonical were united into a single whole.[34]

Evidently, the method propounded by Spinoza involves an extraordinarily arduous historico-literary study of the Bible. On the other hand, it was in principle a method that could be employed by any individual willing to undertake the task. Nevertheless, an immediate consequence of the application of the method was the possibility, or indeed the likelihood, that there would be numerous divergent conclusions reached about the genuine meaning of any single scriptural passage. Disparities in the particular skills or reasonableness of each interpreter would account for the differences in the interpretations offered by each of them. But no proposed interpretation could be dismissed casually if it were reached in accordance with the procedures of the method. What Spinoza's method for the interpretation of Scripture guarantees is that "freedom of judgment" on religious or theological matters would be encouraged; at the same time it ensures that the authority of received schools of interpretation would be eroded, since any individual's exercise of the "natural light" is accorded precedence.[35]

---

34. *TTP*, 3.99–102/142–45. Having enunciated in Chapter 7 the procedures for interpreting Scripture, Spinoza applies the method to various books of the Bible in Chapters 8–13 of the treatise. It is obvious, however, that the teachings of Scripture cited in Chapters 1–6 of *TTP* are exempted from the application of the method. That fact is most apparent in light of the conclusion in Chapter 8 that it is "contrary to reason" to attribute authorship of the Pentateuch to Moses, whereas throughout the first six chapters of *TTP* the Mosaic authorship of the Pentateuch is nowhere challenged. In other words, there is no "historical study" of the Pentateuch as would be prescribed by the method announced in Chapter 7. Rather the conviction that Moses wrote the Pentateuch is presupposed. The curious shift in attention between Chapters 1–6 and Chapters 7–15 (and its consequences) is a matter of grave importance to the *theologico-political* character of the treatise. But that issue requires an analysis that exceeds the present consideration of the relation between Spinoza and "the Enlightenment."

35. See, e.g., *TTP*, 3.117/159–60: "[T]he supreme authority to explain religion and to make judgments concerning it is vested in each individual, because it belongs to the sphere of individual right. It is, then, far from true that the authority of the Hebrew High Priest in interpreting his country's laws enables us to infer the Pope's authority to interpret religion; on the contrary, a more obvious inference is that the interpretation of religion is vested

To Spinoza, the demand for a method of interpreting the Bible is occasioned by the fact that Scripture "frequently treats of matters that cannot be deduced by the natural light; for it is chiefly made up of historical narratives and revelation," and a regular feature of the historical narratives is the relating of miraculous events.[36] Furthermore, it was determined in Chapter 2 of the *Tractatus* that the narratives containing both prophecies and accounts of miracles had been adapted to the beliefs, judgments, and opinions of the historians who recorded them as well as the prophets who received the revelations.[37] The manners in which those stories have been communicated promote difficulties for interpretation not only because they involve accommodations to the unique circumstances of the addressee(s) but also because the language in which they were composed presents numerous virtually insoluble problems. That is, as Spinoza himself observes, there was no extant "dictionary, nor grammar, nor text-book of rhetoric"[38] to assist one in defining the exact meaning of many Hebrew words. As a result of the often ambiguous nature of the Hebrew language, Spinoza almost despondently acknowledges that "in many instances we either do not know the true meaning of Scripture or we can do no more than make guesses" about it.[39] Whether Spinoza himself believed that one could eventually attain an

---

above all in each individual. And this again affords further proof that our method of Scriptural interpretation is the best. For since the supreme authority for the interpretation of Scripture is vested in each individual, the rule that governs interpretation must be nothing other than the natural light which is common to all, nor any supernatural light, nor any external authority. Nor must this rule be so difficult as not to be available to any but skilled philosophers; it must be suited to the natural and universal ability and capacity of mankind."

Spinoza's remarks about the "supreme authority of individuals" to determine the authentic meaning of Scripture was prepared by an analysis of the suspect character of the received theological traditions of the Hebrew and Roman Catholic faiths; see *TTP*, 3.105/148: "We have thus set out our plan for interpreting Scripture, at the same time demonstrating that this is the only sure road to discovery of its true meaning. I do indeed admit that those are better informed (if there are any) who are in possession of a sure tradition or true explanation transmitted from the prophets themselves, as the Pharisees claim, or those who have a pontiff whose interpretation of Scripture is infallible, as the Roman Catholics boast. However, as we cannot be sure either of the traditions in question or of the authority of the pontiff, we cannot base any certain conclusion on them. The latter is denied by the earliest Christians, the former by the most ancient sect of the Jews; and if, furthermore, we examine the succession of years (to mention nothing else) through which this tradition is traced right back to Moses, which the Pharisees have accepted from their Rabbis, we shall find that it is incorrect, as I shall prove elsewhere. Therefore such a tradition should be regarded with the utmost suspicion."

While Spinoza seems to focus on the problematical status of the Jewish tradition, it should be clear that the Christian tradition becomes implicated as "suspicious" to the extent that it owes its foundations to the Hebrew heritage, as is indicated in the Davidic lineage of Jesus and the "suffering servant" prophecies of Isaiah.

36. *TTP*, 3.98/141.
38. *TTP*, 3.106/149.
37. *TTP*, 3.99/142; also see 3.29–30/73.
39. *TTP*, 3.110/153.

adequate or comprehensive knowledge of the history of the biblical books and their authors, along with an understanding of the changes that occurred in the Hebrew language, is a moot point. The significance of Spinoza's remarks is that they indicate problematical features of Scripture that cannot, for all practical purposes, be resolved even by the methodical use of the "natural light." It follows that such matters should not be accorded any dogmatic significance.

The historico-literary difficulties of interpreting Scripture are compounded by the fact that in the biblical narratives many items are related that simply "surpass human understanding."[40] Unlike the writings of Euclid or any other book in which the author limits himself to examining "things exceedingly simple and perfectly intelligible," scriptural passages contain oddities that strain credulity or prompt men to devise fantastical interpretations of them.[41] It becomes increasingly clear that what the method can achieve with respect to determining the authentic meaning of Scripture is severely curtailed since the form and matter of the Bible frequently pose insurmountable interpretive obstacles. But for Spinoza that realization has one particularly salutary consequence. It means that the genuine significance of scriptural teachings will have to be reducible to a few plain, simple, and universal instructions. Whatever falls outside the immediate sphere of those precepts is subject to the interpretation of each individual, insofar as it might enhance his faith.[42]

The interpretive method supplied in Chapter 7 of the *Tractatus* thus involves three consequences for religious belief. First, one can turn to Scripture, as the Word of God, in order to elicit its moral doctrines, and these can be regarded as divinely originated where they are derived from the Bible itself. Second, the method used to determine the authentic meaning of Scripture is available to anyone who wishes to employ it; hence no extraordinary or supernatural interpretive faculty is required. And third, apart from establishing the few basic tenets that are to be observed by the faithful, Spinoza's method of scriptural interpretation allows for the greatest latitude in accepting or rejecting the authority of biblical passages not deemed essential to faith.

Still, one may ask, What purpose is served in discerning the genuine meaning of a work that is generally regarded by Spinoza as being fundamentally hieroglyphical? Simply stated, religion or theology can have a decisive function in the moral education of human beings. Spinoza is aware that the Bible is a source of moral instruction, and its teachings, as

40. *TTP,* 3.99/142.
41. *TTP,* 3.110/153–54.
42. Compare *TTP,* 3.116–17/159–60 with *TTP,* 3.178–80/225–27; also see Chapter 13 of *TTP.*

divinely inspired, exert considerable influence over the conduct of human affairs. However, he is equally persuaded that preachers, ministers, priests, and certain theologians have abused their authority to interpret the teachings of Scripture to the detriment of those in their charge.[43] Spinoza states flatly to Henry Oldenburg that one of the reasons for composing the *Tractatus* was to promote the freedom of philosophizing, and of saying what one thinks, by exposing the excessive impudence of the theologians, who have suppressed freedom of thought, judgment, and expression.[44] Thus one of the most important effects of Spinoza's method of biblical criticism is that it steers its practitioners away from extreme interpretations of Scripture by encouraging them to reach reasonable or commonsensical conclusions about the Bible's teachings. Therefore the method itself prevents the utilization of Scripture to legitimate extreme theological and political positions. But it also must be understood that the moderating influence of the method owes its origin to an extreme position taken by Spinoza himself at the beginning of the *Tractatus*.

In the first chapter of the *Tractatus*, Spinoza examines the nature of prophecy or revelation, which is taken to be "the sure knowledge of some matter revealed by God to man."[45] However, he commences that investigation with a definition of a prophet as "one who interprets God's revelations to those who cannot attain to certain knowledge of the matters revealed, and can therefore be convinced of them only by simple faith."[46] Spinoza notes that the Hebrew word for prophet, *nabi*, "is always used in Scripture in the sense of interpreter of God, as we gather from Exodus Chapter 7, verse 1."[47] The opening lines of Chapter 1 of the treatise express an orthodox sentiment regarding prophecy and the distinctive status of the prophet. But Spinoza goes on immediately to deduce a most unconventional conclusion about prophetic capacity from his definition of prophecy or revelation.

From the definition given above, it follows that natural knowledge can be called prophecy, for the knowledge that we acquire by the natural light of reason depends

---

43. *TTP*, 3.6–10/50–54.
44. See note 13 Also compare Chapter 20 of *TTP*, which is titled "It Is Shown That in a Free Republic Every Man May Think as He Pleases, and Say What He Thinks."
45. *TTP*, 3.15/59.
46. Ibid.
47. Ibid. Spinoza's ostensible identification of the phenomenon of prophecy with Hebrew prophecy should not distract readers from the fact that any act of prophecy or revelation as a substitute for reason is implicitly under attack in *TTP*. Recall the opening sentence of the treatise: *"Si homines res omnes suas certo consilio regere possent, vel si fortuna ipsis prospera semper foret, nulla superstitione tenerentur"* (*TTP*, 3.5/49). Where men cannot or do not exercise a "sure plan of action" they resort to superstition and the prejudices that attend it.

solely on knowledge of God and of his eternal decrees. However, since this natural knowledge is common to all men—for it rests on foundations common to all men—it is not so highly prized by the multitude who are always eager for what is strange and foreign to their own nature, despising their natural gifts. Therefore prophetic knowledge is taken to exclude ordinary knowledge. Nevertheless, the latter has as much right as any other kind of knowledge to be called divine, since it is dictated to us, as it were, by God's nature in so far as we participate therein, and by God's decrees.[48]

The radical character of Spinoza's understanding of prophecy or revelation is exhibited by his treatment of "natural knowledge," or that which follows from the "natural light of reason," as equivalent in divinity to what uniquely issues from the mouth of the prophet. There is no orthodox theological justification for the equation of "prophecy" and "natural or ordinary knowledge" here advanced by Spinoza.[49] Nevertheless, it would not be misleading to say that the entire theological teaching of the *Tractatus* is founded upon explicit or implicit appeals to the legitimacy of applying the "natural light of reason" to comprehend or interpret "the sure knowledge of some matter revealed by God." In fact, the method of scriptural interpretation devised by Spinoza in Chapter 7 of the *Tractatus* already presupposes the competence of the "natural light of reason" to conduct a historico-literary investigation of the revelations or prophecies communicated through the Bible. For if "the human mind can apprehend the explanations of natural phenomena and inculcate morality," inasmuch as it "partakes of the nature of God,"[50] then surely it is appropriate for the "natural light of reason" to seek an understanding of the genuine significance of Scripture through an examination of the teachings of the Bible.

From the beginning of the treatise, Spinoza introduces the exercise of

---

48. Ibid.
49. See, e.g., *TTP,* 3.16/60 where Spinoza asserts that since "the human mind contains the nature of God within itself in concept, and partakes thereof, and is thereby enabled to form certain basic ideas that explain natural phenomena and inculcate morality, we are justified in asserting that the nature of the mind, insofar as it is thus conceived, is the primary cause of divine revelation." Compare that statement with the teaching of St. Thomas Aquinas in *Summa contra gentiles,* Book 1, Chapters 3, 4, 7, and 8. Whatever affinity exists between reason and faith or revelation, St. Thomas makes plain in Chapter 8 that reason cannot presume to a knowledge of God or the divine nature that is reserved for revelation or faith: "The objects of the senses on which human reason bases its knowledge retain some traces of likeness to God, since they exist and are good. This resemblance is inadequate because it is completely insufficient to manifest the substance of God. . . . [I]t is useful for the human mind to exercise its powers of reasoning, however weak, in this way provided that there is no presumption that it can comprehend or demonstrate [the substance of the divine nature]." On the relation between reason and revelation, see also Maimonides, *The Guide of the Perplexed,* 2.23, 24, 32, 36, and 38.
50. *TTP,* 3.16/60.

reason or "ordinary knowledge" into a sphere from which it otherwise might be barred.[51] Furthermore, the application of reason to scriptural interpretation is made not only feasible but appealing. Rather than submitting to theological doctrines or interpretations of Scripture that traditionally had demanded mere acquiescence by ordinary believers, Spinoza elevates the "natural light of reason" to a position of competence to inquire into the very meaning of faith or theology itself. In a sense, therefore, the application of the "natural light of reason" to scriptural or theological matters is defended by Spinoza as being every bit as pious as accepting revealed dogmas with unquestioning conviction alone.

By advocating the equivalence between "prophecy" and "natural or ordinary knowledge," Spinoza encourages individuals to employ their own judgments in religious concerns. The standard to be observed is one of reasonableness and tolerance rather than zealous faith. What Spinoza's attitude toward "prophecy" or "revelation," and his method of scriptural interpretation, achieve is a loosening of the strictures identified with piety and faithfulness. But for Spinoza that theological liberation is not independent of other considerations. Rather, it has a political corollary. That is, the "freedom of judgment" accorded to individuals in theological matters is identical with the freedom that should be granted

---

51. Ibid.: "[A]s I have just pointed out, all that we clearly and distinctly understand is dictated to us by the idea and nature of God—not indeed in words, but in a far superior way and one that agrees excellently with the nature of the mind, as everyone who has tasted intellectual certainty has doubtless experienced in his own case. However, my main purpose being to treat only what concerns Scripture alone, these few words on the natural light will suffice. So I pass on to treat more fully of other sources of knowledge, and other means by which God reveals to man that which transcends the bounds of natural knowledge—and also that which is within its scope, for there is nothing to prevent God from communicating by other means to man that which we can know by the natural light. However, our discussion must be confined to what is drawn only from Scripture. For what can we say of things transcending the bounds of our intellect except what is transmitted to us by the prophets by word or writing? And since there are no prophets among us today, as far as I know, our only recourse is to peruse the sacred books left to us by the prophets of old, taking care, however, not to make metaphorical interpretations or to attribute anything to the prophets which they themselves did not clearly declare. Now it is important to note here that the Jews never make mention of intermediate or particular causes nor pay any heed to them, but to serve religion and piety or, as it is commonly called, devoutness, they refer everything to God."

This foreshadows the terms of Spinoza's method of scriptural interpretation announced in Chapter 7 of *TTP*. In particular, his remarks concerning the Jews' failure to account for the proximate or intermediate causes of things in their narratives already implies the sufficiency of the "light of reason" in respect to an understanding of the operations of natural phenomena. Furthermore, Spinoza's exhortation to avoid "metaphorical interpretations" presupposes the kind of literary examination of the Bible, e.g., noting discrepancies and ambiguities among passages, that is later enunciated as a procedure in the method of scriptural interpretation. It can be suggested that part of Spinoza's appeal to the "natural light of reason" involves a calculatedly historicist premise: i.e., what the ignorant ancient Jews misunderstood about natural phenomena is now scientifically explicable through reason alone.

to individual citizens without detriment to the public peace; and such was a principal point to be demonstrated in the *Tractatus*.[52] Moreover, the equivalence between "natural or ordinary knowledge" and revelation or prophecy bears directly on theology and politics inasmuch as the teaching of the treatise endorses the identification of divine justice with human justice. For according to Spinoza, whether they are attained through prophecy or the "natural light of reason," divine teachings and precepts do not acquire the force of command directly from God but only through the mediation of those who have the right to dictate commands and issue decrees.[53] Hence "it is only by their mediation," asserts Spinoza, "that we can conceive of God as reigning over men and directing human affairs according to justice and equity . . . for indications of divine justice are to be found only where just men reign."[54] Which divine doctrines or precepts are to be observed as matters of faith can be decided by learning the genuine meaning of Scripture. And now that task is made feasible by Spinoza's method of scriptural interpretation.

BIBLICAL CRITICISM AND "ENLIGHTENED UNIVERSAL FAITH"

Based upon the examination of Scripture conducted in Chapters 7–13, Spinoza concludes in Chapter 14 of the treatise that "he who indiscriminately accepts everything in Scripture as being the universal and absolute teaching about God, and does not distinguish precisely what is adapted to the masses, is bound to confuse the beliefs of the masses with divine doctrines."[55] And though everyone is encouraged to make use of his own judgment in theological matters, there still exist "limits of individual freedom of opinion in regard to faith."[56]

Despite differences of opinion about religious dogma that can arise from one's reliance upon prophecy alone or the "natural light of reason," Spinoza asserts that there is a basic universal teaching communicated throughout both Testaments in the Bible. According to Spinoza,

---

52. See the title page of *TTP* and compare *TTP*, 3.7–11/51–54, 56.
53. *TTP*, 3.231/283.
54. Ibid.
55. *TTP*, 3.173/220. The Latin emphasizes the "vulgar" character of certain doctrines contained in Scripture which Spinoza says must be ignored for a "true comprehension of faith": *Ad veram fidei cognitionem apprime necessarium esse, scire, quod Scriptura accommodata sit non tanquam captui Prophetarum, sed etiam varii, & inconstantis Judaeorum vulgi nemo, qui vel leviter attendit, iqnorare potest; qui enim omnia, quae in Scriptura habentur, promiscue amplectitur, tanquam universalem, & absolutam de Deo doctrinam, nec accurate cognovit, quidnam captui vulgi accommodatum sit, non poterit vulgi opiniones cum divina doctrina non confundere, & hominum commenta & placita pro divina documentis non venditare, Scripturaeque authoritate non abuti.*
56. Ibid., 3.173–74/221.

the sole purpose of Scripture is to teach obedience so that men can "sincerely hearken to God."[57] Furthermore, in both Testaments "Scripture itself tells us quite clearly over and over again what every man should do in order to serve God, declaring that the entire Law consists in this alone, to love one's neighbour."[58] Indeed, in Chapter 12, Spinoza argues emphatically that the very divinity of Scripture was assured because of the constancy of its teaching that "Divine Law."[59] Thus the basis of theology or faith is reduced by Spinoza to the doctrine of obedience to the one principal commandment of God. "He who by God's commandments loves his neighbour as himself is truly obedient and blessed according to the Law" and "Scripture does not require us to believe anything beyond what is necessary for the fulfilling of the said commandment."[60]

In order to obey the commandment enjoined by God, there are certain tenets of a universal faith to which believers must subscribe. That faith, Spinoza concludes, will contain "only those dogmas which obedience to God absolutely demands, and without which such obedience is absolutely impossible. As for other dogmas, every man should embrace those that he, being the best judge of himself, feels will do the most to strengthen his love of justice."[61] Furthermore, adherence to that principle by believers carries the promise of eliminating occasions for controversy within churches or between them.

The few simple tenets of the universal faith enunciated by Spinoza are derived from his study of Scripture and the conclusions he has reached about the authentic meaning of its teaching. What Spinoza calls the "dogmas of the universal faith"[62] may be said to be constitutive of an "enlightened faith" because they are the products of the method of scriptural interpretation announced in Chapter 7 of the *Tractatus*. That method was devised to segregate the prejudiced and superstitious understandings of an ancient people concerning the Bible from those genuine biblical instructions that could be adopted universally by all who wished to be faithful. In order to promote the essential and authentic meaning of Scripture, that is, obedience to the command to love one's neighbor, Spinoza articulates seven dogmas of faith that make obedience to God (and hence salvation) possible.

I can now venture to enumerate the dogmas of the universal faith, the basic teachings which Scripture as a whole intends to convey. These all must be directed (as

---

57. Ibid.
58. Ibid.
59. See Chapter 12 where Spinoza identifies the very "divinity of Scripture" with its constant teaching "to love God and one's neighbor"; *TTP*, 3.165–66/211–12.
60. Ibid.   61. *TTP*, 3.177/224.
62. Ibid.

evidently follows from what we have demonstrated in these two chapters) to this one end: that there is a Supreme Being who loves justice and charity, whom all must obey in order to be saved, and must worship by practising justice and charity to their neighbour. From this, all the tenets of faith can readily be determined, and they are simply as follows: —

1. God, that is, a Supreme Being, exists, supremely just and merciful, the exemplar of the true life. He who knows not, or does not believe, that God exists, cannot obey him or know him as a judge.

2. God is one alone. No one can doubt that this belief is essential for complete devotion, reverence, and love towards God; for devotion, reverence, and love spring only from the preeminence of one over all others.

3. God is omnipresent, and all things are open to him. If it were believed that things could be concealed from God, or if it were not realised that he sees everything, one might doubt, or be unaware of, the uniformity of the justice wherewith he directs everything.

4. God has supreme right and dominion over all things. He is under no compulsion, but acts by his absolute decree and singular grace. All are required to obey him absolutely, while he obeys none.

5. Worship of God and obedience to him consists solely in justice and charity, or love towards one's neighbour.

6. All who obey God by following this way of life, and only those, are saved; others, who live at pleasure's behest, are lost. If men did not firmly believe in this, there is no reason why they should obey God rather than their desires.

7. God forgives repentant sinners. There is no one who does not sin, so that without this belief all would despair of salvation, and there would be no reason to believe that God is merciful. He who firmly believes that God forgives from the mercy and grace whereby he directs all things, and whose heart is thereby more inspired by the love of God, that man verily knows Christ according to the spirit, and Christ is in him.

No one can fail to realise that all these beliefs are essential if men, without exception, are to be capable of obeying God as prescribed by the law explained above; for if any one of these beliefs is nullified, obedience is also nullified.[63]

With respect to the articles of a catholic faith, Spinoza proposes that "faith requires not so much true dogmas as pious dogmas, that is, such as move the heart to obedience."[64] Spinoza also identifies piety with whatever produces obedience to God in men;[65] hence faith and piety become synonymous through their identification with the teaching of obedience to God. And in accordance with a "fundamental principle" observed in the *Tractatus*, Spinoza avers that "faith must be defined as the holding of certain beliefs about God such that, without these beliefs, there cannot be obedience to God, and if this obedience to God is posited, these beliefs are necessarily posited. This definition is so clear, and follows so obviously from what has already been proved, that it needs no explanation."[66]

---

63. *TTP*, 3.177–78/224–25.   64. *TTP*, 3.176/223.
65. *TTP*, 3.160–62/206–8. 66. *TTP*, 3.175/222.
66. *TTP*, 3.175/222.

In general, Spinoza claims that "pious dogmas" are more essential to faith than are true dogmas. In particular, Spinoza allows that one's conviction about the specifics of the articles of faith and piety, for example, whether God "as the exemplar of the true life is fire or spirit or light" and whether "the rewarding of the good and the punishing of the wicked is natural or supernatural," are irrelevant "provided that such belief does not lead to the assumption of greater license to sin, or hinders submission to God."[67] While Spinoza says that the truth or falsity of the fundamental dogmas of faith is not essential for accepting them (though such a claim is already curious, since it would be unusual to abide by what one also knows to be false) and interpretations concerning the precise character of the attributes of God may be varied, he does insist upon one stipulation: *if any one of dogmas of the universal faith is nullified then obedience to God is nullified*. Where obedience to God is eliminated or abandoned then it is not possible for one to be pious or faithful since both presuppose adherence to the injunction "love your neighbor" out of obedience to God. But—and here is the decisive point—the characterization of the divine nature expressed through the seven dogmas of the universal faith presupposes and continues to inculcate a conception of God that Spinoza had previously denounced as vulgar and unphilosophical.

In his discussion of the Divine Law in Chapter 4, Spinoza considered the teachings of Moses, Christ, and Paul the Apostle. There the superiority of Christ's revelations over those of Moses was defended on the view that God revealed himself directly to Christ but to the prophets, like Moses, God was revealed only through the intermediary means of words and images.[68] Such a disparity, Spinoza argues, accounts for the differences between the teachings expressed by Christ and those dictated by Moses. Because Christ "perceived truly and adequately" the things revealed to him, he thus understood them as eternal truths, whereas Moses communicated what was revealed to him as "instructions and precepts, and he ordained them as laws of God. Hence it came about that he imagined God as a ruler, lawgiver, king, merciful, just, and so forth; whereas these are all merely attributes of human nature, and not at all applicable to the divine nature."[69] To illustrate which of the doctrines was more accurate, Spinoza invokes the teaching of the Apostle Paul. For Paul realized that adaptations to the capacities of his audiences determined the style and the content of the teachings he proclaimed. Based on the Pauline model, then, Spinoza concludes "that it is only in concession to the understanding of the multitude and the defectiveness of their

---

67. *TTP,* 3.178/225.
68. *TTP,* 3.64–65/107–8.
69. Ibid.

thought that God is described as a lawgiver or ruler, and is called just, merciful, and so on, and that in reality God acts and governs all things solely from the necessity of his own nature and perfection, and his decrees and volitions are eternal truths always involving necessity [*Concludimus itaque, Deum non nisi ex captu vulgi, & ex solo defectu cogitationis tanquam legislatorem aut principem describi, & justum, misericordem, &c. vocari, Deumque revera ex solius suae naturae, & perfectionis necessitate agere, & omnia dirigere, & ejus denique decreta, & volitiones aeternas esse veritates, semperque necessitatem involvere*]."[70]

Even if one accepts with Spinoza the view that the truth or falsity of the dogmas of faith and the particular characterizations of them (e.g., whether God is omnipresent essentially or potentially) are irrelevant to piety or faith so long as obedience to God is secured, there remains a very troubling feature to Spinoza's account of the fundamental dogmas of the universal faith or "the basic teachings which Scripture as a whole intends to convey." For throughout the seven articles of faith it is explicitly stated or presupposed that God is a king or a sovereign ruler who governs, judges, and shows mercy. In Article 1, God is called "extremely just and merciful"; and those who do not know God or who disbelieve in God's existence "cannot obey him and know him as a judge." The "uniformity of God's justice" in Article 2, which follows from his omnipresence, again casts God as a legislator and judge. The "supreme right and dominion over all things" expressed in Article 4 further identifies God with a king or sovereign ruler. And the explicit identification of God's capacity to forgive sins with God's "mercifulness" is confirmed in Article 7.

Taken together, the seven dogmas of the universal faith are demonstrably vulgar inasmuch as they expressly affirm the conception of God as a judge, a legislator, and a king, one who shows mercy and dispenses justice. All such characterizations of the divine nature were concluded by Spinoza to have been derived *"ex captu vulgi"* and in accordance with "the defectiveness of their thoughts." Thus for Spinoza to identify such views of the divine nature with "the basic teachings which Scripture as a whole intends to convey" is to confirm and promote vulgar prejudices about God. Moreover, to propose such vulgar conceptions about the divine nature is to endorse what is said to be an absurd conception of God. For "in reality," Spinoza contends, "God acts only from the necessity of his own nature and perfection, his decrees and volitions are eternal truths, always involving necessity." God does not legislate, nor does he rule or judge. And to establish the tenets that are requisite for obedience to God upon such apprehensions of the divine attributes is to violate the very premise

70. *TTP*, 3.65/108–9.

with which Chapter 14 of the *Tractatus* begins. For there Spinoza warns that "a true comprehension of faith" would demand the segregation of "what was adapted to the understanding of the masses [*quidnam captui vulgi accommodata sit*]" from the divine doctrines.[71] Yet throughout Chapter 14 Spinoza himself repeats and affirms what he otherwise repudiates as a vulgar way of regarding the being of God.

Ironically, therefore, Spinoza compels his attentive readers to a kind of faithlessness. For he demands his readers to adopt an apprehension of the divine nature which he also tells them is an erroneous conception of God, derived *ex captu vulgi*. Yet he also categorically declares that if any one of the beliefs constitutive of the seven essential dogmas of the universal faith is nullified then obedience to God, and hence piety or faith, is also nullified. One therefore is confronted with a dilemma. Either one is obedient to God and thus faithful or pious by acceding to vulgar (and therefore unenlightened) views concerning the "Supreme Being" or one renounces the vulgarity of such theological beliefs (and therefore is enlightened) but then one cannot be obedient and thus faithful or pious in the way defined by Spinoza.[72]

THE SENSE OF "ENLIGHTENMENT" IN SPINOZA'S TEACHING

The teaching of Spinoza's *Tractatus theologico-politicus* ostensibly engages in enlightenment in a modern sense in three principal respects. First, the declared aim of the treatise is to expose theological or religious prejudices and superstitions that hinder men from attaining an understanding of the authentic meaning of faith, piety, and theology. Second, the vanquishing of such prejudices involves the exercise of "the light of reason" and an appeal to "natural or ordinary knowledge" as distinct

---

71. *TTP,* 3.173/220.
72. The dilemma I cite is not commonly acknowledged by interpreters of the teachings of *TTP.* There are those who admit that Spinoza's language and the conceptions it involves are not strictly philosophical, and so seek to harmonize the vulgar views he expresses with assertions more consistent with the philosophic doctrines of the *Ethica ordine geometrico demonstrata*. One such scholar is Yirmiyahu Yovel; see, e.g., his *Spinoza and Other Heretics: The Marrano of Reason* (Princeton, N.J.: Princeton University Press, 1989), Chapter 5, esp. 145–50. Another who disputes that there are any inconsistencies in Spinoza's teachings is Errol Harris; see his "Is There an Esoteric Teaching in the *Tractatus theologico-politicus?*," in *Mededelingen Vanwege het Spinozahuis* 38 (1978): 1–19, esp. 13–15. Though I believe it is necessary, in order to understand its teaching, to segregate the philosophic statements of *TTP* from the unphilosophic statements contained in that work, it is enough for the present purpose to indicate that the products of the "enlightened biblical criticism" offered in *TTP* continue to reflect a prejudiced and vulgar understanding of the divine nature that could not on Spinoza's reckoning be accepted by any thoughtful or philosophical reader of the treatise.

from any uncommon faculty or source of comprehension. Third, the promised consequence of surmounting theological prejudices is the increased feasibility of securing religious and civil freedoms of thought, judgment, and expression.[73] Furthermore, Spinoza assures us that the liberties secured are to be enjoyed universally: no one may be deprived of such freedoms and anyone may enjoy their benefits.[74]

The apparent openness and universality of Spinoza's teaching suggests affinity between it and the enlightenment doctrine of Kant: that is, "if only freedom be granted, enlightenment is almost sure to follow." Moreover, the enlightenment of which Kant spoke requires the regular "public use of reason as a scholar before the reading public." And in particular, the free and public use of reason concerning religious or theological matters is advocated, nay, demanded, by Kant. But for Kant the kind of enlightenment that attends the public use of reason is also inseparable from the Second Thesis of his "Idea for a Universal History from a Cosmopolitan Point of View" (1784), namely, that it is Nature's purpose for man that reason be fully developed in the whole human race and not just in some individual.[75] If one considers the Kantian doctrine on enlightenment as representing the modern standard, then Spinoza fits only partially into the modern paradigm.

One might well wonder whether Spinoza was a conscious and determined advocate of modern enlightenment or whether his thinking was adapted and applied in ways that he himself would have protested. Whereas Spinoza's contemporaries and successors looked ever increasingly to history as a standard or measure for human development and achievement, Spinoza remained committed to a study of human being in terms of the eternal character of the whole, which he identified with Nature. Such a contrast should call into question Spinoza's support for the basic orientation of modern philosophy.

Spinoza lived in an era marked by revolutions. They were scientific, medical, technological, political, legal, and theological. Reforms were occasioned by more open and public challenges to authorities and traditions. Spinoza cannot be dissociated from that trend. But was his guiding intention identical with that of his Enlightenment contemporaries or successors? Spinoza extols and defends civil as well as religious freedoms, and such liberties were advocated by most Enlightenment figures. But he also consistently argues in support of the constraints that must be placed

---

73. See Chapter 20 of *TTP* as a whole and consider its connection with Chapter 19 in respect of the "command of God" acquiring the force of law only through civil government.
74. *TTP*, 3.246–47/298–99.
75. Kant, *On History*, ed. L. W. Beck, trans. L. W. Beck, R. E. Anchor, and E. L. Fackenheim (New York: Macmillan, 1963), 4–8 and 13.

upon freedoms of speech and deed; for maintenance of the stability of the state is the highest duty that a man can fulfill.[76] Spinoza undisguisedly attacks the forces responsible for intellectual, political, and theological oppression; and Enlightenment thinkers assailed the same groups. But to expose an oppressive force as being oppressive is not the same as providing an account of what it would mean to be free in a true philosophical sense. On the surface, the similarities between the teaching of Spinoza and other Enlightenment thinkers suggest more rather than less common goals and ambitions. But two important factors forestall the simple identification of Spinoza's project in the *Tractatus theologico-politicus* with the program of enlightenment in modernity.

The first and most obvious difference concerns the manner in which Spinoza's teaching was communicated. He chose to write and publish the treatise in Latin, and during his lifetime he attempted to prevent the translation of the treatise into his vernacular language, Dutch. By composing and printing the treatise in Latin, Spinoza effectively precluded any immediate, universal access to his work. It is improbable that he intended his teaching for "the reading public" at large or generally for all literate individuals. Rather, the *Tractatus* was to be available to the community of scholars educated in the "universal language of the learned." And even among that class, Spinoza drew a further line of demarcation. For in the Preface to the treatise, he asked that certain readers ignore his book. Specifically, Spinoza asserted that "the vulgar and all those of like passions with the vulgar" were to be discouraged from reading the *Tractatus*.[77] Whereas the vast majority of Enlightenment writings were published in the authors' native languages, Spinoza published his doctrines in Latin, and in the *Tractatus* he opted to select the *"philosophe lector"* as the intended auditor of his teaching in that work.[78] The other and more

---

76. See *TTP*, 3.194/242 and 3.242/294. Spinoza's concern that citizens be dedicated to the preservation of the state, if only because it is in their interests to do so, still implies that restrictions upon individual liberties are appropriately applied in republics, even against the will of individual citizens. The primacy accorded to the civil authorities reflects the kind of secularization suggested briefly in an earlier section of this paper. The subordination of religious practice to civil governance is a result of Spinoza's "theologico-political" teaching in the treatise. Such secularization, in part, involves the identification of divine justice with human justice, which is the issue addressed in Chapter 20 of *TTP*.

77. *TTP*, 3.12/56: "*Vulgus ergo & omnes, qui cum vulgo iisdem affectibus conflictantur, ad haec legenda non invito, quin potius vellem, ut hunc librum prorsus negligant, quam eundem perverse, ut omnia solent, interpretando, molesti sint, & dum sibi nihil prosunt, aliis obsint, qui liberius philosopharentur, nisi hoc unum obstaret, quod putant rationem debere Theologiae ancillari; nam his hoc opus perquam utile fore confido.*" The explicit connection between an educated reader and one who would share certain passions with the vulgar indicates Spinoza's awareness of a class of readers who may be characterized ironically as the "learned vulgar."

78. *TTP*, 3.12/56.

important difference concerns Spinoza's teaching about the "universal faith," though the actual failure of that doctrine to provide genuine theological enlightenment is connected with the point just mentioned.

When Spinoza defines the convictions that must be believed in order for one to be faithful or pious, that is, to obey God, he conspicuously appeals to a conception of the divine nature that he also elsewhere in the *Tractatus* decries as vulgar and inaccurate. If Spinoza were writing for the common run of people, one could construe such a lapse to be a kind of accommodation. However "vulgar" the religious convictions expressed in the treatise might appear, one could explain them at worst as innocuous flaws and at best as improvements over other exceedingly base depictions of the attributes of the Supreme Being. Referring to God as a ruler, a legislator, or a king expresses an anthropomorphic perspective about the divine nature, but such a view might generally be defended as benign. That kind of interpretation of the inconsistency would be appropriate if Spinoza were writing for unlearned readers. But because he is writing for erudite people his continued use of "vulgar" conceptions about God's nature proves to be rather more intriguing. For if his conclusions about the divine nature are based upon the method for the interpretation of the authentic meaning of Scripture (as he professes they are), then Spinoza's teaching about the universal faith and the convictions essential to it basically amounts to a mitigated form of superstition.

The arguments and conclusions that are presented in Spinoza's *Tractatus theologico-politicus* bear the appearance of an Enlightenment teaching partly because of their heterodox nature. Through his appeals to the "natural light" and "natural or ordinary knowledge," Spinoza seeks to show that (1) the unique character of prophecy or revelation owes more to the imagination than to the intellect of the prophet; (2) natural knowledge contributes to the revelation of God to man; (3) there can be no legitimate claim to the special election of one people over others; (4) the Divine Law is intelligible through our ordinary faculties; (5) the specific religious ordinances of a group of believers, for example, the Hebrews, are not universal in kind and therefore the observance or ignoring of them does not affect faith; and (6) miracles are impossible and thus cannot be cited as authentic proofs of God's existence or providence. Those issues, which are addressed and resolved in Chapters 1–6 of the treatise, involve a criticism of orthodox theological teachings, a challenge to the authority of established traditions and their representatives, an attack upon certain prejudices or superstitions, and a defense of freedom.

Such features tend to persuade students of the treatise of its Enlightenment design and its conformity with the project of a modern enlightenment. But such a conclusion actually is at odds with the teaching of the *Tractatus* precisely insofar as Spinoza's account of the universal faith encourages an unenlightened and vulgar understanding of the nature of the Supreme Being. More particularly, Spinoza's teaching induces one to accept or to adopt a common religious prejudice. For one's obedience to God is not undertaken simply for its own sake. Rather, it is undertaken for the sake of one's salvation: "All who obey God by following this way of life, and only those, are saved" (Article 6 of the "dogmas of the universal faith"). The hope of salvation through obedience to God implies that the Supreme Being is a provident ruler and such providence takes the specific forms of rewarding the obedient, forgiving the sinful—that is, those who disobey but are repentant—and punishing the disobedient who refuse to repent and hence are "lost." But if "in reality," as Spinoza asserts, God acts solely from the necessity of his own nature and his decrees are eternal truths that always involve necessity, then the doctrine of salvation through obedience to God is in fact a vulgar superstition. That is, one cannot obey an eternal necessary truth any more than one can be saved by it.

If one stage of the program of modern enlightenment is synonymous with the public refutation of all theological prejudices and superstitions, then Spinoza does not practice enlightenment in that advanced modern sense. He does not presume that the ascent from darkness to light is feasible for all human beings. Even in a work that is written for the learned, Spinoza is prepared to endorse vulgar superstitions, for he is aware of the fact that even the educated, for example, physicians, lawyers, teachers, magistrates, theologians, and even potential philosophers, may share some prejudices or superstitions with the vulgar. To avoid harming those readers (yet still enhance the legitimacy of obedience that is essential to a democracy by affording it a divine origin[79]), Spinoza propounds the most salutary form of a vulgar superstition. Many readers of the *Tractatus* will accept Spinoza's account of the genuine meaning of faith or piety because its form and content generally are familiar to them. But then they will fail to appreciate that belief in Divine Providence, forgiveness of sins, salvation, and obedience to a God who legislates, rules, and judges is also a vulgar and superstitious teaching from Spinoza's philosophic perspective. Those who can discriminate between vulgar prejudices and philosophic truths also will appreciate that the ascent from darkness to light is a difficult task, often accompanied by pain: a pain that results from the realization that what one once accepted as true is really nothing more than a shadowy opinion. Such a stark contrast between the truth and

---

79. See *TTP*, Chapter 16, esp. 3.184–85/246–47.

one's own opinion is not especially pronounced in modernity. And for that reason, the Enlightenment holds out the promise of a relatively painless advance that nonetheless may not be an ascent. In that crucial respect, Spinoza's form of enlightenment is more akin to that described by Plato than to that advocated by Kant.[80]

80. A significant difference between the ancient (or Platonic) view of enlightenment and the modern (or Kantian) view of "the Enlightenment" concerns their respective attitudes concerning prejudice. See Hans Georg Gadamer, *Truth and Method* (New York: Seabury Press, 1975), 239–44. Whereas the orientation of the modern enlightenment demands the eradication of all prejudices, the ancients understood the positive effects of appealing to certain prejudices where such an appeal would bring benefit. Consider, for example, *Republic* (377a ff., 414c ff.). In Spinoza's case, an appeal to the prejudice that a "legislator God" rewards those who are obedient to his command contributes strongly to the general prospect for civic obedience.

7 Leibniz, Reason, and Evil
PHILIPPE RAYNAUD
Translated by John C. McCarthy

Among the great modern philosophers, Leibniz occupies a singular place.[1] At once he pushed the project of a synthesis between modernity and the classical tradition to its furthest point, and, surpassing Cartesianism and the philosophy of the Enlightenment, announced with greatest clarity the themes that define our own situation. In comparison to Descartes, or Hobbes, or Locke, Leibniz presents himself as a moderate or a conciliator: he means to rescue a portion of the heritage of Plato and Aristotle, he rejects Hobbes's radical nominalism as well as his legal positivism, and he breaks with Cartesian mechanism in order to make a significant place for natural teleology. But this admirer of ancient philosophy is also a brilliant innovator, one who clears the way for the great philosophies of history of the nineteenth century, who introduces into rationalism the notion of the unconscious, and who radically transforms the problem of substance.

Leibniz numbers among those who imposed the idea that philosophy should be essentially *systematic*. This demand conforms to a metaphysical ambition ruled by the principle of sufficient reason, namely, to demonstrate the coherence of the universe, to show that it is ruled by the principle of sufficient reason. Apart from a few exceptions, however, his oeuvre is essentially composed of short treatises and polemical essays, together with a vast correspondence wherein he defends and specifies his views. That there is a paradox here is only apparent. In fact, the diversity of the modes of exposition chosen by Leibniz itself expresses a major feature of his "system": in the same way that the world is constituted by an infinity of monads whose diversity does not impede them from expressing varying perspectives on a *single* world, so there are an indefinite number of

---

1. Sections of the analysis proposed here are drawn from the author's "Théodicée," in *Dictionnaire de philosophie politique*, ed. Philippe Raynaud and Stéphane Rials (Paris: Presses universitaires de France, 1996).

points of access to Leibniz's teaching, all of which lead back to the fundamental theses of his theodicy and monadology. Because the purpose of this essay is to make Leibniz's place in the history of modern philosophy better understood, we shall take our point of departure from his complex and ambivalent relation to Descartes. In this way we hope to make plain the meaning of the novel answers Leibniz imparts to classical problems, before advancing, in conclusion, a few remarks about the destiny of his philosophy.

THE PROBLEM OF FINITUDE FROM DESCARTES TO LEIBNIZ

Even though he has a very different conception of mathematics than does Descartes, Leibniz is commonly included with Spinoza (1632–1677) and Malebranche (1638–1715) among the great Cartesians, because his thought prolongs the mathematical rationalism of the French philosopher, and because many of his most fundamental theses amount to replies to problems posed in the *Meditations on First Philosophy* or the *Principles of Philosophy*. However, on just about every important point Leibniz brushes aside the solutions maintained by Descartes. Indeed, the very nature of his project is different, as is shown by an analysis of the transformation Cartesian themes undergo at his hands.

Let us begin by considering the criticisms Leibniz never ceased to advance against the Cartesian criterion for evidence, and against the notion of a clear and distinct idea. Descartes had sought a fixed point from which it would be possible to traverse and exhaust the domain of the intelligible. He found it in "evidence," which is the property of ideas capable of withstanding the trial of hyperbolic doubt. Evidence so conceived is the source of the great theses of Cartesian philosophy, which presupposes the equivalence—in the theoretical order—of the doubtful and the false. On account of this presupposition, Cartesian philosophy is led to reject virtually all that is essential to the Scholastic and Aristotelian legacy, and not merely the old physics. The arts of the probable (rhetoric, dialectic) find themselves excluded from philosophy, which thereby privileges demonstration more than disputations; and the art of logic appears in Descartes's presentation as a sterile thing, for in claiming to explain "things that are in themselves self-evident" it only obscures them.[2]

On every point Leibniz presents himself as a defender of Scholasticism,

---

2. *Principles of Philosophy* I, §10, in *The Philosophical Writings of Descartes*, ed. John Cottingham, Robert Stoothoff, and Dugald Murdoch (Cambridge and New York: Cambridge University Press, 1985), 1.195–96.

and as a critic of Cartesian *subjectivism*. Methodological doubt does not have the weight Descartes accords to it. There is no advantage to be gained by considering "as false that which is doubtful." "That would not be to deliver oneself from prejudices, it would only be to exchange them."[3] On the one hand, it is vain to believe that we can eliminate all risk of error, since such risk is tied to the "weakness of the human spirit, owing to a lack of attention and memory." On the other hand, the preference granted to doubt is tied to the preference for evidence, which is nothing but a false certainty, because it is only a subjective criterion. Cartesian rules must therefore be reduced to a more modest, but also a "more satisfying and precise," precept: "[I]n regard to each thing one must consider the degree of assent or reservation it deserves, or, more simply, one must examine the reasons for each assertion."[4] This precept assumes that truth admits of degrees, that its discovery passes by the way of logical analysis, and that even in theoretical matters it may sometimes be reasonable to employ "indemonstrables." Logic thus becomes once again the model for science, because the first principle of necessary truths is the principle of *noncontradiction*. It is on this account, for example, that although Leibniz accepts the "ontological proof" of the existence of God, he subordinates it to a preliminary demonstration of the *possibility* of the concept of God. By the same token, he establishes a new continuity between science and the active life, between knowledge and practical judgment, and between reason and faith. For if science may employ indemonstrables, that also means that the initial absence of such principles does not impede one from progressing on the path of reason, without having to "cast into doubt" common beliefs. There is thus with Leibniz, as with Spinoza and Malebranche, something like a "forfeiture of the *cogito*."[5] That Cartesian insight ceases to be for him a "truth of reason"; it is now no more than one of two fundamental "truths of fact." He avers: "I am aware not only of my thinking self, but also of my thoughts; and it is no more true and certain that I think than it is that I think something. Hence, one may rightfully relate all primary truths of fact to these two: *I think*, and *various things are thought by me*. From this it follows not only that I am, but also that I am affected in different ways."[6]

---

3. *Remarques sur la partie générale des principes de Descartes*, on I §2. For an English translation, see "Critical Thoughts on the General Part of the Principles of Descartes," in Leibniz, *Philosophical Papers and Letters*, 2d ed., trans. and ed. Leroy E. Loemker (Dordrecht, The Netherlands: D. Reidel, 1969), 384.

4. Ibid., on I §1. See *Philosophical Papers and Letters*, 384.

5. Martial Gueroult, *Malebranche*, vol. 1, *La vision en Dieu* (Paris: Aubier-Montaigne, 1955), chap. 2, "Déchéance du cogito," 41–61.

6. Leibniz, *Remarques sur la partie générale des principes de Descartes*, I §7. See *Philosophical Papers and Letters*, 385.

As we shall see, Leibniz's ontology and theology are governed by this decision to rehabilitate, at least partially, the philosophy of Aristotle and Scholasticism, a decision that entails a formal objection to Cartesian subjectivism. But Leibniz is no less a "modern" for all of that, insofar as all modern philosophy affirms the power of reason and the primacy of subjectivity. What is more, he opens up paths for modern philosophy that had remained closed to a strict Cartesianism. This paradoxical relationship between Leibniz and Descartes surfaces at every level of the Leibnizian system. To analyze this relationship more closely, let us consider a classic problem among the controversies of the seventeenth century: the status of the discoveries made by Copernicus. For Descartes, the differing hypotheses of Ptolemy, Tycho Brahe, and Copernicus concerning the motions of the earth are originally equivalent, since in any case a body cannot be in motion except in relation to another body that remains at rest.[7] Motion is relative, so that it amounts to the same thing to say that the earth turns around the sun or the reverse; the choice of either hypothesis is simply a matter of convenience. Leibniz agrees with Descartes on this point, but he invests the notion of the convenience of hypotheses with a novel significance. The simple fact that of two hypotheses one makes it possible to give an account of phenomena that would otherwise remain inexplicable suffices for him to grant it genuine superiority: "[T]he truth of an hypothesis is nothing other than its convenience."[8] This formulation is, from a strictly Cartesian point of view, unacceptable, because it does not regard the dubitable as false. It also opens the way to a novel consideration of history and progress,[9] the main lines of which are to be found in the theodicy and monadology. However, even if we detect in Leibniz arguments in favor of a conventionalist conception of knowledge, arguments that would seem to prohibit any apprehension of an absolute in the physical world, so far as he is concerned we can come to know such an absolute knowledge in the domain of physics. It is this thesis that underlies his *dynamics*, which substitutes for the Cartesian thesis of the conservation of *movement* (mv), the constancy of *living force* (mv^2).[10]

This apparent contradiction displays for us just what is original in Leibniz's thought, and what it is that compelled the break with Cartesianism. The philosophy of Descartes may be viewed equally as a teaching,

---

7. *Principles of Philosophy*, III, §15, in *Philosophical Writings*, 1.250.
8. Leibniz, *Dynamica de potentia*, cited by Martial Gueroult, in *Leibniz: Dynamique et métaphysique* (Paris: Aubier, 1955), 102.
9. See on this point Michel Serres, *Le système de Leibniz et ses modèles mathématique* (Paris: Presses universitaires de France, 1967), 213–87, and the discussion below.
10. On Leibniz's dynamics, see Martial Gueroult, *Leibniz: Dynamique et métaphysique*.

established on the basis of self-reflection, about the limits of knowledge (in this way anticipating Kant), and as a dogmatism no less rigorous for being restrained. Clear and distinct ideas are at once *passive*[11] and absolutely true, not subject to relativization through a variation of "points of view." But Descartes's philosophy also implies a radical finitude of the human mind, for it limits the ambition of human reason from the start, thanks to its affirmation of the incomprehensibility of the divine. We can know by reason the "eternal truths" of science, but these are *created* by God, whose unfathomable freedom is thus at the root of rationality. The clarity of ideas, and the certainty admitted by physics and mathematics[12] are, accordingly, but the counterpart to the incapacity of human reason to move beyond the narrow limits allowing philosophy to found the objectivity of finite knowledge. Now it is just this equilibrium that Leibniz overturns. He submits Cartesian intuitionism to a radical critique, and this leads him to modify the status of our knowledge of physics. Yet he is also much more speculatively ambitious than Descartes, thereby forging the way for the Hegelian idea of absolute knowledge. Therefore, Leibniz's dogmatism has the effect of extending the power of understanding and reason far beyond what Descartes had claimed to have achieved, even while presenting itself as a critique of Cartesian subjectivism, which calls radically into question Descartes's confidence in the clarity of human awareness and its ideas.[13]

THE THEODICY

If the heart of Leibniz's ontology is constituted by the *monadology* (which explains how the universe is made up of an infinity of individual substances each of which expresses a particular perspective on the whole), his onto-theology has as its foundation the "theodicy," the object of which is the *justification of God* before those who would hold him responsible for evil, and the basis of which is his resolution of the logical and metaphysical problem of the relations between the necessary and the contingent. The term "theodicy" is a neologism, introduced by Leibniz, and formed from two Greek words, θεός and δίκη, "god" and "justice." Thus it refers to "God's justice": the *Essays in Theodicy on the Goodness*

---

11. Inversely, Leibniz calls into question the idea of the passivity of representation.

12. With Descartes physics has little autonomy in relation to mathematics, a fact connected to his teaching on the creation of the eternal truths: mathematical truths rest on the same footing as the truths of physics.

13. See notably *Meditationes de cognitione, veritate et ideis* (1684); and "Meditations on Knowledge, Truth, and Ideas," in *Philosophical Papers and Letters*, 291–95, for an English translation.

of God, the Freedom of Man, and the Origin of Evil (1710) are a treatise on divine justice, also concerned with entering a plea on God's behalf (cf. the title of the Latin abridgement, *Causa dei asserta per justitiam ejus*).[14] Historically, this work of 1710 is a reply to various objections, posed especially by Bayle. Yet it also forms part of a general discussion among eighteenth-century rationalists; indeed, it takes up once again what was a classical problem for philosophy in its relation to religion.

The thesis of Leibniz's theodicy is at once profound and elegant in its simplicity. It consists in saying that if evil exists it is as counterpart to some greater good, the existence of which can be known by the human mind but not fully comprehended: the actually existing world is not absolutely good, but it is *the best of all possible worlds*. This thesis is posed as the necessary conclusion to an argument that simultaneously satisfies the demands of reason and the demands of faith. Evil exists—it is not merely a human illusion—since without it the notions of sin, the Fall, and salvation would cease to make sense. The world might have been different than it is, or it might not have been at all, because God is the *all-powerful creator* of a world in which *human freedom* is in play. We must admit, then, that this is indeed the *best of all possible worlds*, unless we are prepared to deny the goodness or the omnipotence of God: God cannot but want the best, and he had the power to create the best through an anticipatory calculus of the consequences of different possible choices before the Creation.

The theodicy thus begins from two traditional theses: (1) God is "innocent" of evil, which must accordingly be imputed to human beings. Nevertheless, (2) he is not indifferent to worldly affairs, but seeks, to the contrary, to establish justice in the world, or to reestablish it in the face of human transgression, through his governance. In the shape given it by Leibniz, theodicy is a rationalist answer to the problem of the meaning of existence. In response to this same problem, Kant will be moved to introduce the notion of "the need of reason," which leads to "the postulates of practical reason," which in turn ground our hope in the realization of the sovereign good, without authorizing us on that account to claim that this is the "best of all possible worlds." Leibniz for his part considers that the problem of the meaning of existence is susceptible to a genuinely theoretical solution, given by theodicy. His theory thus responds to a spontaneous tendency of philosophy. Hence we find a "theodicy" already in Book 10 of Plato's *Laws*, for example, wherein the Athenian shows

---

14. "Preface" to the *Theodicy*. For an English translation, see *Theodicy: Essays on the Goodness of God, the Freedom of Man, and the Origin of Evil*, trans. E. M. Huggard (New Haven, Conn.: Yale University Press, 1952), 49–72.

how the city must adopt three beliefs as dogmas: that the gods exist, that they have care for human affairs, and that their justice is incorruptible. With Plato this teaching is indissolubly "philosophical," "theological," and "political." It is directed at the same time against the civic effects of the impiety implicit in merely positive religion, and against the teachings of the "physiologists," who, like Plato, recognize that nature must be understood to be the first principle of things, but who make of nature an incoherent aggregate for want of seeing in it the handwork of an ordering intelligence.

One must also note that in many respects Saint Augustine and his Christian heirs follow in Plato's steps when they strive to show the insufficiency of the earthly city and the necessity of the rule of Providence. Yet one must also add that the Platonic perspective is but one possible philosophical path, and that it itself poses numerous difficulties for the Christian religion to which Leibniz lays claim. With the ancients, Aristotle had shown that the idea of a teleological nature, and of a hierarchical κόσμος was compatible with a god indifferent to the affairs of the world: the world, and a fortiori, the human world, are objects unworthy of god's notice, so that human beings can expect nothing from Providence to make up for the incompleteness or imperfection of nature. From the Christian point of view, on the other hand, two new problems emerge that prevent one from being satisfied by the Platonic theses. The first is born of the idea of a God all powerful and attentive to his creatures. The "responsibility" of such a God is infinitely greater than that of the Platonic "demiurge" (which merely introduces order into a preexisting matter according to a model that precedes it, and is superior to it). Hence the scandal, for Christian souls, of innocent suffering. The second stems from the specificity of the order of grace. The unfolding of this grace presumes a personal relationship between God and his creatures, which renders the rationalist idea of God's impartiality inadequate at the very least. From this is born, for philosophy, a permanent tension between the ideas of nature, of the God of the philosophers, and of the God of Jesus Christ. It is this tension that Leibniz attempts to surmount in establishing the compatibility of God's perfections (his justice, wisdom, and goodness), and in distinguishing necessary truths of reason and contingent truths of fact, a distinction allowing him to conceive of *creation*.

To resolve the problem of theodicy, Leibniz must, as always, first examine and overcome Descartes's position. Yet with Descartes, the question of God's "justice" or of the "justification" of God appears under two different aspects, and receives two distinct if not contradictory answers. On the one hand, Descartes insists, in effect, that God's nature is incomprehensible to us, owing to the radical heterogeneity between finite human understanding and infinite divine understanding. This is the meaning of the theory of the creation of the eternal truths, which absolutely forbids us from placing ourselves among God's "council," and which for Descartes follows from the transcendence of God. "To say that truths are independent of God amounts to speaking of him as though he were a Jupiter or a Saturn, and to subject him to the Styx or to the Fates."[15] For this reason, the solution to a problem such as the meaning and existence of evil is necessarily beyond our reach, because any solution would presume that we could show that God has necessarily acted in accordance with certain principles that would explain the existence of evil. Malebranche and Leibniz, who wish to address this issue, are thus quite logically led to reject the thesis of the creation of eternal truths, and to reduce the distance separating the human and the divine understanding. Nevertheless, there is for Descartes one characteristic of God's nature that we cannot help but know, and on the basis of which we must reason as though he had to act in conformity with truths preexisting the Creation: God must be veracious in order to guarantee human knowledge. The problem of the compatibility of evil and the perfection of God reappears here in a limited form, and *it must receive an answer.* One must explain how *error* is possible if God is at the same time all-powerful and veracious. The answers of Descartes and Leibniz are the same as those that Malebranche and Leibniz extend to the problem of theodicy as a whole: the imperfections in the details contribute to the perfection of the whole, they are the consequence of the simplicity of God's ways, which itself issues from his nature and immutability. Thus God's work, such as it is, is at once the best and the most to be wished for.[16]

From Descartes to Leibniz the rationalist project thus changes nature, completing a cycle one might compare to that which runs from Kant to Hegel: we move from a philosophy of the limits of knowledge to a speculative metaphysics. This metaphysics tends to reduce the distance between human and divine intellect, following a logic at work in the three great "Cartesians," Spinoza, Malebranche, and Leibniz. In "affirming the complete intelligibility to man of God's essence and the essence of things" Spinoza pushes the identity between the nature of human and

---

15. Descartes, "Lettre au P. Mersenne (15 April 1630)"; see *The Philosophical Writings of Descartes*, vol. 3, *Correspondence*, ed. John Cottingham, Robert Stoothoff, Dugald Murdoch, and Anthony Kenny (Cambridge: Cambridge University Press, 1991), 20–23. This thesis of the creation of the eternal truths takes up in a new form the Augustinian interdict that we must look to God's will as the reason for things, but may not look beyond that will to explain his actions. On this point, see below; also see Etienne Gilson, *La liberté chez Descartes et la théologie* (Paris: J. Vrin, 1913), 211–35.

16. On this point, see Martial Gueroult, *Descartes selon l'ordre des raison*, vol. 2, *L'âme et le corps* (Paris: Aubier-Montaigne, 1968), 210–11.

divine understanding to its logical conclusion,[17] but this is at the cost of an open break with the Christian tradition. God is nothing other than Nature itself, whose modes are linked according to the most rigorous necessity. As a result, teleology, contingency, and freedom are shown to be illusions of the human soul. Malebranche and Leibniz, who both wish to demonstrate the compatibility of philosophy and the Christian religion, obviously cannot accept this radical reduction of transcendence. For this reason, each in his way reintroduces a heterogeneity between our understanding and God's that is not simply a matter of degree. From this there follows for both philosophers a forfeiture of clear and distinct ideas, which leads them by a delicate counterpoint to join a philosophy of feeling to the affirmation of the power of the understanding. Besides, the very problem of theodicy has no meaning if we do not admit as premises the contingency of the world and the transcendence of God—correlates of his at least partial incomprehensibility—all the while seeking to reconcile the intrinsic goodness of creation with the observation that evil exists. It is for this reason that Malebranche and Leibniz, each in his way opening a path to an unprecedented affirmation of the integrity of nature, both follow Saint Augustine at least to some degree. Augustine's entire teaching rests on the double affirmation of the omnipotence of God and the intrinsic goodness of his creation. Our problem is, then, to understand how Leibniz's modulation of Christian theology occurs.

For the greatest of the Fathers of the Church, God first appears as the ultimate principal, beyond which it is vain (and sinful) to pursue any other explanation. We may seek the reason for things in his will, but "it is absurd to look beyond his will in order to find a reason, a principle, an order, of his acts surpassing it and not drawn from it."[18] The goodness and the omnipotence of God are thus the radical origin of every being. On the other hand, these qualities cannot express themselves in the world except by means of the goodness of the ways of creation, and by means of the goodness of "nature" itself. The theology of Saint Augustine presents itself, then, as simultaneously an affirmation of transcendence and as a justification of nature. Order is at once that by which God rules things, and that by which he rules himself. Augustine tends, therefore, to minimize the difference between the eternal law of order and the harmonious relations that link the beings of nature in a good and coherent world; however, he also forbids any investigation of the reasons that lead God to create *this particular world*. It is this subtle and unstable equilibrium

---

17. Martial Gueroult, *Spinoza*, vol. 1, *Dieu*, part 1, *Ethique* (Paris: Aubier-Montaigne, 1968), 12.

18. Martial Gueroult, *Malebranche*, vol. 2, *Les cinq abîmes de la Providence*, part 1: *L'ordre et l'occasionnalisme* (Paris: Aubier-Montaigne, 1959), 51–52.

that is ruptured by Leibniz's theodicy, for it rests entirely on the idea of a continuity between the philosophic justification of the Creation, and speculation about the principles that guide the divine creation. It is particularly in his relation to Augustine that Leibniz is to be distinguished from Malebranche.

When he treated the problem of evil, Saint Augustine did not fail to invoke the same arguments as Leibniz in order to show that evil is to a degree nothing other than an illusion, born from our considering only the parts of the whole without taking into consideration its perfection, a perfection that requires moreover some partial defects. Besides, the Christian religion would be meaningless if one could not call evil the counterpart to good, for otherwise it could not make sense either of the Fall or of the Redemption. It is because man can do evil that he can be saved, so that we can say of Adam's sin that it was a "felix culpa," and glorify God that divine grace be given us superabundantly there where sin abounded. But this cannot mean that for Augustine God created *the best of all possible worlds:* the goodness of creation stems simply from the fact that once God resolved to create a world, it could not but conform fully to that which God chose in the perfection of his will. Thus, even if it is true that *our* created universe could not be better than it is, still God could have created *another* universe.[19] Moreover, it is precisely because he thereby preserves the incomprehensibility of God that Augustine, conforming to what one can call his genius for orthodoxy, can affirm both the primacy of the will and power of God, and the proper perfection of created nature: God has truly done what he willed to do, but the fact that the world is not *the best possible* does not at all mean that it is in any way evil.

It is over this point that Leibniz separates himself from Saint Augustine, in order to develop his teaching of the *choice of the best.* This teaching leads him, on the one hand, to distinguish God's *antecedent* and *consequent* will, and on the other, to distinguish three forms of evil: *metaphysical, physical,* and *moral.* That God had chosen to create the "best of worlds" actually proceeds from a simple analysis of the concepts of good and evil, *such as Augustine himself had employed them.* In his polemic against the Manicheans Augustine asserted in effect that evil was nothing but a privation, or a simple lack of being, and that, inversely, God's infinity alone sufficed to explain the inferiority of this (or any other) world to him. Yet, as Leibniz observes, just as the slightest evil includes some element of good, so the slightest good contains some element of evil;[20] and a consideration of

---

19. On all these points, see Martial Gueroult, *Malebranche,* 233–58.
20. *Discours de métaphysique,* §3: "Uti minus malum habet rationem boni, ita minus

God's glory requires us to think that God created the *maximum* good, which is to say, the *best*. As for God's incomprehensibility, it means only that we cannot "know in detail the reasons that moved him to choose this order for the universe" (*Discourse on Metaphysics*, §5). One must therefore distinguish within God's will between the antecedent and the consequent will. The former seeks the good in itself, the latter "moves to combinations, as when one joins a good and an evil" (*Theodicy*, §119). The consequent will results in the choice from among all such combinations of that one wherein the good "surpasses the evil." Therefore God's *final will*, having carried out the combination of all goods and evils possible, would choose that combination most suited to the creation of the best, that is to say, the most perfect, of worlds.[21] What distinguishes Leibniz from Saint Augustine, then, is that continuity is decisive for his thought: the possible worlds are not only different, they are *comparable*, and on that account may be placed on a scale from most to least, depending on the degree that they stray from what is willed by God's wisdom and goodness. This theology of God's glory has as a consequence a rather profound modification of the metaphysical status of evil.

For Leibniz, the intelligibility of evil proceeds from the necessary imperfection of finite creatures. As regards physical evil (pain) and moral evil (sin), his explanations are classic and orthodox. Physical evil is willed by God only as a condition for some good we are prevented from understanding only because we are partial and finite. Moral evil stems from human freedom, which has since the Fall enslaved itself to Satan. More profoundly, however, metaphysical evil (which in itself brings about neither error nor pain, but which is the condition of both) is an eternal consequence of the infinite perfection of God, which has as an ineluctable correlate in any world whatsoever the finitude of creatures. The ultimate source of evil is not sin, but the gradation that separates the superior from the inferior. For the greatest Father of the Church, evil is not tied to the *nature* of things, but rather to their *corruption*, whereas for Leibniz the root of evil is to be found in finitude itself. Therefore, Leibniz's teaching is both faithful to Saint Augustine's theses in that it thinks of evil as *privation*, and radically new, in that sees it as the reverse side of finitude. With Saint Augustine, the primary question is a moral one: "Unde malum faciamus"? How comes it that we do evil? It is on this basis that

---

bonum habet rationem mali (As a lesser evil is relatively good, so a lesser good is relatively evil)." For an English translation, see "Discourse on Metaphysics," *Philosophical Papers and Letters*, 303–30.

21. In the language of contemporary moral philosophy, Leibniz's God is a "consequentialist."

the deficiency of the finite becomes a problem for him. All of Leibniz's energy, on the other hand, is directed toward answering the metaphysical question, "From whence comes evil?" to which he subordinates the moral question."

Clearly it would be vain to hope to advance here an exhaustive analysis of the problems raised by Leibniz's theodicy. At the most we shall try to set out what is essential to it by comparing it briefly with the rival attempt of Malebranche, and by analyzing its moral implications.

Malebranche, like Leibniz, takes exception to the Cartesian theory of the eternal truths. So he begins from the same question: How does one reconcile the existence of evil with the perfection of God? Accordingly, he inquires after the law of divine combination that results in the creation of this world. But he distinguishes himself from Leibniz by an intransigent theocentrism, which leads him to a strict subordination of the perfection of the *work* to the perfection of the *paths* chosen by the creator. For Malebranche, God cannot but act for the sake of his own glory, and this presumes that there are *means* compatible with his perfection. Hence the supreme principle of the *simplicity* of his ways, which impedes God from acting other than by general and constant intentions. It is for this reason that the world includes real imperfections, even though it is just as good as it can be, for these imperfections are the consequence of the general laws established by God's will, and are no less disordered for so being. "The visible world would be more perfect if the lands and the seas were formed in a more just manner, and if, being smaller, they could maintain just as many human beings, and if rain were more regular and the earth more fertile; in a word, if there were not so many monstrosities and disorders" (*Méditations chrétiennes*, Entretien V, §11). By the same token, as Ferdinand Alquié has shown, Malebranche, whose every writing is animated by an apologetic intention, opens the way to the idea of the clockmaker God of the Enlightenment,[23] because his position logically implies a certain indifference of God to the particular, just as it favors a morality founded upon the primacy of technique. The regularity of the laws of nature testify to God's greatness, but they make evil possible; and the real imperfection of the created world must lead us to improve upon it by conforming us to his order. All of this follows from Malebranche's

---

22. Paul Ricoeur, *Le mal: Un défi à la philosophie et à la théologie* (Geneva: Labor et Fides, 1986), 22–28. From the point of view of the Augustinian tradition, there is doubtless something shocking in all this, since it compounds the error born of the question of the "best of all possible worlds": in the same way that the world can be good, because it is created by God, without being "the best," a created nature can be good even in being inferior to another (and a fortiori to God).

23. Ferdinand Alquié, *Le cartesiannisme de Malebranche* (Paris: J. Vrin, 1974).

distinction between the nature and order of the world. From this point of view, Voltaire will be the great heir of Malebranche. His "deism" does not prevent him from recognizing the irreducibility of evil, both physical and moral. He also proves, in his *Candide*, to be the most caustic (and one of the most profound) of Leibniz's critics. God is great and powerful; his laws are good and intelligible; but it is false or unintelligible to say that our world is "the best of all possible worlds."

Thus in the controversy between Leibniz and Malebranche over the ultimate principle of divine combinatorics—simplicity of ways or perfection of the work—there are in fact two paths that open up for modern philosophy. The first, which is dominant in the French Enlightenment, leads to the rationalism of universal rules, tempered by a philosophy of feeling and by an acute awareness of the irreducibility of evil. The second, which will flourish in German Idealism, and especially with Hegel, tends to make of the irrational a moment in the unfolding of reason. It is this latter aspiration that is born with Leibniz through his affirmation of the *principle of reason*, the principle of contingent truths, which allows (divine) reason to realize itself through the (apparent) irrationality of natural events and human actions.[24]

Accordingly, the Augustinian conception of the relations between nature and grace also undergoes an important transformation in Leibniz's thought, which can be seen very clearly in the way he treats the notion of the "City of God." The harmony between the "physical kingdom of nature" and the "moral kingdom of grace" "causes things to lead to grace by the very ways of nature" (*Monadology*, §88): the arrival of the City of God merges with the formation of a *moral world*, which is realized without any rupture with the world of nature.[25] The theologian concerned with orthodoxy will doubtless greet this suggestion with an indignation similar to that provoked by the notions of metaphysical evil and the best of all

---

24. This should not lead to a misinterpretation of the sense of the divergence between Leibniz and Malebranche. Both principles we have been discussing are present in both thinkers, even though they are weighted differently. For Leibniz, the simplicity of God's ways does indeed form part of the "rules of perfection of divine conduct," but these must be balanced with "the wealth of the effects" (*Discours de métaphysique*, §5). Inversely, for Malebranche, even if a better world could be conceived, God clearly would not have created it, since that would have derogated from the principle of the simplicity of his ways, and in this sense the created world is in fact the best possible. Besides, both authors know perfectly well the precise bearing of their difference, as an exchange of letters that took place after the publication of the *Theodicy* attests. See Leibniz, *Die philosophischen Schriften*, ed. C. I. Gerhardt (Hildesheim: Georg Olms, 1960), 1.359–60, and Philippe Raynaud, "Théodicée."

25. *Monadology*, §§84–90; *Discours de la métaphysique*, §§35–37; see also the very fine study of Jacques Rivelaygue, "La *Monadologie* de Leibniz," in *Leçons de métaphysique allemande*, vol. 1, *De Leibniz à Hegel* (Paris: Grasset, 1990).

possible worlds. The philosopher will nevertheless observe that here again Leibniz builds upon arguments present already in an elementary form in Saint Augustine himself. For the latter, if nature is good to the degree that it is uncorrupted, then the laws of nature are the same as those of order: it is difficult to avoid the conclusion that grace is in itself a particular case of order, or at least, that it acts in continuity with nature.[26]

The evocation of the City of God allows us better to understand the way Leibniz transforms the problem of evil, and the governance of Providence. On his reading, for a finite awareness, which is unable to perceive *in concreto* how the created world is from all eternity the best, the arrival of the City of God appears as *progress* and as the result of human *effort* to conform to the moral law and to combat evil. Thus Leibniz's theodicy provokes a development in the philosophy of history, for history is now considered as the place wherein reason, as effective in the world, is actualized. Parallel to this, the theodicy makes a new reconstruction of philosophy possible, beginning from the conflict between metaphysics and finite awareness. Lessing and Kant are the heirs, although with unequal fidelity, of Leibniz's system.

On the other hand, and through an understandable reversal, the strongest objections against Leibniz's philosophy come from the Kantian tradition, which builds upon the radical heterogeneity between finite and divine understanding, and which, by moving the moral problem to the fore, accords a primacy to practical reason. Furthermore, it is significant that Hegel, the most eloquent critic of the "moral vision of the world," should also be one of the greatest of Leibniz's heirs. All the same, it would be a mistake to disregard the practical orientation of Leibniz's philosophy under the pretext that it affirms the universal validity of the principle of reason. From the point of view of the finite subject, the connection of causes and effects is not the equivalent of *fate*, for it presents itself under the form of a law, whether necessary or probable, which makes it possible to foresee the consequences of an act and to bring about an enlightened choice. In this way Leibniz eliminates the sophism of "idle reason." "It is not true that an event occurs whatsoever one does; it will occur if one does that which leads up to it; if the event is written, then the cause that brings it about is written as well. Thus the connection between causes and effects, far from establishing a teaching prejudicial to practice, serves to destroy such a teaching" (*Theodicy*, "Preface"). As a counterpoint to the theodicy, then, Leibniz outlines a moral theory

26. See *contra Faustum*, XXVI, 3, and the remarks of Gueroult, *Malebranche*, 246–49. For the argument of this paragraph, see also Philippe Raynaud, "Théodicée."

whose inspiration is fundamentally "consequentialist," but which, in a thoroughly classical way, considers that our ignorance of God's particular choices entails for us finite beings the duty to submit to the natural law.[27]

THE MONADOLOGY, THE UNCONSCIOUS, AND THE INDIVIDUAL

The theodicy shows that the real world is the best world possible without thereby revealing the particular reasons for God's choice. However, our metaphysical knowledge of the world's constitution does not stop there. Reason demonstrates that the world is constituted by *monads*, that is to say, simple elements differing *qualitatively* from one another, and not only because of their spatial position. The *Monadology* (1714) sets forth Leibniz's system beginning from the most fundamental elements of things (§§ 1–36), in order to reascend in turn to their cause, namely, God (§§ 37–48), and in order, finally, to descend back down toward the world, so as to explain how the world can still be *one whole*, although composed of simple unities qualitatively distinct.[28] Here again, everything begins from the critique of Cartesian difficulties, notably the reduction of matter to extension. And as we have already observed, this critique controls Leibnizian dynamics as a whole:

> What is truly real for [Leibniz] is force, matter being for him nothing but a simple phenomenon. Nor will space be a substance, as it had been for Descartes, but rather a relation between forces. From this follows the constitutive thesis of Leibnizian ontology: beyond appearances, i.e., matter, are points of energy, absolutely simple, out of which everything real is made. It is these points of energy Leibniz names monads; he thereby abolishes the intrinsic difference between matter and spirit, since every reality is monadic; there is between monads only a difference of degree.[29]

The path Leibniz follows is to submit the problem of the simple and the compound to a *logical* analysis: "There must be simple substances because there are compound ones" (§2). This suffices to exclude the possibility that extension be a substance. It also makes space into a mere phenomenon, for space, like time, is infinitely divisible. The monadology leads in turn to the thesis that each monad must possess qualities (§8), and by the same token, qualities "different from every other" (§9). From this flows the *principle of indiscernibles*: two identical things cannot exist

---

27. On this point, see, e.g., René Sève, *Leibniz et l'école moderne du droit naturel* (Paris: Presses universitaires de France, 1989), chap. 4.
28. See Jacques Rivelaygue, "La *Monadologie* de Leibniz."
29. Ibid., 13.

because they could not but be one and the same thing. The entire demonstration presupposes the Aristotelian arguments against the Eleatics and for the reality of change (cf. §8: "if simple substances do not differ at all in their quality, there would be no way to notice any change in things"). Yet Leibniz, who remains a "modern," privileges the reflection of the subject over the change produced in him. The monad will thus be at once *substance*, as that which underlies all changes, and *subject*, since the totality of changes undergone by each monad will be ascribed to its *internal* dynamic (cf. §7: "the monads have no windows through which anything may come in or go out"). The result of this deduction, which rests upon traditional premises, and which partially rehabilitates Aristotle against Descartes, consists in a double philosophical revolution, involving on the one hand the invention of the concept of the *unconscious*, and on the other, the definition of the soul as *endeavor* and no longer as *form*.

The theory of the unconscious, which finds its classic exposition in the "Preface" to the *New Essays on Human Understanding*, is introduced in the *Monadology*, beginning at §14, and developed in §§ 20 to 23. It is based upon a reversal of Descartes's perspective, and consists in understanding thought as originating from nonconscious "perception" rather than from consciousness:

[T]here are a thousand indications causing us to judge that at every moment there is in us an infinity of perceptions, but without apperceptions and without reflection; that is to say, of changes within the soul itself, which we do not apperceive because these impression are either too minute or numerous, or too uniform, having nothing sufficiently distinctive of their own. But joined to others, they do not fail to have their effect, and to constitute themselves in the whole assembly, at least confusedly. (*New Essays*, "Preface")

The "minute" unconscious "perceptions" (like those of the noise of the sea) are of an infinitesimal quantity. They do not become the object of "apperception" (i.e., of awareness) until they attain a certain degree; all the same, they are no less determinative in the series of causes through which the internal dynamism of the substance asserts itself. The "unconscious" is the correlate, in the monadology, of the *principle of sufficient reason*.[30] This suggests that Leibniz's rationalism goes hand in hand with a certain forfeiture of reason. The principle of continuity allows us to distinguish three series of monads, according to the degree of their awareness, that is to say, of the activity they are capable of: simple monads

---

30. Cf. *Monadology*, §22: "since every present state of a simple substance is naturally a consequence of its preceding state, in such a way that the present is great with the future."

know only a succession of states, animals possess memory, and rational souls possess reason and reflection, that which allows them to act on the basis of the representation of a law or rule, and to have awareness of themselves (§§19–30). The notion of "appetition," as a striving toward distinct perception shows, moreover, that this differentiation is hierarchical. The least degree of perception is as well the least degree of activity, that is, of being; and the change from unconscious perception to activity may be represented as *progress*. Yet here again the apparent classicism of Leibniz is nothing but the obverse side of a profound transformation of classical conceptions, as is shown by the use he makes of the notion of *entelechy*.[31] For Aristotle, entelechy designates the state of perfection a being attains when it is no longer in potentiality because it has fully accomplished its essence. For Leibniz, entelechy is the very tendency that pushes the monad to realize itself and to produce all the diversity it is capable of on its own. The end of the monads is no longer to identify themselves with their form, or their common nature, but to develop their internal productivity, their individuality, already contained in the definition of each substance. Perfection lies no longer in the final terminus of the change but in the change itself.

CONCLUSION

Leibniz's system represents, then, a decisive moment in the history of modern philosophy. It does its best to overcome the one-sidedness of the Cartesian conception of subjectivity so as to integrate the heritage of Aristotelian and Scholastic ontology. We have seen, however, that the internal logic of his rationalism leads to a greater distancing from classical philosophy (and Christian orthodoxy) than was the case perhaps even for Descartes. One must also add, in conclusion, that Leibniz opened the way to *all* subsequent currents of modernity, including even those most hostile to dogmatic rationalism. One sees this clearly if one ponders the posterity of the teaching on the unconscious. That teaching presumes, in the first place, that progress in the capacity to act is parallel to the progress from unconscious to conscious perception, or from instinct to understanding. But one might equally well regard the predominance of rationality and calculation as a waning of life, in the same way that instinct, which expresses an originating activity of mind, gives us a comprehension of reality better adapted to the necessities of life than does intelligence. If the rationalist path was followed by the philosophes and the philosophies of progress, the "irrationalist" interpretation of the

31. See Rivelaygue, "La *Monadologie* de Leibniz," 28.

Leibnizian program advances in a subterranean manner in the current that runs from the German romantics to Schopenhauer and Nietzsche.[32] Both currents rejoin, without the advocates of either discipline always knowing, in Freudian psychoanalysis and Weberian sociology.[33] Leibniz is our contemporary.

32. Cf. Nietzsche, "The Gay Science," §357. See Philippe Raynaud, "Nietzsche, la philosophie et les philosophes," in F. Nietzsche, *Oeuvres*, vol. 2, ed. Jean Lacoste (Paris: R. Laffont, 1993), i–xxxiv.

33. See Philippe Raynaud, *Max Weber et les dilemmes de la raison moderne* (Paris: Presses universitaires de France, 1987).

8   Hume's Unnatural Religion (Some Humean Footnotes)

F. J. CROSSON

On the title page of his first publication, *A Treatise on Human Nature* (1739), Hume chose a motto from Tacitus: "Rare those happy times when you can think what you will and are permitted to say what you think." The observation accurately reflected the constraints on the discussion of religion in eighteenth-century England and Scotland, and Hume tells in a well-known letter to a friend in 1737 of revising the *Treatise* for publication and excising his discussion of religious topics (among them that of miracles) because of the possible consequences. Ten years later, when he is preparing the *Essays Concerning Human Understanding* (1748) for the press, he is less fearful of being indiscrete—partly because he has learned something from classical authors about the rhetoric of religious discourse, partly because he has surrendered some of his hopes for public preferment. At any rate, he now (1747) writes to another friend about including his discussion of miracles and of the design argument, Chapters 10 and 11 of the *Essays* (renamed *Enquiry Concerning Human Understanding* in the 1758 edition): "I see not what bad consequences follow, in the present age, from the character of an infidel; especially if a man's conduct be in other respects irreproachable."[1]

By the reference to "the rhetoric of religious discourse," I mean not only the conventional pieties with which Hume learned to surround his critical discussions—for example, the opening and concluding paragraphs of the essays on miracles, on the immortality of the soul, and of the *Dialogues Concerning Natural Religion*—but even more the rhetorical forms themselves in which he henceforth cast his essays on religion. This claim takes Chapters 10 and 11 of the *Enquiry* as forming a complementary pair, complementary not only in their subject matters but in their literary forms.

---

1. *Letters of David Hume*, 2 vols., ed. J. Grieg (Oxford: Oxford University Press, 1932), 1.106. Of course, apart from what might be thought of the character of an infidel, there were social and legal sanctions consequent upon the printing of blasphemous sentiments.

Chapter 10 is a treatise, the famous critical analysis of miracles, which after arguing that the probability of the truth of testimony cannot be assigned independently of the probability of the events reported—and that miracles have a virtually zero probability—concludes as noted with a conventional, if tongue-in-cheek, affirmation that the faith necessary to believe in miracles is itself a miracle that subverts all reason. Chapter 11, without any transition, opens with a narrator "I" who proposes to report a conversation with a friend whose theses, although the narrator can "by no means approve" of them, are yet relevant to the larger "inquiry." Chapter 11, which is entitled "Of a Particular Providence and of a Future State,"[2] in fact says little about these topics directly but rather discourses on what is asserted to be one of their necessary conditions, namely, divine existence as demonstrated by the design argument. The views expressed here are hardly different from those embodied later in the *Dialogues Concerning Natural Religion*. The dialogue form, however, is here utilized much less artfully than in the later work; there are only two characters including the narrator, and most of the space is given over to the anonymous friend.

What is worth remarking is that Chapter 10 deals with positive or popular religion and its foundation, and takes the form of a treatise apparently in *oratio recta*, while Chapter 11 deals with natural religion and its foundation (namely, the design argument) and takes the form of a reported dialogue. Why should the second rather than the first take a dialogue form? Not, I think, as has been said, because the dialogue form is one "in which disagreements could be clearly displayed,"[3] but rather primarily because the dialogue allows the author to recede from view or to hide himself, as Plato's Socrates noted. In Chapter 11[4] the author hides himself only to the extent of speaking as an anonymous "I" who reports the views of an interlocutor, and occasionally makes an objection. Why should Hume want to do that for a discussion of natural religion?

Because it had been acceptable for a long time, and exploited for several centuries before Hume wrote, both to criticize superstition in

---

2. Hume originally entitled this chapter "Of the Practical Consequences of Natural Theology"; cf. Norman Kemp Smith's edition of the *Dialogues Concerning Natural Religion* (Indianapolis, Ind.: Bobbs-Merrill, 1976), 51n1. I shall subsequently refer to the *Dialogues* (DNR) by this edition, as has become common. The pagination appears to be the same in all the revisions and printings from the first in 1935, reviewing which stimulated E. C. Mossner's article "The Enigma of Hume," and helped launch the contemporary interest in Hume's religious views. The best recent critical edition of the *Natural History* and the *Dialogues* is by A. Wayne Colver and J. V. Price (Oxford: Oxford University Press, 1976).

3. H. E. Root, in the "Editor's Introduction" to his edition of *The Natural History of Religion* (Stanford, Calif.: Stanford University Press, 1967), 11.

4. Just as in the only other dialogue Hume published—titled simply "A Dialogue"—at the end of the *Enquiry Concerning the Principles of Morals* (1752).

general and the practices of other religious traditions in particular, and also to characterize religious doctrines as above reason.[5] As long as one was careful not to take examples from the surrounding religious tradition, one was not liable to be denounced, however suspicious some might be. On the other hand, to raise questions about what was common to all religions, namely, the existence of God, and what had been claimed by philosophers as a question decidable by natural reason, namely, the rational arguments for the existence of God, was much more subversive. Reasonable men might disagree about transubstantiation or the relation between faith and works, but not about the existence of a providential God, whose handiwork was only made more apparent as the natural sciences advanced. But the critique in Chapter 11 goes beyond suggesting questions about the cogency of the argument from design. Even if the argument were logically compelling, it would not establish the existence of a God whose providence goes further than the orderliness of nature, namely, a God of "particular providence," one who intervenes in history.[6]

So if we read Chapters 10 and 11 as a unit, we find that they make a radical cut between "popular" religion and philosophical religion, between the God of miracles and particular providence, and the God of the philosophers. Each of these two forms of theism must stand on its own—they do not reinforce each other—and neither stands on very solid ground.

What Hume did in Chapters 10 and 11 of the *Enquiry*, I want to say, he repeated in the two works that he wrote soon afterward, the *Natural History of Religion* (1757) and the *Dialogues Concerning Natural Religion* (1779).[7] The *Natural History* is a treatise that deals with popular, not philosophical, religion, while the *Dialogues* are a reported conversation on the design argument in which Hume does not speak in his own voice, that is to say, is not the narrator of the conversation as he apparently is in his two previous dialogues. Although I think that parallel relations are clear once they are remarked, the fact that the *Dialogues* were not published until some twenty years later, after Hume's death, has

---

5. E.g., Montaigne, *An Apology for Raymond Sebond*; Descartes, *Discourse on Method*; etc.

6. This is also an implicit theme of the *De Natura Deorum*, that the god or gods of the (Epicurean and Stoic) philosophers, even if their existence were demonstrated, would not support the traditional religious practices.

7. The *Dialogues* were being composed in 1751, as we know from Hume's correspondence, and were revised by him several times before being published three years after his death; see Appendix C of N. K. Smith's edition on the stages of composition. On the composition and suppression of the first edition of the *Natural History* and its subsequent publication, see E. C. Mossner, "Hume's Four Dissertations: An Essay in Biography and Bibliography," *Modern Philosophy* 48 (1950): 35–57.

made the parallelism less salient. But unless one takes it into account, one is liable to misinterpret Hume's own views. For example, in the *Natural History* there are half a dozen favorable references in passing to the design argument (the argument is never discussed directly), and few critical remarks about it.[8] The reader might think (and a number of modern readers have so thought) that Hume accepts the design argument or at least does not reject it. But if the *Dialogues* is taken as a diptych to the *Natural History*, then it is clear that Hume is simply not opening more than one front at a time. Philosophical demonstrations simply have nothing to do with the origin or the justification of ordinary religiousness. Positive religion is one thing and natural religion is another, and the one needs different assessment (both rhetorically and logically) than the other.

So let us look first at the *Natural History of Religion* and then at the *Dialogues*.

THE SOURCES OF POPULAR PIETY

The opening sentence of the *Natural History* introduces a distinction between the reasons for and the causes of religion, between the questions "concerning its foundation in reason, and that concerning its origin in human nature."[9] The first question, it is said, "admits of the most obvious, at least the clearest solution," namely, the evident design character of the whole frame of nature, about which "no rational enquirer can, after serious reflection, suspend his belief a moment." But the order of nature is not the source of religiousness, Hume claims against the Deists, nor on the other hand does it spring from "an original instinct or primary impression of nature" (21). Religion is not natural to man—as is shown, he says, by the facts that it is not universally found among all nations and ages, and that it does not have a fixed and determinate object. So one must give an account of the genesis of religion that neither presupposes that early man had inferred the existence of God nor that man

---

8. The careful reader will note that the ground is laid for criticism. Consider, for example, the beginning of Chapter 2, where Hume remarks that "to persons of a certain turn of mind, it may not appear altogether absurd, that several independent beings ... might conspire in the execution and contrivance of one regular plan; yet is this a merely arbitrary supposition, which even if allowed possible, must be confessed neither to be supported by probability nor necessity." Having conceded this, however, he immediately proceeds to give a counterexample.

9. *The Natural History of Religion*, ed. H. E. Root (Stanford, Calif.: Stanford University Press, 1967), 21. (Henceforth NHR; subsequent page references to this work will be to this edition.) A similar distinction is made in the opening sentence of the classical work that most influenced Hume's writings on religion, Cicero's *De Natura Deorum*.

is by nature a religious being, that is to say, by nature inclined toward the worship of a deity. Indeed, such an account should not even presuppose that there is a God.[10]

Hume proceeds to trace its origin rather to a weakness in human nature, namely, an inordinately fearful concern about what will befall us tomorrow, hence with the unknown causes of those future events; and the conjunction of this concern with a "universal tendency among mankind to conceive all beings like themselves" results in the conceiving of these causes as having sentiment and intelligence (29). Conceiving of the unknown causes of our good and bad fortune anthropomorphically, as conscious, intentional agents, we ascribe to them the same passions and thoughts as human persons, and so are led to try to influence their attitudes toward us. So it is not out of the experience of a "universal presence" or through observation and reflection that religion arises, but from our emotions, from "an anxious fear of future events" (65).[11] And its object is not some observed or known cause of events, but an imaginary object, an invisible cause of the events about which we fear and hope.

Given this account of the origin of religion, and so the rejection of the Deistic attempt to trace its origin to the perception of the order of nature, Hume proceeds to argue that it is both logical to expect, and confirmed by all our historical data, that polytheism was the first form of religion. It is not the unity and order of nature that lies at the foundation of religion, but rather the disorder or unpredictability of the events of human life, the things that happen to us individually and collectively and constitute our misery or good fortune. What the perplexing variation of connection between action and reward suggests is that there are multiple conflicting causes, not one consistent agent. So, concludes Hume, we are "necessarily led into polytheism" (27).

No more is the genesis of "theism" (monotheism[12]) out of this original polytheism a matter of men's observation and reflection. Rather, the exaggerated worship and praise to which religion inclines human beings leads to the magnifying of one divinity as higher and more glorious than all the others. From fear of his powerful displeasure and from fear of admitting to ourselves that he might not have control over future events, any suggestion of limitations of power and knowledge becomes

---

10. Hence James Collins considered Hume to be the first philosopher of religion in the modern sense of the term; see James Collins, *The Emergence of Philosophy of Religion* (New Haven, Conn.: Yale University Press, 1967).

11. Thus his account is what we would call psychological, like that of the Epicurean Velleius in the *De Natura Deorum*.

12. Hume never uses this term in NHR, nor does he use "polytheism" after Chapter 9.

unthinkable in praising him. And, as this process reinforces itself over time, it ends by elevating one supreme divinity over mere messengers and mediators, and thus finally arrives at the maximal theism of an infinitely perfect being, creator of the world.

Thus far, even a contemporary might have found these views, if rather untraditional, at least not subversive of the established religion.[13] Indeed, the first chapter of the *History* ("That Polytheism was the primary Religion of Man") explicitly suggests the development of religion from lower to higher, from polytheism to monotheism, by language such as the following:

[I]f we consider the improvement of human society, from rude beginnings to a state of greater perfection, polytheism or idolatry was, and necessarily must have been, the first and most ancient religion of mankind. (23)

[A]ccording to the natural progress of human thought, the ignorant multitude must first entertain some groveling and familiar notion of superior powers, before they stretch their conception to that perfect Being.... (24)

The mind rises gradually, from inferior to superior ... [in a] natural progress of thought.... (24)

But these presuppositions, on the basis of which we have been following the evolution of polytheism into theism, are suddenly not merely questioned but reversed by Chapter 8, which is the middle chapter of the book. The title of the chapter is "Flux and Reflux of Polytheism and Theism"; and Hume tells us there that "men have a natural tendency to rise from idolatry to theism, and to sink again from theism into idolatry" (46–47), and that "so great is the propensity, in this alternate revolution of human sentiments, to return back to idolatry, that the utmost precaution is not able effectually to prevent it" (48).[14] Hume seems to have indicated the singularity of this chapter by placing it in the center of the fifteen chapters.[15]

---

13. Hume is very sparing with the term "Christianity"—which can include the established religion—and its variants in NHR: it occurs only three times, if I am not mistaken, and never in a favorable reference (except ironically): 45, 53, and 68n1.

14. To give this thesis greater plausibility—which it needs—Hume takes great care with his language. The thesis gains plausibility if we understand it to be claiming that there is a tendency for theism to supplement its worship of one invisible God by visible or representable mediators (angels, saints, the Virgin Mary): what Hume terms "idolatry." Hence in later revisions of the text, he carefully changes "idolatry" to "polytheism" in the early chapters, conjoins the terms in the middle chapters, and does not use the term "polytheism" after Chapter 9, but only "idolatry" and other synonyms.

15. Why should Hume bother to do this, if he did? It has to be remembered that his readers were divided not only into religionists and "bystanders" (57) whom he wanted to understand him in different ways, but also into the vulgar and the few (a division largely but not completely coincident with the former). One way to reach his intended audience, if it consisted of careful, thoughtful readers, would be by employing the patterns of the work to

Two other claims, made in Chapters 4 and 12, also subvert the opening picture of an evolution from lower to higher forms of religion.[16] Chapter 4 (quite in contrast to its title, "Deities not considered as creators or formers of the world") asserts that the so-called gods of polytheism are rather more like the elves and fairies of our ancestors, that is, not truly deities at all. Indeed, Hume says, such pagans are closer to atheists than they are to genuine theists. It is, he says, "a fallacy, merely from the casual resemblance of names, without any conformity of meaning, to rank such opposite opinions under the same denomination" (33). Polytheism and theism are thus not two species of the same genus, related as lower and higher, but disparate. (This is obviously related to Hume's thesis that religion is not a disposition natural to man, because it has no precise determinate object.[17]) In addition, Chapter 4 introduces in connection with its depreciation of polytheism and the power of its divinities an alternative account of the origin of the universe, namely, by generation, an account that is developed at length in the *Dialogues Concerning Natural Religion* as the major alternative to the argument from design.[18]

Chapter 12 is the concluding chapter of four chapters that deal with the comparison between idolatry and theism. If it is read with care, it reveals clearly that the author's view is that modern religion is no less absurd than ancient religion. Still, the chapter concludes explicitly that the human consequences of idolatry are less corrupting, so that of the two, idolatry laid the lighter yoke upon life and mind. Far from popular the-

---

emphasize some parts over others, just as some ancient writers used, e.g., chiasmic pattern for increment of meaning. Knowledgeable readers may expect that if an author's views are at variance with established institutions and beliefs, and there are social consequences for contravening them, then he will not say so directly; he may indicate his real views by the structure, by qualification, by irony, by modifying subsequently what had been stated earlier.

16. There is another curious pattern in the footnotes of the final edition revised by Hume. Listed sequentially, the number of footnotes in successive chapters is: 0-1-2-25-4-1-3-0-11-5-0-25-6-5-0. It happens that Chapters 4 and 12 have more footnotes than all the other chapters of each half of the treatise put together—they each have 25. It also happens that each of them announces views both unusual and central to Hume's argument: Chapter 4 that polytheism is not a form of theism, and Chapter 12 that theism is not superior to polytheism or idolatry in its reasonableness.

17. It is thus puzzling that Keith Yandell maintains that in NHR Hume argues for a natural "propensity to minimal theism," since Hume denies that polytheism is a form of theism, minimal or otherwise. It is also puzzling that in an essay that takes the NHR as central to understanding Hume, he does not deal with polytheism, although the discussion of the latter outweighs that of theism in NHR. See K. Yandell, "Hume on Religion," in *Hume: A Reevaluation*, ed. D. W. Livingston and J. T. King (New York: Fordham University Press, 1976).

18. In fact, Hume suggests that it probably is the case that somewhere in this universe polytheism is true, that somewhere there has come into being "a species of intelligent creatures, of more refined substance and greater authority than the rest" (53, 36 n. 2), there being no contradiction in such a conception. There is merely no ground for supposing that this has happened on our planet.

ism being an advance upon and superior to mythological religion, idolatry scores higher on Hume's card.

So if the opening chapter suggests that there are two species of theism, that there is a progress from the one to the other, and that the later stage is higher, we can say that those opening impressions are subverted in sequence, in Chapters 4, 8, and 12. The final chapter draws the conclusion: if there is no significant distinction between ancient and modern religion (one is not higher nor lower, nor more or less absurd), then the prudent thing to do is to suspend judgment[19] on "the whole . . . subject." We can maintain the suspension only by "opposing one species of superstition to another [and] set them a quarreling; while we ourselves, during their fury and contention, happily make our escape into the calm, though obscure, regions of philosophy" (76). This counsel implies that we have nothing before us in this whole subject except comparable superstitions, and that "we" recognize that. To recognize that, of course, requires that the case against any superiority or uniqueness of Christianity has been understood. It requires that we become one of the few "bystanders" (57) to whom the work is primarily addressed.

THE JUSTIFICATION FOR NATURAL RELIGION

The *Natural History of Religion* is not a straightforward, unfeigned enquiry into the origins of religion, although a recent editor of the work describes it as "in the form of straight exposition" (11) in which we have no reason to doubt "Hume's philosophical sincerity and honesty" (16). In fairness, it is right to note that he explicitly disclaims any concern with "questions of biographical interest" such as "whether Hume retained genuine respect for 'the primary principles of genuine Theism and Religion' or whether he was merely willing, at times, to work within the conventions of his age." Rather, he says, "what we are left with [after setting aside biographical questions] is the argument itself" (9).

I do not want to deprecate the role of analysis in assessing an argument but rather to raise the question of whether we can always know what an author's argument is without attending to the issue of whether different audiences are being implicitly addressed. It is always possible to dissect an

---

19. The counsel to suspend judgment seems at variance with the opening paragraph of NHR which says no reflective enquirer can do so. (See James Noxon, "Hume's Concern with Religion," *Southwestern Journal of Philosophy* 7 [1976], 71, as against Yandell, "Hume on Religion," 113, who cites the opening statement without remarking on the closing one.) The inconsistency might be mitigated by taking the later counsel as referring to suspending judgment about popular religions, i.e., superstitions, and the former as referring to the design argument. This construal defers the question of Hume's inconsistency about suspending belief to the *Dialogues* where the issue reappears.

argument out of a text, and that may be useful and very important to do, but it is another question to ask how the author means it to be taken. No difference is more fundamental for the author of the *Natural History of Religion* than that between the vulgar and the few, and it is at least fair to reflect on whether an author intends to address both audiences in the same way, to the same purpose.[20]

Perhaps one of the reasons why this issue has often not been given sufficient attention is that an influential model of language does not make it salient. A contemporary British philosopher writes, "The task of the philosopher [of language] is to obtain some stable conception of this triangle of speaker, language, and world."[21] What is left out in this picture is a fourth element, namely, the addressee(s). In construing the meaning of an expression, it may be safe to ignore that element if there is only one (specific or generic) addressee, if in effect the words are meant to have the same meaning for all readers or hearers.

These brief remarks are a prologue to the examination of the *Dialogues Concerning Natural Religion*, which both contemporary readers[22] and Hume himself[23] rank among his most carefully written works. It is the more remarkable that it has received the most diverse interpretations and that there is no agreement about what Hume's position on the issues discussed was.

Let me briefly summarize the *Dialogues*. They consist of a conversation recounted by a schoolboy, Pamphilus, to a friend, in which three interlocutors discuss questions of God's nature and existence. The character of the interlocutors is characterized by Pamphilus as "the accurate philosophical turn of Cleanthes . . . the careless scepticism of Philo [and] . . . the rigid inflexible orthodoxy of Demea" (128). (Of course one has to take those descriptions as coming from a youth, and one who is in fact a student and protegé of Cleanthes.) Cleanthes is an "empirical theist" who defends the argument from design as the only foundation for a reasonable religiousness. Philo criticizes it, offers alternative hypotheses for the apparent order of the world, and shows that, in any case, no moral or

---

20. The differences between believer and atheist are of course discussed freely today, but the sort of language that Hume commonly uses to refer to differences between the vulgar or the many and the few is considered inappropriate or "elitist."

21. Simon Blackburn, *Spreading the Word* (Oxford: Oxford University Press, 1984), 3. Contrast Augustine's definition of "word": Verbum uniuscuiuque rei signum, quod ab audiente possit intelligi, a loquente prolatum (*De Dialectica* 5.7.6)..

22. E.g., Terence Penelhum, *Hume* (London: Macmillan, 1975), 171: " . . . beyond any question the greatest work on philosophy of religion in the English language."

23. He writes to Adam Smith in 1776, "On revising them [the *Dialogues*] . . . I find that nothing can be more cautiously and more artfully written" (*Letters*, 2.334). Smith appears to have had reservations about the artfulness, since he declined to assent to his friend's request to publish them after Hume died.

religious attributes of God can be inferred from the design argument. Demea, who thinks Philo is on his side, offers an a priori argument for God's existence (from contingency and necessity), and after a lethal critique by Cleanthes, admits that his religiousness is really founded on the experience of evil and suffering in the world. At the end of Part 11, he leaves, and in the last part, 12, Philo appears to change his attitude toward the design argument—he now seems to accept it—and hence to reach some kind of consensus with Cleanthes. The work ends with Pamphilus commenting to his friend that he (Pamphilus) thought the position of Cleanthes was nearest to the truth.

The question "Who [among the interlocutors of the dialogue] speaks for Hume?" has preoccupied at least a third of the large number of essays on the *Dialogues* in the last fifteen or twenty years.[24] Of the four characters—Pamphilus, the schoolboy narrator of the discussion; Demea, the pious and orthodox; Cleanthes, the empirical philosopher; and Philo, the skeptical challenger—only Demea has never been identified as Hume's spokesman by anyone.[25]

It is tempting to propose that one of the reasons for the disagreements about what Hume intended is that some have read the *Dialogues* as Demea might, literally and unsuspiciously; some like Cleanthes, focusing concentratedly on the analysis of the design argument; and some like Philo, conscious always of the differences between the interlocutors.[26] Perhaps one could suggest that the best way to read the work would be successively as Demea-, Cleanthes-, and Philo-like, passing to the subsequent hermeneutic only when the motive is appropriate.

However that may be, to refer to different levels of understanding is not merely or primarily to refer to the ironical remarks of Hume in his other writings on religion and of Philo here—an irony commonly noted by some and denied by others—but rather to the difference of levels in-

---

24. It was E. C. Mossner who launched this question; see Note 2 above. I am grateful to my research assistant Barbara Sain for reviewing some 120 articles from this period on the subject of Hume's writings on religion. It is interesting that there has been an increase in attention to the dramatic and rhetorical aspects of the *Dialogues* in the secondary literature. See, e.g., Michael Morrisoe, "Rhetorical Method in Hume's Works on Religion," *Philosophy and Rhetoric* 2 (1969): 121–38, and "Hume's Rhetorical Strategy," *Texas Studies in Literature and Language* 11 (1970): 963–74; A. G. Vink, "The Literary and Dramatic Character of Hume's *Dialogues Concerning Natural Religion*," *Religious Studies* 22 (1986): 387–96.

25. See the surveys in DNR 58–59; John Bricke, "On the Interpretation of Hume's *Dialogues*," *Religious Studies* 11 (1975): 2–3; and J. Noxon, "Hume's Agnosticism," *Philosophical Review* 73 (1964): 250ff.

26. In keeping with their personae, Cleanthes becomes aware (199) sometime before Demea does (213) that Philo has been playing a double role. But then Cleanthes has been alert from the beginning to the possibility of purposeful ambiguity in Philo's pious affirmations (132).

stituted by the form of the work; for example, in a dialogue, to whom is what is said addressed? Some remarks have their irony, their double meaning, built in, on their face, so to speak: it does not depend on character or context.[27] If we take into account the form of a work—for example, the dramatic structure of a dialogue—then different meanings of what is said may derive not only from what is said but to whom and when and in what circumstances it is said. It certainly cannot be assumed in a dialogue that what a speaker says can be taken as what the author thinks. But this is often overlooked. Consider the following hermeneutical principle: "[O]ne must assume that, no matter who the speaker, those arguments which seem most cogent, are probably to be ascribed to Hume."[28]

So before the question "Who speaks for Hume?" we have to place a prior issue: What Philo says to Demea and what he says to Cleanthes and what he says to Pamphilus may have to be evaluated differently. If Philo is always taken as speaking candidly and uniformly, then we arrive at the contradictions or inconsistencies that so many commentators have found in the *Dialogues*. Moreover, in a dialogue with more than two interlocutors, one may also have to consider how the different speeches might be taken by the listener(s). For example, it is perfectly clear that the speeches of Philo through Part 11 are not only a running criticism of Cleanthes and the design argument but that they are intended to sound orthodox to Demea. Philo makes an explicit point several times of allying himself with Demea, not only in the critical responses to Cleanthes but in the vivid descriptions of the evil that men suffer in this world. (The only

---

27. Consider the following, from NHR: "Were there a religion (and we may suspect Mahometanism of this inconsistence) which sometime painted the Deity in the most sublime colours, as the creator of heaven and earth; sometimes degraded him nearly to the level with human creatures in his powers and faculties; while at the same time it ascribed to him suitable infirmities, passions, and partialities, of the moral kind: That religion, after it was extinct, would also be cited as an instance of those contradictions, which arise from the gross, vulgar, natural conceptions of mankind, opposed to their continual propensity towards flattery and exaggeration. Nothing indeed would prove more strongly the divine origin of any religion, than to find (and happily this is the case with Christianity) that it is free from a contradiction, so incident to human nature"(45). Or from DNR: "What truth so obvious, so certain, as the being of a God, which the most ignorant ages have acknowledged ..." (128).

28. J. Bricke, "On the Interpretation of Hume's Dialogues," 17. W. Salmon, "A New Look at Hume's *Dialogues*," *Philosophical Studies* 33 (1978), thinks that the *Dialogues* are presented by Hume as a discussion of the nature, rather than the existence of, God. It is true that Pamphilus thus describes the issue (128) and Demea also at times (141, 142), but it is also clear—and asserted (e.g., 143, 146)—that the issue is whether or not a deity exists. This is one of the many points in which Hume's strategy is illuminated by comparing it with that of Cicero in the *De Natura Deorum*, a work that had far more influence on the *Dialogues* than did Newton, Clarke, or Butler. On the parallels between the two works, see J. V. Price, "Empirical Theists in Cicero and Hume," *Texas Studies in Language and Literature* 5 (1963): 255–64, and "Sceptics in Cicero and Hume," *Journal of History of Ideas* 25 (1964): 97–106.

brief exception is at the end of Part 9, when Philo allows himself to endorse the criticisms that Cleanthes has made of Demea's metaphysical argument. But this is followed immediately by their duet of lamentation on the evils in the world, introduced by Demea's admission that his belief is not based on the refuted arguments but on the human situation.)

The fact that the dialogue of Cicero *On the Nature of the Gods* served as Hume's model in more ways than one—not only in form but in content—means that it may be worthwhile to look at some ways in which he departs from his model. One way in which he changes the dramatic structure is by having one of the interlocutors, Demea, leave before the end of the dialogue. The most discussed question among recent commentators has been why there appears to be a change, indeed to some a reversal,[29] in the position of Philo at the end of the dialogue (Part 12). He now seems to accept the design argument which has heretofore been the object of his unrelenting critique. It would appear likely that these two changes are connected. How?

In the first eleven parts, as noted earlier, Philo seeks to ally himself with Demea by implying that his criticisms of Cleanthes's design argument are meant to support a pious orthodoxy. (Compare the way in which Socrates often seems to ally himself with his interlocutors, e.g., Euthyphro.) This is why Cleanthes is brought forward as critic of Demea's metaphysical argument rather than leaving that role to Philo.[30] But after Philo and Demea join in magnifying the evil in the world in the first half of Part 10, Philo goes on to suggest the argument from evil and the difficulty that this causes for an empirical theist[31] like Cleanthes. Cleanthes responds (11) by proposing the "new hypothesis" of a finite God to account for evil, and Philo shows that this would still leave us with the same difficulty of inferring the existence of a benevolent and providential God—even finite—from the reality of the evil around us. As he warms to his argument he even draws the conclusion that the more powerful God is taken to be, the more must we think him responsible for the evil. At this point (the end of Part 11) Demea, who has been silent since the first

---

29. See, e.g., Terence Penelhum, "Natural Beliefs and Religious Beliefs in Hume's Philosophy," *Philosophical Quarterly* 33 (1983): 166–81; and J. Noxon, "Hume's Agnosticism," 251. Contrast Stewart Sutherland, "Penelhum on Hume," *Philosophical Quarterly* 33 (1983): 182–86, who argues that it is Cleanthes who changes in Part 12.

30. In Hume's original version, Philo only adds to Cleanthes's critique a very mild "observation" about the psychology of those who are attracted by metaphysical arguments through confusing them with the a priori method of mathematics. Only in one of his last revisions did he broaden this.

31. I.e., one who aspires to demonstrate that the cause of the order of nature coincides with the God of religion—which requires, as Philo emphasizes, the inferring of particular providence and moral intent from the empirical data.

section of 10, at last comes to see that Philo has not been his ally all along, and he shortly finds "some pretence" to depart.

And now a change does take place, but it is not a material change in Philo's position. He has never denied the appearance of order in the world, only that a designer was the best or even a very probable explanation of it. His own preference, if he had to defend a position, would be to argue for an internal principle of order like that of organisms (174), which, he agrees with Aristotle as against Thomas Aquinas, does not presuppose mind or design (179, 146). But now that Demea is gone, he can behave toward Cleanthes just the way he has behaved toward Demea: by stating his position in such a way as to maximize the area of agreement, to suggest his alliance with Cleanthes.

He readily concedes that not only is it logically possible to pose the hypothesis of a designer (he has all along conceded that much, arguing only that the confirmation for it was very weak and that such a designer is not the God of popular religion), but that the semblance of finality engages a strong propensity in us. "A purpose, an intention, or design strikes everywhere the most careless, the most stupid thinker" (214).[32] If there is a cause of order, analogous to that of organisms or of thought, isn't it merely balking at words to refuse to call it "mind" or "intelligence" or even "God"? But—and now he steps back from the debate—isn't the whole question a matter of words anyway, a verbal dispute? The theist will agree that the analogy with human design is very remote and hypothetical, the atheist will agree that there is some "remote inconceivable" analogy between whatever explains the order of nature and whatever explains "the rotting of a turnip, the generation of an animal, and the structure of human thought" (218).

Where then, cry I [Philo] to both these antagonists, is the subject of your dispute? The theist allows, that the original intelligence is very different from human reason: The atheist allows, that the original principle of order bears some remote analogy to it. Will you quarrel, Gentlemen, about [that] . . . which admits not of any precise meaning, nor consequently of any determination?

When I read this passage, I cannot understand those commentators who say that Hume is defending a "minimal theism" at the end of the *Dialogues*. The conclusion is that no rigorous resolution is possible in estimating *how* similar the world is to a machine, or *how* similar its hypothetical designer would be to human designers. What leads to the difference between the two antagonists is not the empirical evidence or the logic of the argument, but the inclinations that carry each one beyond the evidence.

---

32. See Note 27 above. That the propensity is not natural, however, appears from the opposition between "natural inclination" and "religious motives" (221).

What I want to argue, then, is that the only change in Part 12 is rhetorical, that Philo is behaving toward Cleanthes just the way he had behaved toward Demea in the first speeches of Part 1. Just as he had allied himself with Demea to attack Cleanthes's rational religiousness, so now he allies himself with Cleanthes to attack Demea's vulgar religiousness. His "reversal" is less substantive than it has appeared to some commentators, because it is not the admission of any data or inference that he had not admitted before, but only in the way in which he describes the argument. Not only does this seem evident in the language just cited (and even more in the summary conclusion at the end of the dialogue), but there are other signs of the shift. One is the change in vocabulary that appears in 12. Philo now denounces, in a duet with Cleanthes, the "bigots" and the "vulgar superstitions" that Cleanthes calls "false religion" (224). In fact Philo uses the pejorative term "superstition" 10 times in Part 12, but he has not used it even once before.[33] "True religion" appears for the first time as opposed to "bigoted credulity" or "popular religion" or "vulgar superstitions." Clearly, Philo feels able to use now a vocabulary that he can share with Cleanthes but could not share with Demea, just as previously the two of them have spoken of the "theistic hypothesis" or of the "hypothesis of design," while Demea spoke only of "perfect evidence" (145) and "infallible demonstration" (188).[34]

Moreover, Philo reiterates his earlier insistence that for a philosophical theist like Cleanthes, there is no way of inferring a providential and just and good God on the basis of the human situation. Even if there is order in nature, there is none in human life and history that bears witness to a just God, as Job long ago complained. Cleanthes makes no reply except to say that religion still offers the most agreeable picture that "human imagination" can suggest (224).

True, in his last words in the *Dialogues* Philo returns to recommending philosophical skepticism as the most essential step toward being a "sound, believing Christian."[35] He explicitly notes that he is addressing this remark to Pamphilus—which tells us something about his perception of the latter. But this position, which he has maintained from his opening remarks in Part 1, is perfectly consistent with the claim that philosophical theism does not arrive at the Christian God.

So what is Philo's position in the end? Well, that neither theism nor

---

33. 219, 220, 222, 226.
34. Thus, "hypothesis of experimental theism" (165), "of design" (169), of the "soul of the world" (170), of the "Epicurean hypothesis"(182), and of course of the "religious hypothesis" (138, 216). See also 172, 174, 180, 183, and 200.
35. This is only the second time he has used the word "Christian" and the only one that could be taken as commendatory (160, 228).

atheism is proved or refuted by the admission of there being some principle that accounts for the order of nature; one can live with either in peace[36] so long as it is conceded that the inclination to assent to the proposition that God exists is motivated not by the evidence, but by temperament and early training: "If this proposition be not capable of extension, variation or more particular explication: If it afford no inference that affects human life, or can be the source of any action or forbearance. ...[W]hat can the most inquisitive, contemplative, *and religious* man do more than give a plain, philosophical assent to the proposition"(227; emphasis mine).

Does Philo speak for Hume? I agree with Norman Kemp Smith and E. C. Mossner that he does,[37] *provided* that we weigh his remarks not by looking for a merely logical consistency but by considering when and to whom he says what he does. Apart from the reading suggested here, there is a curious bit of evidence in another departure of Hume from his Ciceronian and classical dialogue models.

After the passage quoted earlier in which Philo distinguishes himself from *both* the atheist and the theist ("Where then, cry I to both these antagonists . . ."), Hume added a note to the text that endorses the judgment that both dogmatist and skeptic go beyond the evidence available to them, and insists that the difference between them is merely verbal.[38] The note says, in effect: "What Philo is claiming here is correct." All the same it is a curious interjection.

Hume's own view can then be summarized on the basis of this reading as follows. Theism is a possible hypothesis to explain the apparent order of nature, just as is that of atheism—coupled, say, with the hypothesis of an internal principle of order—but there is no possibility of *proving* either hypothesis. That is why, in his letters and published essays, he declined to believe that there really were atheists (who *know* there is no

---

36. When Hume is speaking in his own voice (NHR 42) he quotes Francis Bacon's well-known remark as "A little philosophy makes men atheists: A great deal reconciles them to religion." But his Cleanthes quotes the same passage as "a little philosophy makes a man an atheist: A great deal converts him to religion" (DNR 139). In Bacon's original essay, "Of Atheism," the text runs: "It is true, that a little philosophy inclineth man's mind to atheism; but depth in philosophy bringeth men's minds about to religion"; see *The Works of Francis Bacon* (London: Longmans, 1861), 6.413.

37. Many, perhaps most commentators deny this, e.g., John Bricke, "On the Interpretation of Hume's *Dialogues*."

38. 219. J. V. Price in his edition of the *Dialogues* puts this note in the text on the ground that "Hume, in preparing a final draft of the work, was conscious of the incongruity of a discursive note in a dialogue"; *Dialogues Concerning Natural Religion*, 251. Stanley Tweyman has noted (*Scepticism and Belief in Hume's Dialogues Concerning Natural Religion* (Nijhoff: Dordrecht, 1986) that Part 12 of the *Enquiry Concerning Human Understanding* prescribes the antidote to dogmatism that is administered to Cleanthes.

God), except self-styled ones.[39] This position can be described as a strong, that is, impregnable agnosticism, because given the absolutely singular nature of the case—creating and/or ordering a world—we have no possible basis for compelling demonstration. All demonstration involving cause and effect rests for its cogency on experience, reason in this mode being "nothing but a species of experience" (150) and we do not have sufficient experience of other worlds to draw reliable conclusions.

Moreover, as we have seen, even if we allowed the possibility of the theistic hypothesis being true, no consequences would follow for popular religion, which must assume a particular providence and a just and good God to justify its practice (prayer, sacrifice, etc.). The data for such an inference are simply not consistent. If we *assumed* the existence of such a God, it is *possible* that such an assumption could be made consistent—especially if we abandoned infinity and omnipotence—with our conflicting experience of suffering and injustice (205). But then we are in the region of sheer conjecture, unsupported by prior evidence.

Religion is unnatural then in two ways. First, it is not a natural inclination, as is shown by the fact that it is not universal and has no specific object. Second, it is unnatural in the sense that it has no foundation in reason, contrary to the Deists of the Enlightenment. There is a philosophical kind of religiousness, namely, the mere assent to the proposition that God exists, but it is not motivated by any compelling evidence, it entails no consequences for human life, and it teaches no way of life other than that of ordinary, unreligious morality. Moreover, popular or vulgar religion in fact has historically had nothing but bad consequences for human beings.[40] So neither in its causes nor in its reasons nor in its consequences are there rational grounds for religiousness.

So with Hume, the confidence in proving the existence of the God of Christianity, which seemed to be introduced by Descartes and for which the progress of science had come to be the primary foundation, came to an end. Kant agreed, and instead sought to reinterpret rational morality as requiring the presupposition of God's existence. The philosophy of religion took a new turn, or rather recast an old one. The philosophy of religion directed itself to the genealogy of religiousness, to trying to understand why human beings have this propensity toward piety and worship.

---

39. Cf. the often-cited incident related by Diderot to Samuel Romilly in which Hume is said to have told Baron d'Holbach that he had never met an atheist (DNR, 39–40). He certainly knew himself of men who styled themselves atheists. Cf. NHR 36n. On the sense of "atheism" in Hume's time, see David Berman, "David Hume and the Suppression of Atheism," *Journal of the History of Philosophy* 21 (1983): 375–87.

40. This is an argument that Hume places toward the end of both the *History* (Chapter 14) and the *Dialogues* (Part 12).

Cicero had long ago, in the opening sentence of the *De Nature Deorum*, suggested that if we cannot learn about the existence and nature of the divine from such an inquiry, we shall at least learn something about man.[41] Through Feuerbach and Marx and Nietzsche and the rise of anthropology and psychoanalysis the quest to understand religion as a curious human creation grew.

RELIGION AND FAITH

I want to end by remarking briefly on some differences between the conception of religion and of faith that Hume takes as his target and the conception of religiousness and faith in another tradition, that of Thomas Aquinas.

Why did Hume seek to understand the nature of religiousness by writing a history? A century before he wrote, the emergence of the "state of nature" theories of Hobbes and Locke had opened up the question of whether things that had previously been assumed to be natural to man— for example, being a political animal—were not rather the result of developments in history (or prehistory as we would say). That question expanded as more human properties—for example, language and moral obligations[42]—came to seem susceptible of historical rather than natural explanation. Justice, Hume argued, is "artificial," which does not mean that it is arbitrary—it is extremely useful if not necessary to human society—but that it is not a natural, innate obligation. History came more and more to seem capable of giving an account of what had been called human nature. Hume was consistent in seeing that if this were the case with respect to religion, then the development from polytheism to theism could just as well reverse itself.

Thomas Aquinas, following the classical tradition, denied that there is any dichotomy between the things that human beings bring into existence and those that are natural. What is natural to us is not merely our genetic endowment, but the human goods to which we are innately inclined, even though we may have to experiment and invent in order to discover the proper way to realize those goods. So he can agree with Hume that religion is a phenomenon human in origin, and not founded

---

41. "There is no question of importance whose decision is not compriz'd in the science of man; and there is none, which can be decided with any certainty, before we become acquainted with that science"; Hume, *A Treatise of Human Nature*, ed. L. A. Selby-Bigge, 2d ed., ed. P. H. Nidditch (Oxford: Oxford University Press, 1981), xvi. See E. C. Mossner, "The Religion of David Hume," *Journal of the History of Ideas* 39 (1978): 653–63.

42. So, e.g., Hume argues that there is no natural obligation to obey promises, but that the utility of posing such an obligation has come to be seen; *Treatise of Human Nature*, 2.5 to end.

on any philosophical arguments for the existence of divinity. But he can also locate religion in a yet unshaped innate inclination of human beings to realize their need for help in achieving their good[43] without their being clear about what that good truly is or how to seek the help. Religion is as natural as that aspiration and that realization are, and it unfolds as the attempt, profoundly shaped by the society we grow up in, to say and do what is needful in order to stand in the right relation to that superior nature "which men call divine."[44]

Undeveloped man may indeed seek his good in the gifts of fortune, and implore the aid of imaginary powers, just as justice may first come into view as helping one's friends and harming one's enemies. But thoughtful reason, over time, exercises some measure of pruning and clarifying the good we seek. Homer's Achilles learns that death is not the greatest of all evils or life the greatest of all goods, and Homer's Odysseus that death at home is preferable to immortal pleasures in exile. So religion can be a natural virtue without having to emerge automatically, provided we delineate it from the normative state toward which it inclines. Then we shall say that far from being characterized by a concern with the good and bad fortune of future events, true religiousness teaches us not to worry about the morrow.

As for the Enlightenment notion of a higher form of "true religion" or "true theism," Hume surely thought that superior to ritualistic religion of any kind. "To know God," says Philo to Cleanthes (quoting Seneca), "is to worship Him: it is to think rightly and reverently of Him." That view may commend itself to one for whom nothing is present to the mind but its impressions, but if man is an embodied spirit, his reverence must be more than mental, and religiousness must incarnate the devotion of the soul in corporeal expression. Only so long can it exist in the soul itself.[45] Religiousness for Aquinas is not thinking rightly about God, it is placing the good that God wills for us first in our lives, and part of that good we seek is doing things that acknowledge his holiness, his being above us, as the child honors her father and mother by kissing them goodnight on the way to bed. The action does not so much express the inward disposition as bring it to life, sustain it in existence. Everything is made more perfect by subjection to its superior, Aquinas wrote:[46] body to soul, child to parent, disciple to teacher, man to God. If man is the greatest thing in the universe, then religiousness, which entails the acknowledgment of

---

43. *Summa theologiae* 2.2.85.1.
44. Cf. Cicero's definition of *religio*, repeated by Aquinas in *Summa theologiae* 2.2.80.1.
45. Hume in fact has some perceptive things to say about the religious function of ceremonies; see DNR, p. 13.
46. *Summa theologiae* 2.2.81.7.

superiority, cannot be a virtue: that seems to have been the view of Hume and many of his successors. For then indeed *pietas* would have no other object than our parents and the community that has endowed us with what humanity we have.

Cleanthes says that "Locke seems to have been the first Christian, who ventured openly to assert, that faith was nothing but a species of reason, that religion was only a branch of philosophy" (DNR 138). Faith in this view is simply the belief that God exists. Many find it natural so to think today. If someone says, "Do you believe in God?," we commonly take that to mean "Do you think that God exists?" Faith is often taken—as Hume's term "the religious hypothesis" suggests—as tantamount to the belief that God exists.

But for Aquinas, faith is not fundamentally belief *that* some proposition p is true. Faith is, in his conception, a "theological virtue," it has God as its object, it reaches God: it is believing God. *Credere est credere aliud.* Faith, we could say, is believing G that p. It is not primarily a "propositional attitude," it is not believing that p, or believing other human beings; it is believing God when he speaks to us in the words of men, as Saint Augustine discovered in the Garden.

Making sense of that understanding of faith requires understanding it in the context of time and being and creation, to which Augustine devoted the last three books of the *Confessions*.[47] But that is too far afield for now.

---

47. See F. J. Crosson, "Structure and Meaning in St. Augustine's Confessions," *Proceedings of the American Catholic Philosophical Association*, vol. 63 (Washington, D.C.: American Catholic Philosophical Association, 1989), 84–97.

9 Poetry and Praxis in Rousseau's *Emile:* Human Rights and the Sentiment of Humanity[1]

TERENCE E. MARSHALL

The first histories, the first speeches, the first laws were in verse; poetry was discovered before prose; that had to be so, since the passions spoke before reason.... Concerning the manner by which the first societies were bound together, was it astonishing that one placed the first histories in verse and that one sang the first laws?... A language which has only articulations and sound possesses accordingly only half of its wealth; it conveys ideas, it is true, but to convey sentiments, images, it needs moreover a rhythm and resonances, that is to say a melody. —*Essay on the Origin of Languages*, Chapter 12

While several phases span the Enlightenment, all seem to culminate in Kant's Copernican Revolution in philosophy, and all seem unified under Kant's synoptic apophthegm, "sapere aude."[2] Yet as Kant acknowledged, and as has since been carefully shown, the critical philosophy originating from Königsburg is particularly formed by the thought of the Enlightenment's first great modern opponent, Jean-Jacques Rousseau.[3] Kant's synoptic statement, intended to cover the Enlightenment's differing phases,

---

1. Page citations of the *Emile* refer to the Edition Garnier Frères (Paris, 1964). Unless otherwise indicated, all other citations of Rousseau are from *Oeuvres complètes*, abbreviated *O.C.* (Paris: Bibliothèque de la Pléiade, 1959–1995). An earlier version of this article was published in French as "Poésie et praxis dans l'*Emile* de J.-J. Rousseau: Les droits de l'homme et le sentiment de l'humanité," *Revue des sciences philosophiques et théologiques* 76, no. 4 (1992). I am indebted to the Earhart Foundation for graciously providing assistance for the preparation of this study.
2. Immanuel Kant, "Beantwortung der Frage: Was Ist Aufklarung?," in *Kants Gesammelte Schriften*, ed Preussischen Akademie der Wissenschaften (Berlin: Walter De Gruyter, 1902–1983), 8.35.
3. Immanuel Kant, "Fragmente aus Kants Nachlass," in *Immanuel Kants sammtliche Werke*, 8 vols., ed. G. Hartenstein (Leipzig: Leopold Voss, 1867–1868), 8.618, 624, and 630. Cf. Ernst Cassirer, *Kant's Life and Thought* (New Haven, Conn.: Yale University Press, 1981), 87–90; and esp. Richard L. Velkley, *Freedom and the End of Reason: On the Moral Foundation of Kant's Critical Philosophy* (Chicago: University of Chicago Press, 1989).

may thereby obscure a problem whose scope its earlier moments do not comprehend and which Kant's critical philosophy does not fathom.

Following Rousseau's own indications, Kant found the most profound and comprehensive expression of his predecessor's thought not in the *Social Contract*, nor in the *Discourses*, but in the *Emile*. It has been well noted that, for the founder of German idealism, the *Emile* held an importance in the history of philosophy tantamount to that of the French Revolution in the history of politics.[4] Ordinarily this judgment is deemed applicable less to philosophy *stricto sensu* than to its practical dimension. But to the extent that Kant followed Bacon and Descartes in considering theory as subservient to practice, one may more precisely appreciate therein his idea of Rousseau, on the basis of the *Emile*, as "the Newton of the moral universe."[5]

Notwithstanding its decisive imprint on German philosophy, however, the *Emile* is rarely read integrally in a philosophical spirit, and is more recognized for its literary qualities than for its meticulous reasoning. Indeed, in that section of the book reputed to be most fundamental, "The Profession of Faith," Rousseau himself stipulates that his argument there is not, strictly speaking, philosophical.[6] And with respect to its practical significance, the Citizen of Geneva criticizes the folly of those who, misperceiving it as a pedagogical manual, would seek to apply it in deed.[7]

But by affirming that the *Emile* is strictly neither philosophical nor practical, the author of the book evokes a mystery concerning the grounds of the philosophical and practical traditions it inaugurates. Certainly, with respect to theoretical significance, it is clear that Rousseau in this work seeks to perform the educational experiment suggested by Descartes for overcoming prejudice and discovering the natural vision of the world.[8] Moreover, with respect to practical import, Rousseau specifies that, while the pedagogy presented in the *Emile* is not intended for implementation, one will nonetheless find in this work the grounds of

4. Allan Bloom, "The Education of Democratic Man: Emile," *Daedalus* 107, no. 3 (1978): 135–36. See also Edna Kryger, *La notion de liberté chez Rousseau et ses répercussions sur Kant* (Paris: Nizet, 1979); Jean Ferrari, *Les sources francaises de la philosophie de Kant* (Paris: Klincksieck, 1979); and Cassirer, *Kant's Life and Thought*, 86–87.

5. Immanuel Kant, "Fragmente aus Kants Nachlass," 630; cf. 624. See Rousseau, *Emile* (Paris: Editions Garnier Frères, 1964), 214.

6. *Emile*, 320, 323–24, 347, 353–55, and 359–60, in comparison with 109, 209, 302, and 333.

7. *Lettres ecrites de la Montagne* 5, in *O.C.* 3.783; *Lettre à Philbert Cramer*, October 13, 1764, in *Correspondance générale de J.-J. Rousseau*, 20 vols., ed. Théophile Dufour (Paris: Armand Colin, 1929), 11.339. Cf. *Emile*, 430.

8. Descartes, *Discours de la méthode* 2, in *Oeuvres et lettres* (Paris: Bibliothèque de la Pléïade, 1953), 133–34.

the political principles formulated in the *Social Contract*.[9] And his book subtitled "Principles of Political Right," far from outlining a utopia, is destined to form the practical judgment not only of jurists but of a new prince, perhaps the founder of a new republican order which will follow the European revolutions that the *Emile* foresees in the century to come.[10] In this sense, Rousseau leads his reader to believe that what he calls his "principal work" conceals both philosophic and practical aspirations. Thus, to uncover them might disclose, if not the natural vision of the world, then at least that vision, anterior to critical philosophy, that elucidates both the problem of Enlightenment and the ideas of rights that critical philosophy has since inspired.

In his own explanations, Rousseau furthermore emphasizes that his book on education is intended to vindicate Providence against what, because of Rousseau, would soon be called the nihilism of the Enlightenment.[11] But in that case, could faith in Providence, and not philosophy, be the ground of Rousseau's teaching? Conforming to its practical aim, the *Emile* begins not aporetically but assertorically: "Tout est bien sortant des mains de l'Auteur des choses; tout dégénère entre les mains de l'homme." "The Author of things," it seems, must be the Supreme Being, and as author he brings to mind the biblical God. But approximately at the work's literal center, Rousseau's creation the Savoyard Vicar questions the biblical doctrine of creation, and thus indicates that "the Author of things" is no more the God of the Bible than he is the *demiurgos* of Plato's *Timaeus*.[12] The book's central passages thereby reveal more clearly than does the assertoric beginning that the beginning is an enigma. If

---

9. *Lettre à Duchesne*, May 23, 1762, in *Correspondance générale de J.-J. Rousseau*, 7.233; *Lettres ecrites de la Montagne* 6, in O.C. 3.806; *Dialogues Rousseau juge de Jean-Jacques*, in O.C. 1.932–33; *Confessions* 9, in O.C. 1.407. Cf. *Emile*, 584ff.

10. *Emile*, 224, in comparison with *Fragments politiques*, in O.C. 3.474. See also *Lettres ecrites de la Montagne* 6, in O.C. 3.810; and *Confessions* 11, in O.C. 1.565. Cf. "Dédicace de Maximilien Robespierre aux manes de Jean-Jacques Rousseau," in Hippolyte Buffenoire, *Le prestige de Jean-Jacques Rousseau* (Paris: Emile-Paul, 1909), 433–34; Roger Barny, *Prélude idéologique à la Révolution Française: Le rousseauisme avant 1789* (Paris: Les Belles Lettres, 1985); and Mona Ozouf, *L'homme régénéré: Essais sur la révolution française* (Paris: Gallimard, 1989), 116–57.

11. *Dialogues Rousseau juge de Jean-Jacques*, in O.C. 1.818, 934–35, 943, 967–69, and 971; *Les rêveries du promeneur solitaire* 3, in O.C. 1.1015–19. Cf. *Emile*, 5, 9–11, 12, 23–25, 321–23, 356–57, and 386–89; also note 14 below. Used in a philosophical sense, the term "nihilism" appears to originate toward the end of the eighteenth century with Jacobi's critique, influenced by Rousseau, of modern rationalism. See F. H. Jacobi, *Sendschreiben an Fichte* (1799), in *Werke*, ed. G. Fleisher (Leipzig: 1812–1825), 3.44. Cf. Martin Heidegger, *Nietzsche* (Pfullingen: Verlag Günter Neske, 1961), 2.1.1; Stanley Rosen, *Nihilism* (New Haven, Conn.: Yale University Press, 1969), 78; and Leo Strauss, *Das Erkenntnisproblem in der Philosophischen Lehre Fr. H. Jacobi* (Ph.D. diss., Hamburg, 1921).

12. *Emile*, 335 and 346–47 Cf. 356–57, 385, and 388, in relation to 65, 99, and 106–9.

not the God of Abraham and Jesus, "*Quid sit Deus?*" If the world was not created *ex nihilo*, what is meant by the "Author of things"?

Obscuring these first questions, the beginning immediately orients the reader toward aporiae of a different sort. If man is by nature good, and if his natural goodness is due to divine artifice, what causes the evil emerging through man's artifice? Further, if seeking to remain natural in the midst of man's artifices means "tout irait plus mal encore," how, then, might nature's providential goodness continue to inform the artificial state that must henceforth be both created and sustained?

In a passage of the *Social Contract*, recalling the Greek idea that heroes are "divine," Rousseau describes as a god the lawgiver who creates the conventional whole that is the political community.[13] By contrast, the *Emile*'s beginning refers to the natural whole (*le tout*) and affirms that it is the latter that is good. The *Emile*'s author thus immediately reminds the reader of the dispute over optimism and pessimism conjured by Leibniz's *Theodicy* and Voltaire's *Candide*.[14] He thereby increasingly induces attentive readers to wonder: If, contrary to the Enlightenment's teaching, the whole is good, what is the good informing the whole if it also differs from the good both of the Hebrew prophets and of Greek philosophy?

The mystery that Rousseau evokes, concerning the ground of his thought on rights, recalls his argument that the propagation of philosophy ineluctably erodes the spirit required to sustain customs or morals, which are "the real constitution of the state."[15] If Rousseau seeks to forge a republican spirit to resist such erosion and constitute "the unshakable keystone" for the rights of humanity, it would thereby be consistent with his critique of Enlightenment to obscure the philosophical foundation of his teaching:

---

13. *Du contrat social*, 2.7. Cf. *Emile*, 23–24.

14. The *Emile* is part of a series of exchanges with Voltaire over this question, which in their case refers to the Enlightenment's project to master nature according to man's will, as opposed to the traditional view subordinating human will or desire to natural or to divine limits. After the publication in 1755 of the *Discours sur l'origine de l'inégalité*, wherein the Citizen of Geneva defends the principle of natural goodness, Voltaire had sent to Rousseau his *Poème sur le Désastre de Lisbonne, ou examen de cet axiome: "tout est bien."* Rousseau responded with his *Letter on Providence* (August 18, 1756), to which Voltaire in turn promised a reply. In 1761 Voltaire published *Candide*, ridiculing the optimist thesis. The following year Rousseau answered with the *Emile*. See the author's translation of the *Letter on Providence* in *The Collected Writings of Rousseau*, ed. Roger Masters and Christopher Kelly (Hanover, N.H.: University Press of New England, 1992), 3.192, 196–97, and notes 1, 3, 43, and 44. Cf. Leibniz, *Essais de Théodicée*, 1.7–9; and Alexander Pope, *An Essay on Man*, 1.294. See also Plato, *Timaeus* 30b 5ff.; *Laws* 899d ff., 903b 9–10; Proclus, *Ten Problems Concerning Providence*; and note 27 below.

15. *Du contrat social*, 2.12, in relation to the thesis of the *Discours sur les sciences et les arts*, in *O.C.* 3.10, 16. Cf. the *Préface à Narcisse* and the *Lettre à d'Alembert sur les spectacles*, which amplify the argument of the first *Discours*.

"Always reasoning is the mania of small minds. Strong souls have another language; it is by this language that one persuades and causes to act.... Clothe reason with a body if you wish to make it felt. Make the language of the mind pass by the heart, in order that it may be heard."[16]

Should it be true, as Rousseau helped persuade Kant, that theory is subordinate to the ends of practice, then for Rousseau it would follow that publishing his theory of practice must be done in a manner attuned to achieving these ends. "The knowledge of what can be agreeable or disagreeable to men is necessary not only to someone who needs them but also to the one who wishes to be useful to them; it is even important to please them in order to serve them; and the art of writing is anything but an idle study when one employs it to make the truth heard."[17] If, however, contrary to the Enlightenment and Kant, Rousseau further thought that a contradiction exists between the ends specific to theory and to action, then it would be morally necessary for Rousseau's acts of publication to dissimulate his theoretical vision, just as such a necessity applies to the Vicar in relation to his congregation, to Sophie in relation even to her lover, and finally to the mentor in relation to Emile.

Take an opposite route with your pupil; let him always believe he is the master, and let it always be you who is it. There is no subjugation so perfect as the one which retains the appearance of liberty; one thus captures the will itself.... No doubt he should only do what he wills; but he should only will what you will that he should do; he should not take a step that you have not foreseen; he should not open his mouth without your knowing what he is going to say.[18]

Emile's transparence and his teacher's ruses only reflect the inevitable difference Rousseau observes between the perceptions of "l'homme de génie" and "l'homme du commun."[19] Such a difference could only be overcome if the latter ascends to the former. But Rousseau avers that he knew of "only two classes that are really distinct: the one of people who

---

16. *Emile*, 398 and 401 Cf. 426–27, in relation to 110, 121, 185, 189–90, 218, 296, 298, 470, 489, 493, and 497.
17. Ibid., 426. Cf. 116, 121, 134, 142–45, 161, and 237; *Les rêveries du promeneur solitaire* 4, in *O.C.* 1.1028ff.; *Du contrat social*, 2.7. Cf. the author's "Art d'écrire et pratique politique de Jean-Jacques Rousseau," *Revue de métaphysique et de morale* 89, nos. 2–3 (1984): 232–61 and 322–47, and errata in 90, no. 1 (1985): 143. In *Jean-Jacques Rousseau: La transparence et l'obstacle* (Paris: Gallimard, 1971), Jean Starobinski attributes Emile's "transparence" to the author of his being, thus overlooking the very thesis of the *Discours sur les sciences et les arts* while beginning his analysis therewith.
18. *Emile*, 121, in relation to 110, 496, and 498. Cf. 64–69, 71, 80, 85–86, 135, 172, 180, 185, 192, 198, 200, 202–3, 209, 249, 254–55, 257, 276–77, 295, 318, 388–90, 392–94, 396, 404, 406, 409, 414, 426, 443, 486, 489, 516–517, 528, 545, 549, and 552.
19. Ibid., 26, 79, 99–102, 180–81, 265, 293, 497, and 514. Cf. *Dictionnaire de musique*, 2 vols. (Paris: Art et Culture, 1977), 1.272 ("Génie"); *Du contrat social*, 2.7.

think, the other of those who do not think."[20] The idea of equality, which mediates Emile and his master, conduces the former to blink this distinction, while he who dissimulates it must never forget it.

Make of them your equals in order that they become it; and if they still cannot raise themselves up to you, descend to them without shame or scruple.... Even less must the pupil suppose that the master intentionally allows him to fall into these traps and tenders these snares to his simplicity. What therefore should he do to avoid these two inconveniences at the same time? What is best and most natural: be simple and true like him.[21]

The obstacle to true communication between the personae of this philosophical novel may be the same as exists not only between the Legislator and the citizens he forms, but perhaps between Rousseau and his readers as well.[22]

In this case, more than embellishing the reasoning they accompany, the literary qualities of the *Emile* would, like the book's title, encapsulate insights their charms obscure.[23] If indeed "it is only appropriate to men to be instructed by fables," then elucidating this fable destined for adults must be undertaken in a way analogous to seeking the thought concealed in the words of a poem.[24]

The *Emile* would then be a work of philosophy similar to such other revolutionary books as Plato's *Republic*, Bacon's *Wisdom of the Ancients*, or Nietzsche's *Zarathustra*, which coalesce philosophy and poetry with a view to forming a new state of mind, and to supplanting the prior education furnished by Homer, the Bible, or the *Encyclopedia*.[25] Just as these

---

20. *Emile*, 518. Cf. 306, 321, 435, 454, and 542.

21. Ibid., 294. Cf. 193, 196, 280, 295, 406, and 417. Concerning the governor's dissimulations, see also 392 in relation to 72, 121, 124, 126, 134–35, 144, 153–54, 172, 178, 255–56, 266, 278, 295–96, 316–17, 388, 394, and 408–9.

22. *Du contrat social* 2.7, in *O.C.* 3.383. Cf. *Emile*, 9–11, 121, 145, 193, 196, 292–94, 312, and 392–93; *Observations*, in *O.C.* 3.46, in relation to *Préface d'une seconde lettre à Bordes*, in *O.C.* 3.105–6; *Les rêveries du promeneur politaire* 4, in *O.C.* 1.1028ff. in comparison with 1047 and with *Lettres à Malesherbes*, in *O.C.* 1.1141.

23. *Emile*, 110, in relation to 106–8, 121, 200, 284–85, 296, 298, 350, 358, 396, 398, 409, 426, and 494–95.

Cf. Kant's remark, "I have to read Rousseau until the beauty of his expression no longer disturbs me. Only then can I view him rationally." See Paul Schilpp, *Kant's Pre-Critical Ethics* (Chicago and Evanston: Northwestern University Press, 1960), 618. Cf. Cassirer, *Kant's Life and Thought*, 88, where Cassirer affirms peremptorily that Kant "is no prisoner of this charm." Concerning the book's title, see the author's "Rousseau Translations: A Review Essay," *Political Theory* 10, no. 1 (1982): 111–14.

24. *Emile*, 298, in relation to 110, 312, and 358 Cf. 83, 87, 121, 188, 200, 202, 296, 396–98, 401, 409, and 495. Cf. note 76 below.

25. With respect to the intent to replace the educational teachings of Locke and Plato, see *Emile*, 2, 10, and 452; with respect to the Bible, see 210 and 373; with respect to Homer,

antecedents provide models to emulate, notably the aristocratic warrior, the philosopher, the gentleman, the saint, or the enlightened bourgeois, the *Emile* presents an image of the common man, such as to make of him, paradoxically, an ideal. Thereby the *Emile* would aim at transforming perceptions of this man, hitherto discerned as lacking in refinement and imbued with vulgar prejudices, in order to render popular government a desirable object that even educated persons would seek to establish and defend.[26]

However this may be, in seeking to vindicate Providence against the Enlightenment's nihilism, Rousseau articulates a new reason for human practice and responds thereby to the "pessimistic" cosmology promulgated by Bayle, d'Holbach, and Voltaire.[27] In so doing, and contrary to the Enlightenment philosophies that suppress imagination, Rousseau here infuses it with a theoretical and practical function that is profoundly novel. "It is the imagination," he says, "which extends for us the measure of the possible, whether for good or evil, and which consequently excites and nourishes desires by the hope of satisfying them."[28]

From its first page, this work of imagination "excites and nourishes" desire both by evoking man's separation from his nature and the possibility of somehow recovering his original unity. The obstacle to finding this unity is life in common, which by the hierarchy of classes and the division

---

consider the engravings introducing the books of the *Emile*, as well as the parallels between Rousseau and Chiron in Book 2, and also 516, where Rousseau, in comparing himself with the father of "Telemachus," replaces Ulysses.

26. *Emile*, 430, in relation to 409 and 470. Cf. 10–11, 110, 210, 212, 406, 424, 426, and 585. Concerning the *Emile*'s influence, see Barny, *Prélude idéologique à la Révolution francaise*, 8–9, 15, and passim; Ozouf, *L'homme régénéré*; Robert Darnton, *The Great Cat Massacre* (New York: Random House, 1984), 241–52; Cassirer, *Kant's Life and Thought*, 84–90; Velkley, *Freedom and the End of Reason: On the Moral Foundation of Kant's Critical Philosophy*; and Albert Béguin, *L'ame romantique et le rêve: Essai sur le romantisme allemand et la poésie française* (Paris: Librairie José Corti, 1991), 65, 77, and 81.

27. *Emile*, 386–89, in comparison with 93, 223, 278–79, 310, 313, 361–63, 377, 385, and 494; *Dialogues Rousseau juge de Jean-Jacques*, in *O.C.* 1.934–35, 971, 1015–19, and note 1 (to 1016) at 1782–1783 concerning d'Holbach and the nihilism of the modern philosophers. Concerning the correspondence between Rousseau and Voltaire on this question, see note 14 above and esp., in response to Voltaire's *Poème sur le Désastre à Lisbonne*, Rousseau's *Letter to Voltaire on Providence* (August 18, 1756), in *O.C.* 4.1059ff. See also d'Holbach, *Le bon sens* (Paris: Editions Rationalistes, 1971), chaps. 87, 93, 105, and 108. For the Baron d'Holbach's influence on the Marquis de Sade, see *Le bons sens*, 239, 241, 246, and 249. Compare note 46 below.

28. *Emile*, 64 See 76, 85–88, 179, 256, 272, 323, 388, 393, 396, 403, 406, 410, 415, 494–95, 568, and 570. Cf. Descartes, *Discours de la méthode*, 129–30; *Les passions de l'ame*, arts. 70–78; Hobbes, *Leviathan*, 1.2, 1.8; and Kant, *Kritik der Urteilskraft*, sec. 83. Cf. also Carnes Lord, *Education and Culture in the Political Thought of Aristotle* (Ithaca, N.Y.: Cornell University Press, 1982), 20–22.

of labor establishes within men the contradictory sentiments of domination and servility, or of duty and desire.[29] The instrument of this quest for lost unity is the very principle of human action, self love (*amour de soi*); and the direction of the quest is indicated by the poet-philosopher, perhaps "the author of things," he "who knows the art of sounding hearts while working to form them."[30] But if self love is the ground of action, the idea one has of one's self can orient the conscious action of this principle.[31] Through his work on education, Rousseau seeks to revise ideas about what is humanity, whether in terms of human nature or of principles of the equality and liberty of men.[32]

To accomplish this revision of perception, Rousseau distinguishes within the principle of human action, or *amour de soi*, two sources of its activity: sentiment and sensation. Whereas the Encyclopedists explain the former by the latter, Rousseau observes, for example, that as an expression of *amour-propre* and as a modification of *amour de soi*, the phenomenon of pride is perceived as neither a sight nor a sound, nor a taste nor a smell nor a touch.[33] And yet such an irreducible sentiment is more expressive of what one is than are any of the five particular senses. The latter are affected and drawn by objects beyond the self; but if *amour de soi* is the foundation of sentiment, its object, however mediated externally, will somehow always be its origin.

Just as the imagination can either augment or diminish sensual desires, the same is true of its effect on sentiments. Recollecting to the reader the classic distinction between necessary and unnecessary wants, Rousseau seeks, by novel means, to limit the sensual desires with a view

---

29. *Emile*, 70. Cf. 11, 83, 124–25, 135, 212, 215, 217–18, 223–24, 236, 247, 260, 265, 538, 559, and 581–82.

30. Ibid., 266. Cf. 5, 11, 12, 23–25, 170, 223, 247, 249, 256, 282, 332, 335, 337, 340–42, 346–47, 356, 388, 393, and 567. See also *Du contrat social*, 2.7 and 2.12; *Essai sur l'origine des langues*, chaps. 1, 2, 7, 12, 15, and 20; and *De l'imitation théâtrale: Essai tiré des Dialogues de Platon*, in *Oeuvres complètes de J.-J. Rousseau*. (Paris: Librairie de L. Hachette et Cie., 1862), 1.369, on the quarrel between philosophy and poetry. Paradoxically both Plato and Rousseau, famous for their critiques of poetry, reintroduce it in the City, but in Plato's case as handmaiden to philosophy and in Rousseau's case as both obstacle and emulator thereto. Cf. Marc Eigeldinger, "*Les rêveries*, solitude et poésie," in *Jean-Jacques Rousseau: Quatre etudes* (Neuchâtel: Editions de la Baconnière, 1978), 119 and 122; and Rousseau's disciple Gaston Bachelard, *La poétique de la rêverie* (Paris: Presses Universitaires de France, 1960), 160: "L'exploit du poète au sommet de sa rêverie cosmique est de constituer un cosmos de la parole"; cf. 143.

31. *Emile*, 246–50, 256–57, 266, and 279.

32. Ibid., 200, in comparison with 9, 11, 80, 93, 99, 110, 202, 209, 212, 247–250, 319, 392, 396, 401, and 605. Consider the effect of Rousseau's project on the idea of *Bildung* in Kant's *Kritik der Urteilskraft*, sec. 83, and in Hegel's *Phänomenologie des Geistes*, 6.B.

33. See *Emile*, 247–49, 256, 272–73, and 357, in comparison with *Dialogues Rousseau juge de Jean-Jacques*, in *O.C.* 1.805ff.; *Notes sur "De l'Esprit" d'Helvétius*, in *O.C.* 4.1121ff.

to conserving the integrity of the source of what one is. Beyond necessity, the imagination may touch and bestir the sentiments to the point where the pleasure they seek supersedes and masters the desire for somatic pleasures.[34] Human independence or liberty depends, it seems, on such mastery before the objects to which, otherwise, the desires would be subjugated.[35]

But with respect to this freedom, a reflection on the differences among natural, moral, and civil liberty doubly reveals the work performed by imagination within the ideas Rousseau transmits concerning the principles of right. "The imagination," he says, "which plays so much havoc among us, does not speak to savage hearts.... [T]he savage lives in himself; the sociable man, always outside himself knows how to live only in the opinion of others; and it is, so to speak, from their judgment alone that he draws the sentiment of his own existence."[36] If *"l'homme sociable"* is *"toujours hors de lui,"* then no less than the "bourgeois," such a common man as the citizen must forget his natural origins, just as Rousseau must recollect them.[37]

The good is initially defined as the object of desire; but there is a difference between natural desire and that which is artificially conceived. The object of natural desire, or of *l'amour de soi-même*, is what a being lacks for self sufficiency. But social man, *ex hypothesei*, cannot be self-sufficient. "The natural man is entirely for himself; he is the numerical unity, the absolute whole who only has a relation to himself or to his like. The civil man is only a fractional unity which depends on the denominator, and whose value is in his relation to the whole, which is the social body. Good social institutions are those which know how best to denature man, remove from him his absolute existence in order to give him a relative one,

---

34. *Emile*, 72–73, 251, 253–56, 272–73, 358, 388, 393, 406, 409–10, 424, 494, 509, and 512–14.

35. Ibid., 280, 341–42, and 354–58, in comparison with 93, 99, 182, 185, 212, 279, 289, and 303. On the question of *amour-propre* and virtue, for a common misinterpretation of Rousseau on this point in relation to Kant, see John Zammito, *The Genesis of Kant's Critique of Judgment* (Chicago: University of Chicago Press, 1992), 331. On the question of being (*être*) and Rousseau's resuscitation and transformation thereof in relation to Bacon's and the Enlightenment's rejection of this category, consider *Emile*, 10 and context, and compare Friedrich Hölderlin, "Rousseau" and "Der Rhein," in *Sämtliche Werke* (Stuttgart: Kohlhammer Verlag, 1953), 2.12–13 and 149–56, and Martin Heidegger's *Destruktion* of *Dasein*, in *Kant und das Problem der Metaphysik*, Vierte, Erweiterte Auflage (Frankfurt am Main: Vittorio Klostermann Verlag, 1973), Einleitung, and in *Hölderlins Hymnen "Germanien" und "Der Rhein"* (Frankfurt am Main: Vittorio Klostermann Verlag, 1980), 1.2 and 2.

36. *Discours sur l'origine de l'inégalité*, in *O.C.* 3.158 and 193.

37. *Emile*, 165, 239–40, 304–6, 422, 453, and 514–15, in comparison with 5 and 9–11; *Discours sur l'origine de l'inégalité*, in *O.C.* 3.122–23 and 125; *Les rêveries du promeneur solitaire* 4, in *O.C.* 1.1028, on Rousseau's "dictamen," in comparison with 1047 and with *Lettres à Malesherbes*, in *O.C.* 1.1136–37.

and to transport the I [*le moi*] into the common unity; in such a way that each particular no longer believes himself one, but part of the unity, and is no longer sensitive except in the whole."[38]

Emile will therefore have a spirit whose imagination, formed "little by little" by his mentor to estrange it from its origins, must simultaneously "nourish" his desires and obscure their object.[39] "The source of all the passions is sensibility; the imagination determines their bent. . . . If it were only necessary to listen to penchants and follow their directions, that would soon be done: but there are so many contradictions between the rights of nature and our social laws, that to conciliate them it is necessary to dodge and tergiversate incessantly; it is necessary to employ much art to prevent social man from being altogether artificial."[40]

Book 4, where the latter citation appears, is illustrated at its center by an engraving of Orpheus "teaching men the worship of the gods." Thus, the book, where the "Profession of Faith of the Savoyard Vicar" appears, transmits a new prophecy, comparable to Book 10 of Plato's Laws.[41] Yet the beginning of Book 4 deals not with theology, but with the human passions, notably with eros, with *amour de soi-même* and *amour-propre*.[42] While the Profession of Faith follows the passages in Book 4 devoted to the teaching of rhetoric, the beginning of the book has already betokened the necessity of employing particular care when speaking of eros.[43]

Since in the beginning one is entire and eros comes to be only when one is incomplete, eros exists when one is alienated from one's self.[44] It

---

38. *Emile*, 9, 95–96, 99–100, 200, 271, 336, 388, and 393.

39. Ibid., 38, 43–44, 47–49, 53, 92–93, 96, 122, 124, 132, 134, 136, 151, 185, 192, 198, 215, 223–24, 232, 246, 248, 253–61, 274, 304, 316, 392–93, 396, 401, 406, 409, 414, 449, 531, and 567. Concerning the imagination, see, e.g., 64, 76, 85–88, 179, and 256. Cf. Descartes, *Discours de la méthode*, 132–34, 136, 138, 140, 157, 171, and 175; Martin Heidegger, *Kant und das Problem der Metaphysik*, Chapter 2, first paragraph.

40. *Emile*, 256 and 393. The word "*tergiverser*," as the context suggests, can mean "equivocate." Cf. 253–55, 259–62, 272, 290–91, 406, 409, 415–16, 425, 453, 493, and 571.

41. Ibid., 359. See 355 in relation to 331–32, and 346 in relation to 341, 349, and 353. Cf. Avicenna, "On the Division of the Rational Sciences," in *Medieval Political Philosophy: A Sourcebook*, ed. Ralph Lerner and Muhsin Mahdi (Glencoe, Ill.: Free Press, 1963), 97; Thomas Pangle, "The Political Psychology of Religion in Plato's Laws," *American Political Science Review* 70, no. 4 (1976): 1059ff.

42. *Emile*, 245–47 and 249–60.

43. Ibid., 246 and 253–55. On rhetoric in this regard, see 302 in relation to 106–8, 110, 256, 296, 298, 316, and 388–93. Cf. *La nouvelle Héloïse*, Seconde Préface, in *O.C.* 2.11–30; *Le devin du village*, in *O.C.* 2.1102–3. As these instances reflect, Rousseau seeks to replace Socrates as master of *erotika*. See the allusions to Plato's *Symposium* in *La nouvelle Héloïse*, 2.11, in *O.C.* 2.223, and *Emile*, 429.

44. *Emile* 415 in comparison with 350, 392–94, 405–6, 409–10, 425, 436, 449, 455, 495–96, and 498. Cf. 63, 276, 337, 423, 429, 437, 456, 462, 468, and 472–73, in comparison with Plato, *Symposium* 189d–e, 191d–e, 192e–193b, 200e ff., and 205e–212b. Cf. the tension and the drama created by the separation motif as the keynote of *La nouvelle Héloïse*,

therefore aims beyond historical being and toward the original unity.[45] The study of eros involves that of the desire for the whole that completes it. In the beginning, prior to the effects of art or convention, this whole is natural. But in the case of a being alienated from his nature, the liberation of eros hazards liberating tyrannical desires, without a recognition of their original limits. Just as Orpheus's hymns tamed the savage beasts, Book 4 of the *Emile* reveals how eros can be civilized by a musical language forming an image, indeed a vision, concerning the whole in relation to which desire, ever incomplete and thus properly in tension, will orient its self.[46]

According to Francis Bacon, Orpheus represents philosophy.[47] But as was noted, according to Rousseau "the true function of the observer and the philosopher" is knowing "the art of sounding hearts while working to form them."[48] Just as the genesis of ancient philosophy occurs with the discovery of nature, Rousseau, in opposition to antiquity and early modernity, constructs a new philosophy on the basis of his attempt to recover what he

---

1.1, 31. Compare the analogous motif in Hegel's *Phänomenelogie des Geistes*, 4.A, and the more complete form thereof indicated in *Emile*, 5, 9–11, 120–21, 179, 393, and 453.

45. Consider the question of language, time consciousness, and being as indicated by the citation of Ovid at *Emile* 58 in relation to 61–71, 99, 259, and 356. The citation of Ovid, at the moment when the child begins to speak and thus to apprehend past and future time, refers to exile from one's origins. The recollection thereof is a leitmotif of the *Emile*, as indicated by the engravings from Homer representing the themes of each book and concluding with an image from the *Odyssey*. This leitmotif points to the recovery of the principle of being, in the sentiment of existence, as outlined in the *Lettres à Malesherbes*, in *O.C.* 1.1136–37, and in Rousseau's "first philosophy," *Les rêveries du promeneur solitaire* 5, in *O.C.* 1.1047.

46. *Emile* 359 in comparison with 63, 65, and 356. Concerning Orpheus's music in relation to *eros* and the regime, see Plato, *Laws* 2.669d ff., and consider Rousseau's restatement of *Laws* 2 and *Republic* 10 in *De l'imitation théâtrale: Essai tiré des Dialogues de Platon*, 358ff. Cf. "Extrait sur un morceau de *l'Orphée* de M. le Chevalier Gluck," in Rousseau's *Dictionnaire de musique* (Paris: Art et Culture, 1977), 2.375–79, in comparison with 1.183–84, 234–36, 253, 257, and 272. See Horace, *Ars poetica*, ll. 385ff.; Béguin, *L'ame romantique et le rêve*, 64–65 and 77. Cf. note 27 above on Sade.

47. *The Wisdom of the Ancients*, in Francis Bacon, *Selected Writings* (New York: Modern Library, 1955), 410–13. Cf. *Discours sur les sciences et les arts*, in *O.C.* 3.29, where Rousseau calls Bacon "le plus grand, peut-être, des philosophes." See also Timothy Paterson, "Bacon's Myth of Orpheus: Power as a Goal of Science in *Of the Wisdom of the Ancients*," *Interpretation* 16, no. 3 (1989): 427–44; and Howard B. White, *Peace among the Willows: The Political Philosophy of Francis Bacon* (The Hague: Martinus Nijhoff, 1968), 207–17.

48. *Emile*, 266. See also 424–25 in comparison with 121, 272, 280, and 393; *Du contrat social* (first version), in *O.C.* 3.285 and 288, and *Du contrat social*, 2.7 and 2.12; *Essai sur l'origine des langues*, Chapters 12, 15, and 20; *De l'imitation théâtrale*, 369. Cf. Percy Shelley, "Defense of Poetry," in *Shelley's Poetry and Prose* (New York: Norton, 1977), 482, 492. Concerning the relation of Orpheus and Pygmalion, see Jerry Weinberger, *Science, Faith, and Politics: Francis Bacon and the Utopian Roots of the Modern Age* (Ithaca, N.Y.: Cornell University Press, 1985), 162–63, and cf. Rousseau, *Pygmalion*, in *O.C.* 2.1224–31. Cf. Nietzsche, *Jenseits von Gut und Böse. Vorspeil einer Philosophie der Zukunft*, aph. 56, 61, 62, 269, 292, and 295.

is. But while this quest for his nature discloses what conventions obscure, the fourth book is concerned with the genesis of eros, which is separated from nature and a fortiori determined by relations to another. Since these relations are necessary to the social spirit, Book 4 prepares for entry into the world of customs or morals, or that of the forgetfulness of origins.[49]

Because eros exists when not satisfied, the very dividedness of man implied by association gives rise to eros. But civil association is in turn maintained by conserving the incompleteness or tension of eros. Since the latter is sustained by the forbidden, that seducer who divines the mystery of eros, the poet-legislator, "occupies himself in secret" with artfully tracing and maintaining moral taboos.[50]

Given that the separation from nature is accompanied by the rise of the passions, Book 4 is concerned with forming these passions. "Here then is another apprenticeship to undertake, and this apprenticeship is more painful than the first: for nature delivers us from the ills it imposes on us, or else teaches us to bear them; but it tells us nothing for those which come from us; it abandons us to ourselves."[51] The image of Orpheus, chosen to represent the principal subject of Book 4, indicates that the teaching found there is addressed to life in the underground world of the Cave.[52] Comparable to the charms of the Orphic hymns, Rousseau's art of writing seeks to forge a civic spirit that is pleased by its alienation.

49. *Emile* 415, in comparison with 84, 88, 92, 121, 172, 219, 250–52, 255–57, 276, 316–17, 354–55, 359, 387, 397–98, and 423. On the question of forgetfulness induced by Orpheus's music, see Francis Bacon, *The Wisdom of the Ancients*, 411–12. On the association of Orpheus with both Dionysus and Apollo, see Pindar, *Pythian Odes* 4.177, cited by Thomas Pangle, in Pangle, *The Laws of Plato* (New York: Basic Books, 1980), 520n23. Cf. Friedrich Nietzsche, *Die Geburt der Tragödie*, secs. 1–4 and 16, on the Apollinian and the Dionysian.

50. *Du contrat social*, 2.12, in *O.C.* 3.394. Cf. *Emile*, 121. Cf. Aristophanes' speech in Plato, *Symposium* 192d–193d, and Rousseau's allusions to Aristophanes in *La nouvelle Héloïse*, 2.17, in *O.C.* 2.252; *Lettres ecrites de la Montagne* 5, in *O.C.* 3.797; and *De l'imitation théâtrale*, 369.

51. *Emile*, 567, in ironic allusion to the *Emile*'s epigraph, drawn from Seneca's *De ira* 2.13. Cf. 11, 66, 74, 258–59, 318, 514–15, 561, 565, and 600. See also note "b" to 414 of the Pléiade edition of the *Emile*, in *O.C.* 4.1404–5.

52. Consider *Emile*, 359–60, in relation to 99, 259–61, and 319, and *Dictionnaire de musique*, 1.313: "Le caractère du mode lydien étoit animé, piquant, triste cependant, pathétique et propre à la mollesse, c'est pourquoi Platon le bannit de sa *République*. C'est sur ce mode qu'Orphée apprivoisoit, dit-on, les bêtes mêmes, et qu'Amphion bâtit les murs de Thebes." Cf. *L'etat de guerre*, in *O.C.* 3.608–9. Rousseau constructs the walls of the Social Contract, his *communio*, on the basis of a musical *pathétique*, the *lydien grave* or Aeolian mode, which accords with the harsh requirements of civic virtue. See *Dictionnaire de musique*, 1.247, 313, and 331, in relation to *Emile* 303, 336, 532, 540, 548–49, 567, and 571, where the separation from Sophie and the desire to find her again contribute to forgetting the natural sentiments thanks to the pleasures and pangs of love. Analogous to the quest for Eurydice, the desire for Sophie, or this ideal compared to Eucharis (525), eclipses the *sophia* sought by philosophy at the same time that this imaginary ideal serves to tame the Dionysian *eros* of a civil man. Concerning Sophie as Circe, see 527 in relation to the frontispiece of Book 5. On the Cave and music, see notes 53, 76, 77, and 78 below.

On the basis of this aesthetic emerge the new principles of right presented in Book 5 and in the *Social Contract*.⁵³

But if the good is both what is natural and the object of desire, how could Rousseau hope to induce his readers to desire being alienated from the good and toward the community?⁵⁴ The inducements outlined in the *Social Contract* 1.8 correspond to those criticized in the *Discourse on Inequality*. In conformity with the Vicar's enthymemes, they lead to forgetting more precise arguments, contrary to these inducements, furnished in the earlier books of the *Emile*.⁵⁵ Yet, just as those anterior arguments are obscured by the alluring charm of Books 4 and 5, this same charm conduces no less to forgetting the antecedent lessons on the art of governing.⁵⁶ In the first three books, and notably in Book 2 on the Promethean Chiron, Rousseau had revealed how one can find, in the very

---

53. "Let us show (our violent interlocutor) in perfected art the reparation of the ills that beginning art caused to nature," in *Du contrat social* (first version), in *O.C.* 3.288. Concerning the Cave, compare ibid. 288–89 and *Du contrat social*, 1.l, with Plato, *Republic* 357a–367e and 514a–c. Cf. *De l'imitation théâtrale*, 358ff., where Rousseau reexamines the themes of *Republic* 10 and *Laws* 2. In what seems to have been an early draft for a preface to his *Institutions politiques*, Rousseau had envisioned commencing by an "Examen de la République de Platon." See *O.C.* 3.473. Cf. *Emile*, 10, 93, 121, 202, 217, 276, 304, 385, 389, 393, 403–4, 567, 570, and 583. Just as the *Emile* was designed in part to replace Plato's *Republic*, so the *Social Contract*, conceived as a sequel to the *Emile*, begins by an allusion to the inhabitants of the Cave.

54. *Emile*, 5, 7, 9, 11, 99, 349, 425, 431, 453, and 456; *Lettre à Philopolis*, in *O.C.* 3.232; *Lettre à Christophe de Beaumont*, in *O.C.* 4.935–36; *Lettres a Malesherbes*, in *O.C.* 1.1136–37; *Dialogues Rousseau juge de Jean-Jacques*, in *O.C.* 1.819; *Les rêveries du promeneur solitaire*, in *O.C.* 1.1047, 1083, in comparison with *Du contrat social*, 1.8.

55. In *Du contrat social*, 1.8, Rousseau emphasizes moral freedom (*"la morale"*) over *"le physique."* But within *"la morale,"* he is silent about the difference between the happiness of the sentiment of existence (*le moral*) and the *"frêle bonheur"* of a moral man (*"la morale"*). Cf. *Lettres à Malesherbes*, in *O.C.* 1.1137, written when Rousseau was correcting the proofs for the *Social Contract* and the *Emile*, and see *Emile*, 259. Concerning Rousseau's irony with respect to the spirit of community, see *Emile*, 442 and 597, in relation to 93, 99, and 280–81. Concerning agriculture and alienation, cf. the differences between the *Emile*, 216 and 226, and the *Discours sur l'origine de l'inégalité*, in *O.C.* 3.171. For the consistency between the two works, see *Emile*, 5 and 9–11, and esp. p. 223, in the very context of the praise of agriculture. The fact that Rousseau did not change his view between the *Second Discourse* and the *Emile* is specified in the *Lettres à Malesherbes*, in *O.C.* 1.1135–36; *Dialogues*, in *O.C.* 1.932; *Lettre à Beaumont*, in *O.C.* 4.928; and *Rêveries*, in *O.C.* 1.1019. Concerning his paradoxes, see *Emile*, 82 and 104; *Dialogues*, in *O.C.* 1.829; and *Lettre a Philopolis*, in *O.C.* 3.230. On the differences between Rousseau and the Savoyard Vicar, see *Emile*, 93, 99, 108, 247–48, 275, and 287, in relation to 320, 341, 351, 353–57, and 567. In Book 3 Rousseau demonstrates the art of writing which will mediate between his vision and that of the Vicar. See 187, 203–4, 207–9, 213–14, 220, 222–23, 236, and 238–40. Cf. Immanuel Kant, *Mutmasslicher Anfang der Menschengeschichte*, in *Kants gesammelte Schriften*, 8.116–17, where the founder of critical philosophy infers that the *Emile* seeks to "end the conflict between the natural and the moral." Cf. *Kritik der Urteilskraft*, sec. 83. In this sense, Kant reads Rousseau as Emile understands his governor. Cf. *Emile*, 422–24.

56. *Emile*, 83, 95–96, 110, 115–16, 121–22, 128, 147, and 150. Cf. 255, 276, 392–93, 396, 398, and 401.

sources of modern thought, the instrument for channeling eros away from its natural object. This inconspicuous device for reorienting the spirit is conceived as a composite of dogmatic skepticism, utilitarianism, refined epicureanism, compassion, egalitarianism, and pride (*amour-propre*). Rousseau calls this composition the principle of humanity.[57]

Although the dogmatic skepticism underlying modern thought represents a peril for customs or morals, nonetheless, the very repudiation by skepticism of the love of wisdom (*philia tes sophias*) can also seal the mind's alienation within the Cave, and thereby serve to reestablish morals on an "unshakable" foundation.[58] Rejecting metaphysics, or the inquiry into primary questions, dogmatic skepticism conducts its adepts to believe only in what they can sense. Thus, in place of the Socratic question, "What is . . . ?" ("*ti esti?*"), Emile is led to ask, in response to any proposition for inquiry, "What's the use of that ?"[59] Being utilitarian, Emile's ideas will become "precise and limited" ("*nettes et bornées*"). While imagining his skeptical mind to be open and free, his inquiries will be limited to what is practical, concerned only with this "reality," and thus renouncing a priori any reflection on the premises of his thought.[60]

Contrary to the partisans of Enlightenment, however, Rousseau emphasizes that the utilitarianism they propagate is insufficient for founding properly a civil constitution. Acknowledging no other motive than self-interest, utilitarianism unalloyed detaches men by egotism and seems only to associate them through relations established by necessity or force.[61] Thus, according to Rousseau, the Enlightenment vitiates traditional morals by the liberation of egotistical passions, and thereby prepares for a new despotism by daring and enlightened men no longer respecting any moral limit on exercising their power.[62] To overcome the interestedness dividing men in private affairs, Rousseau seeks by his art to awaken a public spiritedness that unites them.

57. Ibid., 62–65, 89–90, 93, 95, 99, 121, 259, 263, 276, 303, 392, 472–73, and 506.
58. *Du contrat social* 2.12; *Emile*, 82–83, 184–85, 191, 255, 259, 355, and 359, in comparison with 202, 214, 229, 237, 298, 316–17, 322, 324, 346, 360, 377, 386, and 419. See *Discours sur les sciences et les arts*, in *O.C.* 3.9; *Discours sur l'origine de l'inégalité*, in *O.C.* 3.127, in relation to Descartes, *Discours de la méthode*, 1.130.
59. *Emile*, 204. See 202–3 in relation to 93, 121, 200–201, 217, and 392–96. On dogmatic skepticism, see 184–85, 191, 322, 324, 327, 380, 383, and 385, and compare with 306 on the inevitability of thought, and with 386–89 on Pierre Bayle. Cf. *Discours sur les sciences et les arts*, in *O.C.* 3.9 and 18–19, on the problem of Pyrrhonism for practice.
60. *Emile*, 146, 177, 217, 221, 223, 239, 242, 295, 392, 394, 419, 422, 458–60, 481, 497–98, 501, and 518 Cf. 22. On forgetfulness, see 316–17, 354–55, 359, 387, 397–98, and 423, in relation to 84, 92–93, 120–21, 202, 217, 251–55, and 276.
61. Ibid., 386–89, in comparison with 93, 223, 286, 355, 377, 385, 494, and 509. Cf. *Dialogues*, in *O.C.* 1.934–35, 971.
62. *Emile*, 389; *Dialogues*, in *O.C.* 1.971, 1015–19; *Discours sur les sciences et les arts*, in *O.C.* 3.9–11, 14–15; *Du contrat social* (first version), in *O.C.* 3.283–89.

Already in Book 2 of the *Emile* Rousseau indicates that, to be effective, the utilitarian principle of the social contract depends on an antecedent "interior sentiment," which "would impose [this commitment] as a law of conscience." He adds of contracts: "Whoever keeps his promises only for his own profit is hardly more bound than if he has promised nothing; or at most, he is in the position to violate it like the tennis players who delay using a bisque only to await the moment for using it with more advantage."[63] Though according to Rousseau the aim of action is pleasure, there is a difference between the pleasure of the sentiments and that of the senses. The sufferings that an athlete—or a politician—endures to achieve victory indicate that the desire for the first kind of pleasure can master that for the second, just as love for one person can overpower the desire for any other.[64]

Yet the pleasures of sentiment composing the "fragile happiness" of civil man differ from those of the natural man.[65] Thus, the practical aesthetics of the governor conspires with his scientific method to induce, through the stratagem of a negative education, the oblivion of natural happiness. Instead of unifying men by the classic pursuit of a common object of desire, Rousseau advances a principle of social unity based on the imagination of what one wishes to evade.

> The sight of a happy man inspires in others less love than envy. One would gladly accuse him of usurping a right that he does not have by giving himself an exclusive happiness. And *amour-propre* suffers anew in making us feel that this man has no need of us. But who does not pity the unfortunate that he sees suffer? Who would not want to deliver him from his ills if it only cost a wish for that? The imagination puts us in the place of the miserable rather than in that of the happy man; we feel that one of these states touches us more closely than the other.[66]

This "interior sentiment," the "law of conscience," is reminiscent of the Hobbesian principle of fear as the foundation of civil right. Nonetheless, recalling his critique of Hobbesian fear as the ground of practice,

---

63. *Emile* 93. See 99, 178, 247, 261, 278–79, 303–4, 385, 389, and 403–4.
64. Ibid., 403, 406, 409, 436, and 494–95, in comparison with 8, 42, 62–64, 72–73, 250–51, 355, and 551. See *Dialogues*, in *O.C.* 1.805ff.
65. *Emile*, 200, 259, in comparison with 9–11, 70, 93, 99, 110, 202, 209, 212, 343, 351, 392, 396, and 409. See also 239–40, 304–6, 393, 418, 431, 435, 438–39, and 514.
66. Ibid., 259, in comparison with 255. While the negative education implies giving no doctrines and allowing the pupil to discover things on his own, the governor surreptitiously shapes the sentiments which in turn determine the pupil's ideas. Cf. 93, 121, 193, 196–97, 202, 212, 217, 237, 276, 295, 392–94, 404–6, 441, 551, and 564. Thus, contrary to Jean Starobinski's thesis in *La transparence et l'obstacle*, Rousseau's perception of "la condition humaine" requires him to veil his thoughts about the ends. See 12, 281, 417, and the double meaning of his remark (585) that "it is necessary to know what ought to be in order to judge well concerning what is." Cf. 422–24 in relation to 494–95. Cf. the essay by the distinguished semiologist Tzevetan Todorov, *Frêle Bonheur: Essai sur Rousseau* (Paris: Hachette,

Rousseau specifies that pity for others' suffering is in fact a manifold sentiment, compounded of pain and pleasure.

> Pity is sweet, because in putting oneself in the place of someone who is suffering, one yet feels the pleasure of not suffering as he does.... If the first sentiment that strikes him is an object of sadness, the first return to himself is a sentiment of pleasure. In seeing from how many evils he is exempt, he feels himself happier than he thought himself to be. He shares the pains of his fellows; but this sharing is voluntary and sweet. He enjoys simultaneously the pity he has for their ills and the happiness which exempts him from them; he feels himself in that condition of strength [*force*] which extends us beyond ourselves, and makes us bear elsewhere the activity superfluous to our well-being.[67]

In this way, the "fragile happiness" of the sentiment of humanity is a refraction of the sentiment of existence of the natural man.[68]

Yet to suffer from the suffering of others depends, according to Rousseau, on an act of imagination, wherein one identifies with another. Pity would therefore be both an expression of *amour de soi-même* and also an alienation from it.

> Indeed, how do we let ourselves be moved to pity if not by transporting ourselves outside of ourselves and identifying ourselves with the suffering animal, by leaving, so to speak, our being to take on its own? We suffer only to the extent that we judge that it suffers; it is not in ourselves, it is in him that we suffer. Thus, no one becomes sensitive until his imagination is animated and begins to transport him outside of himself.[69]

In order to evoke the sentiment of humanity by means of the imagination, the poet-lawgiver must remove the obstacles to one's capacity in thought to identify with another. Egalitarianism and the sentiment of humanity thus complement each other in this political strategy.[70] Moreover,

---

1985), 64–72, who on this point follows Starobinski and who in other respects interprets Rousseau in the spirit of Kant. See note 55 above.

67. *Emile*, 259–60, 270. See 262, 301, 303, 341, 343, 350, 440, 442, 449, 429, and 522, in comparison with *Rêveries* 6, in *O.C.* 1.1051–52. The self-pity marking the beginning of the *Rêveries* establishes a separation not only between Rousseau and most readers but also between his pity's object, the "Citizen of Geneva," and the subject feeling the compound sentiment of pity. Such an internal diremption anticipates going beyond the City, or the sentiment of humanity, to rediscover in *Rêveries* 5 the sentiment of existence.

68. *Emile*, 9, 11, and 336, in comparison with 13, 40, 46, 325, 342, 353, 357, 442, and 587; *Lettres à Malesherbes*, in *O.C.* 1.1139–43; *Rêveries* 5, in *O.C.* 1.1047. Cf. Martin Heidegger, *Sein und Zeit* (Tübingen: Max Niemeyer Verlag, 1979), 176, on "die Verfallenheit des Daseins" and "dem Mitdasein Anderer im Man völlig"; also *Die Grundbegriffe der Metaphysik Welt-Endlichkeit-Einsamkeit* (Frankfurt am Main: Vittorio Klostermann Verlag, 1983), 1.1.16–18.

69. *Emile*, 261. See also 93, 98–99, 176, 185, 222, 256–57, 304, 349–52, 401, 419, and 423.

70. Ibid., 263. See 12, 70, 73, 193, 196, 217–18, 224–25, 236, 260, 279–80, 294, 319, and 417.

such an egalitarianism draws individuals together in accord with the psychological requirement that civil liberty be founded on moral sentiments that are neither despotic nor servile toward others.

However, to the extent that through human association self love is ineluctably transformed into *amour-propre*, this metamorphosis properly guided allows what was the principle of honor, in the ancien régime, to become paradoxically the guardian of equality in a popular government. Association with another he says, is

> the point where *amour de soi* changes into *amour-propre*, and where begin to be born all the passions which derive from that one. But to decide if those of these passions which will dominate in his character will be humane and gentle or cruel and malfeasant, if they will be passions of benevolence and commiseration or of envy and covetousness, it is necessary to know what place he will feel himself to have among men.[71]

Humane sentiments are, therefore, also an expression of *amour-propre*. Yet,

> let us extend *amour-propre* over other beings. We shall transform it into virtue, and there is no man's heart in which this virtue does not have its root. The less the object of our cares is immediately involved with ourselves, the less the illusion of particular interest is to be feared. The more one generalizes this interest, the more it becomes equitable; and the love of mankind is nothing other in ourselves than the love of justice.[72]

Indeed, the idea of the equal dignity of men, which flatters and pleases the *amour-propre* of the greatest number, should be easier to propagate than is the classical, hierarchical idea of distributive justice. Moreover, the same idea of the dignity of men, linked to the sentiment of humanity or to pity "generalized and extended to the whole of mankind," unites individuals by a "common sentiment of existence"; "for each is a part of his species and not of another individual."[73] Cultivating the sentiment of humanity through pity and *amour-propre* will thus establish the "unity" of the "*moi commun*," which mediates the particular and the general good.[74]

In both the *Essay on the Origin of Languages* and the *Emile*, Rousseau at

---

71. Ibid., 279.
72. Ibid., 303. See also 210, 290, 292, 313, 317, 336, 357, 370, 390, 397–98, 440, 487, 493–95, 497, 503, 505, 509, 545, and 556–57. Cf. *Economie politique*, in *O.C.* 3.254–55; *Discours sur l'origine de l'inégalité*, in *O.C.* 3.189.
73. *Emile*, 303. See note 68 above.
74. Ibid., 9, 11, 259–61, 279, 303, and 336. See *Economie politique*, in *O.C.* 3.252, 254–55. The parallel movement from Hegel's *Phänomenologie* to the *Grundlinien der Philosophie des Rechts* abstracts, in the synthesis of the constituting *Idee*, from the difference and the tension between Emile and his governor or from the Emilean illusion thereon. The same abstraction continues in Marx's theory of *praxis*, which ignores the problem in Rousseau that alienation originates not in property, or in having, but in association itself.

first argues that written speech abstracts from the accents of vocal expression. And while writings may transmit ideas, "accent is the soul of speech; it gives it sentiment and truth."[75] But in his reflections on language, whether in these two writings or in the *Nouvelle Héloïse*, his plays, or his writings on music, Rousseau explores "*la phrase pittoresque,*" "*la phrase sentimentale,*" "*la phrase musicale,*" in a word, as he says in his notebook in 1754: "Comment être poète en prose?"[76] Through adept use of punctuation, sonorities, and allusive images, Rousseau seeks to provide an unobtrusively rhythmic and lyrical quality to his texts, reproducing the effects of the mixolydien mode, or the *pathétique* that he ascribes to Orpheus.[77]

In this way, the tone of Rousseau's language, conceived in order "to perfect reason by sentiment," seeks to conjure a particular passion, compassion, and to attach it, by the octosyllabic and alexandrine cadence of his political writings, to a form of *amour-propre* compatible with the idea of equality.[78] Since the principle of political reasoning will be a sentiment, Rousseau engenders a novel *poésie*, differing from that of the "bourgeois" theater derived from Diderot and Voltaire. The latter's art had been designed, by its skeptical irony, to disarm the soul and, in reason's name, to liberate desires attached to the senses or to their interests.[79] By contrast, Rousseau seeks to develop an aesthetic aimed at furnishing the soul with a new élan. Contrary to the art promulgated by Diderot and Voltaire, Rousseau argues first that one

---

75. *Emile*, 56. Cf. 45, 72, 147, 161, 302, 372, 381, 385, 401, 405, 430, 463, 470–73, 486–89, and 493; *Essai sur l'origine des langues*, chaps. 2–5, 7, and 12–15; *Dictionnaire de musique*, 1.33–37.

76. Cited in "Notes et variantes" to *La nouvelle Héloïse*, in *O.C.* 2.1359. See also 1360–61, in comparison with *La nouvelle Héloïse*, 1.48, 2.16; *Confessions* 4, in *O.C.* 1.157; *Ebauches des Confessions*, in *O.C.* 1.1153–54; *Emile*, 116 and 424–26; *Correspondance génerale de J.-J Rousseau*, 4.22, 5.129. Cf. Gustave Lanson, *L'Art de la prose* (Paris: Fayard, 1909), 201: "[Rousseau] a été vraiment un grand musicien, et, en un temps où le vers ne savait plus chanter, il a orchestré sa prose avec éclat."

77. See *Dictionnaire de musique*, 1.313, in comparison with 247 and 331, and the citations in note 52 above. Cf. Pierre-Maurice Masson, "Contribution à l'etude de la prose métrique dans *La Nouvelle Héloïse*," *Annales de la Société Jean-Jacques Rousseau* 5 (1910): 259–71; Jean-Louis Lecercle, *Rousseau et l'art du roman* (Paris: Armand Colin, 1969), chaps. 5 and 6; "Notes et variantes" to *La nouvelle Héloïse*, in *O.C.* 2.1360.

78. *Emile*, 237, 259–66; "Notes et variantes" to *La nouvelle Héloïse*, in *O.C.* 2.1359; Pierre-Maurice Masson, "Contribution à l'etude de la prose métrique dans *La Nouvelle Héloïse*," 263; Michel Launay, "L'art de l'ecrivain politique dans le *Contrat Social*," Actes du Colloque de Dijon sur le *Contrat Social, mai* 1962 (l'Université de Dijon, 1964), 30.351–78; Marie-Hélène Cotoni, *La lettre de Jean-Jacques Rousseau à Christophe de Beaumont: Etude stylistique* (Paris: Les Belles Lettres, 1977), Chapters 5 and 6.

79. *Discours sur les sciences et les arts*, in *O.C.* 3.9, 15, 21, and 27; *Emile*, 386–89 and 453, in comparison with 494–95; *Lettre à d'Alembert sur les spectacles* (Paris: Garnier-Flammarion, 1967), 49, 70, 80–128, and 232–50; *Préface à Narcisse*, in *O.C.* 2.965, 974.

offer to young people spectacles which restrain them, and not spectacles which arouse them. Mislead their nascent imagination by objects which, far from inflaming, repress the activity of their senses.... [T]he durable impression that he receives from an object comes to him less from the object itself than from the point of view under which one brings him to recollect it. It is by thus arranging examples, lessons and images that you will long blunt the needle of the senses and mislead nature by following its own directions.[80]

Through the selection of images to form the memory, such a moderation of sensual desire gives latitude to the sentiments and to their formation in turn. Correspondingly, the imagination may bestir the sentiments' eros and in its wake bring together lovers, families, and communities.

There is no true love without enthusiasm, and no enthusiasm without an object of perfection, real or chimerical but always existing in the imagination. What will enflame lovers for whom this perfection is no longer anything, and who see in what they love only the object for sensual pleasure? No, it is not thus that the soul is warmed and delivered to these sublime transports which constitute the delirium of lovers and the charm of their passion. All is only illusion in love, I admit; but what is real are the sentiments with which it animates us for the truly beautiful that it causes us to love. This beauty is not in the object one loves; it is the work of our errors. What of it? Does one sacrifice any less all his low sentiments to this imaginary model?[81]

This new *poésie*, destined to form a taste seeking pleasure in the beautiful and repelled by the ignoble, nonetheless incorporates a democratic moral entailing profoundly different effects from those of classical tragedy. While the latter provokes fear and pity in order to purge the disorientations imposed by emotion upon the intellect, Rousseau's art aspires to awaken certain passions in order to master others. "One has a hold on the passions only by means of the passions; it is by their empire that their tyranny must be combated."[82] In accord with this, Rousseau's poetic lan-

---

80. *Emile*, 272–73. Cf. 110, 254–56, 296, 298, 393, 396, 409–10, and 494–95. In Book 3, Rousseau discreetly displays the power of his art by providing, without warning or comment, a series of alternative, persuasive portrayals of the same phenomenon. See 175, 186–87, 203, 207–9, 213–14, 220, 222–23, 236, and 238–40. Books 4 and 5 then provide the poetic version thereof, based on the theory of reflexive ideas indicatedm in the note at 353–54. To consider how Rousseau's art shapes the transcendental imagination underlying Kant's thought, see Eva Brann, *The World of the Imagination, Sum, and Substance* (Savage, Md.: Rowman & Littlefield, 1991), 89ff.; and Richard Velkley, *Freedom and the End of Reason: On the Moral Foundation of Kant's Critical Philosophy*. Cf. Kant, *Kritik der Urteilskraft*, sec. 83.
81. *Emile*, 494–95. Cf. 9–11, 64, 99, 256, 272, 393–94, 401, 406, 409, 415, 539–42, 548, 567, 585, and 597.
82. Ibid., 406–7. See 424 on taste and "ce qui flatte ou choque le coeur humain"; also see 79–80, 93, 121, 135, 153, 209, 266, 274, 299, 330, 340, 388, 392, 395–98, 409, 416, 426, 430, 489, 562–63, and 568. With respect to classical poetry, see *Lettre à d'Alembert sur les spectacles*, 70–84, 92–93. Cf. Aristotle, *Poetics* 1449b 24–1450b 8 in relation to 1448b–1449a; *Nicomachean Ethics* 1175b 5–25; *Politics* 1341b 35–1342b 15. Cf. Laurence

guage does not promote a catharsis leading its auditors better to reflect on human things. The "truth" that Rousseau defends is less found in his words than in the sentiments that the tone of his discourse both represents and evokes. As noted, "accent is the soul of speech; it gives it sentiment and truth. The accent lies less than the word."[83]

Rousseau could thus insist on his veracity, despite the fables through which he transmits his idea of right. "Sensible men," he says, "ought to regard history as a tissue of fables, whose moral is very appropriate to the human heart."[84] Like a composer who, by music, moves his auditors without their comprehending the foundation of the art they hear, Rousseau seeks by the accents of his prose to touch the sensibility of his readers in order subliminally to transform and orient their perception, their judgment, and ultimately their conduct.[85] Thus, the aporetic prelude of the *Social Contract*—"Man is born free, and everywhere he is in bondage"—arouses less curiosity than righteous indignation. And this very disposition impedes pondering inordinately over the sequel: "What can render [this change] legitimate? I believe I can resolve this question." In accord with Rousseau's critique of Enlightenment, the charm of his aesthetics makes the pleasure of moral indignation, of "the good witness of oneself," or of *amour-propre*, the guardian of political judgment, which when linked to dogmatic skepticism would require, in order to be rethought and overcome, a cruelty toward oneself.[86] The natural inclination to

---

Berns, "Aristotle's *Poetics*," in *Ancients and Moderns*, ed. Joseph Cropsey (New York: Basic Books, 1964), 70–87; Carnes Lord, *Education and Culture in the Political Thought of Aristotle* (Ithaca, N.Y.: Cornell University Press, 1982).

83. *Emile*, 56. See note 75 above; also see *Emile*, 255 and 486–89; *Lettre à d'Alembert sur les spectacles*, 72–74, 78, and 82; *La nouvelle Héloïse*, 1.48, in *O.C.* 2.131–35; *Rêveries* 4, in *O.C.* 1.1028–33, 1037.

84. *Emile*, 172. See also 106, 110, 284–85, 297–98, and 317. Cf. Aristotle, *Poetics* 1451b 4, where Aristotle says "poetry is more philosophic and more serious than history," and *Nicomachean Ethics* 1140a 17, where he says "*poiesis* and *praxis* are other" and that *praxis* is the concern of *phronesis* and thus of political philosophy rather than of poetry (see also 1140b 2–8). By contrast, Rousseau's poetics prepares for the modern philosophy of history through, not only Herder, but also Kant's *Kritik der Urteilskraft*, sec. 83.

85. See notes 52 and 77–78 above. Cf. *Emile*, 284–85, on the historian's art of reporting "the facts without judging them, but ... (in a way) suited to making us judge them ourselves," in relation to 106–8, on the problem of what is an historical "fact," and to the remarks on fables and history at 110, 172, 296, 298. See also 56, 121, 237, 266, 279, and 585; and *Rêveries* 4, in *O.C.* 1.1029, 1031, on "fictions which have a moral objective" and on "the moral truth, a hundred times more respectable than that of the facts." For considering how these texts explain the movement away from the scientific study of human things and toward the modern theory of praxis, see the author's "Perception politique et théorie de la connaissance dans l'oeuvre de Jean-Jacques Rousseau," *Revue française de science politique*, 29, no. 4–5 (1979): 605–64.

86. Concerning "le bon témoignage de soi-même" in relation to critical judgment, see *Emile* 341, 351, 355–58, and compare with 184, 239, 279, 303, 316, 322, 360, 377, 386,

avoid such cruelty provides the durable wellspring of the Enlightenment's second wave, leading to the transcendental aesthetics of critical philosophy.

Yet the consequence of thus anchoring citizens' rights in the sentiment of humanity is manifested not only by their supersession of self-interest and scientific rationalism as the foundations of political perception. It is also manifested by the abnegation of deliberative reasoning or of the moderation it presumes, and favors, alternatively, political judgments that are categorical, general, indeed universal.[87] As the very *arche* of practical judgment, the sentiment of humanity, unlike classical generosity, has no measure beyond itself.[88]

Impressed by the perception of "inequalities," the moral indignation reflexively evoked by the sentiment of humanity would hardly be disposed to seek or deliberate over the true nature of an apparent injustice. Its principle of practical reason is no more the love of wisdom than it is interested calculation. Critical judgment will therefore orient itself not by prudence nor by nature but by asymptotically seeking an ideal, which is justified by the extent to which the ideal is logically or conceptually possible. Yet, says Rousseau in speaking of Emile, "I do not desire . . . that one lie to him, by falsely affirming that the object depicted to him exists; but if he is pleased by the image, he will soon wish for himself an original. From the wish to the supposition, the trajectory is easy; it is a matter of some skillful descriptions which, under features more perceptible to the senses, will give to this imaginary object a greater air of truth."[89] Whether in love or politics, to imagine thus and believe that the object of desire is possible arouses the hope, and thereby the attempt, to realize it. In this way, the power of the idea of historical progress would issue in new forms

---

389, and 419. With respect to Emile and Sophie themselves in this regard, see 483, 493, 495, 497–98, 502–6, 532–33, 539, 543, 554, 556, 566–68, and 608. Cf. Nietzsche, *Jenseits von Gut und Böse*, aph. 229.

87. *Emile* 303, 588–89, and 597, in relation to 70–71 and 280–81. Consider how this is consistent with the argument on the proper diversity of tastes, at 424. See also *Du contrat social*, 2.6, in O.C. 3.378–80 and *Discours sur l'origine de l'inégalité*, in O.C. 3.222–23, in comparison with Aristotle, *Nicomachean Ethics* 1133b 30–1134a 15, 1137b 10–25, and 1141b 15–1145a 12.

88. See *Emile*, 423–25 and 280–81, on moderation and pity, in comparison with Aristotle, *Nicomachean Ethics* 1119b 7–1122a 20 and 1138b 18–30ff; *Rhetoric* 1385b 12–1386b 8; *Poetics* 1449b 27 and 1453a 3–15. On the difference between Christian charity and modern humanity, see Howard B. White, *Peace among the Willows*, 21–23; and Richard Kennington, "Descartes and Mastery of Nature," in *Organism, Medicine, and Metaphysics*, ed. S. F. Spicker (Dordrecht, Holland: D. Reidel, 1978), 202–6.

89. *Emile*, 409. See 175, 250, 400, 415, 448, 455, 472, 487, 493–98, 509, 513, 527–28, 540, 545, 548, 551, 560, and 569. Cf. Kant, *Kritik der Praktischen Vernunft* (Hamburg: Felix Meiner Verlag, 1967), Erster Teil 1, Buch 1, Hauptstück. 1.51–54.

among those of Rousseau's disciples, such as Kant, alienated like Emile from his teacher's idea of natural limits.[90]

Faced with those who are disposed to deliberate on a different basis and whose deliberations reach conclusions which thus do not seem humane, the partisan of humanity, far from being disposed to examine their reasoning, will be inclined to judge his opponents as being, at best, "insensitive."[91] In this way, the *amour-propre* attached to the sentiment of humanity leads to a democratic version of the contempt manifested by the noble in the face of vulgarity. Since "sensitive souls" (*âmes sensibles*) and "bourgeois" souls will not perceive human things in the same way, there could not be a genuine communication between them. And the same is true of their relations with those habituated to deliberate prudently over public affairs. The establishment of the conditions of dialogue, or of communication, would first require eliminating these differences, superseding them through the instauration of the single party of humanity.[92]

Yet, given its egalitarian premises, the idea of the possibility of this instauration, inscribed in the sentiments of its partisans, embitters all the more their perception of refractory opponents. Thus arises the acrimony that criticisms can have of the "egoistic," commercial society promoted by the constitutional thought of the early Enlightenment.[93] Indeed, if the critic's ground of judgment is aesthetic sensibility, he will be all the more contented to repudiate his adversaries, reasons as either simply benighted

---

90. Kant, *Mutmasslicher Anfang der Menschengeschichte*, 116–17; *Metaphysiche Anfangsgründe der Rechtslehre*, *Die Metaphysik der Sitten*, part 1, conclusion; *Idee zu Einer Allgemeinen Geschichte in Weltbürgerlicher Absicht*, eighth and ninth theses; *Kritik der Praktischen Vernunft*, 3–5, 154–56, 174; Marx and Engels, *The German Ideology* (New York: International Publishers, 1969), 20, 22, 26; *Economic and Philosophical Manuscripts*, in *Marx's Concept of Man*, ed. Erich Fromm (New York: Frederick Ungar, 1966), 126, 130, and 134–40. Just as pp. 303 and 588–89 of the *Emile* anticipate Kantian formal rights, similarly pages 70, 212, 217, 247, and 280 foreshadow the socialist critique of "formal rights" in the name of "concrete rights." Abstracting from psychology, or from human nature, each of these successors glosses the tension, highlighted by Rousseau, between the progress of the individual and the progress of the species. See *Discours sur l'origine de l'inégalité*, in *O.C.* 3.162, 171, and 205; *Dialogues*, in *O.C.* 1.934–35.

91. *Emile*, 267. Cf. 147, 317, 339, and 425; *Dialogues*, in *O.C.* 1.672.

92. *Emile*, 266, 486–89; *Du contrat social* 4.7–8; *Economie politique*, in *O.C.* 3.252–55; *Dialogues*, in *O.C.* 1.768–70, 973–75. Unlike the Socratic dialogue, Rousseauian civil communication depends upon an affinity of sentiments. See *Essai sur l'origine des langues*, chap. 12, in comparison with *Discours sur l'origine de l'inégalité*, in *O.C.* 3.147–48. In his *Theorie des Kommunikativen Handelns* (Frankfurt am Main: Suhrkamp, 1981), Jürgen Habermas follows the orientation inaugurated by Rousseau. Concerning the problem of communication as revealed by the Socratic dialogue, see Leo Strauss, *The City and Man* (Chicago: Rand McNally, 1964), 50–60.

93. *Emile*, 280, in comparison with 70, 218, 224–26, and 236. See also *Discours sur l'origine de l'inégalité*, in *O.C.* 3.164, 178, 187, 193–94, and 202–8.

or else as duplicitously concealing a self-interested or exploitative motive. Ill-disposed to exploring the accuracy of opposing conclusions, he would be inclined rather to deform their basis and to criticize instead the character of those who reach them. And if piqued in turn, his interlocutor's indignation would only reinforce the barrier to reasoned exchange.

Conscious of such a problem, Rousseau presents it good naturedly in the romantic comedy of Book 5 of the *Emile*.[94] He thus discretely indicates the limits of his political solution. If the truth is found primarily in accents and not in thought, then beyond the art of the *gouverneur*-poet there is no escaping these misunderstandings. In the immediate context, while attenuating appeals to sensual pleasure, his musical aesthetic also ensnares people's intellects by the agreeable sentiments it awakens. Thus subjected to sentiment, thought in its most profound activity seems restricted to discerning and appreciating the different states of soul bestirred and modulated by this art.[95]

Yet, a part of Book 5's charm is found through Emile's partial apprehension of what the words of Sophie and others dissemble. Rousseau thereby furnishes to the cautious reader a thread leading to the ground of the perceptions, not of Emile, but of the author himself.[96] But to grasp a pleasantry beyond the charm that Emile perceives indicates a difference, between guilelessness and dissimulation, that aesthetic discernment alone cannot comprehend. In this sense, the verisimilitude of Rousseau's perception, concealed by his words, escapes his tonality or accent as well. Such alleged veracity would have to be grasped and appraised, not by sensibility, but by an altogether different principle of judgment.

But recollecting this principle allows for appreciating the problem

---

94. See *Emile*, 539, where Rousseau, like the augur of *Le devin du village*, takes the role of love's intermediary. Cf. 543, 564–68, and 608–14. Cf. Plato, *Symposium*, 177e, with *Emile*, 276–79, 337, 389, 429–30, 452, 456, 462, 472–73, 486–87, 493–94, 504, 541, 545, 569, and 570; *La nouvelle Héloïse*, 2.11, in *O.C.* 2.223.

95. Consider the self-reflexive activity of the citizen based on the formation indicated by *Emile*, 9–11, 56, 110, 121, 237, 239–40, 393, 401, and 494–95; and compare *Rêveries* 1, in *O.C.* 1.1000–1001: "Je ferai sur moi-même à quelque égard les opérations que font les physiciens sur l'air pour en connaître l'état journalier. J'appliquerai le baromettre à mon âme."

96. See *Emile*, 246 in comparison with 516, where the governor replaces Emile as "Ulysses." Cf. 121 and generally in Book 2 on the difference between Chiron's wisdom and his pupil's perceptions; also see 58–59 in relation to 86, 88, 101, 103–4, 177, 189, 192, 203, and 299 concerning the difference between words and ideas. On the thread leading from the student's perceptions to those of his teacher, see *Emile et Sophie*, in *O.C.* 4.923; *Ebauches des confessions*, in *O.C.* 1.1153; and *Dialogues*, in *O.C.* 1.666 and 973, to "fournir à ceux qui viendront après nous un fil qui les guide dans ce labyrinthe." On the movement from the *Confessions* through the *Dialogues* to the *Rêveries*, see *Rêveries* 1, in *O.C.* 1.1000–1001 in relation to 998.

and meaning of the commercial republic in a way that the sentiment of humanity ignores. This problem had indeed been broached by Montesquieu in the *Spirit of the Laws*, when he introduced his treatment of commerce by a poem dedicated to the daughters of Zeus.[97] It appears there that the self-interest abetted by the commercial society risks removing all poetry, all eros, from human life. In this work Montesquieu seems to hesitate between the élan encouraged by the republic of virtue, and the pedestrian but steady life of a regime devoted to commerce. In order to surmount this irresolution, Rousseau commits himself to establishing principles of right that will be no less sure, but that will conserve something of the humanity that Montesquieu seems to have placed in doubt.

Yet, corresponding to Montesquieu's apparent hesitations, the first wave of modernity proceeds through various currents, one deriving from an ontological utilitarianism, but another issuing from, at most, a prudential version thereof.[98] By reducing the modernity that he criticizes to the first variation alone, Rousseau radicalizes it. And it is on the basis of this constricted judgment of modern liberalism that he generates his novel project. What is thus obscured is the practical reason that led some to adopt a version of the constitutional project that Rousseau and his disciples reject. If the unalloyed union of ethical and intellectual virtues is too rare by itself to be effectual, then the interests and ambitions that stimulate the greatest number must be mastered by means other than classical education alone. As Montesquieu observes, the commercial society introduces among the greatest number a moderate behavior, which produces effects in politics analogous to those of true self-mastery. By multiplying interests and diminishing the scope of each, the commercial society diminishes as well the vehemence of passions attached to them, and thereby conducts ordinary men to be less despotic and more reasonable than they might otherwise be.

Certainly, Rousseau observed that, for Montesquieu and the Moderns,

---

97. *De l'esprit des lois*, Book 20. See Thomas Pangle, *Montesquieu's Philosophy of Liberalism* (Chicago: University of Chicago Press, 1973), 202–3, 208, and 219ff.; David Lowenthal, "Montesquieu and the Classics," in Cropsey, ed., *Ancients and Moderns*, 258–87.

98. See *Emile*, 430–31, in relation to 266 and 280–81. Cf. the author's "Les droits de l'homme et la politique constitutionnelle: Un dialogue franco-américain à l'époque révolutionnaire," in *La philosophie et la Révolution française*, ed. B. Bourgeois and J. D'Hondt (Paris: Librairie J. Vrin, 1993), 29–48; "La raison pratique et le constitutionnalisme américain," *Revue francaise de science politique* 38, no. 6 (1988): 906–23; "John Locke et la philosophie constitutionnelle," *Revue de synthèse* 106 (1985): 355–66; William Kristol, "The Problem of the Separation of Powers: *Federalist* 47–51," in *Saving the Revolution: The Federalist Papers and the American Founding*, ed. Charles Kesler (New York: Free Press, 1987), 100–30; Harvey C. Mansfield Jr., *America's Constitutional Soul* (Baltimore: Johns Hopkins University Press, 1991), 115–27.

this reasonableness, this "prudence," is at bottom only determined by an enervating desire for security and comfort.[99] Yet for some, and contrary to Montesquieu, such reasonableness echoes another practical reason than that founded upon an enfeebling anxiety. For these, the best guarantee of a nondespotic or free regime would be to find latitude within it for this other, deliberative reason, differing from that of the Enlightenment.[100] What bears recalling, moreover, is not only this idea of reason, but also the nobility of character of which it is the indispensable complement and measure.

However this may be, when Rousseau criticizes philosophy in the name of practice, the poetry that he establishes as horizon for the new *praxis* obscures simultaneously this other reason and the foundation of his own philosophy. "Respect therefore your species," he says, "remember that it is composed essentially of a collection of peoples; that when all the kings and all the philosophers would be removed from them, it would hardly be apparent, and things would not be any worse for it."[101] As much by its spell as by its logic, his pen radiates the itinerary circumscribing the career of rationalism under German critical philosophy. The cunning of this charm, and its extension over the modern spirit, were acknowledged by Nietzsche when he sought to surmount it in *Beyond Good and Evil.*[102] And seeking to fathom its enduring penetration induced Bergson later to observe that "the most powerful of the influences exercised

---

99. See *De l'esprit des lois,* 11.6, and compare *Emile,* 584–85. Rousseau's punctilious study of Montesquieu is revealed in some six hundred pages of manuscript notes on *De l'esprit des lois,* prepared when he served as secretary to Madame Dupin at the Chateau de Chenonceaux and preserved in the Archives de la famille Dupin at the Bibliothèque Municipale de Bordeaux. I am grateful to Madame H. de Bellaigue and to Monsieur Louis Desgraves for their assistance in obtaining a copy of this manuscript in preparation for a future study.

100. Alexander Hamilton, James Madison, and John Jay, *The Federalist,* ed. Jacob Cooke (New York: Meridian Books, 1965), 59–60, 62, 340–41, 374, 384, 425, and 482–83, in comparison with Aristotle, *Nicomachean Ethics* 1144a 22–1145a 12 and *Politics* 1296a5–20. Concerning the commercial republic as opposed to the virtuous polity, it is noteworthy that, despite Aristotle's criticism of commerce, he praises most highly, among the praiseworthy regimes, the commercial republic of Carthage. See Abram Shulsky, "The 'Infrastructure' of Aristotle's *Politics:* Aristotle on Economics and Politics," in *Essays on the Foundations of Aristotelian Political Science,* ed. Carnes Lord and David O'Connor (Berkeley and Los Angeles: University of California Press, 1991), 74–111.

101. *Emile,* 266. Cf. 184–85, 232, 291–93, 298–99, 307, 322–23, 348, 353, 355, 378, 431, and 433. Cf. Kant, *Fragmente aus Kants Nachlass,* 618, 624, 630; Luc Ferry, *Homo aestheticus* (Paris: Bernard Grasset, 1990). See Susan Meld Shell, *The Rights of Reason: A Study of Kant's Philosophy and Politics* (Toronto: University of Toronto Press, 1980), 20–32; Richard Velkley, *Freedom and the End of Reason: On the Moral Foundation of Kant's Critical Philosophy,* passim; Eva Brann, *The World of the Imagination,* 89ff.

102. *Jenseits von Gut und Böse,* Part 1, "Von den Vorurteilen der Philosophen," in comparison with *Der Wille zur Macht,* aph 98–101. Cf. in this light André Gide, *L'immoraliste.*

on the human spirit since Descartes—in whatever way moreover that one judges it—is incontestably that of Jean-Jacques Rousseau."[103]

Yet if, as these authors once again reveal, scientific reason is insufficient for grasping what is human in man, and if the poetic art masks by its charm the genius at its source, a different reason would be desired to disclose what eludes its other two forms. Anterior to either science or aesthetics, this other reason would be wanted for judging the principles of beauty or of right that inspire practice, whether for good or for ill. To appreciate the problem of unifying *humanité* with justice, one would in effect have to discern the several components of this "unity" in the thought of Rousseau. But to identify properly these elements, it would be first necessary to recollect an idea of the truth—lack of forgetfulness (*aletheia*)—which is antecedent to the thought of either Descartes or Rousseau. By such an archeology of the intellect one might thus divine, beyond the Orphic mysteries of the *Emile*, the primary ground of political philosophy.[104]

---

103. Henri Bergson, *Ecrits et paroles* (Paris: Presses Universitaires de France, 1958), 2.419. See also *Les deux sources de la morale et de la religion* (Paris: Presses Universitaires de France, 1988), 38, 300. Cf. Nietzsche, *Jenseits von Gut und Böse*, aph. 229, in comparison with *Der Wille zur Macht*, aph. 62, 92, 101, 106, and 1021. It bears noting that Nietzsche's philosophic project remains within the horizon of an aesthetic perception.

104. See the texts associated with notes 49 and 58 above; also see *Discours sur l'origine de l'inégalité*, in *O.C.* 3.207; *Emile*, 355, 359, 387, 392, and 398, in comparison with 121, 255, 259, 422–24, 426, and 429. Cf. Aristotle, *Nicomachean Ethics*, 1095a 30–35, 1139b 20–35, 1142a 15–30, 1142b 27–35, 1143a 12–16, 1143b 10ff., and 1143b 34–37, and Aristotle, *Metaphysics*, 1072b 4, in relation to Plato, *Symposium* 174a–b, 200a–b, 201e, 202c–204d, 214e, 216d–e, 221b, 221e, and 223d.

10   Lessing at God's Left Hand

KENNETH L. SCHMITZ

Gotthold Ephraim Lessing (1729–1781) stands to the Enlightenment in Germany as does no single figure in the British or French Enlightenment. But whereas the Encyclopedists mark the ripeness of the French movement, Lessing goes beyond its first maturity in fruitful and suggestive ways. Nowhere in his writings has this critical turning point been more succinctly expressed than in the oft-quoted passage about God's two hands. The passage is known to many English readers more through Sören Kierkegaard's citation of it than from Lessing's own work. It occurs originally in a late work of Lessing's, *Eine Duplik,* which was written early in 1778 just before the outbreak of a furious exchange with a Lutheran theologian, Hauptpastor Johann Melchior Goeze of Hamburg. Lessing had published what he had alleged to be fragments of an anonymous author (although Lessing actually knew them to be the work of Hermann Samuel Reimarus, a vigorous Deist and opponent of Christianity). Pastor Goeze was to attack Lessing directly; but before that controversy broke out another defender of Lutheran orthodoxy, Johann Dietrich Ress, attacked the reputedly "Anonymous" author directly and Lessing only indirectly. Superintendent Ress accused the unnamed author of attacking the credibility of Holy Scripture and of undermining traditional (i.e., Lutheran) Christianity by pointing out alleged contradictions among the Gospel accounts of the Resurrection.[1]

---

1. *Eine Duplik.* Lessing had in the previous year published *Ein Mehreres aus den Papieren des Ungenannten* (Fragments of an unnamed), but Lessing had actually known who the "unnamed" author was: Hermann Samuel Reimarus. To these fragments, he had attached his own "Editorial Counterpositions." Lessing now refuses to call the present work *A Rejoinder* (Eine Replik). A "Duply" (obsolete in English, *OED*) is the fourth in a series of statements. In this controversy there were (1) the original *Fragments* with (2) Lessing's own "Counterpositions"; these were followed by (3) a *Defense of the History of the Resurrection* (December 1777), authored by the Lutheran superintendent at Wolfenbüttel, Johann Dietrich Ress. Ress set out to refute the "Unnamed One's" charges, made in the fifth *Fragment,* that the accounts of the Evangelists contradicted one another. Ress denied the alleged contradictions and proposed his own "harmony" among the Gospels. (4) Finally, in this, the fourth of the series, Lessing set forth his own examination of ten alleged contradictions in the Gospels. He argued,

In the foreword to his reply Lessing sets forth the standard for judging among the parties to such a controversy. He tells us that the party who, however keenly yet modestly, opposes another while honestly trying to get at the truth, "is infinitely more worthy than one who defends the best and noblest truth out of prejudice and by decrying his opponent in a trite and vulgar manner."[2] More is at stake obviously than the objectivity of truth. Lessing continues: "A person's worth is determined not by the truth which is in his possession, or is thought to be, but by the honest effort which he has made to get behind that truth. For his powers are broadened not through possession but through search for the truth, and his growing perfection consists in the search alone. Possession puts one at ease, makes one lazy, turns one proud."[3] And so Lessing dares to say: "If God held the whole of truth enclosed in His right hand, and in His left only the ever-driven striving after truth, although with the proviso, that I should always and ever be in error, and if He then said to me: 'Choose!' In all humility I would fall down before His left hand and say: 'Father, grant me this! Surely, the truth in its purity is for You alone!'"[4] Lessing attends to the left hand, but we ought not to forget that its partner is the right. And so we ought perhaps also to ask what Lessing thinks God has in his right hand. For that might well tell us something of what for Lessing would count as truth.

---

moreover, that Ress had missed the point and therefore did not warrant a reply in the strict sense (*Replik*), since Lessing's fourth counterposition had already argued the case that the truth of the Christian religion did not stand or fall on the correctness of the Gospel accounts. Hence: "*Duplik* nicht *Replik*" (*G. E. Lessing's gesammelte Werke in zwei Bänden* [Leipzig: Göschen-'sch, 1855], 2.293b, n3; hereafter cited as *LGW*). Lessing is nothing if not "*feinsinnig.*"

2. Ibid. (*LGW* 2.271a): "Ein Mann, der Unwahrheit unter entgegengesetzter Ueberzeugung in guter Absicht eben so scharfsinnig als bescheiden durchzusetzen sucht, ist unendlich mehr werth, als ein Mann, der die beste, edelste Wahrheit aus Vorurtheil mit Beschreiung seiner Gegner auf alltägliche Weise vertheidigt."

3. Ibid.: "Nicht die Wahrheit, in deren Besitz irgend ein Mensch ist, oder zu seyn vermeint,* sondern die aufrichtige Mühe, die er angewandt* hat, hinter die Wahrheit zu kommen, macht den Werth des Menschen. Denn nicht durch den Besitz, sondern durch die Nachforschung der Wahrheit erweitern sich seine Kräfte, worin allein* seine immer wachsende Vollkommenheit besteht. Der Besitz macht ruhig, träge, stolz." (*Helmut Thielicke, "Vernunft und Existenz bei Lessing. Das Unbedingte in der Geschichte," in *Lessing und die Zeit der Aufklärung* [Göttingen: Vandenhoeck & Ruprecht, 1968], reads "vermeinet," "aufgewandt," and "alle," respectively. There are partial English translations in Henry Chadwick, *Lessing's Theological Writings* [London: Adam and Charle. Black, 1956], and in Henry E. Allison, *Lessing and the Enlightenment* [Ann Arbor: University of Michigan Press, 1966].)

4. Ibid.: "Wenn Gott in seiner Rechten alle Wahrheit, und in seiner Linken den einzigen immer regen Trieb nach Wahrheit, obschon mit dem Zusatze, mich immer und ewig zu irren, verschlossen hielte und spräche mir: wähle! Ich fiele ihm mit Demuth in seine Linke und sagte: Vater gieb! die reine Wahrheit ist ja doch nur für dich allein!" (partial English translations in Chadwick, *Lessing's Theological Writings,* and in Allison, *Lessing and the Enlightenment*).

The image is ultimately biblical, of course. It occurs in various contexts throughout the Scriptures. Usually, the right hand of God is the source of power.[5] Through its mighty power the right hand of God is also a place of protection and support for those who love and revere him.[6] It is a place of refreshment and joy.[7] The right hand of God is filled with righteousness.[8] In the Old Testament (OT) the right hand of God is a place of honor, and this attribute is especially emphasized in the New Testament (NT) with reference to Christ.[9] Indeed, Revelation depicts Christ as alone worthy to take the scroll with the seven seals from the right hand of God, since all authority and power in heaven and on earth are given to him.[10]

The symbolism of the left hand is less uniform in the Scriptures. It is sometimes coupled with the right hand,[11] but the association of the word "left" with the word "dark" lends a certain bent toward a pejorative sense. Nowhere is this sense more pronounced than where we are told (Matthew 25.33ff.) that at the Last Judgment Christ in his glory will separate the gathered peoples "as a shepherd separates the sheep from the goats, and he will place the sheep at his right hand, but the goats at the left. Then the King will say to those at his right hand, Come. . . . Then he will say to those at his left hand, Depart from me. . . ."[12] Lessing certainly did not choose to wander in the outer darkness offered by such a biblical left hand; and while there are goats aplenty in Lessing's theological world,

---

5. E.g.: Psalm 20.6 ([the Lord saves] "with mighty victories by His right hand"); Isaiah 62.8 ("by His right hand and by His mighty arm"); Matthew 26.64 ([Jesus speaks:] "Hereafter you will see the Son of man seated at the right hand of Power"). Cf. Luke 22.69.

6. Psalm 18.35 ("Thy right hand upholds me"); Isaiah 41.10 ("I will uphold you with My victorious right hand"). Cf. Hebrews 8.1 ([Our High Priest, Christ,] "has his place at the right [hand] of the throne of divine majesty in the heavens, and he is minister of the sanctuary").

7. Psalm 16.11 ("at Thy right hand are everlasting pleasures").

8. Psalm 48.10 ("Your right hand is full of righteousness"). Cf. Isaiah 41.10 ("I uphold you with the right hand of my righteousness").

9. Acts 5.31 ("God exalted Him [Christ] at [or "by"] his right hand to be Leader and Savior"); Ephesians 1.19ff. ("according to the working of His great might, which He accomplished in Christ when He raised him from the dead and made him sit at His right hand in the heavenly places, far above . . ."). Cf. Acts 7.55, Romans 8.34, Colossians 3.1, Hebrews 1.3., and 1 Peter 3.22. In the OT, see Psalms 111.1 ("Sit at My right hand, while I make your enemies your foot stool"); cf. Matthew 22.44.

10. Revelation 5.7 ([the Lamb, Christ,] "went and took the scroll from the right hand of Him Who was seated on the throne").

11. 2 Corinthians 6.7 ("with the weapons of righteousness for the right hand and for the left").

12. It should be noted that the judgment is not made on the basis of merely superficial and inactive "knowledge" of the way to salvation, but on living in accordance with God's offering. After "Come!" the text enjoins: "For I was hungry and you fed me, thirsty . . . etc."

there is no evidence that he numbered himself among them. When, in all modesty, Lessing declined the shining right hand, it seems fair to say that the twilight of mixed truth and error seemed to him to be more appropriate to the human condition. But what precisely did he take that condition to be?

Kierkegaard's use of Lessing's text makes that condition strikingly clear, and also perhaps what some later thinkers thought was in God's right hand. For Kierkegaard cites Lessing's text with keen irony as a polemic against Hegel and a weapon against all rationalist attempts to claim absolute knowledge. To Kierkegaard's mind, a logical system is possible, and a thinker may take petty pride in it as a private possession; but an actual, existential system is not possible. The claim to have constructed an absolute system of existence leads to idolatry, to a purported truth that claims to possess more than God has in his right hand. Indeed, if I might dare to improve upon Kierkegaard: the Absolute System has three hands, whereas God has only two. For there is the left hand of becoming (Lessing's search), the right hand (in which God holds pure truth), and the pretentious claim to absolute truth (in the possession of the System). For the System holds in its third hand more than God has in both his hands. Hear Kierkegaard out:

> When Lessing wrote these words the System was presumably not finished; alas! and now Lessing is dead. Were he living in these times, now that the System is almost finished, or at least under construction, and will be finished by next Sunday—believe me, Lessing would have stretched out both his hands to lay hold of it. He would not have had the leisure, nor the manners, nor the exuberance, thus in jest as if to play odd and even with God, and in earnest to choose the left hand. But then, the System also has more to offer than God had in both hands; this very moment it has more, to say nothing of next Sunday, when it is quite certain to be finished.[13]

Now, this is all good fun! And like all good fun it is serious fun. Kierkegaard's irony is displayed under the pseudonym of Johannes Climacus with the title *Concluding Unscientific Postscript to the "Philosophical Fragments."* Not only does the title carry the echo of Lessing's own publication of the Reimarus *Fragments* (also, by the way, published in a sort of pseudonymous fashion); but Kierkegaard's own earlier work, entitled *Philosophical Fragments*, raises the very question that so concerned Lessing, especially in his later years. For Kierkegaard asks: "Can [an historical

---

13. *Concluding Unscientific Postscript to the "Philosopical Fragments"* (Princeton, N.J.: Princeton University Press, 1941 [cited from *A Kierkegaard Anthology*, ed. R. Bretall (New York: Modern Library, 1936), 195]).

point of departure—and here we must bear in mind the historical witness that grounds Christianity—]have any other than a mere historical interest; is it possible to base an eternal happiness upon historical knowledge?"[14]

We can confidently maintain that one of the staples of Lessing's thought is that he answered "No!" It is not possible to base a reasonable understanding and the certitude of faith nor the hope of eternal happiness upon mere historical reports. And so Lessing confesses that he cannot cross the "broad ditch" from the probability of historical accounts to the sure grasp of eternal truth: such a transfer amounts to an illicit transit from one kind of statement to another (*metábasis eis állo génos*), from the probable, contingent, and factual to the certain, necessary, and eternal.[15]

And yet Lessing is never so simple. The major difficulty of interpreting Lessing is that he is something of a protean figure, passing between the older fully formed Deism of the eighteenth-century Enlightenment and those events that follow after him, and in part at least from him. I say that he passes between, since—it seems to me—Lessing himself does not seem to have moved gradually from the position of a classical Deist and Rationalist to that of a postclassical German Idealist or a new kind of Christian. He is transitional only from our point of view, not from his own. From his viewpoint, it seems to me, the mature Lessing (say, from 1750 on) is shot through with the unresolved tensions of his age; and he is interesting to us because many of these tensions are still in play. No doubt, this is why Lessing scholarship feeds upon itself to a remarkable

---

14. Theilicke, in "Vernunft und Existenz," 100–115, esp. 103–6, presents a subtle and closely reasoned argument for the relation between Lessing and Kierkegaard in terms of the certitude needed for whatever will fulfill one's "essential being." Recall, too, the "broad ditch" over which Lessing confesses he cannot leap: the gap between history and a more-than-historical certitude. For "Lessing's Ditch," see *On the Proof of the Spirit and of Power*, in *Gotthold Ephraim Lessings sämttiche Schrifte*, 23 vols., ed. Otto F. Lachmann and Franz Muncker (Stuttgart: Göschen, 1886–1924), 13.1–8 (also *LGW*, 2.268a); English translation in Chadwick, *Lessing's Theological Writings*, 54. Günther Rohrmoser, "Lessing und die religionsphilosophische Fragestellung der Aufklärung," in *Lessing und die Zeit der Aufklärung* (Göttingen: Vandenhoeck & Ruprecht, 1968), 117–29, takes Lessing's basic problem to be that of the "ditch," the separation of necessary truths of reason from contingent truths of history. Cf. also K. L. Schmitz, "Natural Religion, Morality, and Lessing's Ditch," in *Proceedings of the American Catholic Philosophical Association*, vol. 65 (Washington, D.C.: American Catholic Philosophical Association, 1991), 55–73.

15. See preceding note. Whereas Lessing cannot cross the ditch, Kierkegaard champions a transcendent Teacher, Christ, who breaks into human consciousness with fresh and original news, unlike Socrates who only draws out of mankind what has been there all along. Lessing appears to be a good deal closer to Kierkegaard's Socrates than to Kierkegaard's Christ. But, as we shall see, Lessing scholarship is by no means convinced of this identity.

degree, and sometimes reflects the present concerns of the interpreter more than those of Lessing.[16]

No doubt, too, this interplay of unresolved tensions suited Lessing's personality: he could not abide the "all too decisive."[17] His thought is essentially—or should I say, existentially—volatile. H. B. Garland stresses the dramatic character of Lessing's style, a tension that characterizes his theological works as well as his dramas and literary criticism.[18] Karl Barth suggests that what is new in Lessing's sense of revelation arises out of his perception of the dramatic element at work in the process of history.[19] The older literature in large part used to debate the reliance of Lessing upon Leibniz,[20] and whether or not Lessing was a Spinozist.[21] The trend today has shifted to the question of transcendence and immanence,[22] and whether or in what sense Lessing could be said to hold for revelation in any serious sense.[23]

It is quite generally agreed that Lessing is not a systematic thinker.[24]

---

16. In the brief discussion of the secondary literature that follows, I am indebted, especially for characterization of much of the older literature, to Johannes Schneider, "Lessings Stellung zur Theologie" (1953; with Nachtrag 1967), in *Wege der Forschung*, vol. 211 (Darmstadt: Wissenschaftliche Buchgesellschaft, 1968). Schneider observes (293) that many scholars of the nineteenth and twentieth centuries seem to have wanted to understand Lessing better than he understood himself. I have also drawn upon the quite different orientation expressed in the review by Karl Guthke and Heinrich Schneider, in *Gotthold Ephraim Lessing* (Stuttgart: J. B. Metzler, 1967).

17. A remark by Johannes Schneider, in "Lessings Stellung," 295.

18. Guthke and Schneider, in *Lessing*, 64, commend Henry B. Garland's *Lessing: The Founder of Modern German Literature* (London: Macmillan, 1962). As with other positivistically oriented scholars, Garland underplays Lessing's theological writings, but the emphasis upon the dramatic aspect of Lessing's thought is well placed. Indeed, Guthke and Schneider (69) urge that more work be done on Lessing's dramatic and literary output.

19. For Barth, see Johannes Schneider, "Lessings Stellung," 290.

20. See Allison, who in *Lessing and the Enlightenment* champions the influence of Leibniz upon Lessing. Guthke and Schneider (*Lessing*, 68) pass a severe judgment on Allison's work, on the grounds that it does not take into account the shift of problematic in the secondary literature; but theirs seems to me to be too severe a judgment, given Allison's subtitle: *His Philosophy of Religion and Its Relation to Eighteenth-Century Thought.*

21. The discussion was begun by Jacobi's report of a conversation with Lessing, published in Jacobi's *Letters to Moses Mendelssohn on the Subject of Spinoza's Doctrine* (1785). The sharpness of the disagreement is represented by C. Schrempf, *Lessing als Philosoph*, 2d. ed. (Stuttgart: Fromman, 1921), who found Lessing endorsing freedom, whereas G. Spicker, *Lessings Weltanschauung* (Leipzig: Wigand, 1883), maintained that Lessing was a thoroughgoing determinist. See Johannes Schneider, "Lessings Stellung," 291–92; see also Chadwick, *Lessing's Theological Writings*, 46–47.

22. Cf. Manfred Durzak, "Vernunft und Offenbarung im Denken Lessings," in *Poesie und Ratio. Vier Lessing-Studien* (Bad Homburg: Athenäum, 1970), 126ff. Durzak's book will hereafter be cited as *Poesie.*

23. See the discussion below. It is generally agreed that 1931 (the sesquicentennial of Lessing's death) conveniently marks the shift of problematic, though of course in no hard and fast sense.

24. *Kein Systematiker:* Durzak, *Poesie*, 106n4a, takes issue with what he understands to be

He himself protests that he is no theologian, but a mere lover of theology.[25] Johannes Schneider observes that Lessing's arguments are "not the fruit of his principled convictions, but rather investigations and criticisms of the prevailing spiritual currents."[26] In this sense, then, one could say that Lessing's writings are "occasional," that is, that they were called out by the occasion—a new book to review, a play to criticize, a theological opinion to refute. But he was an initiator of controversy, too, as his publication of the *Fragments* clearly shows, and also the *Vindications* or "rehabilitation" of thinkers considered to be heterodox in their Christianity.[27] Indeed, he is a master polemicist who revels in the fight even as he decries the wounds inflicted upon him! Before Nietzsche—and after Petrarch—Lessing gives vigorous expression to *agonistic* thought: new meaning arises neither in gradual development, nor in systematic closure, but in strife and controversy.[28] Lessing warns his brother Karl, who feared that his brother sounded too orthodox, to "bear in mind that I

Johannes Schneider's excessive pressing of the unsystematic form of Lessing's thought and work (see "Lessings Stellung," 293–98). He protests that, although Lessing's writings may be in some sense fragmentary and prompted by various occasions, we still can discern the direction of his thought. Durzak is afraid that such an emphasis will lead to detailed positivistic researches. "*Kleinarbeit*," without much significance for understanding Lessing's thought. Georges Pons, in *Gotthold Ephraim Lessing et le christianisme* (Paris: Didier, 1964), also finds no unified theological system in Lessing's works. So too Helmut Thielicke, in "Vernunft und Existenz," 101, and others. On the other hand, some older scholars who emphasize the dependence upon Leibniz, such as G. Spicker, in *Lessings Weltanschauung* (Leipzig, 1883), point to the posthumously published and somewhat controverted work *The Christianity of Reason* (1752–1753) (in *Lessings Werke*, ed. Lachmann-Muncker, 14.175–78; English translation in Chadwick, *Lessing's Theological Writings*, 99–101), in order to argue that it contains Lessing's first formulation of a metaphysics. Allison also argues strongly for such a view.

25. *Axiomata*, Prefatory Remarks: "Ich bin ein Liebhaber der Theologie und nicht Theolog. Ich habe auf kein gewisses System schwören müssen" (*Lessings Werke*, ed. Petersen and v. Olshausen, 23.164; *LGW*, 2.298). It is interesting to note (as does Garland, in *Lessing: The Founder*) that Lessing even deprecates his own dramatic work in similar fashion: "I am neither an actor nor a creative dramatist [*weder Schauspieler noch Dichter*] . . . I do not feel the quick spring in me . . . I have to force everything up by an artifical system of pressure and pipes." And he protests that it is his critical writing on theater, etc. [*Kritik*] alone that gives value to whatever he has done (*Hamburgische Dramaturgie*, 101–4 Stück; *LGW*, 2.229b.)

26. Guthke and Schneider, *Lessing*, 296.

27. E.g., his *Thoughts on the Moravians* (c. 1751), the *Vindication of Hieronymous Cardanus* (1754), *Berengarius Turonensis* (1770), and *Of Adam Neuser: Some Authentic Accounts* (1774). Lessing carries out a similar enterprise in nontheological matters as well: for example, with the *Rehabilitation of Horace* (1754), and the retrieval of a more adequate understanding of Aristotle's *Poetics* in the *Hamburgische Dramaturgie*, Stück 74ff. (1768) (*LGW*, 2.192b); "Aber das ist grundfalsch! . . . Aristotle couldn't have meant what [Corneille] imagines!" (Stück 76; *LGW*, 2.195b).

28. Durzak, in *Poesie*, 116, dubs Lessing's thought "antithetic." And Barth suggests that Leibniz's motive in publishing Reimarus's *Fragments* was to challenge the faith and to put the Church and theology to the test.

must direct my weapons at my opponents, and that not everything which I write *gymnastikôs* would I also write *dogmatikôs*."[29] And it is just this athletic tactic that has led some interpreters to distinguish between Lessing's exoteric expressions and his purportedly esoteric meaning.[30]

It is not that Lessing had no convictions of his own, but to every conviction—even his own—he immediately applied "the unsparing light of his criticism."[31] Truly, we can speak of the hurricane (*Orkan*) of his critique, which had a considerable influence upon the development of Higher Criticism.[32] Some speak of him as a driven man, driven by a titanic force.[33] Reportedly, the lost manuscript of an early drama on the Faust theme sums up Lessing's impulse to the search for truth.[34] One of the devils declares that an unquenchable thirst for knowledge will send man to Hell more surely than any other passion; but just as the demonic host bursts into triumphant song at the seeming fall of a man, an angel breaks in with the words: "The Godhead has not given to man this noblest of drives in order to make him unhappy: what you devils think you saw and now possess, that is nothing but a phantom."

It is safe to say that Lessing had at least a double meaning as to what is in God's right hand. No doubt, the ideal of a perfect, and perfectly rational, but perfectly inaccessible truth hovers over his passion, and such a truth would properly be in God's right hand and be for God alone. Such a perfect truth would be for Lessing at most an asymptotic ideal. One

---

29. Cited by Allison, in *Lessing and the Enlightenment*, 192n111, from a letter of March 16, 1778. Thielicke, in "Vernunft und Existenz," 114–15, remarks that Lessing's contemporaries also complained of this tactic.

30. Barth remarks that the later Lessing kept his Masonic wisdom to himself. Johannes Schneider, in "Lessings Stellung," 292, reports that some nineteenth-century scholars (e.g., Schwarz, Stahr, Hebler) argued that Lessing used the term "Revelation" only exoterically for the esoteric reference to "Reason." So, too, F. Loofs, in *Lessings Stellung zum Christentum* (Halle, 1910) argues that Lessing used the term to indicate the esoteric religion of nature. While Allison, in *Lessing and the Enlightenment*, 195n12, does not find the exoteric-esoteric distinction helpful, he concedes that Lessing's "positive" remarks about Revelation are to be understood "ironically."

31. Johannes Schneider, "Lessings Stellung," 295. At the same time Schneider insists that Lessing's sole dogma is to base himself on no dogmas.

32. H. Thielicke, "Vernunft und Existenz," 109–10: "Der Sturmwind der historischen Kritik."

33. Hans Urs von Balthasar, *Theodrama, Vol. 2: Dramatis Personae. Man in God*, trans. Graham Harrison (San Francisco: Ignatius Press, 1990), 421, associates Lessing and his Faust with modern Titanism. See his treatment of Lessing also throughout *Theodrama, Vol. 1: Prolegomena*, trans. Graham Harrison (San Francisco: Ignatius Press, 1988).

34. *Hauptmann von Blankenburgs Schreiben vom 14. Mai 1784 über Lessings verlorengegangenen Faust*, in *Werke*, ed. Petersen and Olshausen, vol. 10; and in *LWG*, 1.91b. For Lessing's *Faustfragment*, see *Werke*, vol. 10; and *LGW*, 1.90. See Johannes Schneider, "Lessings Stellung," 297.

might, therefore, call him a nostalgic Rationalist, but distanced from ordinary Rationalism by the unrealizable nature of the ideal. What holds the greater interest for Lessing *engagé*, however, is the imputed truth that the orthodox have reserved for themselves alone—and reserved under the name of God's right hand. So, while Faustian passion must trim its sails to circumstances, self-righteous orthodox possession must be attacked with every weapon at one's disposal. In sum, there can be no doubt that the spirit of criticism moved Lessing as much as any other single motive. He could not stand the status quo. So much, then, for the dynamic form that Lessing's personality and character gave to his thought. It is time to turn to the substance of that thought.

In trying to determine—if not to "fix"—Lessing's views on the important issue of the relation between seeking and finding, between reason and revelation, and between the left and the right hand of God, I have stressed that the protean and polemical quality of his thought poses a major problem. We are adjured to approach Lessing only through Lessing, but that is not easy.[35] Indeed, there are extrinsic cautions as well. The general direction of his thought is determinable in part by the weight put upon the posthumous writings, edited by his brother Karl, who tended to deemphasize the religious remnants and overemphasize the more rationalist pieces in Lessing's written remains. We know that many such manuscripts have not survived.[36]

So, too, Lessing's professed open-endedness gives a quicksilver fluidity to his thought that resists firm, clear determinations of his meaning. No single statement can be taken in isolation from others, nor from the occasion that called it forth and the context in which it has been elaborated. We might put the matter this way: the open never-ending search endorsed by Lessing must become the hermeneutic principle for Lessing interpretation. We must come to see how the open-endedness and the lack of possession themselves become the very herald of truth.

If no single statement can be taken in isolation from his works, it is equally true that his works cannot be taken out of the context in which he framed them. Perhaps it does not oversimplify too much for our present purpose to speak of the theological landscape, as Lessing saw it, in terms

---

35. "Whatever he held to be important must be important to us. What he left unfinished must remain unfinished" (Johannes Schneider, "Lessings Stellung," 294).

36. Chadwick, in *Lessing's Theological Writings*, 28–29, cautions against some of the posthumous writings in that they reflect a more straightforward Deism than Lessing's more subtle view. Johannes Schneider, in "Lessings Stellung," 301, praises the work of Georges Pons, *Lessing et le christianisme*, but warns against too much reliance upon the posthumous works.

of four prevalent positions with regard to reason and revelation. There was first of all the old traditional faith, at its best in the simple form of communities, such as the Moravians, who practiced the moral values of the faith more than they speculated about it.[37] On the far side from them were the Deists who attacked revealed Christianity and substituted a rationalistic religion of nature. This natural religion posited three purportedly demonstrable truths: that there is a Supreme Being; that the soul is immortal; and that rewards or penalties await each individual in an afterlife. In three words: God, immortality, and morality made up the matter of natural religion.

In between were certain orthodox Lutherans and the more recent movement of neology among some Lutheran theologians. The orthodox Lutherans with whom Lessing was in controversy, especially during the last decade of his life, put forward a defense of orthodox Christianity based upon the truth of revelation. Their defense was based upon the inerrancy of Scripture, the realization of the prophecies, the witness of the miracles, and the marvelous spread of Christianity. Neology, on the other hand, brought philosophical considerations into play in order to harmonize reason with revelation and to see both as complementary expressions of one another.

How did Lessing stand with regard to these four tendencies as he understood them? Although Lessing professed respect for a simple traditional faith, he did so on somewhat ambivalent grounds. On the one hand, as just mentioned, he admired the practical results that could be drawn from a simple faith, providing it shed itself of any intellectual pretention. His full evaluation is not so straightforward, however, and his respect had curious limits. Thus, he suggests that the old faith is filled with such absurdities that it will easily fall before the more credible standards of modern thought. In a letter to his brother Karl,[38] he writes candidly:

I only prefer the old orthodoxy (at bottom, tolerant) to the new (at bottom, intolerant) because the former is in manifest conflict with human reason, whereas the latter [neology] might easily take one in. I make agreement with my obvious enemies [the orthodox who were mistakenly taken in by his *Berengarius* book] in order to be able to be the better on my guard against my secret adversaries [the neologists and assorted theologians].

And on May 25th of the same year, he writes a somewhat playful letter,

---

37. In Lessing's view all religion was to be evaluated in terms of its influence upon conduct.
38. March 20, 1777; in *LGW*, 2.415; English translation in Chadwick, *Lessings's Theological Writings*, 13.

ending with the observation that "if the world must be kept going with untruths, then the old ones which are already practicable are just as good as the new ones."[39]

As to the Deists, it is certainly possible to find in Lessing's writings evidence that supports the view that, when all is said and done, Lessing was a Deist and a Rationalist. More recent scholarship tends to reject the view that Lessing is an out-and-out Deist of the garden variety, if such there be; at most he might be called a Deist with a difference, though even that is contestable.[40] Under a somewhat broader category, others have held him to be a Rationalist who has abandoned the notion of revelation.[41]

As to the Lutheran middle ground, Lessing saved his most contemptuous attacks for the neologists who, he was convinced, demeaned reason and poisoned faith by mixing reason and revelation into an unholy stew. They are much too little into theology, and not yet long enough into philosophy.[42] He complains that "[f]aith has become reason, strengthened by miracles and testimony, and reason has become an argumentative faith. The entire revealed religion is nothing but a renewed sanction of

---

39. The German is *gangbar* with the sense "They'll do!"; see *LGW*, 2.417A; English translation in Chadwick, *Lessing's Theological Writings*, 14.

40. While Paul Hazard, in *La Pensée européenne au XVIIIéme siècle de Montesquieu à Lessing* (Paris: A. Fayard, 1946), vol. 2, finds Lessing to be a Deist, he notices the respect that Lessing shows for positive religion, a respect quite absent from Voltaire. Lessing remarks of the latter: "the odious [*abscheulich*] Voltaire [and] his scurrilous scratchings [*Auszüge*]" (from *Anti-Goeze* 6, in *LGW*, 2.319A). Johannes Schneider, in "Lessings Stellung," 292, reports K. Borinski, in *Lessing* (Berlin: Hoffman, 1900), as holding that Lessing opposed the church's "hide and seek," while Paul Wernle, in *Lessing und das Christentum* (Tübingen: Mohr, 1912), complains of Lessing's unheroic and ambiguous position and accuses *him* of playing "hide and seek."

41. F. Loofs, in *Christentum*, argued that Lessing could dispense with the need for a supernatural revelation and still appreciate its positive value. As already indicated, the older research often took Lessing to be an "enlightened" non-Christian. Guthke and Schneider, in *Lessing*, 67, list as holding some variant of this view: Schrempf, Loofs, Fittbogen, Haug, Aner, v. Wiese, and Barth, and more recently Gonzenbach, E. Hirsch, H. Chadwick, von Arx, and various Marxists. They also signal Dilthey's famous Lessing essay (1867), in which Lessing is said to have originated a new *Lebensideal:* "the lived experience of the moral self-certainty of the German bourgeois in the time of the enlightenment and of Absolutism" (62–64). Benno von Wiese (1931) characterized the logic of Lessing's artistic and spiritual development as the gradual progression from the fetters of a received heteronomous religious and social order to the enlightened moral subjectivism of late German classicism (65). Still others point him toward German Idealism.

42. In *Werke*, ed. Rilla, 9.577; cited by Durzak, in *Poesie*, 113: "Ich verdachte ... unsere neumodischen Geistlichen noch mehr, die Theologen viel zu wenig, und Philosophen lange nicht genug sind." The opposition between them and the orthodox is the opposition of *Mistjauche* thrown against *unreiness Wasser*. Allison alludes to Lessing's defense of Leibniz' sincerity: "He believed! If only I still knew what is meant by this word" (ed. Rilla, 7.532).

the religion of reason."[43] And in a subtle mixture of qualified respect and confidential cynicism, he writes to Karl:[44]

> With orthodoxy, thank God, there was a tolerably clear understanding. A curtain had been drawn between it and philosophy, behind which each could go its own way without interfering with the other. But what is happening now? This curtain is being torn down, and under the pretext of making us reasonable Christians we are turned into extremely unreasonable philosophers. I beseech you, dear brother, look rather less at what our modern theologians discard than at what they want to put in its place. We are one in our conviction that our old religious system is false. But I cannot say with you that it is a patchwork of bunglers and half-philosophers. I know of nothing in the world upon the study of which human intelligence has been more acutely shown and exercised. What really is a patchwork of bunglers and half-philosophers is the religious system which they now want to put in place of the old; and with far more influence upon reason and philosophy than the old arrogated to itself.

His most relentless attack, however, was directed against those orthodox Lutheran theologians—Orthodoxists, he calls them—who upheld the inerrancy of Scripture. "Oh, thou, Luther!—Great, misunderstood man! . . . You have saved us from the yoke of tradition, who will save us from the unbearable yoke of the letter?"[45] And again he writes: "The true Lutheran does not wish to be defended by Luther's writings, but by his spirit."[46] Barth saw Lessing's rationalism broadened and deepened in the direction of an autonomous self-subsisting existential consciousness, but acknowledged that one could draw from him the first clear herald of a program of Protestant modernism, not based upon Lutheran faith in revelation, but on the principle of the historical development of the human spirit.[47]

---

43. Lessing's counterposition to Reimarus's first Fragment; in LGW 2.260; English translation in Allison, *Lessing and the Enlightenment*, 93–94; also in Chadwick, *Lessing's Theological Writings*, 19.

44. February 2, 1774; in *LGW* 2.408b–409a; English translation in Chadwick, *Lessing's Theological Writings*, 13.

45. *Eine Parabel;* in *LGW* 2.296b, and in *Werke*, ed. Rilla, 8.160; cited by Durzak, in *Poesie*, 110; also by Allison, in *Lessing and the Enlightenment*, 111–13. Notice the distinction between tradition and a new sense of historical development.

46. *Anti-Goeze* 1; in *LGW* 2.308b. Chadwick, in *Lessing's Theological Writings*, 23, suggests that "with this claim Lessing imported into German Protestantism and many history books the legend that the fundamental principle of the Reformation was the right to exercise unrestricted private judgment. The legend was not entirely his invention." But insofar as it was influential, it contributed to the view that theology was "a collection of interesting opinions which the individual happens to hold because he thinks them probable rather than because he receives them on any supernatural authority" (24).

47. *Die protestantische Theologie im 19. Jahrhundert. Ihre Vorgeschichte und ihre Geschichte* (Zürich, 1947). W. Nigg, in *Das Buch der Ketzer* (Zürich, 1949), sees Lessing as deeply religious but unorthodox, and yet the founder of neo-Protestantism. G. Fittbogen, in *Die Religion Lessings* (Leipzig, 1923), and K. Aner, in *Die Theologie der Lessingzeit* (Halle, 1929), make similar claims, stressing the rationalism inherent in Lessing. (Also see Johannes Schneider,

Recent scholarship, however, has tended to view Lessing's relation to Lutheran Christianity with more sympathy. Otto Mann[48] argues that Lessing can be considered an orthodox Lutheran, providing that we set aside all dogmatic considerations and consider him from an existential point of view as an "apprehending subject, not a comprehended subject." I must confess that that is quite a proviso! Helmut Thielicke, however, has given a much more nuanced reinterpretation of Lessing from this new viewpoint.[49] The issue, of course, is not a new interpretation, but whether that newness can be found in Lessing.

Zscharnak thought it an exaggeration to suppose that Lessing could bring anything new to the "enlightened" theologians of his time.[50] Perhaps, then, we might look elsewhere than at positions and arguments, if we are to discover anything new, and precisely, concerning the relation of reason and revelation, of transcendence and immanence. Durzak warns us that Lessing was not satisfied with the positivistic priority of revelation over reason (defended by the old Lutheran orthodoxy), nor was he satisfied with the simple priority of reason over revelation (defended by Deism, Rationalism, and Neology).[51] Instead, Durzak argues, Lessing goes beyond these dichotomies and dualisms by relativizing revelation.[52] There is something to be said for this interpretation. You will recall that Lessing had indeed proposed—in the *Axiomata* and elsewhere—that revelation came on the scene earlier than Scripture,[53] that we ought to read

---

"Lessings Stellung," 289–93.) Suffice it to say that there has been more interest recently in finding some sense of religiosity in Lessing. Thus, H. Leisegang, in *Lessings Weltanschauung* (Leipzig, 1931), sees Lessing moving in an unsystematic way toward a mystical, personalistic monism. Cf. Johannes Schneider, "Lessings Stellung," 293; Guthke and Schneider, *Lessing*, 67.

48. *Lessing. Sein und Leistung* (Hamburg, 1948); cited by Johannes Schneider, "Lessings Stellung," 287.

49. "Vernunft und Existenz bei Lessing. Das Unbedingte in der Geschichte," in *Lessing und die Zeit der Aufklärung* (Göttingen: Vandenhoeck & Ruprecht, 1968).

50. L. Zscharnak, "Einleitung zu Lessings theologischen Schriften," in *Lessings Werke*, ed. Petersen and Olshausen, vol. 20 (cited by Johannes Schneider, "Lessings Stellung," 292). Chadwick, in *Lessing's Theological Writings*, 32, observes that "the actual arguments are commonplaces, and say little that was not said, perhaps more tediously, by others before him. Locke, for example...."

51. Durzak, *Poesie*, 116ff. Durzak along with others uses the terms "*Irrationalität*" and "*Rationalität*" to contrast transcendent, inspired revelation and the rational religion of nature (109).

52. Durzak, *Poesie*, 118ff. It should be noted that Durzak places a very considerable weight upon the fable of the rings in *Nathan the Wise*, in which the minimalist view of the positive religions is endorsed, and upon *The Education of the Human Race*, in which the educative role of positive religion is underscored.

53. Thus, for example: "In short, the letter is not the spirit, and the Bible is not religion.... And then too there was religion before there was a Bible" (Introduction to the "Counterpositions," in *LGW* 2.259b; English translation in Chardwick, *Lessing's Theological Writings*, 18).

the Bible as we would read Livy or any other historical book,[54] that the Bible is not the sole basis for religious faith because the Bible is not equivalent to religion, nor is "inner" religion equivalent to the historical reports of the Evangelists. The reputed contradictions of the latter leave Lessing untouched, because as he writes many times: "The letter is not the spirit."

But if revelation is relativized, to what is it related? Citing Eichholz,[55] Durzak sums up the relativity of revelation: it precedes reason, but in reflecting back upon it, reason recognizes in revelation its own *not-yet*. This clearly has a basis in Lessing's last great work, *The Education of the Human Race*, in which Lessing recognized the rational value of positive religion, specifically the value of the OT and the NT. The two Testaments have served as provisional "elementary books" toward the education, refinement, and development of the human race. Revelation thus is the means by which the human race has been brought step by step toward its own maturity and autonomy. To be sure, revelation does not in actuality burst into its horizon from without; it only seems to primitive and naive peoples to do so. Rather, what revelation is in truth can be discerned only by the gradual recognition on the part of the human reason of what constitutes the forward movement and self-development of humanity. Revelation, then, is to be understood relative to its educative role.[56]

Whatever the value of this relativization of revelation, there is no doubt of its influence. It permitted Lessing to situate a major category of positive religion within the process of the history and development of mankind. It located revelation within the struggle for humanization. Religion, once it

---

54. In the *Vindication of the Inept Religious*: "Read the Bible just as you read Livy." See also the posthumous publication *The New Hypothesis Concerning the Evangelists Regarded as Merely Human Historians* (1777–78); English translation in Chadwick, *Lessing's Theological Writings*, 65–81.

55. "Die Geschichte als theologisches Problem bei Lessing," in *Theologische Studien und Kritiken* 107 (1936); Durzak, *Poesie*, 129.

56. *The Education of the Human Race* (Chadwick, *Lessing's Theological Writings*, 82ff.): "1. What education is to the individual man, revelation is to the whole human race. 2. Education is revelation coming to the individual man; and revelation is education which has come, and is still coming, to the human race. 3. . . . in theology it may unquestionably be of great advantage, and may remove many difficulties, if revelation be conceived of as an education of the human race. . . . [It is curious, however, that Lessing insists that revelation has brought about changes more quickly than any other means; but he leaves this anomaly unexplained.] 4. Education gives man nothing which he could not also get from within himself; it gives him that which he could get from within himself, only quicker and more easily. In the same way too, revelation gives nothing to the human race which human reason could not arrive at on its own; only it has given, and still gives to it, the most important of these things sooner." Kierkegaard, of course, has quite another "explanation": Christianity is what never was in any man's head; it is absolutely transcendent. Durzak, in *Poesie*, 138–39, argues that even reason is relativized, since reason is not central but is itself subordinate to natural religion, the inner truth that contributes to human development.

was trimmed of its more positivist aspects,[57] could become part of the story of mankind. This was immensely attractive to many. What is more, Lessing wrote his own "gospel." Having set out the impossibility of accepting the fulfillment of prophecies and the performance of miracles that he had not personally observed, had not directly and immediately witnessed, but that were proffered to him on the grounds of others' reports,[58] Lessing wrote his own "apocryphal" *Testament of John* in order to express the new basis for a humanistic reconciliation. It dispenses with the dogmas of Christianity and reduces everything that is essential for a Christian life to the maxim "Little children, love one another." The attractive combination of revelation (understood as instrumental in the development of mankind) and the principle of love (as the essential requirement for humanization) was to move many at the turn of the century from the more passive and external adoption of civil tolerance toward a more internal sense of fraternal love as the essence of modern *humanitas*.[59]

Lessing often stresses the need for "inner truth," which can arise in us without external cause. What Jesus taught is not true because he taught it, but rather he taught it because it is true; but it is a truth accessible from within our rational selves. And Jesus is to be trusted not on account of his own authority, but because he taught the true essentials of a rational religion: *immortality* (which is the basis for the endless character of the search for truth); *purity of heart* (rooted in inwardness), and the primacy of *love* (which crowns the higher morality rooted in the enlightened human subject as distinct from the morality of external rewards and punishments).[60]

There is no doubt, too, that Lessing was enough of an *Aufklärer* to

---

57. In a letter to Mendelssohn (January 9, 1777) he wrote: "I might have thrown away a little too much, which I shall have to retrieve. It is only the fear of dragging all the rubbish back into my house which has so far hindered me from doing this. It is infinitely difficult to know when and where one should stop, and for the vast majority of men the object of their reflection lies at the point at which they become tired of reflecting" (cited by Allison, in *Lessing and the Enlightenment*, 81–82).

58. On the impossibility of accepting historical reports, see *On the Proof of the Spirit and the Power* (in Chadwick, *Lessing's Theological Writings*, 51–56): "Miracles, which I see with my own eyes, and which I have the opportunity to verify for myself, are one thing; miracles, of which I know only from history that others say they have seen them and verified them, are another. ... The problem is that this proof of the spirit and of power no longer has any spirit or power, but has sunk to the level of human testimonies of spirit and power. ..." A concept of truth as immediacy is operative there. Then: "I conclude, and my wish is: May all who are divided by the Gospel of John be reunited by the Testament of John. Admittedly it is apocryphal, this testament. [It was written by Lessing, of course.] But it is not on that account any the less divine." There follows the *Testament of John* (in Chadwick, *Lessing's Theological Writings*, 57–61). For even more radical statements, see the last four selections in Chadwick.

59. In the following century, thinkers as diverse as Ludwig Feuerbach and Auguste Comte promoted their own version of human love as the highest value and as central to human development.

60. Cf. Durzak, *Poesie*, 130.

make autonomy a primary value, and that he balked at outside authority, which he took to be a kind of heteronomy. He writes: "I judge no one, in order to be judged by no one."[61] And yet Lessing did not seek idiosyncracy: he sought a kind of truth. Indeed, universality for Lessing is purchased by freedom from the contingency of history. For he seeks the kind of universal significance that holds good for rational self-development, and not the kind of generalization that is drawn from historical or empirically objective data. Thielicke makes much of Lessing's search for that kind of certitude upon which he could found the hoped-for happiness essential to his being. Lessing sought to find it, we are told, not in the ordination of his rational subjectivity to truth in the form of objective dogmas, but rather in the orientation of his existential subjectivity toward the objectively uncertain, inwardly passionate search for the truth; not in the quest for dogmatic certitude, but in the search for personal truth.

It can be said, then, that Lessing is in the process of transforming the very notion of truth into whatever is significant in the development of one's own selfhood: it is the transformation from an objectively dogmatic to a subjectively effective notion of truth. But it also seems to me that we must not press Lessing too far in the direction of Kierkegaard.[62] Nevertheless, the bulk of Thielicke's argument is a profound probing of the nature of Lessing's "inner truth." There can be no doubt that, just as Lessing has opened up a path for "enlightened humanism," so too has he played a part in carrying forward in fresh ways—largely through the polemic with established theology—the long modern journey of the human mind within itself. That modern interior journey is not to be identified without qualification with the even longer journey of the Christian spirit.[63] Lessing's journey continued the journey of self-criticism begun by Descartes and directed toward rational self-enlightenment. It is the journey of self-understanding and self-development, and it is meant to

---

61. *Eine Duplik;* in *LGW* 2.270b. Also: "Damn not, so that you too will not be damned" (in *Anti-Goeze* 1; *LGW* 2.308b). Thielicke, in "Vernunft und Existenz," 103, generalizes: "What I here call 'Existenz' is with Lessing thoroughly determined by the fact that I am the bearer of the Logos. Over against this is history, the heteronomous and irrational Outer, which threatens the Logos-structure of my essential being." On universality, see 103.

62. Thielicke, "Vernunft und Existenz," 111–12, recognizes, of course, the ultimate difference between the two thinkers. At any rate, it seems safe to say that the "person" who is the hoped-for goal of Kierkegaard's objectively uncertain, passionately inward "becoming" is Christ, whereas Lessing is less definite and seems rather to seek his own self-development, along with that of the race.

63. The interior journey of a St. Augustine or a St. Bernard involves prayer and the desire to have the soul lifted up before God; the methodical inward journey of Descartes, on the other hand, is intended to reach safe harbor in the *ego cogito* as the foundation of human certitude. I have drawn the distinction in "The Geography of the Person," *Communio* 13, no. 1 (Spring 1986): 38–39.

hold not just for Lessing but for all others who reach out for modern Enlightenment. And so Thielicke is right in holding that for Lessing truth is a kind of inward process that moves the inner self along the path toward a greater realization of the self's own power.

Lessing's inner self stood in constant interplay with the outer world of history and society. It is necessary to keep the inner direction of Lessing in tension with that outer world. The universality he sought was not merely the negative freedom from the contingency of history and the externality of social life. For Lessing, the inner remained bound in antithetic fashion to the outer. Universality had at the very least the significance that the reflective discovery of human reason and the educative instrumentality of revelation held for the humanization of others as well as himself. No doubt, the inward had dominance over the outward, but not—it seems to me—in quite the sense in which we nowadays speak of "existential subjectivity." It is not "*Existenz*" but "historical development" that is the central concern of Lessing's endless search. Lessing may have been on the way toward existential subjectivity, but he was a thinker of his own century and he was moved by its currents. That century's canon of objective truth is not put quite so far out of play as the concepts of "existential subjectivity" and *Existenz* might suggest.

The older scholarship was not entirely wrong in tracing the influence of Leibniz upon Lessing. There are many aspects in his thought that are the result of the transformation of Leibnizian ideas: the capacity of discovery from within recalls the monad; the trust in God is less a deeply "existential" religious faith than it is a rational conviction of the fitness of things that recalls the preestablished harmony; the overriding Leibnizian distinction between contingent truths of fact and necessary truths of reason provides the logical basis for Lessing's depreciation of historical Christianity; the notion of the continuity of development from within is not wholly unlike the career of the monad's appetition and perceptions; Leibniz's cosmopolitan rationalism that sought to find room for apparently incompatible aspects is not unlike Lessing's attempt to accommodate positive religion; and finally, the ideal of truth as immediate and clear presence with consequent certitude still hovers as an unattainable yet not absent norm over Lessing's search.[64]

I will conclude with two summary remarks. I find Lessing to be a self held by the tension of four coordinates in the matrix of his somewhat

---

64. Cf. Allison, *Lessing and the Enlightenment*, 4. Allison may well have overstated Lessing's dependence upon Leibniz and Wolff, or rather understated other influences, but the influence is undoubtedly there.

unsystematic yet persistent search. Imagine a four-pointed cross. At the top is Reason, and directly below it is Revelation; on the right is the Outer World of nature, society, and history, and on the left is the Inner World of self. But the coordinates are not static; they vibrate with their interplay. Now one, now another moves toward the center, while others resist. This is the first remark, and the second is like unto it.

For, by patient watching we can discern a movement of the whole cross toward the upper and the left coordinates: toward the rationalization and the interiorization of human life. The whole cross is in movement toward the upper left. Only one part of the dynamism consists in the interplay among the four coordinates; but the overriding source of dynamism is provided by the movement of the whole cross; for this total movement betrays the primary energy of the unending search. For with Lessing *the movement itself possesses the supreme value.* It is this primacy of movement that joins Lessing at once to his modern past and to the future he will not live to see. It is this continual movement of the whole that stamps Lessing as thinking within the context of modern liberalism in its classical sense.

Lessing's century and the century preceding him saw the great debate over the primacy of motion.[65] It was fiercely debated whether natural motion needed an extrinsic, transcendent cause. Some metaphysicians thought so, while others did not; but natural science went on its way filling out the understanding of nature according to the measure of motion and its autonomous intelligibility. The technology that was developed from the scientifically determined laws of nature merely confirmed the rightness of a scientific enquiry whose gold standard and currency was that of motion as such. For the modern sciences of nature were not the same as the older philosophy of nature. The latter was the study of mobile being, whereas the new sciences were a study of motion qua motion.

The rapid and remarkable successes of the sciences of nature had overflowed into social thought as well.[66] Or perhaps it is better to say that the complete process of modernization is borne up by both the idea and the experience of the primary value of motion: its consideration as absolute in all areas of reality and human life. For the primacy of motion did not remain in the natural order alone, either in actuality or in thought. Social and political thought in the seventeenth century is dominated by

---

65. See Michael Buckley, *At the Origins of Modern Atheism* (New Haven, Conn.: Yale University Press, 1987).

66. See my "Is Liberalism Good Enough?" in *Liberalism and the Good*, ed. R. Bruce Douglass et al. (New York: Routledge, 1990), 86–104. The radical character of classical liberalism is not the power to choose, but "the power to unchoose," to invalidate past choices. It is this that accounts for the high value put upon novelty, change for the sake of change.

the notion of *conatus*, according to which human affairs were determined by an active force of the will, whether free or not. And so it was inevitable that history as the (moral) story of human agency should come to be reinterpreted in accordance with the primacy of motion. Deeds became events, actions became facts, and the historical order gave way to the primacy of motion.

The principle of historical development spread quickly, and by the end of the eighteenth century it was quite generally acknowledged that everything had a history. The primacy of the principle of historical development gave rise to the earth sciences, to paleontology, eventually to the historical study of biology, culture, art, politics, and even religion itself. The eternal was submitted to the temporal—and in some authors the historical account was accepted as the more adequate explanation. With the general turn to history, the primacy of motion began to take on a specific character: objectively, it was the notion of the development of the human race, and subjectively, it was signaled by Lessing's search for the truth of self-development and self-identity. It is paradoxical that Lessing should have played such a role in the furthering of the historical principle, given his frequent strictures against the reliability of merely probable historical reports. It is true that Lessing all but discounted the rationalist view of history as a set of merely probable contingent propositions, and treated them as the husk that covered the rational kernel of truth. But what he endorsed was not the objectivist rationalistic view of historical probability, but the principle of development in history. This transformation in the meaning of development and history accords neither with the older more static rationalism of his immediate past (say, with Leibniz), nor with the newer existential subjectivity of the immediate future (say, with Kierkegaard), but is, rather, the pervasive principle of historical development applied to the human self and to the role that religion is reputed to have played in that self-development and in the development of the race. It is this legacy that Lessing has left to his heirs and to those also who stand partly in the mixed light and shadow he has cast.

11 Kant and the Mythic Roots of Morality[1]

JOHN R. SILBER

The transcendence on which great philosophy depends, that ability to write and think, as Spinoza said, *sub specie aeternitatis*, can never be fully attained. Indeed, the finest philosopher may be the one who, rather than withdrawing from the movements of his times, includes all of them in his intellectual grasp and assigns to each its proper weight and influence.

Immanuel Kant was such a philosopher: revolutionary thinker in the age of revolution, quintessential child of the eighteenth century. He caught the spirit of the Enlightenment in writing "*Sapere aude!* 'Have courage to use your *own* reason!'—that is the motto of enlightenment,"[2]

---

1. This essay is a lightly revised version of "Kant and the Mythic Roots of Morality," which first appeared in *Dialecta* 35 (1981): 167–93.
2. Immanuel Kant, *Was ist Aufklärung* KGS 8, 35; Beck 286. In this essay, I have abbreviated the titles of the works cited as shown below. I have usually cited both the German text and an English translation.

KGS	*Kant's Gesammelte Schriften* (Königlich Preussische Akademie der Wissenschaften).
Gr	*Grundlegung zur Metaphysik der Sitten* (KGS 4).
Paton	*The Moral Law, or Kant's Groundwork of the Metaphysic of Morals*, trans. H. J. Paton (London, 1948).
KdrV	*Kritik der reinen Vernunft* (KGS 3).
Smith	*A Translation of Kant's Critique of Pure Reason*, trans. N. Kemp Smith (London, 1929).
KdpV	*Kritik der praktischen Vernunft* (KGS 5).
Beck	*Critique of Practical Reason and Other Writings in Moral Philosophy*, trans. L. W. Beck (Chicago, 1949).
Rel	*Die Religion innerhalb der Grenzen der blossen Vernunft* (KGS 6).
Greene	*Religion within the Limits of Reason Alone*, trans. T. M. Greene and H. H. Hudson (New York, 1960).
Abbott	*Kant's Critique of Practical Reason and Other Works on the Theory of Ethics*, trans. T. K. Abbott (London, 1948).
A	*Anthropologie in pragmatischer Hinsicht* (KGS 7).
Gregor	*Anthropology from a Pragmatic Point of View*, trans. Mary J. Gregor (The Hague, 1974).
TuP	*Über den Gemeinspruch: Das mag in der Theorie richtig sein, taugt aber nicht für die Praxis* (KGS 8).
TaP	*On the Old Saw: That May Be Right in Theory But It Won't Work in Practice*, trans. E. B. Ashton (Philadelphia, 1974).

and in Kant we find most of the complex and often conflicting movements that gave the eighteenth century its distinctive character, held in a balance of extraordinary coherence.

A pietism that emphasized moral practice over abstract theology—a religious tradition that asserted the still powerful influence of the Christian Weltanschauung—was dominant in Kant's home and in his early schooling. Reflecting the intellectual balance of the eighteenth century, the influence of this powerful motivational force was checked in Kant by the rising influence of a new Weltanschauung based on Newtonian science, to which Kant was himself a significant contributor. Kant believed that "the heavens declare the glory of God," but those "starry heavens above" continued to fill Kant's mind "with ever new and increasing admiration and awe" not through revealed mystery but through Newton's revelation of a God of reason who had created a natural order devoid of mystery and miracle that was comprehensible through man's reason. As Pope had written:

> Nature and Nature's laws lay hid in night:
> God said, *Let Newton be!* And all was light.

THE BALANCE OF WORLD VIEWS IN THE ENLIGHTENMENT

The most significant intellectual work of the eighteenth century involved the assimilation of the Christian and Newtonian worldviews into some coherent or at least plausible synthesis.

But the Enlightenment is not to be understood simply as an age of reason, any more than the seventeenth century, dominated though it was by Descartes. As Carl Becker correctly observed, the thirteenth century, the century of Dante and Saint Thomas, could with equal or greater plausibility be called the Age of Reason. Any true Age of Faith, which at its

---

KdU *Kritik der Urteilskraft* (KGS 5).
EEin *KdU, Erste Einleitung* (KGS 20).
Haden *First Introduction to the Critique of Judgment*, trans. James Haden (New York, 1965).
CoaJ *Kant's Critique of Aesthetic Judgment*, trans. J. C. Meredith (Oxford, 1911).
CotJ *Kant's Critique of Teleological Judgment*, trans. J. C. Meredith (Oxford, 1928).
MdS *Die Metaphysik der Sitten* (KGS 6).
MoM *The Doctrine of Virtue, Part 11 of the Metaphysic of Morals*, trans. Mary J. Gregor (Philadelphia, 1971).
VüE *Eine Vorlesung Kants über Ethik*, ed. Paul Menzer (Berlin, 1924).
LoE *Lectures on Ethics*, trans. Louis Infield (London, 1930).
Päd *Über die Pädogogik* (KGS 9).
Ed *Education* (Ann Arbor, 1960).
Streit *Streit der Fakultäten* (KGS 7).
Hist. *On History*, ed. L. W. Beck (Indianapolis, 1963).

core is instinctual, had reached and long passed its climax by the thirteenth century. In a true age of faith, questions do not arise, for there is no basis for doubt. In an age of faith the religious Weltanschauung appears factual and mundane: the faithful would no more wonder about the existence of God or ask for proof of his existence than middle-class Victorian children would wonder if their parents were married and ask to see their marriage license.[3] And if in such an age an imponderable question should arise, all doubt would be dispelled with Tertullian's response, *credo quia absurdum.* In an age of faith we believe what has been told us by our fathers and by their fathers before them. The character of such an age is expressed by the chorus in Euripides's *Bacchae:*

> Beyond the old beliefs,
> no thought, no act shall go. Small, small is the cost,
> to believe in this:
> whatever is god is strong; whatever long time has sanctioned, that is a law
>   forever;
> the law tradition makes is the law of nature.[4]

By this criterion, the thirteenth century could hardly be described as the Age of Faith; it was rather an age of increasing doubt in which justification by reason became increasingly important to the preservation of faith and faith became increasingly dependent upon justification by reason. As Becker writes:

> Thus it was possible for the 13th century, employing a highly intricate dialectic supported on occasion by a symbolic interpretation, to justify the ways of God to man. Paradise lost and paradise regained—such was the theme of the drama of existence as understood in that age; and all the best minds of the time were devoted to its explication. Theology related and expounded the history of the world. Philosophy was the science that rationalized and reconciled nature and history. Logic provided both theology and philosophy with an adequate methodology.[5]

In an age of reason, like the thirteenth century and the two following centuries, reason was sufficiently effective in service to the tradition of faith, the Christian worldview, that reason was able to check the doubts of the most penetrating critics of the mythic tradition.

But in the seventeenth century, the scientific method, that mixture of rationalism and empiricism, that melting of Baconian observation of nature and Cartesian clarity of mathematical thought, triumphed in New-

---

3. Such an age of faith might more aptly be called an age of credulity.
4. Euripides, *The Bacchae,* ll. 891–99, trans. William Arrowsmith (Chicago: University of Chicago Press, 1959), 194.
5. Carl Becker, *The Heavenly City of the Eighteenth-Century Philosophers* (New Haven, Conn.: Yale University Press, 1932), 10.

ton's *Principia*. The implications of the Newtonian synthesis were so profound that they struck at and loosened the roots of the Christian Weltanschauung itself. From the point of view of traditional Christian theology, reason, which in the thirteenth century had been a faithful handmaiden, had become first a rebellious servant and finally a dangerous usurper.

The new world view was given the name of Newtonianism because, as Becker sums up,

> Newton, more than any other man had banished mystery from the world by discovering a "universal law of nature," thus demonstrating, what others had only asserted, that the universe was rational and intelligible through and through, and capable, therefore, of being subdued to the uses of men.[6]

Newton, a lifelong believer in traditional Christianity, said: "I do not know what I appear to the world, but to myself I seem to have been only a boy playing on the seashore, and diverting myself and now and then finding a smoother pebble or prettier shell than ordinary, whilst the great ocean of Truth lay all undiscovered before me."[7] But Newton's younger contemporary, Alexander Pope, offered in the *Dunciad* a dramatic assessment of the unintended impact that Newton had had on the intellectual life of his age:

> See skulking Truth to her old cavern fled,
> Mountains of Casuistry heap'd o'er her head!
> Philosophy, that lean'd on Heav'n before,
> Shrinks to her second cause, and is no more.
> Physic of Metaphysic begs defense,
> And Metaphysic calls for aid on Sense!
> See Mystery to Mathematics fly!
> In vain! They gaze, turn giddy, rave and die.
> *Religion blushing veils her sacred fires*
> *And unawares morality expires.*[8]

The scientific Weltanschauung only began in the early seventeenth century to take form in the public mind. But everywhere in the eighteenth century, men and women who lacked the mathematical and scientific education to read Newton with understanding read of Newton's views in popular restatements. And even those who had never read on the subject spoke freely of it.

Intoxicated by the apparent simplicity, elegance, and power of the Newtonian synthesis, philosophers and intellectuals of the eighteenth

---

6. Ibid., 60.
7. Sir David Brewster, *Memoirs of the Life, Writings, and Discoveries of Sir Isaac Newton*, 2 vols. (Edinburgh: T. Constable, 1855), 2.407.
8. Alexander Pope, *The Dunciad* (1743), 4.641–50; italics mine.

century "renounced the authority of church and Bible, but exhibited a naive faith in the authority of nature and reason."[9] The Laws of God metamorphosed into the Laws of Nature, disclosed not by revelation but by reason and sense. In a world free from the miraculous lay the opportunity for human advancement and perfectibility.

Among the literate, the scientific worldview gradually displaced the Christian worldview as the dominant climate of opinion. Aristophanes' commentary on the collapse of Greek religion in the face of natural philosophy at the end of the fifth century B.C. was, as Becker remarked, equally descriptive of this transition from the medieval to the scientific worldview: "Whirl is king, having cast out Zeus."

Newtonianism held forth the promise of understanding and ultimate control of nature, but it placed in doubt the spiritual and moral foundations on which the meaning of human existence depends. The fear that Pope had expressed of the eclipse of religion and the expiration of morality was widely shared. The emergence of the scientific worldview revealed implications destructive to religion and morality that, in turn, gave rise to a new appreciation of the religious worldview and thereby, as in the thirteenth century but with perhaps greater urgency, pressed theological issues on the minds of the most advanced thinkers of the age.

As the century wore on, even the most skeptical—fearing the consequences of the new philosophy—restrained their skepticism. Those less skeptical offered religious interpretations of the new philosophy. In sense experience, for example, Bishop George Berkeley found the *divine* language of nature that could be read by thoughtful, rational men to reveal knowledge of the real world, which was also the world of God. A similar view was expressed by Hume, through the *persona* of Cleanthes, in his *Dialogues Concerning Natural Religion.* Cleanthes points out that the mind of man is congruous with the Author of Nature who has so arranged the grandeur of the universe that the mind of man can comprehend it. Natural law does not, thus, cease to be God's law; but the law is immanent in Nature rather than imposed upon it. As Newton put it, "These Principles I consider not as occult Qualities, supposed to result from the specific Forms of Things, but as general Laws of Nature, by which the Things themselves are form'd."[10]

But if nature was the expression of God, and moved in accordance with inexorable laws, then whatever evil exists in the world was the consequence of God's creation, the result of either his incompetence or his

---

9. Becker, *Heavenly City,* 30.
10. Sir William Dampier, *A History of Science and Its Relations with Philosophy and Religion,* 3d ed. (Cambridge: Cambridge University Press, 1942), 183–84.

indifference, if not of his malevolence. This dilemma posed by the new philosophy drove many to reconsider the relationship of reason and religion, the very question that had preoccupied the great Scholastic philosophers of the later Middle Ages. But now the apparent moral indifference of the universe, which seemed to many the inescapable consequence of the work of Newton and his followers, posed a terrible dilemma for thinkers who feared that Whirl might truly be king, and that by a cruel irony truth itself might overthrow virtue. Concerned about the effect that his *Dialogues* might have, Hume voluntarily withheld them from publication during his lifetime and he revised published work so that, as he said in 1737, "it shall give as little offense as possible."[11]

Diderot, like Hume, also wrote works he refused to publish. But unlike Hume he was personally distressed by his inability to find "any sufficient reason for virtuous conduct, his heart unable to renounce the conviction that nothing is better in this world than to be a good man."[12] Diderot could intellectually articulate, but could not ultimately believe, the moral indifference that appeared to follow from the Newtonian philosophy. Diderot was profoundly troubled by his inability to establish morality on a rational foundation, and was not content to attack the Christian faith and doctrine without offering something positive and superior to take its place. Diderot concluded, "It is not enough to know more than they [theologians] do; it is necessary to show them that we are better, and that *philosophy makes more good men than sufficient or efficacious grace*."[13] To put it another way, Diderot was troubled by his inability to incorporate what he regarded as the new truths discovered by Newton and others into a satisfactory and comprehensive synthesis that could do for his age what Thomism had done for the later Middle Ages.

Although Diderot devoted years of effort to the establishment of morality on rational foundations, he never wrote on the subject. He said, "I have not even dared to write the first line; I say to myself, if I do not come out of the attempt victorious, I become the apologist of wickedness; I will have betrayed the cause of virtue . . . I do not feel equal to this sublime work; I have uselessly consecrated my whole life to it."[14]

Diderot may have been unusual in honestly recognizing his inability to solve the problem he had framed, but he was right—and hardly alone—

11. J. H. Burton, *Life and Correspondence of David Hume*, 2 vols. (Edinburgh, 1846; reprint, New York: B. Franklin, 1967), 1.64; Becker, *Heavenly City*, 38.
12. Becker, *Heavenly City*, 80. Note the expression of Diderot's view in Kant's famous statement, "It is impossible to conceive anything at all in the world, or even out of it, which can be taken as good without qualification, except a *good will*" (Gr, 393; Paton, 61). This point is elaborated below.
13. Diderot, *Oeuvres* (1875–1877), 19.464; Becker, *Heavenly City*, 81.
14. Diderot, *Oeuvres*, 23.45; Becker, *Heavenly City*, 80.

in his diagnosis: the eighteenth century lacked a comprehensive and coherent worldview, and its construction was the central intellectual project of the age. As Becker rightly concludes, "[T]he underlying preconceptions of 18th-Century thought were still, allowance made for certain important alterations in the bias, essentially the same as those of the 13th Century . . . the *philosophes* demolished the heavenly city of St. Augustine only to rebuild it with more up-to-date material."[15]

While the philosophes welcomed Newtonianism, and while they sought through the use of reason to understand the laws of nature and thereby to gain control of it, they nevertheless recognized that an adequate natural philosophy must also provide guidance for the affairs of men and give meaning to human life. In the opinion of the most sensitive of the philosophes, one could not abandon the mythic roots of Christianity until the problem of evil had been dealt with and a rational foundation for morality had been provided. Diderot framed the problem: a "sufficient reason for just conduct" must be found.

KANT'S RESPONSE TO DIDEROT'S DILEMMA

Clearly, it is in this spirit that Kant wrote his first *Critique* and established the limits of knowledge "in order to make room for faith."[16] In particular, it was in this spirit that Kant sought not to discover or invent morality, but to complete that "sublime work" that Diderot found beyond his powers—that is, "to seek out and establish *the supreme principle of morality*"[17] and the principles and doctrines of religion on the basis of reason, and to ensure that the laws of practical reason have "access to the human mind and an influence on its maxims."[18]

Kant recognized, perhaps more clearly than Diderot, that there was no going back. No one, least of all Kant, could minimize the appeal of the new scientific Weltanschauung. As a contributor to the Newtonian philosophy, he recognized, like King Canute, that he could not hold back the tide, even though he was as concerned as Diderot to save morality and the essential tenets of the Christian religion. Christianity proclaimed a good news that could be understood by the most ordinary person. As Becker said,

No interpretation of the life of mankind ever more exactly reflected the experience or more effectively responded to the hopes of average men. . . . The importance of the Christian story was that it announced with authority (whether truly or not matters little) that the life of man has significance, a universal significance

---

15. Becker, *Heavenly City*, 31.
17. Gr, 392; Paton, 60.
16. KdrV, 5.Bxxx; Smith, 29.
18. KdpV, 5.151; Beck, 249.

transcending and including the temporal experience of the individual. This was the secret of its enduring strength, that it irradiated pessimism with hope: it liberated the mind of man from the cycles in which classical philosophy had enclosed it as in prison, and by transferring the golden age from the past to the future substituted an optimistic for a disillusioned view of human destiny.[19]

That Kant was concerned to preserve this good news for the average man through a rational interpretation of the Christian message is obvious, even from the most casual reading of Part 1, Book 2, and Part 2 of the *Critique of Practical Reason*. And though less obvious, this concern is still evident in his *Religion Within the Limits of Reason Alone*. Where the Christian religion reassured each individual, no matter how common, of his infinite worth as a child of God—the hairs of whose head were numbered and whose life counted more than those of sparrows, no one of which fell without God's knowledge—Kant enunciated the secular good news of the moral worth of the individual personality that was beyond all price.

Thus he began the *Groundwork of the Metaphysic of Morals* with these words: "It is impossible to conceive of anything at all in the world, or even out of it, which can be taken as good without qualification, except a *good will*." "A good will," he continued, "seems to constitute the indispensable condition of our very worthiness to be happy."[20] The human will is transcendentally free from determination by alien and antecedent influences (free, that is, according to Kant's negative definition of freedom) and also free in the positive sense of possessing the potentiality for freedom either in its fulfilled mode as autonomy or in its deficient mode as heteronomy. Because of its unconditioned and self-determining nature, the will possesses whatever moral qualities it might have (whether good or evil) without qualification. The moral law defines the conditions of personal fulfillment and those conditions are recognized as part of the given nature of any and every person. A being lacking either transcendental freedom or the potentiality of autonomy or heteronomy lacks the conditions essential to being a person, but one who has these characteristics is a self-determining cause and totally responsible for whatever he makes of himself in the process of exercising his freedom. Autonomy is achieved by acting in accordance with the moral law and for its sake, that is, by acting in accordance with the principle of universality that by virtue of its universality ensures the individual's transcendence of particular motives for action. The individual by his volition establishes a moral worth that becomes the basis for his right to happiness: "Man *himself* must make or have made himself into whatever, in a moral sense, whether

19. Becker, *Heavenly City*, 126, 128.
20. Gr, 393; Paton, 61.

good or evil, he is or is to become. Either condition must be an effect of his free choice; for otherwise he could not be held responsible for it and could therefore be morally neither good nor evil."[21]

Observing society and history without distortion, Kant recognized that there was nothing to guarantee distribution of happiness in this world on the basis of moral deserts. And consequently, Kant argued that consistent volition requires that the free moral individual should will that there be a God and personal immortality.[22] Thus, having established the supreme principle of morality, Kant used that principle in its full development to establish religion on the basis of reason alone.[23] Under this interpretation freedom of the moral agent is not undermined by the introduction of God and immortality. There are no independent theoretical proofs for their existence; there is only a moral proof that follows as a condition of consistent volition from the recognition of one's duty.[24]

Since every person is possessed of freedom, the achievement of a good will is within the potentiality of each person. To this extent, there is good news for every person. But there is no guarantee of happiness. A person of good will who has made a consistent effort to universalize the maxims of his acts, to put himself in the place and point of view of another, to treat humanity, whether himself or another, always as an end in itself and never as a means merely—that is, a person who has achieved "honesty, integrity, in the innermost depths of the self, both in relation to one's self and in actions towards others as the supreme maxim of one's life"—has established a worthiness to be happy. Such a person has established, Kant says, "the only proof in the consciousness of a man that he has character."[25] This is both the most and the least that can be demanded of a person. To do less than this is to fail morally; to do more is impossible.

In this context failure is not defined by the occurrence of specifically

---

21. Rel, 44; Greene, 40. The responsibility for the origin of evil is thus transferred from God to man. It is a possibility that is introduced by freedom and, though not logically or causally necessary, appears to be an ineluctable consequence of human volition.

22. KdpV, 5.143; Beck, 245.

23. For a fuller explication of these views, see John R. Silber, "The Metaphysical Importance of the Highest Good as the Canon of Pure Reason in Kant's Philosophy," *University of Texas Studies in Literature and Language* 1, no. 2 (1959), 240ff.; and John R. Silber, "The Importance of the Highest Good in Kant's Ethics," *Ethics* 73 (1963): 179–97.

24. KdpV, 5.129; Beck, 232.

25. A, 295; Gregor, 166. The English translation is my own, though I here cite Gregor's translation. The words "honesty," "sincerity," or "integrity," singly and alone, inadequately translate "*Wahrhaftigkeit.*" In this context, its meaning encompasses not only "honesty," but also "sincerity" (*Aufrichtigkeit*), "conscientiousness" (*Gewissenhaftigkeit*), and "integrity" (an English word for which there is no single German equivalent). "Integrity," however, which presupposes a consistent and dependable moral character through time—as contrasted with sincerity, an instant virtue—most adequately conveys the full meaning of "*Wahrhaftigkeit*" as used by Kant.

immoral acts but only by the loss of a genuinely moral disposition or that *Wahrhaftigkeit* in relation to one's self and in actions toward others as one's supreme rule of life. A person who has achieved an essentially good will by making reason practical in his life and by subordinating his sensible interests to the achievement of rational action has clearly demonstrated his commitment to a universe that is also rational. That is, he is committed by his acts and his consistent volition to a universe in which there is God and immortality. Having willed the ends, the morally good person likewise wills the means.

This does not prove theoretically the existence of God or the immortality of the soul, but it establishes God and immortality as part of a context of coherence and meaning in the life of the individual that becomes in itself, Kant believed, a powerful motive for moral conduct. If our dignity and self-respect as free moral persons is well established, says Kant, "so that a man fears nothing more than to find himself upon self-examination to be worthless and contemptible in his own eyes, every good moral disposition can be grafted on to this self-respect, for the consciousness of freedom is the best, indeed the only, guard that can keep ignoble and corrupting influences from bursting in upon the mind."[26]

Within this general framework Kant believed that he had brought about the synthesis of the Christian and the Newtonian worldviews and concluded the *Critique of Practical Reason* with those famous lines:

Two things fill the mind and with ever new and increasing admiration and awe, the oftener and more steadily they are reflected on: the starry heavens above me and the moral law within me. . . . The former begins from the place I occupy in the external world of sense, and it broadens the connection in which I stand into an unbounded magnitude of worlds beyond worlds . . . and into the limitless times of their periodic motion, their beginning and continuance. The latter begins from my invisible self, my personality, and exhibits me in a world which has true infinity but which is comprehensible only to the understanding—a world with which I recognize myself as existing in a universal and necessary . . . connection, and thereby also in connection with all those visible worlds. The former view of a countless multitude of worlds annihilates, as it were, my importance as an animal creature. . . . The latter, on the contrary, infinitely raises my worth as that of an intelligence by my personality, in which the moral law reveals a life independent of all animality and even of the whole world of sense—at least so far as it may be inferred from the purposive destination assigned to my existence by this law, a destination which is not restricted to the conditions and limits of this life but reaches into the infinite.[27]

Diderot asked for a sufficient reason for just conduct. He said it was necessary to demonstrate that philosophy makes more good men than

26. KdpV, 5.161; Beck, 258.
27. KdpV, 5.161–62; Beck, 258–59.

sufficient or efficacious grace. Kant's reply may be summarized as follows: If we reflect rationally on the presuppositions of our natures as persons, of our ability to function as responsible, accountable individuals, we become aware of our freedom and the law of its fulfillment. We recognize that through the fulfillment of our freedom in autonomy we establish our infinite worth, our ultimate significance, on the basis of which we can expect whatever significance and fulfillment the universe has to offer will in fact be ours.

In Prelude 4 of *Fear and Trembling*, Kierkegaard was later to observe, "When the child must be weaned, the mother has stronger food in readiness, lest the child should perish."[28] Was this the stronger food that Diderot had insisted upon before the Christian worldview could safely be swept away? Had Kant succeeded in procuring for the categorical imperative and moral law "admittance to the will of man and influence over practice?"[29] Could one say of Kant's moral philosophy not only that it was true in theory but that it also worked in practice? That is, had Kant provided a sufficient motivation for moral conduct?

Although Kant made a place for religion, it is not at all clear that his religion had effective motivational force. For Kant's religion is devoid of mythic roots: all its doctrines are subjected to rational, essentially secular interpretations. The synthesis of Christian and Newtonian thought was genuine enough for Kant, and the motivational force that derived from Kant's religious upbringing continued to exert its influence on Kant long after he had completed his process of demythologizing Christianity. Kant continued, throughout his life, to speak at times with religious fervor, as in the passage, quoted above "on the starry heavens above and the moral law within," or as in his moving apostrophes to Duty and Sincerity.[30]

Kant's religious fervor did not derive from his demythologized religion within the limits of reason alone. It came rather from the emotionally and mythically rich pietism of his parental home. Kant could hear

---

28. Kierkegaard, *Fear and Trembling*, trans. Walter Lowrie (Princeton, N.J.: Princeton University Press, 1969), 29.

29. Gr, 389; Paton, 57.

30. "O Sincerity! Thou Astraea, that hast fled from earth to heaven, how mayest thou (the basis of conscience and hence of all inner religion) be drawn down thence to us again?" (Rel, 190; Greene, 178); and "Duty! Thou sublime and mighty name that dost embrace nothing charming or insinuating but requirest submission and yet seekest not to move the will by threatening aught that would arose natural aversion or terror but only holdest forth a law which of itself finds entrance into the mind and yet gains reluctant reverence (though not always obedience)—a law before which all inclinations are dumb even though they secretly work against it: what origin is there worthy of thee, and where is to be found the root of thy noble descent which proudly rejects all kinship with the inclinations and from which to be descended is the indispensable condition of the only worth which men can give themselves?" (KdpV, 5.86; Beck, 193).

the voice of duty as if it were the voice of God because he had heard the voice of God issue the categorical imperative: "Be ye perfect, as your Father in heaven is perfect." The refined stem of Kant's rational ethics had been grafted onto the hardy emotional root of Christianity. What effect would the demythologized religion of reason alone, itself derivative from a rational theory of ethics, exert on individuals devoid of childhood nurture in the mythic religious tradition?

No one can question the success of Kant's philosophical horticulture. His grafting of a secular interpretation onto mythic Christianity was brilliant. Those reared in a mythic religious tradition have, generation after generation, developed from childhood to adulthood along essentially Kantian lines. As children they have spoken as children, articulating their moral obligation in essentially religious terms as commands of God, but on maturing, they have put away the myths of childhood and continued to do their duty as the requirement of practical reason and to reinterpret the religion of their childhood in a secular, demythologized form.

The theological movement of the nineteenth and twentieth centuries from Schweitzer to Bultmann and Tillich illustrates the feasibility of Kant's program. But we must also note the inability of demythologized branches of Christianity to reproduce themselves. The Unitarian Church and the Congregational Church in the United States, for example, have not been able to recruit sufficient numbers of ministers from their own congregations but have had to draw for their ministry on the mythically richer traditions of the Baptist, Methodist, Lutheran, and other evangelical traditions. In recent years, following the Second Vatican Council and steps toward the demythologizing of Catholicism, it has become increasingly difficult for the Catholic Church to recruit individuals for its religious orders and for the parish priesthood. Whitehead, in *The Adventures of Ideas*, pointed out that the platonic idea of *psyche* had been without widespread influence until it was given motivational force through the Christian idea of soul. Had not Kant perhaps reduced the Christian idea of soul to an equally abstract and motivationally inert concept of personality?

This is the position taken by Reinhold Niebuhr. In *An Interpretation of Christian Ethics*, he wrote,

No rational moral idealism can create moral conduct. It can provide principles of criticism and reasons; but such norms do not contain a dynamic for their realization.... Rationalism not only suppresses the emotional supports of moral action unduly, but it has failed dismally in encouraging men toward the realization of the ideals which it has projected.[31]

---

31. Reinhold Niebuhr, *An Interpretation of Christian Ethics* (New York: Harper and Row, 1935), 206.

Niebuhr would grant, I think, that Kant answered a part of Diderot's concern in that he offered a reason for just conduct. But Niebuhr would deny that Kant offered a *sufficient* reason—a "philosophy [that] makes more good men than sufficient or efficacious grace." Niebuhr would categorically deny that Kant had provided sufficient incentives for moral action.

MORAL INCENTIVE IN KANT'S ETHICS

Although Niebuhr may be correct in his conclusion, it is clear that Kant, no less than his critics, is aware of the insufficiency of the moral law and the categorical imperative as static formulae. For the purpose of moral life, Kant insists, they "require in addition a power of judgment sharpened by experience, partly in order to distinguish the cases to which they apply, partly to procure for them admittance to the will of man and influence over practice."[32] Judgment, Kant insists, must provide the incentive that moves the will to do that which it knows it ought to do. Kant's recognition of the need to provide moral incentives is seen in his distinction between the moral law and the categorical imperative.

Kant observed that if men had holy wills, that is, if they were pure rational beings, they would act in accordance with the moral law without overcoming temptation. They would have neither obligations nor the need of incentives to follow the moral law because it would be the descriptive law of their behavior. Men are not pure, rational beings; the human will consists not merely of practical reason (*Wille*) but also of the faculty of desire (*Willkür*). *Willkür*, free and self-determining, confronts both the demands of reason and the desires of sensibility; it is tempted to act in accordance with the appeals of the latter, while it is obligated to act in accordance with the principle of the former. The moral law for pure, rational beings thus becomes the categorical imperative for men who, being both rational and sensible beings, require some sensible incentive for fulfilling the demands of reason.

In order to determine action in accordance with the categorical imperative, practical reason must gain control over the desires and inclinations that compete with it for determination of the will. And since reason cannot control nonrational desires and pleasures by means of argument, it must control them by means of pleasures and desires that the moral law itself can effect in the will. In order to fulfill the demands of the categorical imperative, the human will as a dynamic, unitary faculty must be able

---

32. Gr, 389; Paton, 57. I have dealt with the role of judgment in the application of the moral law at greater length in "Verfahrensformalismus in Kants Ethik," *Akten des 4. Internationalen Kant-Kongresses, Teil III* (Berlin, 1974), 149–85: "Procedural Formalism in Kant's Ethics," *Review of Metaphysics* 28, no. 2 (1974): 197–236.

to find pleasure or delight in the fulfillment of duty. Thus, Kant argues that "if we are to will actions for which reason by itself prescribes an 'ought' to a rational, yet sensuously affected, being, it is admittedly necessary that reason should have a power of *infusing a feeling of pleasure* or satisfaction in the fulfillment of duty, and consequently that it should possess a kind of causality by which it can determine sensibility in accordance with rational principles."[33] Reason must be able not merely to legislate the law for the human will; it must also be able to produce in the will a sensible incentive to fulfill the law.

It is here that judgment enters as the power of the mind to provide a priori principles for the feeling of pleasure and pain. It is that power or ability of reason to produce a feeling of pleasure in sensibility associated with the fulfillment of duty.[34] In providing for a moral incentive, Kant must show how judgment can win acceptance for the moral law in the human will. He must answer the question, How can judgment—as reason in its dynamic employment—be an efficient cause in the determination of an effect (a feeling) in sensibility? That is, he must answer the question, How can reason be practical?[35]

Before considering Kant's answer to this question, we must be sure the question is correctly interpreted. In the first place, it must not be understood as a question of whether or not reason can be practical. Freedom of the will—which involves the actual capacity of reason to be practical through the production of incentives—is presupposed in the experience of obligation from which Kantian ethics begins.[36] That reason is practical, that man does take an interest in enacting the demands of the moral law, is a fact of human experience for which no additional proof is required.[37]

In the second place, granting that reason is practical, we must not suppose that a direct theoretical explanation of how it is practical is possible. The question How is reason practical? is identical to the question How is freedom possible? to which no direct answer can be given. These questions are identical because to explain how reason can be practical requires one to show "how a law in itself can be the direct determining ground of the will"[38] while the capacity of the will to act in terms of the idea of law is precisely what is meant by freedom. As Kant puts it, "a free will and the will under moral laws are one and the same."[39] Hence, any explanation of the way in which the moral law can determine the will

---

33. Gr, 460; Paton, 128.
34. KdU, 245–46: CoaJ, 91–92. See also Gr, 389; Paton, 57.
35. Gr, 459–61; Paton, 127–29.   36. KdpV, 532; Beck, 143.
37. Gr, 460; Paton, 128.
38. KdpV, 5.72; Beck, 180. See also Gr, 459; Paton, 127.
39. Gr, 447, 88, 413; Paton, 114, 80, 108.

necessarily involves an explanation of freedom. Once we grant that these are identical questions, we must agree with Kant that no explanation for either is possible, since both require an explanation of freedom. In order to *explain* something theoretically, one must make it determinate by reference to the spatial and/or temporal conditions that necessitate it; the idea of freedom, however, presupposes an independence from all alien or antecedent causes and therefore the absence of the very factors that make possible a theoretical explanation.[40]

Thus, in asking how reason or judgment can provide an incentive for the will, we are not questioning that it can, nor are we seeking a direct theoretical explanation of the conditions by which it does so. Rather, we seek to know (1) what kind of feeling is produced in the will by judgment whereby the will takes a sensible interest in the fulfillment of the moral law? (2) How can Kant introduce feeling into his ethical theory as an incentive of the will without destroying the categorical imperative and inheriting the difficulties of ethical empiricism? And (3) presuming that Kant can satisfy the previous issues, what practical means can judgment employ in providing moral incentives?

On the first question—what kind of feeling is produced by moral judgments—Kant stresses that the feeling in question is different in kind from other feelings in that it is not aroused by material objects. In the *Critique of Judgment*, he enumerates three varieties of delight: delight in the agreeable, delight in the beautiful, and delight in the good. Delight in the good results from the activity of reason whereby the object (the morally good) is demanded and made attractive by reference to the moral law. Thus Kant's introduction of feeling into moral experience does not reduce his ethics to the empirical level. Feeling can be aroused not only by sensation in the judgment of something as agreeable, or by the play of imagination and understanding in the judgment of something as beautiful; it can be aroused also by a concept—the moral law—in the judgment of something as good. The moral law (as an expression of *Wille*) produces an incentive in *Willkür* that is moral feeling, the delight or sensible interest taken in an object that is good.

As to the second question, the introduction of this incentive does not undermine the theory of the categorical imperative. Moral feeling, the sensible incentive that moves the will (*Willkür*) to the fulfillment of duty, does not reduce Kant's theory to one of ethical empiricism, because moral feeling is rationally, not empirically, determined. Moral feeling is the *effect* of the moral law on the will, not the *cause* of the moral law. One's desire to be happy or to avoid unhappiness cannot be the incentive that

---

40. KdpV, 5.96; Beck, 202. Gr, 461, 163; Paton, 129–31.

leads one to obey the law. Whatever satisfaction one derives from fulfilling one's moral obligation, and whatever suffering one experiences from a guilty conscience for having failed to do so, are the effects of one's virtue, not the causes of it.[41]

Our central concern here is to understand Kant's answer to the third question: What practical means or devices can judgment employ in providing moral incentives and are these incentives adequate? We must recognize at the outset that Kant offers techniques for the cultivation rather than the creation of moral feeling, for moral feeling is presupposed in every moral person. "Since any consciousness of obligation has moral feeling at its basis," Kant argues, "as that which makes us aware of the necessitation present in the concept of duty, there can be no duty to have moral feeling or to acquire it. It is inherent in every man (as a moral being). Our obligation with regard to moral feeling can be only to *cultivate* and strengthen it by our wonder at its inscrutable source."[42]

Recognizing its proper task as the cultivation rather than the creation of moral feeling, judgment may enlarge the moral incentive of each individual by any of the following techniques: by directing the will's attention to the elegance of rational thought,[43] to the beauties of nature,[44] to the beauties of art,[45] to the sublime,[46] to the examination of the lives of good men,[47] and to practices in moral casuistry.[48]

THE LIMITS OF MORAL INCENTIVE

These various means for the cultivation of moral feeling and the encouragement of moral conduct are ingenious and imaginative but not convincing. There is on Kant's theory an inescapable dilemma inherent in moral education. If incentives and inducements are introduced to determine the will, they destroy in the process its freedom and thereby the will itself. On the other hand, if the moral incentives are merely inducements, guiding threads to encourage moral volition, they are insufficient. That is, if one wishes a moral incentive that provides a truly sufficient reason for just conduct, an incentive sufficiently strong to ensure

---

41. TuP, 283–84; TaP, 50–51. Cf. KdpV, 5.76; Beck, 184. Since the issues raised by questions A and B are considered at length in the section on "Moral Feeling" in my essay "The Ethical Significance of Kant's *Religion*," in Greene, lxxix–cxxxiv, I shall not elaborate these issues here.

42. MdS, 399–400; MoM, 59–60.   43. KdU, 366; CotJ, 12.
44. MdS, 443; MoM, 109.
45. KdU, 232–33, 298–99; CoaJ, 75–76, 157; see sections 41, 59, and 60.
46. KdU, 257–63; CoaJ, 106–13.
47. KdpV, 5.76–77; Beck, 184–85.
48. KdpV, 5.152–56; Beck, 250–53; cf. MdS, 428–40; MoM, 92–106.

moral action, one cannot help but adopt an incentive so strong that it will either buy off or scare off the moral agent, and thus destroy his freedom. Morality is ineluctably contingent upon the exercise of freedom and cannot be guaranteed by force or sufficient incentive.

It was for this reason that Kant stressed the importance for morality of the fact that there is no theoretical proof of God and immortality. For if there were, the freedom of mankind would be destroyed and moral action would be determined simply by fear of Hell or hope of Heaven.[49] Consistent with his ethical theory, Kant recognized in *Über die Pädagogik* that "if we wish to establish morality, we must abolish punishment. Morality is something so sacred and sublime that we must not degrade it by placing it in the same rank as discipline."[50]

After making this sound observation, Kant proceeded to contradict himself by introducing and approving *moral* punishment. Apparently Kant failed to recognize that moral punishment, the denial by the parent of love or respect for the child, is from the child's point of view more terrifying and severe than any reasonable form of physical punishment and can be just as heteronomous as a beating.[51] This irregularity aside, Kant is basically consistent in holding that no program of education that accorded with his ethical theory could develop moral persons by means of social and psychological influences that would undermine the freedom of the students and destroy them as moral beings. Whatever man is in a moral sense, whether good or evil, must be a condition of his free choice. From this it follows that "whatever his previous deportment may have been, whatever the natural causes may have been influencing him and whether these causes were to be found within him or outside him, his action is yet free and determined by none of these causes; hence [his action] can and must always be judged as an original use of his will."[52]

The inscrutable and irreducible nature of freedom that we comprehend only to the extent that we recognize its incomprehensibility precludes Kant's development of sufficient moral incentives or a genuine theory of education that is determinative of personal character.

He proposes in lieu of a theory of education a two-stage educational process that first encourages legality of action by insisting that the student act in accordance with the moral law and train his judgment in assessing

---

49. Päd, 494–95; Ed, 112. Kant would agree with Kierkegaard that faith presupposes an objective uncertainty.
50. Päd, 481; Ed, 84.
51. Päd, 482–84; Ed, 87–91.
52. Rel, 41; Greene 36 Cf. Rel, 44; Greene 40. This, Kant adds, is the basis of original sin: it originates in the individual. Niebuhr, incidentally, offers an identical interpretation; see Niebuhr, *An Interpretation*, 89–90.

his actions and those of others in terms of conformity to law. A second stage follows in which moral feeling is developed, in which the moral individual's growing sense of his own worth as a free moral person becomes itself the dominant incentive to action.[53]

In this two-stage process, Kant suggests, the metamorphosis of freedom will occur and the natural person, having become accustomed to acting in accordance with the moral law and to judging others in terms of that standard, will discover in himself a growing sense of his own dignity as a moral person and eventually desire above all else to become worthy in his own eyes.

Though Kant cannot, while preserving freedom, offer a genuine educational theory, he may nevertheless offer educational counsel to assist in practice. On this view Kant does not have, strictly speaking, a pedagogy, but merely offers observations on training, cultivation, and education. Kant's educational program is better understood in Aristotelian terms as a natural process of entelechy in which the individual, after being subjected to a series of educational influences, is not *made* moral but simply becomes a moral person. Just as in puberty the child suddenly and dramatically becomes sexually potent, so the moral person, attending the voice of conscience, naturally but inexplicably ceases to be led by the inclinations that dominated his infancy and answers to the voice of his own practical reason. Kant would hold that reason and freedom are immanent in the human being from birth and that the unfolding of moral capacity is no more remarkable, and no more comprehensible, than the capacity for rationality in any of its other employments.

On Kant's theory, the moral individual cannot be "programmed" by sociological or educational techniques. To brainwash is to destroy freedom, not to build it. To educate, by contrast, is to develop the capacity for freedom that may yet express itself in ways that are either good or evil. Since the student's actions are his own and the responsibility for them radically his own, the teacher can never be blamed for the wrong actions of the student nor credited for his achievements. Recognizing the inscrutable depths of freedom, Kant cannot claim to know the conditions under which freedom is developed and its autonomous expression assured. Thus, Kant can offer only nostrums for moral instruction, including even his ludicrous suggestion, noted by Beck, that the life of Anne Boleyn might exemplify for children innocence punished.[54]

How, then, does one provide sufficient reason for moral conduct? If

---

53. KdpV, 5.152, 159–60; Beck 250, 256–57.
54. L. W. Beck, *Essays on Hume and Kant* (New Haven, Conn.: Yale University Press, 1978), 202. KdpV, 5.156; Beck, 253.

one accepts Kant's understanding of moral conduct, there is no way to *make* men morally good and worthy of happiness. Strictly speaking, they make themselves morally good and worthy by their own acts. The teacher in a moral community provides oxygen for the tiny spark of reason until it bursts spontaneously into fire. Freedom is potential from the start, and education is no more than guardian and encourager of the flame. Programs are developed, exercises are completed, and free moral persons emerge as if by a process of moral entelechy.

In his concern to provide an adequate foundation for moral conduct, Kant was occasionally swept away by the extravagance and utopianism of the eighteenth century. At the close of his *Lectures on Ethics* he proposed an educational program to bring about the systematic betterment of mankind on a worldwide scale. Holding that the ultimate destiny of mankind is his moral perfection, Kant asks: "How then is moral perfection to be sought? Wherein lies our hope?" And he answers:

In education and in nothing else. Education must be adapted to all the ends of nature both civil and domestic. . . . Let education be conceived on right lines, let natural gifts be developed as they should, let character be formed on moral principles, and in time the effects of this will reach even the seat of government, when princes themselves are educated by teachers fitted for the task. . . . But the ruler cannot do it alone; men of all ranks in the state would have to be similarly trained; then would the state be built on a firm foundation. . . . Justice and equity, the authority, not of governments, but of conscience within us, will then rule the world. This is the destined final end, the highest moral perfection to which the human race can attain.[55]

But for the most part Kant held his enthusiasm in check. His more characteristic and certainly more consistent view of the limits of education was clearly stated in the *Anthropologie* and serves as a correction to the panegyric just quoted:

Man must . . . be *educated* to be good. But those who are supposed to educate him are again men who are themselves still involved in the crudity of nature and are supposed to bring about what they themselves are in need of. . . . But since he needs, for his moral education, *good* men who must themselves have been educated for it, and since none of these are free from (innate or acquired) corruption, the problem of moral education for *our species* remains unsolved even in principle and not merely in degree.[56]

Finally, Kant only partially succeeds in solving the problem framed by Diderot. Kant, like Pentheus, must refuse to acknowledge God except as an afterthought of consistent volition. Kant cannot but fail to offer ade-

---

55. VüE, 318–19; LoE, 252–53.
56. A, 325, 327; Gregor, 186, 188.

quate incentives for ethical conduct, for if they were adequate they would destroy the freedom of the moral person. Hence, he offers a limited educational curriculum incapable of reshaping history but capable in some cases of developing morally sound individuals.

Kant discovered that his theory of morality contained the implication that it is impossible to *make* men morally good. Hence, while he was successful in meeting Diderot's concern to establish morality on a rational basis, he was unable to deal adequately with the other aspect of Diderot's concern: that philosophy make "more good men than sufficient or efficacious grace." This concern, Kant would argue, is mistaken. It is a consequence of Diderot's confusion. Do we wish to encourage moral conduct, that is, true morality? If so, virtue must be the free expression of the moral person. Or do we wish rather to encourage conformity to the moral law, that is, mere legality? The latter can be motivated through laws and social pressure; the former can only be nurtured.

Similarly, Kant can answer a part of Niebuhr's concern. The moral law does in fact contain a mechanism for its realization: it produces moral feeling and thereby provides some emotional support for moral action. On the other hand, that support is so attenuated that Niebuhr might reasonably conclude that it "has failed dismally in encouraging men toward the realization of the ideals which it has projected."

ETHICAL ORTHODOXY IN RELIGIOUS EDUCATION

But why did Kant reject a middle course? Why should we not rear the young child in a mythic tradition—as Kant himself had been reared—and after the mythic religion with its powerful motivational power had been established only then introduce the process of rational pruning and grafting? Kant did not reject the mythic religion of his childhood either from personal whim or from prejudice against religion as such. It is a logical condition of Kant's theory of ethics that morality be introduced without the threat of punishment or the inducement of reward. Thus, ethics and moral education must precede rather than follow religion and religious education. As Kant says, "[T]he religion which is founded merely on theology can never contain anything of morality, hence we derive no feelings from it but fear on the one hand, and hope of reward on the other, and this produces merely a superstitious cult."[57]

On ethical grounds, consistent with the implications of his moral theory, Kant would restrict the child's experience of God and his participation in religious practices. When God was explained to children in

---

57. Päd, 494–95; Ed, 112.

eighteenth-century religion, He was presented on the same footing as any other fact and was characterized as a being who knows the human heart and who directly rewards and punishes it according to its intent. Presented thus, the presence of God in the consciousness of the child destroys its freedom. Consequently, Kant recommends that children be reared in their earliest years in the absence of religious rites and without hearing the name of God. Instead, they should be given instruction about the ends and aims of mankind, about the order and beauty of nature; their judgment should be exercised, and they should be provided with a wider knowledge of the universe and its laws. "Then only might be revealed to them for the first time the idea of a supreme being—a law giver."[58]

Having established religion on the foundation of ethics, Kant is consistent in holding that education should progress from ethics to religion: "Morality must come first and theology follow; and that is religion."[59] "Religion is the law in us, in so far as it derives emphasis from a Law-giver and a Judge above us. It is morality applied to the knowledge of God."[60] "Religion without moral conscientiousness is a service of superstition."[61]

In practice, nevertheless, Kant reluctantly recommends the introduction of religious education into early childhood education. This, however, is only because it is absolutely necessary in order to prevent the miseducation that children would receive in their daily lives through contact with morally corrupting religious ideas. The religious education Kant would offer to counteract this problem is not, of course, an education in Christianity or in any mythic religion. It would be education—even for the youngest child—in the demythologized religion of reason alone. Rejecting the advice of Saint Paul that a child be taught as a child and allowed to grow to adulthood before putting off childish things, Kant proposes to teach the ethical religion of reason to the little child as if it were a little man or woman.

With an eighteenth-century confidence that nature does nothing without purpose and is organized to ensure the maximum efficiency of means, Kant concluded that man had not been created for happiness but for a moral pilgrimage that could establish his dignity, and his worthiness to be happy.

Kant could find no way to use historical Christianity as a foundation for ethics. Christianity was presented to the public in many varieties of religious orthodoxy, each of which contained elements inimical to Kant's moral orthodoxy. But Kant had no way of imposing his moral orthodoxy

---

58. Päd, 493; Ed, 110.
60. Päd, 494; Ed, 111.
59. Päd, 495; Ed, 112.
61. Päd, 495; Ed, 113.

on any branch of the Christian church. Unable to make over the culture of his day, Kant was forced to accept it as a limiting condition for his theory of moral education. He concluded that a sound moral education would have to proceed with the simultaneous introduction of a morally orthodox interpretation of Christianity that would be understood as a derivative rather than as a foundation of morality.

THE NECESSITY OF FREEDOM

As if these obstacles were not enough, there was an additional problem that Kant did not anticipate. The Christian worldview was being gradually eclipsed by the scientific. Even if Kant had proposed to ground moral education on historical Christianity, he would have found that project swept away by subsequent cultural changes. The project could not have succeeded in the climate of opinion of the nineteenth and twentieth centuries, in which the scientific worldview was enormously strengthened by the work of Darwin, Freud, Einstein, and their many brilliant collaborators and successors. Concomitantly, and without any direct encouragement from Kant, Christianity was rationalized and demythologized. As it gained in sophistication, Christianity lost much of its appeal to the average person. The scientific worldview was indifferent to the ultimate questions concerning the meaning of life, and left these to the realm of uncertainty. The civilization based on the Christian worldview was dissolving into smaller and competing social elements. Each of these could claim to be validated by the scientific worldview, whose presumption of value neutrality led to ethical relativism, and to some extent encouraged an intellectual climate of political and moral anarchy and nihilism.

The pervasive influence of the scientific worldview in the twentieth century as the implications of value neutrality and ethical relativism were applied with extraordinary crassness to justify the opinions and beliefs of any and everyone has contributed to the disintegration of the social and legal order. The individual's respect for law and the discipline that the moral person imposes on himself in the fulfillment of his freedom have been extensively undermined by social relativism and indifferentism.

Kant did not have the option of proposing the imposition of a religion contrived to achieve ethical orthodoxy, which could provide the motivational force of a mythic religion. Kant was, of course, aware of this possibility from his reading of Plato.

Plato had proposed in the fourth century B.C. a scheme of general education whereby a society might be transformed and an ideal state of ideal citizens brought into existence. In order to achieve this social objective, Plato proposed a new mythic religion whose tenets were consistent with the aims of the state. He proposed a great fable in which all citizens of his republic would be nurtured. They would be taught to believe that God had made men of three basic substances: gold, silver, or iron and bronze. They would come to believe on faith, as if it were a mundane truth, that their natures were thus differentiated at birth. Those of gold would become rulers; those of silver, auxiliaries; and those of bronze or iron, farmers or craftsmen.[62]

Plato recognized that the first, and possibly even the second, generation of persons nurtured in this new religion would likely not believe it. In order to ensure the workability of the ideal state, Plato recommended finally[63] that all citizens over ten years of age be sent out into the countryside so that the children, removed from the ways of their parents, might be brought up in accordance with the institutions of the new state and so believe its newly developed religious myth.

By getting rid of everyone who was bound by older traditions, and by introducing a new orthodoxy fully congruent with the aims of the state, Plato proposed nothing less than a pervasive totalitarianism. He offered in support of his moral theory an educational system that appeared more capable than "sufficient or efficacious grace" in the production of good men.

Plato's proposal to invent mythic roots as incentives to moral conduct was not, however, acceptable to Kant. It involved not merely the propagation of falsehoods and a mistaken concept of the good as homogeneous, but its success required also a totalitarian state that destroyed freedom and hence the possibility of morality. In providing moral incentives, Kant was not concerned to encourage mere legality; rather, he was concerned to encourage true morality. Plato's proposal to force men by thought control and regimentation to act in accordance with law could at best produce persons who conformed to law and who were brainwashed to believe that they were therefore happy. But Plato's citizen could not possibly be morally good or worthy of happiness by virtue of this heteronomously determined choice. To force moral goodness (in the Kantian sense of the term) is as impossible as to force love: each must be the expression of the free individual, or it is nothing.[64]

Kant demonstrated the falseness of Plato's ethical position and that of the Stoics by proving the heterogeneity of the good. He showed that the plausibility of the Platonic and Stoic concept of good depended on the assumption of a homogeneous concept of the good in which virtue and

---

62. Plato, *The Republic*, 3.414–15; trans. F. M. Cornford (New York, 1945), 106–7.
63. Ibid., 7.540–41; Cornford, 262–63.
64. In noting the totalitarian implications of the Platonic program, I wish to distance myself from the analysis by Professor Popper, who, in *The Open Society and Its Enemies*, tried to

happiness are conflated.[65] Once the mistaken notion of a homogeneous good is corrected, Plato's theory of motivation is destroyed. The individual no longer automatically desires to do the good as a means to both virtue and happiness; rather, he finds himself torn between the appeals of happiness (the natural good) and the demands of moral obligation on which depend his virtue (the moral good) and his worthiness to be happy. Quite often, moreover, he finds that the moral good can be attained only at the sacrifice of the natural good. Thus, Plato fails to offer any genuinely moral incentive. He appears to encourage moral action but in fact encourages only legality of action by means of coercion.

Although Kant exposed a fundamental confusion in Plato's concept of the good and demolished Plato's theory of motivation, which derived its plausibility from that confused notion, Kant did not and could not refute the efficacy of Plato's educational proposal. He understood that it was entirely possible to change human behavior by a totalitarian educational program.

Unfortunately, subsequent history has amply shown that Plato's theory of totalitarian education works effectively in practice. In the twentieth century we have witnessed many examples of societies that have produced remarkable changes in the social and moral order through the techniques of totalitarianism. Once the government assumes the role of a Dostoyevskian Grand Inquisitor who "saves" mankind from freedom in order to ensure the well-being and happiness of all, the technological advances of modern science are available to make easier and swifter the fulfillment of the totalitarian project.

Marx, Lenin, Stalin, and Mao all proposed and all, save Marx, established educational programs with the scope and thoroughness of Plato's scheme, programs that put down the mythic roots of their secular religions. They project a new vision of society and of man within that society. That vision is indoctrinated into the child as a mythic religion, and the child comes to consciousness in an ethos in which the state is watching and judging and will reward and punish him. The diabolical religion of National Socialism was inculcated in the same way—by terror and totalitarianism. It incorporated Norse sagas into a new state religion whose end remained Ragnarok.

---

credit Plato with ideas that lay behind Hitler's National Socialism. It was Plato's position that the state should serve the individual and guarantee his greatest personal fulfillment. It is highly anachronistic and irresponsible for a scholar to attribute to Plato an abuse of democratic freedoms and a support of totalitarian schemes of which he had no knowledge and about which he had no intentions.

65. John R. Silber, "The Copernican Revolution in Ethics: The Good Reexamined," *KantStudien* 51 (1959–1960): 85–101.

However benign or malignant their objectives, these totalitarian states have inculcated contrived mythic religions that promise to "free mankind." But the freedom that is promised is not the freedom more precious than life itself, the freedom that makes possible "all that makes life worthwhile,"[66] the freedom on which human dignity and one's worthiness to be happy are grounded. Rather, it is only a counterfeit freedom of mere conformity to party objective, a legality devoid of autonomy.

It would appear that Kant stood between two worlds—one dying and the other powerless during his lifetime to be born. The civilization based on mythic Christianity was dissolving in the solvent of the scientific worldview and the neoreligions of socialism were as yet scarcely emerging. Kant could not subvert the ethical by introducing the coercive motivations of mythic religion. But he was by no means indifferent to the need for moral incentive. He thus presented a theory of ethics of maximal rational purity, grounded in human freedom and the law of its expression, and revealing the human person as a being worthy beyond price. Those who understand and accept Kant's conception of man are immunized against the temptations of the secular heterodoxies, the totalitarian schemes for human betterment without freedom.

Kant's ethics has its mythic roots: but they lie rather in Christian pietism than in reason. And his fully developed ethical theory proscribes the use of any mythic religion that is not subject to the test of ethical orthodoxy. By eschewing mythic roots, Kant's theory only lost what it could never really have had. Having reached the limits of reason in providing moral incentive, Kant stopped. And perhaps he did enough: his ethical theory clearly provides the principles of criticism and procedural guidance for personal and political conduct. Although the force of moral feeling produced by reason may be weak, it continually gives rise to the conviction that freedom is the natural end of mankind and that each of us should subordinate life itself to those principles that make life worthwhile.

The limited incentive of moral feeling is perhaps best understood as a moral sea anchor that, although incapable of providing the motive power to move a ship to harbor, may yet prevent its foundering on the rocks.

66. KdpV, 5.159; Beck 256.

12 The Enlightenment Project in Twentieth-Century Philosophy

NICHOLAS CAPALDI

INTRODUCTION

My essay has three aims: to illustrate how the Enlightenment Project continues to dominate the intellectual life of the twentieth century, to identify its philosophical elements, and to explore its cultural consequences.

What is the Enlightenment Project? The Enlightenment Project is the attempt to define, explain, and control the human predicament through the use of scientific technology.[1] This project originated among the French philosophes during the eighteenth century, among whom the most influential were Diderot, d'Alembert, La Mettrie, Condillac, Helvetius, d'Holbach, Turgot, and Condorcet.

This project has three philosophical elements: metaphysical, epistemological, and axiological.

1. Its metaphysics is Aristotelianism without teleology, faith or tradition. The product of this is scientism, and the consequence of scientism is the loss of philosophical consciousness.

2. Its epistemology is Aristotle's epistemology without the metaphysics and without a soul or an active intellect. The product of this is empiricism,[2] and the consequences of empiricism are a corrosive skepticism or a politicized epistemology.

3. Its axiology can be characterized as Aristotelian natural right without nature or as natural law without God. The consequence of this is the turning of natural rights theory into a form of ideological rhetoric.

---

1. See Carl Becker, *The Heavenly City of the Eighteenth-Century Philosophers* (New Haven, Conn.: Yale University Press, 1962), Chapter 4, for an exposition of the position that the dream of a technological utopia is the common inheritance of liberals, socialists, and Marxists.

2. "Immediately after Aristotle comes Locke; for it is not necessary to count the other philosophers who have written on the same subject"; Condillac, *Extrait raisonné du Traité des Sensations* (Paris: F. Alcan, 1921), 32.

257

In what follows, I shall examine each of these elements both in their original Enlightenment context and in the context of twentieth-century philosophy. I shall stress the extent to which positivism and analytic philosophy[3] maintain the Enlightenment Project, but the influence is even wider.

METAPHYSICS

Let us turn to metaphysics. It is generally said that the Enlightenment replaced authority, faith, and tradition with reason. It is also said that the Enlightenment identified reason with physical science. Philosophically, this amounts to the following contentions:

1. The world is self-explanatory.
2. Human beings are to be understood in the same way as we understand the world.
3. The world is to be understood as a mechanical system devoid of purpose and captured within the formulas of Newtonian mechanics.

The first two points are part of traditional Aristotelian metaphysics.[4] The third point is new, it is in opposition to traditional Aristotelianism, and it is the source of incoherence within the Enlightenment program. It is precisely the attempt to combine a deteleologized Aristotelianism with mechanism and determinism that ultimately renders the Enlightenment Project incoherent.

There are two standard objections to the idea of a wholly mechanistic-naturalistic world view: (a) science is not self-explanatory and (b) mechanistic science renders both human action and cognition unintelligible. What stands behind these objections? Two millennia of philosophical literature! In addition, two centuries of scientific debate had made clear

---

3. "Rorty thinks there was a 'hidden agenda' behind the central problems in analytic philosophy: the defense of the values of science, democracy and art on the part of secular intellectuals"; see *Post-Analytic Philosophy*, ed. John Rajchman and Cornel West (New York: Columbia University Press, 1985), Preface, xii.

In "Solidarity or Objectivity?," Richard Rorty claims that "[t]here is, in short, nothing wrong with the hopes of thee Enlightenment. . . . I have sought to distinguish these institutions and practices from the philosophical justifications for them provided by partisans of objectivity, and to suggest an alternative justification"; see Rajchman and West, eds., *Post-Analytic Philosophy*, 16.

4. This statement has to be carefully qualified. Aristotle does not have a reductive view of human beings, and he insisted that on the human level there are truths that are not to be found on the merely organic or inorganic level. In addition, Aristotle holds the methodological position that there must be different methods for different objects of investigation. At the same time, Aristotle sees human beings as part of a seamless web or continuous natural order. It is the postulation of a different conception of natural order in the modern period that significantly alters the very meaning of the view that human beings are a part of nature.

that mechanistic science is not a self-sufficient explanation of either the world or of human nature. It was clear to both Newton and Leibniz that the laws of nature did not explain themselves; it was clear to Descartes that human nature could not be explained mechanistically; it was clear to both Hume and his Scottish critics that without appeal to either divine guarantees or tradition and custom there was no way to ensure that the human thought process accurately modeled the world; it was clear to both Hume and Kant that the practice and intelligibility of science required a background of assumptions and norms that science itself could not explain; and it was clear to Hobbes, Locke, and Adam Smith that social, political, and economic stability required both some version of theism and some appeal to traditional authority. In short, it is impossible to read and understand the greatest minds even of the seventeenth and eighteenth centuries and to take seriously the third metaphysical contention. It is precisely the power of these objections that accounts for the intellectual appeal of Deism during the eighteenth century. How all of this gets ignored is something we shall have to ask.

It is generally agreed that it is during the Enlightenment that a commitment to scientism first crystallizes into a dogmatic program. Proponents of this program like d'Alembert among others point back to the inspiration of Bacon, Descartes, and Hobbes. Thus it is tempting to suggest that the program was already present in much earlier thinkers but that the program was obfuscated for any number of reasons. Let me indicate why this temptation ought to some extent to be resisted.

First, one must not confuse science with scientism. To advocate the importance of science for helping us to understand the world and to advocate the practical importance of a scientifically based technology is not to believe that physical science is intellectually autonomous or self-explanatory. To believe in the intellectual autonomy of science is to be an advocate of scientism. Bacon, Descartes, Hobbes, and others all defend the importance of science, but none of them advocates scientism. On the contrary, there is an explicit rejection in each of what we here call scientism.

Second, even among some of the philosophes there is an explicit awareness of the limits of science. As d'Alembert expressed it, "[T]he supreme Intelligence has drawn a veil before our feeble vision which we try in vain to remove."[5] It is specifically among a subset of the members of the philosophes that we find the advocacy of scientism, specifically in Condillac, d'Holbach, La Mettrie, and so on.[6]

5. D'Alembert, *Mélanges littérature d'histoire et de philosophie* (1759), 4 vols., 4.63–64.
6. Ernst Cassirer has argued that d'Holbach and La Mettrie reflect "a retrogression into

Third, it is only and specifically during the Enlightenment that an "anti-systematic" philosophy is advocated.[7] To be anti-system, like the later anti-metaphysical stance of the positivists, is explicitly to refuse to deal with the philosophical issues raised by scientism. In some cases, for example, d'Alembert and Diderot,[8] the refusal reflects genuine perplexity; in other cases, for instance, advocates of the Enlightenment Project like d'Holbach, La Mettrie, and others, this signals an attempt to discredit or delegitimate those issues.

Fourth, and most important, in their attempt to delegitimate the fundamental philosophical issues broached by the advocacy of scientism, defenders of the Enlightenment Project will develop a historicist posture. We shall be discussing that posture shortly, but what is important to note is that the historicist posture is unique to the Enlightenment Program. In short, while there is an undoubted line of development from Bacon and Descartes to the philosophes what is unique and original to advocates of the Enlightenment Project is both the anti-system approach to philosophy and the historicist posture.

What arguments or counterarguments were offered to offset the standing critique of the naturalistic-mechanical worldview? The answer is none! What the eighteeth century, specifically the French philosophes, offered instead was a historicist rhetoric and a methodological pose. Whenever challenged, the first line of defense for the mechanistic-naturalistic thesis was the claim that scientific progress would in some unspecified manner meet these objections. In a ironic sort of way, a providential history without God became a substitute for argument.

One of the first theorists in the eighteenth century to suggest a historicized teleology was Turgot.[9] Turgot's thesis was later to be refined into attempts to formulate laws of development. The most important figures to continue Turgot's work into the nineteenth century were Fourier, Saint-

---

that dogmatic mode of thinking which the leading scientific minds of the eighteenth century oppose and endeavor to eliminate"; see *The Philosophy of the Enlightenment* (Boston: Beacon Press, 1955), 55.

7. The "esprit de système" is specifically attacked in d'Alembert's *Preliminary Discourse to the Encyclopedia of Diderot*, trans. and ed. Richard N. Schwab and Walter T. Rex (Indianapolis, Ind.: Bobbs-Merrill, 1963), and in Condillac's *Treatise on Systems*, in *Philosophical Writings of Etienne Bonnot, Abbé de Condillac*, trans. Franklin Philip and Harlan Lane (Hillsdale, N.J.: Erlbaum, 1982).

8. See Diderot's novel *Jack the Fatalist*.

9. Turgot published two essays in 1750 dealing with his philosophy of history: "Philosophic Panorama of the Progress of the Human Mind," and "Plan of Two Discourses on Universal History"; see *Turgot on Progress, Sociology, and Economics*, ed. Ronald L. Meek (Cambridge: Cambridge University Press, 1973). See also Buffon, *Histoire naturelle* (Paris, 1765), vol. 13; and Yves Goguet, *De l'origine des loix, des arts, et des sciences* (1758).

Simon, and Comte. Comte is an important figure for our story because he serves as the connecting link to the positivists, and he was so cited in their manifesto to be mentioned below.

It is during the Enlightenment that we see the equating of the history of philosophy with the history of science and the rhetoric of progressive scientific histories without any rational substantiation. It is important to recognize that this is a story and not an argument. As Montaigne had already made clear, there is no way of standing outside history and seeing that science is progressing.[10]

This progressive historicism is a crucial part of intellectual history. While it is certainly clear that the philosophes inherited from Bacon and Descartes the notions of salvation through physical and even a social technology, it was the philosophes who openly proclaimed that physical science could define and totally explain humanity as well. Whereas their predecessors had recognized the metaphysical and epistemological limits of scientific explanation, the philosophes sought to overcome those limits through the notion of the historical progress of science.

In order to give some indication of the distance between their predecessors and the philosophes, we shall cite the latter's methodological pose, that is, the belief that one can step outside of all contexts and critically evaluate all practices by means of a wholly dispassionate reason that is its own ground of legitimation. Ironically, Descartes himself had wisely refrained from applying this superrationalism to the human and social world and had even insisted that the use of this kind of reason presupposed the acceptance of commonsense traditional moral and social practices. But by the end of the eighteenth century this superrationalism was adopted without any restraints and applied to every facet of human endeavor. This is reflected in Condorcet's statement that "all errors in politics and morals are based on philosophic errors, which, again, are allied to physical errors. There exists neither a religious system, nor a supernatural extravagance, which is not founded on ignorance of the laws of nature."[11]

What we see in Condorcet's remark is the view that scientism entails the existence of a special kind of social knowledge, modeled after physical science, such that the first result of that social science will be an explanation

---

10. The full skeptical challenge to the idea of scientific progress is to be found in Montaigne's *Apology of Raimond Sebond*. For the importance of Montaigne's influence in subsequent discussion, see Richard Popkin, *The History of Scepticism* (New York: Humanities Press, 1964).

11. Antoine-Nicolas de Condorcet, "The Ninth Stage: From Descartes to the Foundation of the French Republic," in *Sketch for a Historical Picture of the Progress of the Human Mind*, trans. June Barraclough (New York: Noonday Press, 1955), 163.

of why individuals oppose scientism. What we are promised is a scientific delegitimation of the opposition to scientism. What we are not given is a logical refutation of the arguments against scientism.

Defenders of the Enlightenment Project respond to these criticisms with a plea for scientific tolerance coupled with the claim that traditional views of human nature are idols or obstacles to accepting the new scientific view. We are told such things as people could not previously imagine standing at the antipodes or we are told by now canonic episodes like those who refused to look through Galileo's telescope. In short, there is a story about scientific progress with a special kind of rhetoric that is supposed to establish the legitimacy of turning subjects into objects, and an important component of that story is a "scientific" account of why people oppose scientism. The history of ideas comes gradually to be construed as a historical progression in which earlier ideas are only worthwhile to the extent that they reflect the current "mature" intellectual agenda. Condorcet's *History* is just such a work. Instead of responding to the critics' arguments, proponents of the Enlightenment program employ the rhetoric of scientific progress to delegitimate their opposition.

Since there are no arguments, we are forced to look for what other considerations led people to take this program seriously. One consideration is that the naturalistic-mechanistic worldview allows for a social technology that could in principle solve all human problems.[12] Hence, the enthusiasm for mechanistic science. Mechanistic views of human nature are attractive because they are compatible with the idea that human beings are either a tabula rasa or fundamentally good. Hence, human beings could be either caused to be good or obstacles to their natural goodness could be removed. It was no accident that freedom in the modern world came to be defined, in one version, as the absence of external constraints. In an analogous way, rationality could seemingly be promoted either mechanically or by removing constraints such as the belief in religion, authority, custom, or tradition. This has the added benefit of reinforcing the progressive-scientific story by seemingly providing a naturalistic account of why it has taken so long to arrive at the superrationalism of the Enlightenment.

The other consideration is that given the economic and social challenges of the modern world. It seemed to many of those impatient to alter the status quo that a wholesale rejection of authority, tradition, and the religious institutions that seemed to support the status quo was the

---

12. "But with these well known conclusions of the materialistic system, we only have so far its outside, not its real conceptual core. For, paradoxical as it may appear at first glance, this core is not to be found in natural philosophy, but in ethics"; Cassirer, *Philosophy of the Enlightenment*, 69.

quickest way to achieve reform; hence, the enthusiasm for a seemingly liberated reason. Since traditional institutions had justified themselves on the grounds that they embody a certain wisdom about human shortcomings, mechanistic theories about the natural goodness of human nature will seem doubly attractive to critics of the status quo.

The desire for reform presupposes some norms. Not only is it unclear how norms can have a place in a mechanistic and nonteleological universe, but until the scientific work is completed there is no way to confirm one's expectation that science will justify one's policy preferences. But, as we have argued, the proponents of the Enlightenment Project have no rationale other than their agenda of political reform.[13]

To put the issue succinctly, there are two difficulties or two versions of the same difficulty with the practical part of the Enlightenment Project. First, it is not clear how there can be norms at all in the world that is neither theistically, nor teleologically, nor conventionally defined. Second, it is not clear by what standards progress of any kind, either moral or scientific, is to be measured. The critics of the Enlightenment Project have always rejected "progress" because all suggested or imaginable standards of what constitutes "progress" lie outside the realm of science. The advocates of the Enlightenment Project not only believe that such standards are available, but they also believe that knowledge of them is itself progressive. The standards will be defined, apparently, "as we advance towards them and the[ir] validity . . . can be verified only in the process of attaining them."[14] In the end, what science declares to be "progress" will become the definition of "progress." It is precisely because advocates of

---

13. The official position of analytic philosophers is that their theoretical positions are held independent of practical concerns. We note, in response, that (1) even if theoretical positions are independent of practical ones, this does not show that practical positions are independent of theoretical ones, some relationship between analytic philosophy and Enlightenment values is still possible; (2) even if theoretical positions are independent of practical ones, this by itself does not show that analytic philosophers hold theoretical views independent of practical ones, for it is always open to someone to suggest the hypothesis that when push came to shove analytic philosophers consistently opted for solutions compatible with certain practical commitments; that is, analytic philosophers may not have practiced what they preached; (3) we shall show that the relationship worked both ways, specifically in Carnap and Popper; (4) the belief that a theoretical position can be held coherently without reference to prior practical or evaluative concerns is itself a controversial thesis, one held by analytic philosophers to be sure, but a thesis never established by analytic philosophers; the latter remains an assertion and not an argument. This thesis is but a restatement of scientism or Aristotelianism without teleology, faith, or convention.

14. E. H. Carr, *What Is History* (New York: Knopf, 1962), quoted by Morris Ginsberg in his article "Progress in the Modern Era," in *Dictionary of the History of Ideas*, ed. Philip P. Wiener (New York: Charles Scribner's Sons, 1973), 3.637. See also the previous article by E. R. Dodds, "Progress in Classical Antiquity." The classic works on progress are J. B. Bury, *The Idea of Progress* (London, 1920), and J. Baillie, *The Belief in Progress* (New York: Charles Scribner's Sons, 1951).

the Enlightenment Project offered no argument and could not offer any argument that we have characterized their presentation as a historicized methodological pose.

What supporters of the Enlightenment Project end up doing is adopting two complimentary discourses. On the one hand, they speak from within our common heritage by invoking intellectual and political norms when needed, and, on the other hand, they reserve the right seemingly to step outside the common heritage into the atmosphere of a contextless reason in order to amend or reject the common heritage when they deem it is necessary. We are told at one and the same time that science is the whole truth about everything and that we can never be sure that we have the whole truth. Both the speech within and the speech without are billed as provisional, but what is not provisional is the assumption that scientific progress will show that the two speeches are ultimately coherent and that there is some kind of historical progression from one to the other. The historicization of the two discourses serve jointly to deflect counterargument, but not to answer it. There is, in short, a special rhetoric developed to compensate for the lack of a philosophical argument.

In making the claim that science is self-justifying, one is asserting something about the totality of knowledge, something about our role within or awareness of that totality, and something about our current incomplete state of knowledge and its relation to that totality. All of these assertions are forms of the problem of self-reference, that is, issues about how a totality is to be understood and by whom, how a totality can make sense of itself, or how we are to understand our role within the totality.

Instead of having solved those problems, proponents of the Enlightenment Project claimed that progress in science will eventually dissolve those problems. This response is itself problematic because there does not appear to be any consensus prior to reaching total knowledge on whether we are in fact making progress. Nor does there seem to be any nontautological or non-question-begging way of establishing in the mean time that science is progressing. In the end what proponents of the Enlightenment Project ask us to do is to suspend philosophical inquiry on the most fundamental metaphysical problem, namely, the problem of self-reference. This suspension is usually coupled with the castigation of those who offer nonscientistic metaphysics. What emerges is a bizarre conversation in which we are (a) asked to accept a position on grounds of intellectual faith alone, (b) criticized for offering any alterative account to that position, and (c) when we inquire into the basis of that criticism, we are told, somewhat impatiently, that the future of scientific progress will clarify these matters.

We use the world "impatient" advisedly. Having espoused scientism, proponents of the Enlightenment Project consistently seek for "scientific" solutions to the intellectual problems generated by that espousal. The proponents have no choice but to do this. They are in an important intellectual sense trapped within a certain framework. They are, therefore, not in a position to discuss that framework. Unfortunately for them, there are others, most notably the entire Western philosophical tradition other than proponents of the Enlightenment Project, who do want to talk about and to challenge the acceptability of that framework. The critics can hardly accept quasi-scientific speculations as answers when the critics are dubious about scientism in the first place, and most especially the ·critics are not going to accept dubious and unsubstantiated historical-progressive claims on behalf of scientism. Because of the espousal of scientism, proponents of the Enlightenment Project are intellectually unable, and therefore unwilling, to discuss their metaphysical starting point.

The suspension of philosophical inquiry on the most fundamental metaphysical problem, the problem of self-reference, has had remarkable intellectual consequences. The first consequence has been the refusal and the inability to deal with issues about totality and self-reference; the second consequence has been the institutionalization of a historical mythology that turns a systematic blind eye to the fact that the whole of the Western philosophical tradition is against the Enlightenment Project. Because of these two consequences, and some others we shall be discussing later, we shall characterize the Enlightenment Project in general and analytic philosophy in particular as exhibiting and promoting the loss of philosophical consciousness.

The primary twentieth-century heirs of the Enlightenment Project are positivism and analytic philosophy. In support of this thesis, we cite the following. First, positivists self-consciously proclaimed their link to the Enlightenment.[15] As Neurath expressed it, the *International Encyclopedia of Unified Science* is the direct counterpart to the *Encyclopedie* begun under the direction of Diderot in the eighteenth century.

Second, in his introductory article in the *Encyclopedia*, Neurath presents a historical account of Western thought and the role of positivism within it. That is, instead of responding to objections to the project, positivists offer a historicist reading of their relationship to their predecessors and current critics.

15. "[W]hen Philip Frank summarized the main achievements of Mach's philosophy in an article published in 1917, he first pointed to the idea of the unity of science. . . . Secondly, . . . he praised Mach for being the philosopher who preserved the heritage of the Enlightenment for our time"; see Rudolf Haller, *Questions on Wittgenstein* (London: Routledge, 1988), 39.

Third, within that historicist account, Neurath specifically invokes the critique of systems found in d'Alembert and in Condillac's *Traité des systèmes*.[16]

Fourth, the programmatic nature of positivism and its self-conscious historical links with the past, as well as a progressive reading of the history of Western thought, are also to be found in the 1929 Vienna Circle "manifesto" entitled "The Scientific Conception of the World." As in the case of Neurath's *Encyclopedia* article, one of the major figures cited as Comte. Comte was not only a nineteenth-century positivist but a connecting link with Turgot's notion of scientific progress.

Fifth, if one were to ask who were the major preservers of scientism and materialism in the nineteenth century, surely the names of Spencer, Feuerbach, and Marx would come to mind. Those are precisely the names cited by Neurath in both the manifesto and in his opening article.

As Carnap said, the three main programmatic features of the Vienna Circle were a denial of supernaturalism, a belief in progress, and the contention that scientific technology was the key to progress. In fact, every point that I have made so far about the Enlightenment Project is specifically present in the work of Carnap: (1) a critique of religion;[17] (2) the endorsement of scientism;[18] (3) the endorsement of the Enlightenment Project;[19] (4) the persistent refusal to deal with the issue of self-reference;[20] (5) a similar refusal to address the philosophical arguments against scientism;[21] (6) the desire to be a scientific technician but of an indeterminate sort;[22] (7) the exhibiting of two levels of rhetoric: "All of us in the [Vienna] Circle were strongly interested in social and political progress. Most of us . . . were socialists. But we liked to keep our philosophical work separated from our political aims";[23] (8) the embracing of a progressive historicism: "[There is a] connection between our philosophical activity and the great historical processes going on in the world:

---

16. Otto Neurath, "Unified Science as Encyclopedic Integration," *International Encyclopedia of Unified Science* (Chicago: University of Chicago Press, 1938), 2.

17. Arthur Schilpp, ed., *The Philosophy of Rudolf Carnap*, vol. 11 of *The Library of Living Philosophers* (LaSalle, Ill.: Open Court, 1963), 7.

18. As Bertrand Russell once put it, "[W]hatever knowledge is attainable, must be attained by scientific methods; and what science cannot discover, mankind cannot know"; see *History of Western Philosophy* (New York: Simon and Schuster, 1946), 862–63. More recently, Michael Dummett has expressed this commitment as follows: "[American analytic philosophers] . . . are unanimous in regarding philosophy, with Quine, as at least cognate with the natural sciences, as part of the same general enterprise as they"; see Dummett, "Can Analytical Philosophy Be Systematic, and Ought It to Be?," in *Truth and Other Enigmas* (Cambridge, Mass.: Harvard University Press, 1978), 438. See also Schilpp, ed., *Philosophy of Carnap*, 38.

19. Schilpp, ed., *Philosophy of Carnap*, 7.
20. Ibid., 9. 21. Ibid., 8.
22. Ibid., 10–11. 23. Ibid., 23.

Philosophy leads to an improvement in scientific ways of thinking and thereby to a better understanding of all that is going on in the world, both in nature and in society; this understanding serves in turn to improve human life";[24] (9) and a belief in and proclamation of the unity of science, understood as the reduction of subjects to objects.[25]

We have identified the problem of totality as the main metaphysical problem evaded by the Enlightenment Project. There are several significant examples of this evasion in analytic philosophy. First, in his theory of types, Russell postulated an infinite hierarchy but he could not explain where in the hierarchy he was standing when he asserted the existence of the infinite hierarchy. Logicism eventually had to be abandoned. This problem reemerged in Gödel, in the liar paradox, and in the status of modal logic. Second, Quine has maintained that no individual statement can be tested against experience; rather, all of knowledge as a whole confronts experience. Of course, Quine cannot explain the status or the truth or the meaning of his statement about the whole of our knowledge since no individual statement can stand on its own. It is not that we have any trouble understanding, or even accepting, Quine's statement, but rather it is the case that it is not clear what sense it could make for Quine. Third, in the long debate within analytic philosophy of science intended to establish the autonomous nature of science (Popper, Kuhn, Feyerabend, et al.), it was finally concluded that this could not be done directly but that we needed a historical theory to determine when scientific progress takes place, that is, when one theory is said legitimately to replace another. Once more, serious metaphysical issues were evaded through a historicist stratagem.

EPISTEMOLOGY

Let us now turn to the epistemological dimension of the Enlightenment Project. As in its metaphysics, so in its epistemology, the Enlightenment represents a truncated if not a perverse form of Aristotelianism. In its traditional Aristotelian form, knowledge is to be understood as the internal abstraction of the external and objective structure of the world. The continuity of the subject and the object is maintained through an organic account of knowledge acquisition and the teleological nature of both the world and that process.

The Enlightenment version of Aristotelian epistemology is empiricist. This means two things. First, it means the substitution of mechanical

---

24. Ibid., 23–24.
25. Ibid., 52.

models for teleological ones. Second, it denies in principle that there is anything like an active intellect.[26]

Assertions about the continuity of human nature and physical nature come to mean something different in the light of the scientific revolution. In the mechanical and deterministic scientific worldview, nature is bereft of consciousness and purpose. Yet human nature seems to have both consciousness and purpose. The problem of empiricism is to explain how consciousness and purpose can arise from inanimate nature, that is, how the "physical" can give rise to the "mental." In the seventeenth and eighteenth centuries it was assumed by Hobbes, Locke, and their followers that an as yet undiscovered physiological mechanism was responsible for the transition. The modern epistemological predicament, then, is that although we are in one way conscious of how our minds work and of the norms generated within the conscious mind about how the external physical world works, we still do not know how the physical world generates the conscious mind. As long as we do not know that we cannot be sure of either the continuity of mind with the physical world or whether the intellectual and moral norms generated within the conscious mind accurately tell us about the physical world. This is not only a theoretical problem, it is a serious practical one for the Enlightenment Project because everything depends upon an accurate view of the physical world.

Part of the reason that there is no physiological account available is that there is no clear idea or consensus on what it is that is being explained. Specifically, there is no consensus on what is traditionally referred to as the "mental." Proponents of the Enlightenment Project see this lack of consensus as a problem to be resolved scientifically; critics of the Enlightenment Project maintain that resolving what "mental" means is a philosophical (specifically metaphysical) problem that is prior to science. Since proponents of the Enlightenment Project subscribe to scientism, they cannot accept or even listen to what the critics are saying.

To the extent that there is any internal processing of data, the internal processing must be understood as mechanical or as reducible to mechanical parts. The great failure of Enlightenment epistemology, epitomized in Hume's admission in the *Treatise* of his dissatisfaction with his own account of the self, is the failure either (1) to do away with the self or (2) to account for the physiological generation of the "mental" from the "physical" or (3) to conceive philosophically how there could even be a scientific account of that generation. In short, Enlightenment epistemology could neither do away with the active intellect nor reduce it to mechanical parts.

26. See Condillac, *Extrait raissoné*.

The problems that plague Enlightenment epistemology in particular plague all of Enlightenment psychology. Recall that the second major contention of the Enlightenment Project is that human beings are to be understood in the same way as we understand the natural world. In claiming that how we understand the world is fundamental and that how we understand ourselves is derivative, the proponents of the Enlightenment Project became committed to the position that subjects can be reduced to objects, that is, that the subject matter of the purported social sciences is not different in kind from the subject matter of the physical sciences. This position is not only consistent with the claim of Enlightenment epistemology that the "mental" is somehow generated by the "physical," it is consistent with the claim of Enlightenment axiology that human nature must be amenable to an externally imposed social technology.

Enlightenment psychology in particular and programmatic Enlightenment social science in general were not the product of an explication of the actual empirical accomplishments of the social sciences. Rather, these were conclusions from unargued philosophical premises and a political agenda. In practice, this led to two programs: either a militant reductivism or a miraculous functional dualism. By "functional dualism" is meant the contention that physical processes at one level were perfectly coordinated with conscious processes at another level, that is, a dualism of mechanism and teleology. This dualism is "miraculous" because without some appeal to God[27] it is difficult to see why a deterministic system should also function coincidentally as a teleological one. Locke believed that God could make matter "think," but within the Enlightenment Project no appeal to theistic notions was permitted. So, just as the Enlightenment Project required a providential history without God, so it required a miraculous psychological dualism without God. The Enlightenment Project never succeeded in explaining, either in its epistemology or in its psychology, how the human subject could be understood without appeal to teleology of some kind and at some level.

Curiously, those who proposed such programs, from Locke to d'Holbach or La Mettrie or Condillac, rarely if ever conducted experimentation. Rather, they engaged in intellectual speculation about the possibility of such experiments. Not only were these speculations unsuccessful as research projects but they remained mysterious since no one could explain even in principle what such experiments would be like. What emerged from this was the character of the philosopher as quasi-scientific technician, but a technician of an indeterminable kind.

---

27. Note that even Spinoza, who was among the first to propose such a miraculous dualism, found room for God in his system.

Returning to the ambitions of Enlightenment epistemology, namely, to delegitimate nonscientific claims and to provide a microcosmic account of the growth of knowledge, we find that it failed on both counts. In fact, rather than providing independent support for scientism, Enlightenment epistemology had to invoke the claim that the future of scientific progress would render intelligible its speculative research programs with regard to cognitive psychology. Here we seem to be moving in a circle. Scientism is defended in terms of an allegedly progressive view of the scientific development; the progress of science is defended by an allegedly scientific account of epistemology or knowledge acquisition; and the allegedly scientific epistemology is defended by an appeal to the future of science. Given this circle, it is not surprising that Enlightenment epistemology could not come to the rescue of Enlightenment metaphysics. In this respect, Enlightenment epistemology could not resolve traditional epistemological perplexities, and it most especially could not resolve them without at least a covert appeal to the metaphysics of scientism and its attendant view of historical progress.

In addition, Enlightenment epistemology generated new problems by its attempt to eliminate the activities of the subject. It is important to note that these problems in cognitive psychology or philosophical psychology are not timeless problems but problems specifically necessitated by the presuppositions of the Enlightenment Project. Moreover, Enlightenment epistemology, by tying itself to the requirement that there be a "scientific" account of cognition, and by failing to provide such an account, threatened to delegitimate the very possibility of knowledge. In short, empiricism leads when consistently pressed to a corrosive skepticism.

It is important to note that proponents of the Enlightenment Project did not consistently press empiricism. They never really doubted the existence of genuine knowledge. In the absence of the final and certified product, the proponents fell back upon customary beliefs. Here we return to the point we made earlier about adopting two complimentary discourses. That is, they spoke from within our common heritage, invoking consensual intellectual and axiological norms when needed, and they still reserved the philosophical privilege of seemingly stepping outside of the common heritage to amend or reject items within that common heritage when they deemed it necessary. Failure to be consistent combined with the advocacy of a social and political agenda led to a politicization of epistemology. By this is meant the selective use of epistemological doctrines in the service of particular social and political agendas.

In the early part of the twentieth century, analytic philosophers began with the eighteenth-century introspective model, but, after repeating all of its errors in déjà vu fashion, they then moved to replace introspective epistemology with the philosophy of language. It seems that the very nature of the introspective approach invokes an internal subject that is not an object. Language, on the other hand, appeared to be an object in the world. As Carnap put it, "[L]anguage phenomena are events *within* the world, not something that refers to the world from outside."[28] This move to language also seemingly supports scientism:

1. Language is a natural object.
2. Natural objects are explained scientifically.
3. Hence language can be explained scientifically.
4. All philosophical issues are expressed in language.
5. Hence, too, at some level philosophical discourse can be explained scientifically.
6. Hence, all metaphysics can be replaced with or subsumed under science.

The trouble with the linguistic program is that it too raised all of the old problems. First, Gödel made clear that there could not be a mechanical model for the most celebrated of all linguistic systems, namely, mathematics. Then, Wittgenstein was to make clear that language could not be explained without appeal to the users of language as well as the culture of the users. Finally, Wittgenstein was to argue that the very notion of a mechanical model for explaining the user of language was inherently unintelligible.[29]

The problems within the analytic philosophy of language are identical to the problems of self-consciousness within Enlightenment and positivist epistemology. Scientific philosophers can only construe consciousness as itself an object. But if consciousness were an object, then there would have to be another subject conscious of that consciousness. So to the infinite fact is added yet another "fact." Unfortunately, the added "fact" belies the existence of the original infinite fact that was supposed to be all-encompassing. Scientific philosophers have been unable to collapse the subject (or mind) into the object (or body), and hence any attempt they make to capture the awareness of the totality, that is, to capture the subject's part in all of this, fails.[30]

---

28. Schilpp, ed., *Philosophy of Carnap*, 29.
29. See Richard McDonough, "Wittgenstein's Critique of Mechanistic Atomism," *Philosophical Investigations* 14, no. 3 (July 1991): 231–51.
30. Analytic philosophical psychology is dominated by a mechanistic paradigm. See, e.g.,
  (1) J. Fodor, *Psychosemantics: The Problem of Meaning and the Philosophy of Mind* (Cambridge, Mass.: MIT Press, 1987), 119.
  (2) D. Dennett, *Brainstorms* (Cambridge, Mass.: MIT Press, 1981), 107.
  (3) J. Searle, *Minds, Brains, and Science* (Cambridge: Cambridge University Press, 1984), 145.

The only modern philosopher working within the broad confines of Aristotelianism who was able to deal coherently with the problem of self-reference was Hegel. However, from the Enlightenment point of view, Hegel is unacceptable because he collapsed the object into the subject, and embraced teleology in opposition to materialism. This means that Hegel rejected the materialism on which the Enlightenment Program of social reform through social technology is based. In addition, Hegel eschewed the kind of substantive individualism with which supporters of the Enlightenment often interpreted newly emerging liberal values. In this respect and others, it is no accident that the twentieth-century revival of the Enlightenment Project comes with Russell's rejection of Hegel.

Fodor and other analytic defenders of the Enlightenment Project protest that such mechanical modeling deserves the respect of being treated as a scientific hypothesis and should not be rejected a priori. Unfortunately, Fodor and his supporters have been no more successful than their nineteenth-century predecessors in making clear the experimental intelligibility of these projects.[31]

I believe that I can explain the logic of what is happening here. In embracing the scientism of the Enlightenment Project, analytic philosophers are in the position of having to maintain that philosophy, if it is to be meaningful, must be a science or a part of science. The question we face, then, is what kind of science or part of science can philosophy be?

There are two kinds of explanations in science: eliminations and explorations. First, in hard or physical science we find elimination. When we theorize from an elimination point of view there is an explicit substitution of new ideas for old ideas. Elimination is a form of radical replacement through innovation. All forms of reductionism are forms of elimination. One example is the elimination of Ptolemy's geocentric view of the universe and its replacement by Copernicus's heliocentric view of the universe. Another example is the elimination of traditional theories of disease by the discovery of microbes. Elimination is a form of thinking

---

(4) S. Stich, *From Folk Psychology to Cognitive Science: The Case against Belief* (Cambridge, Mass.: MIT Press, 1983), 231.

(5) P. M. Churchland, *Scientific Realism and the Plasticity of Mind* (Cambridge: Cambridge University Press, 1979), 6.

(6) P. S. Churchland, *Neurophilosophy* (Cambridge, Mass.: MIT Press, 1986), 461–62.

(7) F. Dretske, *Knowledge and the Flow of Information* (Cambridge, Mass.: MIT Press, 1981), 186–88.

31. According to Colin McGinn ("Can We Solve the Mind-Body Problem?" *Mind* 97 [1989]), "We have, it seems, no understanding whatsoever how... brains are the... causal basis of consciousness" (349). The problem, according to McGinn, "resists even articulate formulations" (354), and we seem to be "bang up against the limits of our ability to understand the world" (354).

that makes sense if there is some prior and conventionally agreed-upon framework in terms of which we can judge that one new theory is better than an old theory.

The early history of analytic philosophy, especially in its positivistic phase, can be viewed as subscribing to the view that all correct thinking is eliminative thinking. Certainly in the early Russell and in the positivism of the Vienna Circle one sees an optimism about how science is the successful elimination of superstition and nonsense and how philosophy is the overseer of the transition period to a totally scientific worldview.

The major difficulty with elimination is one that we have already touched upon, and that is that there must be some independent criterion in terms of which we can judge an elimination to be successful. Analytic philosophers, because of their commitment to scientism, originally believed that science bore the mark of its own validity. Therefore, in order to decide when one theory has successfully eliminated another, we can look to science itself. Within physical science we, presumably, find examples of "successful" reductions of one theory to another or eliminations of one theory in favor of another. So it would seem to be the case that it is a simple matter to extract the criteria for such success. Unfortunately, this turns out not to be the case. Instead of being a minor technical problem of specifying when reduction-elimination was successful, it turned out that there was no consensus on when elimination was successful without appeal to nontechnical criteria.[32]

Russell's *Principia Mathematica* and Wittgenstein's *Tractatus* are the high-water mark of the notion that philosophy as the logic of science is to be a form of elimination. The failure of logicism and the results of Gödel's theorem show the impossibility of carrying out the kind of reduction and elimination that analytic philosophy originally thought possible. In logic, in mathematics, and in science there are a priori elements (semantic notions, conventions, appeals to common sense or to intuitions, etc.) that cannot be eliminated in a straightforward and unambiguous fashion. Hence, if philosophy is to be a science, or the logic of science, it must appeal to some other version of scientific thinking.

This brings us to exploration. In exploration we begin with our ordinary understanding of how things work and then go on to speculate on what might be the hidden structure behind those workings. In time, we

---

32. "Analytic philosophy has great accomplishments, to be sure; but those accomplishments are negative. Like logical positivism (itself just one species of analytic philosophy), analytic philosophy has succeeded in destroying the very problem with which it started. Each of the efforts to solve that problem, or even to say exactly what could count as a solution to that problem, has failed"; Hilary Putnam, "After Empiricism," *Partisan Review* (1984), reprinted in Rajchman and West, eds., *Post-Analytic Philosophy*, 28.

come to change our ordinary understanding. The new understanding does not evolve from or elaborate the old understanding; rather, it replaces it by appeal to underlying structures. The underlying structures are discovered by following out the implications of some hypothetical model about those structures. Our ordinary understanding is a necessary but temporary scaffolding to be taken down when the construction is completed; it is indispensable but revisable in the light of the discovery of underlying structures.

Exploration is a mode of thinking sometimes found in the physical sciences and is exemplified, for example, in the use of the atomic theory to explain chemical behavior or the behavior of gases. But exploration is also preeminently the mode of thought of academic social science. By alleged analogy with physical science, the social sciences have persistently sought to discover the hidden structure behind the everyday understanding of social activities. From Durkheim to Marx, Freud, the functionalists, Chomsky, and so on, social scientists have persistently sought to reveal a structural level of which we are not immediately aware. Exploration, then, stresses the search for structure rather than the search for meaning, the search for the formal elements underlying the everyday world rather than believing that the everyday world can constitute its own level of understanding.

The single most important development in the evolution of analytic philosophy is the transition from the view that philosophy is elimination to the view that philosophy is exploration. Put another way, analytic philosophy turns philosophy into an alleged social science. The widely hailed rejection of positivism is the symbol of this transition.

Symptomatic of this transition is the emphasis on the continuity of science and common sense. Of course, we must be careful to keep in mind that "continuous" is being used here metaphorically, and we would have to specify it more carefully. Jonah, after all, was continuous with the whale. To explore is to begin with common sense and then to transcend it by the use of science. What is happening here is that analytic philosophy engages in intellectual practices that are indistinguishable from the social sciences, where the social sciences are construed as explorations along the lines of the physical sciences.

Nevertheless, there is a problem with exploration. Exploration on its own is inherently incoherent. This incoherence can be seen on two levels. First, before one can investigate the alleged hidden structure of a social practice, one must clearly identify the social practice itself. No analysis can proceed unless there is a clear conception of the fundamental entities that are the subject matter of analysis. However, a social practice is an intersubjectively shared framework of norms within which we interpret what we are doing. In order to identify the social practice, therefore, one must specify clearly the intersubjectively shared framework of norms. Since the framework is intersubjective, no specification of the framework is legitimate that does not accord with previous historical practice. Thus we are brought to the same point, namely, that thinking can only proceed against a background of shared assumptions.

The entire argument about the incoherence of unanchored exploration can be articulated at an even higher level. No technical form of thinking (including logic, mathematics, and physical science) can itself be understood except by appeal to something that is pretechnical (e.g., common sense). Technical thinking, no matter how valuable within its limited sphere, can never replace pretechnical thinking. Rival hypotheses in technical discourse must ultimately be judged by appeal to pretechnical norms. Nor can one develop a technical account of pretechnical reasoning, for, on pain of incoherence, there would be no possible way to judge the adequacy of the proffered technical account.

Having chosen science as their model, analytic philosophers are unable to resolve their dilemma. Unable to choose among alternative explorations, they offer either an infinite chain of supplementary explorations, or they propose explorations of the process of choosing among explorations, or they suggest explorations of the hidden structure behind the explorations of their opponents. In short, they have fallen into an abyss of exploration from which there is no exit. Whereas in hard science the process of exploratory thinking leads, when successful, to the discovery of new and previously hidden entities, the case in both the alleged social sciences and in philosophy is merely the substitution of one new jargon for another. There are endless new techniques but no new facts; the analytic technician always hopes to escape the limitations of technique with more technique; in this, he confuses technique with science. The riders and the tunes change, but the carousel's progress is illusory.

The other consequence of this kind of thinking is the delegitimation and relativization of reason. Taken to its logical conclusion, the inability to choose leads to a corrosive skepticism.[33] Instead of having to respond to the arguments of their critics, all practitioners of exploration offer an exploration of the hidden structure behind their critics' views.

33. As examples of corrosive skepticism, I note that both Quine and Kripke have become skeptical about meaning. See Saul Kripke, *Wittgenstein on Rules and Private Language* (Oxford: Blackwell, 1982). Colin McGinn claims that we cannot solve the mind-body problem (see Note 31); there has been a reemergence of eliminativism in analytic philosophical psychology such that commonsense views about ourselves are denigrated as examples of a misguided folk psychology (see Note 30); there is continued skepticism about freedom and responsibility.

This is what we identified earlier as Condorcet's promised "scientific" delegitimation of the opposition to scientism. Unfortunately, since explorations cannot be confirmed or disconfirmed, they delegitimate everything.

The only alternative is a disingenuously politicized epistemology. By his own admission, Karl Popper's notion of falsification did not derive from a study of science but originated politically. That is, according to Popper himself, it was the desire to refute the views of both Marxists and Freudians that led him to formulate the principle of falsifiability. This is a clear case of political preference dictating technical doctrines.[34]

As the position of analytic philosophy vis-à-vis science evolved from a naive empiricist form of elimination into a more open-ended form of exploration, the connection between analytic philosophy and liberalism became even more apparent. In the absence of strict empirical confirmation, other criteria closely resembling liberal political values were substituted. We note that in analytic ethical theorizing the traditional moral agent gets replaced by an economic agent, and that the economic agent seems to make decisions using the model of neoclassical economics. Analogously, when analytic philosophers surrender naive empiricism and are forced to specify criteria to be used in the evaluation of rival hypotheses, the criteria turn out to be the sort one would expect of a neoclassical economist!

The assimilation of philosophy to general theoretical science is frequently thought to deprive philosophy of its normative or critical role in telling us how we *ought* to think.... Such views ... tend to exaggerate the purely factual nature of science; those who hold them fail to see that science is also a discipline of enormous normative scope. Legislative postulation, the general mode of scientific hypothesis, is essentially a matter of human proposal and decision. Theory is not simply and unequivocally "determined by the facts," but instead involves theory-wide "practical" considerations of simplicity, convenience, utility, and efficacy, which have become increasingly recognized for their important role in theory construction. Thus the problem of deciding what is best or most desirable of alternative views of the same set of "facts," so to speak—deciding what we ought to think—is a regular feature of standard scientific operating procedure.[35]

We note in passing the close similarity of the foregoing criteria to Ben-

---

34. Popper is a great admirer of Mill's *On Liberty*. One of Popper's early followers who later became a critic was Paul Feyerabend, also an admirer of Mill's essay. Feyerabend, who was a political anarchist, tended to construe science and scientific practice from the political perspective of anarchism. For an interesting discussion of Popper on this point, see Struan Jacobs's *Science and British Liberalism: Locke, Bentham, Mill, and Popper* (London: Avebury, 1991).

35. George D. Romanos, *Quine and Analytic Philosophy* (Cambridge, Mass.: MIT Press, 1983), 193.

tham's felicific calculus for determining the value of pleasure and pain, specifically Bentham's criteria of fecundity, purity, and extent.[36]

AXIOLOGY

The most serious consequences of the Enlightenment Project have been in social policy.

We have already touched briefly on the axiological problems faced by the Enlightenment Project. The most obvious, but not the most fundamental, issue is how proponents of the Enlightenment Project could claim scientific support for particular moral, social, economic, and political policies prior to the achievement of certifiable results within specific social sciences. It certainly seemed as if the policies came first and the alleged "scientific evidence" was fashioned later. At the very least there is the appearance of disingenuousness. The suspicion of disingenuousness merely reinforces the perception of the politicization of epistemology.

The foregoing difficulty, which we can characterize as moral, is also reinforced when we turn to the fundamental logical problem within the axiology of the Enlightenment Project. Having eschewed teleology, God, and custom, what would the metaphysical or ontological status of a norm be?

Here the metaphysical problems of the Enlightenment Project lead to axiological problems. Put bluntly, how can there be norms (values, goods, "the good," etc.) in the first place?

Not only do the metaphysical problems of the Enlightenment lead to axiological problems, but the epistemological problems do so as well. If there are norms, what is their cognitive status? How do we apprehend norms? Are norms to be construed as facts of a special kind, or, if they are not, just how are the norms related to the facts?

There is one unusually disturbing and perplexing axiological problem for the Enlightenment Project. That problem is the loss of the self. As we stressed in our discussion of epistemology, proponents of the Enlightenment Project denied the existence of an active intellect with special and unique functions. As we stressed in our discussion of both metaphysics and epistemology, proponents of the Enlightenment Project deny the existence of a subject that is not an object or not reducible to a collection of objects. Most especially this amounts to the denial of the idea of a free and personally responsible individual soul that emerged out of the Greco-Roman and Judeo-Christian worldview.

---

36. See Jeremy Bentham, *An Introduction to the Principles of Morals and Legislation*, ed. J. J. Burns and H. L. A. Hart (London: Athlone, 1970), Chapter 5.

The denial of the self thus serves a number of important and interrelated purposes for the Enlightenment Project. Metaphysically, it reinforces the claim that the physical world is primary. In a very important sense, the entire Western intellectual tradition prior to the Enlightenment had made self-understanding primary. Coincidentally, it is a further attack on the theistic contention of a unique volitional being. Epistemologically, the denial of the self reinforces the claim that knowledge is nothing but the grasping of an external structure. Failure to grasp the structure cannot be attributed to any act of the will but becomes in principle explainable in terms of further objective structures. This gives a tremendous boost to rationalist optimism. Finally, the denial of the self serves the axiological function of providing for an objective social technology that does not depend upon human attitudes that are not externally manipulable. Put in other terms, intellectual virtue would not depend upon moral virtue, nor could there be a failure of the will, and there would be no problem of freedom of the will.

The Enlightenment Project is the attempt to engage in social reconstruction on the basis of a purely scientific reason. It is this attitude that explains the radical transformation of Locke's ideas and even Rousseau's ideas in the hands of the philosophes and their followers.

The clearest example of this is to be found in Helvetius's *De l'esprit* (1758). Starting with Locke's epistemological claim that all knowledge originates in experience and that the human mind at birth is a tabula rasa, Helvetius goes on to embrace an extreme form of environmental determinism. This should remind us of Rawls's veil of ignorance. All differences in beliefs, attitudes, values, and the like, are solely the result of historical and environmental accident.[37] From this, it was concluded that all human beings are fundamentally identical and therefore equal. All forms of social hierarchy, privilege, and differences in power and influence were deemed the result of historical accident and denounced as unjust. In its place was substituted the notion that all individuals, when properly educated, are equally competent judges. Participatory democracy is therefore the only form of government compatible with the fundamental equality of human nature.

What Helvetius did not see is that his reading of Locke was also compatible with totalitarianism. First, if there were basic truths about human nature that dictated specific social arrangements, then why should these practices not be forthwith instituted by an enlightened elite? Further, the

---

37. "Even the willingness to make an effort, to try, and so to be deserving in the ordinary sense is itself dependent upon happy family and social circumstances"; John Rawls, *A Theory of Justice* (Cambridge, Mass.: Harvard University Press, 1971), 74.

people were only to be trusted if they were properly educated and had undergone a deprogramming therapy that cleansed them of the misperceptions from which they suffered as the result of" previous oppressive governments. Allowing the people to debate public policy issues in their current state of mind ran the risk of their intellectual exploitation by scoundrels. It might be necessary to have a "temporary" dictatorship until the therapeutic process was completed, and even then political debate could be dispensed with in favor of scientific discussion among the informed experts followed by public reeducation.

Environmental determinism had also to be qualified by and made compatible with the assumption that a secularized natural law would continue to discover that all human beings shared the same basic goals. When these goals had been presumed to originate with God, as was the case in Locke and traditional natural law, it was not necessary to explain

1. why there were goals in the first place,
2. why these goals were common and universal to all human beings, and
3. why these goals could harmoniously coexist both within the same individual and among an entire community.

Moreover, within traditional theologically based versions of natural law some consideration had been given to the inner conflicts we all experience and to potential social conflicts. Perfect justice was to be achieved in the next life so that all we could hope for in this world was a harmony of private interests. When natural law is shorn of its theological framework, it becomes problematic why human beings should be believed to have natural goals at all, especially given a commitment to strong environmental determinism. It also becomes problematic to assume that if there are goals they would be common to all human beings, especially in the presence of differing histories. Finally, and most important, how can there be scientific public policy and social reconstruction unless there is some natural harmony or guarantee of a lack of ultimate conflict?

Once the belief in God is surrendered, the adherence to a secularized natural law doctrine requires some substitute to guarantee the convergence toward a common interest. The logic of the argument will inevitably drive theorists to the conclusion that there must be a common or group interest that subsumes all of the individual interests so that ultimate fulfillment on the part of the individual can only be achieved within some absolute social and political framework. Modern totalitarianism is thus born. In that pivotal work, "*What Is the Third Estate?*," the Abbé Sieyes had asserted that the nation "is prior to everything, it is the source of everything . . . its will is always the supreme law." It should therefore come as no surprise that in the twentieth century Carnap would assert his "conviction that the great problems of the organization of the economy and the organization of the world at the present time, in the era of industrialization, cannot possibly be solved by the 'interplay of forces,' but require rational planning. For the organization of the economy this means socialism in some form; for the organization of the world it means a gradual development towards a world government."[38]

Totalitarian democracy, as Talmon has dubbed this development, substitutes the idea of a common good for the traditional idea of a harmony of interests. At the same time, it seemingly solves one of the serious problems of the new secularized natural law. Instead of having to establish that each individual has a built-in goal (as opposed to historically acquired ones) and instead of having to prove that each individual's "natural" goal is compatible with those of every other individual, the new totalitarian has merely to establish what the common goal is. Establishing this common goal was never done in any objective or scientific way, despite the scientific pretensions of the age. Instead, each and every revolutionary individual or faction was free to propose whatever was wanted. Carnap's economic views were certainly not based on empirical investigation, nor were they formally abstracted from the work of economists, certainly not the economists in either Vienna or at the University of Chicago!

The new scientific basis for the reconstruction of society becomes an empty formula into which anyone can plug any variable. Instead of establishing the common good objectively, rival theorists employ the notion of environmental determinism as an exploration to discredit their rivals. Whatever a rival proposed was the result of past miseducation and prejudice. One's own proposal wins by default. This is the sense in which it can be claimed that no coherent or consistent political philosophy animates the actors in the Enlightenment tradition. Rather, they are capable of disguising their political, social, and economic ambitions behind the rhetoric of a fanatical devotion to the common good. With the loss of philosophical consciousness has come the final degradation of philosophy, for it is now only a mask for politics.

Contemporary analytic political theory fares no better. Hiding behind Rawls's veil of ignorance, a perfect example of groundless exploration and environmental determinism, one can arrive either at Rawls's own preference for mild welfare liberalism, or Nozick's preference for a more classical liberalism, or Dworkin's unabashed embrace of elitist socialism.[39] In each case, we find natural rights theory turned into a form of ideological rhetoric.

---

38. Schilpp, ed., *Philosophy of Carnap*, 83.
39. "This [Rawls's book] is certainly the model of social justice that has governed the

There is a relationship between analytic philosophy and politics. We maintain the historical and sociological thesis that analytic philosophy is a product of the cultural movement known as the Enlightenment, and we have characterized that movement in terms of the attempt to use science and technology both to define and to solve human moral, social, and political problems. Hence, we wish to suggest that a previous political agenda informs the cultural context in which analytic philosophy flourished. We are not suggesting that this is all there is to analytic philosophy, nor are we suggesting that recognizing this cultural context automatically discredits analytic philosophy, nor are we suggesting that all those who have identified themselves as analytic philosophers consciously operate in their philosophical endeavors to advance this political agenda. We do, however, wish to suggest that in order to understand any philosophical movement some consideration must be given to its cultural context,[40] and

---

advocacy of R. H. Tawney and Richard Titmus and that holds the Labour Party together"; quote from Stuart Hampshire, in his review of the book, "A New Philosophy of the Just Society," in the *New York Review of Books*, February 24, 1972. Dworkin has said "in a way, we're [i.e., Rawls, Nozick, and Dworkin] all working the same street ... liberalism ... the theory that makes the content of justice independent of any particular theory of human virtue or excellence"; Bryan Magee, *Men of Ideas* (New York: Oxford University Press, 1982), 223.

40. Space limitations prevent its development here, but we believe that a case can be made for a continuous development, suitably qualified, stretching from Hobbes, Spinoza (e.g., see Feuer), and Locke to the philosophes to Bentham to Russell and to the positivists. This development would be analogous to the development we have described in metaphysics and epistemology from Bacon and Descartes through the philosophes to Carnap, etc.

Carnap, for example, was not only inspired by Russell's general philosophical vision but by his political positions as well. "I am in complete agreement with the aims for which you are fighting at present: serious negotiations, instead of the Cold War, no bomb-testing, no fall-out shelters" (Letter from Carnap to Russell, dated May 12, 1962).

The most programmatic member of the Circle, Otto Neurath, was actively involved in the Social Democratic Party in Bavaria, and he articulated in unequivocal fashion the utopian goals of social engineering. Specifically, Neurath argued that after seeing the fruits of central economic planning during wartime (in World War I), market economies would be replaced by a communal economy. "In a socialist economy the living standards and wages of everybody will be fixed by ... decrees ... they will not be decided by contract" (Otto Neurath, "Through War Economy to Economy in Kind" in *Empiricism and Sociology* [Dordrecht: Reidel, 1973]).

Even epistemological issues were not immune to political considerations. According to Anders Wedberg, "[T]hrough the influence of the ideas of Otto Neurath, which in turn were inspired by Marxism, Carnap began in the early 1930's to regard methodological solipsism with a certain disapproval" (Wedberg, *History of Philosophy*, 3 vols. [Oxford: Oxford University Press, 1984], 3.222).

Another positivist who shared Neurath's enthusiasm for planning was Hans Reichenbach. Reichenbach had been a leader of the Socialist Youth Movement in Germany. In his book *The Rise of Scientific Philosophy* (Berkeley and Los Angeles: University of California Press, 1951), Reichenbach praised Marx specifically for Marx's critique of Hegelian idealism, Marx's empiricism, and most especially Marx's advocacy of applying science to the social world.

One of the clearest and most direct expressions of the link between analytic philosophy

we do want to maintain that a great deal of what analytic philosophers have done and have failed to do is illuminated by recognizing the cultural context of the Enlightenment Project.

---

and liberalism understood as the advocacy of social technology is to be found in the works of Karl Popper. "Man can know: thus he can be free.... This is the formula which explains the link between epistemological optimism and the ideas of liberalism." Karl Popper made this statement at the annual Philosophical Lecture read before the British Academy on January 20, 1960. It was reprinted in *Conjectures and Refutations: The Growth of Scientific Philosophy* (New York: Harper and Row, 1962), 6. According to Popper, the belief in objective truth or epistemological realism is equated with the belief in liberal social technology. He believes that the rise of science and technology since the Renaissance leads to the epistemological optimism of the liberal mind.

Contributors

Paul J. Bagley received his Ph.D. from Trinity College, Dublin, and is a member of the Philosophy faculty at Loyola College in Maryland. He has been a visiting lecturer at the Katholieke Universiteit Leuven, and is currently President of the North American Spinoza Society. His publications include "On the Practice of Esotericism," *Journal of the History of Ideas* (1993), "Descartes, Triangles, and the Existence of God," *Philosophical Forum* (1995), "Harris, Strauss, and Esotericism in Spinoza's *Tractatus theologico-politicus*," *Interpretation: A Journal of Political Philosophy* (1996), "On the Moral Philosophy of René Descartes: Or How Morals Are Derived from Method," *Tijdschrift voor Filosofie* (1996), and "Religious Salvation and Civic Welfare: '*Salus*' in Spinoza's *Tractatus theologico-politicus*," *Studia Spinozana* (1997).

Nicholas Capaldi is McFarlin Professor of Philosophy and Director of Legal Studies at the University of Tulsa. He is the author of six books, and over sixty articles, and has edited five anthologies. A former editor of *Public Affairs Quarterly* and member of numerous editorial boards, he is currently editor-in-chief of the Peter Lang series, Masterworks in the Western Tradition. He is a long-time student of the Enlightenment, noted for such studies as *Hume's Place in Moral Philosophy* (1989). His forthcoming book, based upon the article he contributed to this volume, is *The Enlightenment Project in the Analytic Conversation* (Kluwer, 1998).

Frederick J. Crosson is Cavanaugh Professor of Humanities at the University of Notre Dame. He has edited five books and published over forty articles.

Pamela A. Kraus is Lecturer at St. John's College, Annapolis, where she also serves as editor of the *St. John's Review*. She has published on Descartes and Locke.

Richard H. Kennington studied at the Sorbonne and the University of Chicago before receiving his Ph.D. from the New School for Social Research. He joined the faculty of The Catholic University of America in 1975, and retired in 1996. He has written on Bacon, Descartes, Spinoza, Hans Blumenberg, and Leo Strauss. In addition, he is editor of *The Philosophy of Baruch Spinoza* (1985) and *The Philosophy of Immanual Kant* (1985).

Alan Charles Kors is Professor of History at the University of Pennsylvania, where he teaches early modern intellectual history. He is the author of several books on the seventeenth and eighteenth centuries, and is currently editor-in-chief of the *Oxford Encyclopedia of the Enlightenment*.

Robert P. Kraynak is Professor of Political Science at Colgate University. He is the author of *History and Modernity in the Thought of Thomas Hobbes* (1990) and numerous articles on modern liberalism. He is writing a book-length study, "Christianity and Liberal Democracy," which will be delivered as the Frank M. Covey Jr., Loyola Lectures in Political Analysis in 1998, to be published by Notre Dame University Press.

Terence E. Marshall is Maître de Conférences at the University of Paris X, Nanterre. He has published, both in French and English, on Rousseau, on ancient and modern political philosophy, including several studies of Rousseau, and on constitutional theory. His books include *Classicisme et modernité* (1989), *Vie et institutions politiques des Etats-Unis* (1989), and *Théorie et pratique du gouvernement constitutionnel: la France et les Etats-Unis* (1992).

John C. McCarthy is Associate Professor of Philosophy at The Catholic University of America. Among his publications are essays on Augustine and Aquinas, and several studies of Husserlian phenomenology understood as a response to the heritage of early modern philosophy.

Philippe Raynaud, "agrégé" in philosophy, and in political science, and "docteur d'état en science politique," is Professor of Political Science at the University of Lille, II. He is on the editorial boards of the journals *Esprit, Commentaire*, and *Le Débat*. Among his publications are *Terrorisme et démocratie* (with François Furet and Antoine Liniers, 1985), and *Max Weber et les dilemmes de la raison moderne* (1987, 1996). Together with Stéphane Rials he has edited a *Dictionnaire de philosophie politique* (1996).

Kenneth L. Schmitz is Professor Emeritus of Philosophy, and Fellow of Trinity College, in the University of Toronto, where he received his Ph.D. in 1952. The recipient of Humboldt grants and a Canada Council Research Grant, he has also been President of the Hegel Society of America, the Metaphysical Society of America, and the American Catholic Philosophical Association. His numerous publications have focused on the philosophies of Kant and Hegel, the philosophy of religion, aesthetics, and philosophical issues in theology. Books include *The Gift: Creation* (1982), and *At the Center of the Human Drama: The Philosophical Anthropology of Karol Wojtyla/Pope John Paul II* (1993).

John Silber is Chancellor of Boston University. He received his Ph.D. from Yale University, where he held his first academic position. For many years a member of the faculty of the University of Texas, he became the seventh President of Boston University in 1971, a position he held until 1996. Aside from his publications in philosophy, and especially on the philosophy of Kant, he has written on education, and social and foreign policy, including a book, *Straight Shooting* (1989). He has a distinguished record of public service, having served on board and commission memberships at local, state, and national levels. He has been decorated by the governments of France, Germany, and Israel.

Selected Bibliography

Alembert, Jean le Rond d'. *Preliminary Discourse to the Encyclopedia of Diderot.* Translated and edited by Richard N. Schwab and Walter E. Rex. Indianapolis, Ind.: Bobbs-Merrill, 1963.
———. *Mélanges de littérature, d'histoire, et de philosophie.* 4 vols. Amsterdam, 1759.
Allison, Henry E. *Lessing and the Enlightenment: His Philosophy of Religion and Its Relation to Eighteenth-Century Thought.* Ann Arbor: University of Michigan Press, 1966.
Alquié, Ferdinand. *La découverte métaphysique de l'homme chez Descartes.* Paris: Presses universitaires de France, 1950.
———. *Le cartesiannisme de Malebranche.* Paris: J. Vrin, 1974.
Alquié, Ferdinand, ed. *Discours de la methode,* by René Descartes. In *Oeuvres philosophiques,* vol. 1. Paris: Editions Garnier Frères, 1963.
Aner, K. *Die Theologie der Lessingzeit.* Halle: Niemeyer, 1929.
Avicenna. "On the Division of the Rational Sciences." Translated by Muhsin Mahdi. In *Medieval Political Philosophy: A Sourcebook,* edited by Ralph Lerner and Muhsin Mahdi. Glencoe, Ill.: Free Press, 1963.
Bachelard, Gaston. *La poétique de la rêverie.* Paris: Presses universitaires de France, 1960.
Bacon, Francis. *The New Organon and Related Writings.* Edited by Fulton H. Anderson. Indianapolis, Ind.: Bobbs-Merrill, 1960.
———. *Selected Writings of Francis Bacon.* Introduction and notes by Hugh G. Dick. New York: Modern Library, 1955.
———. *The Works of Francis Bacon.* 14 vols. Edited by J. Spedding, R. L. Ellis, and D. Heath. London: Longmans and Co., 1857–1870. Reprint, Stuttgart-Bad Canstatt: Frohmann-Holzboog, 1963.
Baillie, J. *The Belief in Progress.* New York: Charles Scribner's Sons, 1951.
Baird, A. W. S. "Inconsistencies in Pascal's Conception of Scientific Knowledge." *Aumla* 24 (1965).
———. "Pascal's Idea of Nature." *Isis* 61 (1970).
———. *Studies in Pascal's Ethics.* The Hague: Martinus Nijhoff, 1975.
Balthasar, Hans Urs, von. "Pascal." In *Studies in Theological Style: Lay Styles.* Vol. 3 of *The Glory of the Lord: A Theological Aesthetics.* Translated by Andrew Louth et al. San Francisco: Ignatius Press, 1986.
———. *Theodrama.* Vol. 1, *Prolegomena.* Translated by Graham Harrison. San Francisco: Ignatius Press, 1988.
———. *Theodrama.* Vol. 2, *Dramatis Personae: Man in God.* Translated by Graham Harrison. San Francisco: Ignatius Press, 1990.
Barny, Roger. *Prélude idéologique à la révolution française: Le rousseauisme avant 1789.* Paris: Les Belles Lettres, 1985.

Barth, Karl. *Die protestantische Theologie im 19. Jahrhundert. Ihre Vorgeschichte und ihre Geschichte.* Zurich: Evangelischer Verlag, 1947.
Baudin, E. *Études historiques et critiques sur la philosophie de Pascal.* Vol. 1, *Pascal et Descartes.* Neuchâtel, Switzerland: Éditions de la Baconnière, 1946.
Bayle, Pierre. *An Historical and Critical Dictionary.* 4 vols. London, 1710.
Beccaria, Cesare. *On Crimes and Punishments.* Edited and translated by Henry Paolucci. Indianapolis, Ind.: Bobbs-Merrill, 1963.
Beck, Lewis White. *Essays on Hume and Kant.* New Haven, Conn.: Yale University Press, 1978.
Becker, Carl. *The Heavenly City of the Eighteenth-Century Philosophers.* New Haven, Conn.: Yale University Press, 1962.
Béguin, Albert. *L'âme romantique et le rêve: Essai sur le romantisme allemand et la poésie française.* Paris: José Corti, 1991.
Beitzinger, A. J. "Pascal on Justice, Force, and Law." *Review of Politics* 46 (1984).
Bentham, Jeremy. *An Introduction to the Principles of Morals and Legislation.* Edited by J. J. Burns and H. L. A. Hart. London: Athlone, 1970.
Bergson, Henri. *Ecrits et paroles.* Paris: Presses universitaires de France, 1958.
——. *Les deux sources de la morale et de la religion.* Paris: Presses universitaires de France, 1988.
Berman, David. "David Hume and the Suppression of Atheism." *Journal of the History of Philosophy* 21 (1983).
——. *A History of Atheism in Britain: From Hobbes to Russell.* New York: Croom Helm, 1988.
Berns, Laurence. "Aristotle's *Poetics*." In *Ancients and Moderns,* edited by Joseph Cropsey. New York: Basic Books, 1964.
Beyssade, J.-M. "Certitude et fondemont: L'évidence de la raison et la véracité divine dans la métaphysique du *Discours de la méthode.*" In *Le Discours et sa méthode,* edited by Nicolas Grimaldi and Jean-Luc Marion. Paris: Presses universitaires de France, 1987.
Blackburn, Simon. *Spreading the Word.* Oxford: Oxford University Press, 1984.
Bloom, Allan. "The Education of Democratic Man: Emile." *Daedulus* 107 (1978).
Blumenberg, Hans. *The Legitimacy of the Modern Age.* Translated by Robert N. Wallace. Cambridge, Mass.: MIT Press, 1983.
Boriski, K. *Lessing.* Berlin: Hoffmann, 1900.
Bourgeois, B., and J. D'Hondt. *La philosophie et la révolution française.* Paris: J. Vrin, 1993.
Boyle, Robert. "The Excellency and Grounds of the Corpuscular or Mechanical Philosophy." In *The Works,* vol. 4, edited by Thomas Birch. London, 1674. Reprint, Hildesheim: Georg Olms, 1966.
Brann, Eva. *The World of the Imagination, Sum, and Substance.* Savage, Md.: Rowman and Littlefield, 1991.
Brewster, Sir David. *Memoirs of the Life, Writings, and Discoveries of Sir Isaac Newton.* 2 vols. Edinburgh: T. Constable and Co., 1855.
Bricke, John. "On the Interpretation of Hume's *Dialogues.*" *Religious Studies* 11 (1975).
Brockliss, L. W. *French Higher Education in the Seventeenth and Eighteenth Centuries: A Cultural History.* Oxford: Oxford University Press, 1987.
Broome, J. H. *Pascal.* New York: Barnes and Noble, 1965.
Browne, Thomas. *Miracles Works Above and Contrary to Nature.* London, 1683.
Brunschvicg, Léon. *Descartes et Pascal: Lecteurs de Montaigne.* New York: Brentano, 1944.

———. *Blaise Pascal*. Paris: J. Vrin, 1953.
Buckley, Michael. *At the Origins of Modern Atheism*. New Haven, Conn.: Yale University Press, 1987.
Buffenoire, Hippolyte. *Le prestige de Jean-Jacques Rousseau*. Paris: Emile-Paul, 1909.
Buffon, George Louis Leclerc, Comte de. *Histoire naturelle*. 64 vols. Paris, 1799–1801.
Burns, Timothy, ed. *Francis Fukuyama and His Critics*. Lanham, Md.: Rowman and Littlefield, 1994.
Burton, J. H. *Life and Correspondence of David Hume*. 2 vols. Edinburgh, 1846. Reprint, New York: B. Franklin, 1967.
Burtt, Edwin A. *The Metaphysical Foundations of Modern Physical Science*. Garden City, N.Y.: Doubleday, 1954.
Bury, J. B. *The Idea of Progress: An Inquiry into Its Origin and Growth*. London: Macmillan, 1920.
Butler, Joseph. *Five Sermons . . . and a Dissertation upon the Nature of Virtue*. Edited by Steward M. Brown Jr. Indianapolis, Ind.: Bobbs-Merrill, 1950.
Carr, E. H. *What Is History?* New York: Knopf, 1962.
Carraud, Vincent. "Le refus Pascalien des preuves métaphysiques de l'existence de Dieu." *Revue des sciences philosophiques et théologiques* 75 (1991).
Cassirer, Ernst. *Kant's Life and Thought*. New Haven, Conn.: Yale University Press, 1981.
———. *The Philosophy of the Enlightenment*. Boston: Beacon Press, 1955.
Caton, Hiram. "Analytic History of Philosophy: The Case of Descartes." *Philosophical Forum* 12 (1981).
———. "Will and Reason in Descartes' Theory of Error." *Journal of Philosophy* 72 (1975).
Chartier, R., et al. *L'éducation en France du XVIe au XVIIIe siècle*. Paris: Societé d'édition d'enseignement supérieur, 1976.
Chastellux, François-Jean, marquis de. *De la félicité publique; ou, Considérations sur le sort des hommes dans les différentes époques de l'histoire*. 2 vols. Amsterdam, 1772.
Churchland, Patricia S. *Neurophilosophy*. Cambridge, Mass.: MIT Press, 1986.
Churchland, Paul M. *Scientific Realism and the Plasticity of Mind*. Cambridge: Cambridge University Press, 1976.
Colie, Rosalie L. "Spinoza and the Early English Deists." *Journal of the History of Ideas* 20 (1959).
Collins, James. *The Emergence of Philosophy of Religion*. New Haven, Conn.: Yale University Press, 1967.
Compère, M.-M., and D. Julia. *Les collèges français: 16e–18e siècles*. Paris: Institut National de Recherche Pédagogique, 1984.
Condillac, Etienne Bonnot de. *Extrait raisonné du Traité des sensations*. Paris: F. Alcan, 1921.
———. *Philosophical Writings of Etienne Bonnot, Abbé de Condillac*. Translated by Franklin Philip and Harlan Lane. Hillsdale, N.J.: Erlbaum, 1982.
Condorcet, Jean-Antoine-Nicolas, Marquis de. *Sketch for a Historical Picture of the Progress of the Human Mind*. Translated by June Barraclough. New York: Noonday Press, 1955.
Cotoni, Marie-Hélène. *La lettre de Jean-Jaques Rousseau à Christophe de Beaumont: Etude stylistique*. Paris: Les Belles Lettres, 1977.
Crosson, F. J. "Structure and Meaning in St. Augustine's Confessions." In *Proceed-

ings of the American Catholic Philosophical Association, vol. 63. Washington, D.C.: American Catholic Philosophical Association, 1989.

Curley, Edwin. "Cohérence ou incohérence du *Discours*." In *Le Discours et sa méthode*, edited by Nicholas Grimaldi and Jean Luc Marion. Paris: Presses universitaires de France, 1987.

Dampier, Sir William. *A History of Science and Its Relations with Philosophy and Religion*. 3d ed. Cambridge: Cambridge University Press, 1942.

Darnton, Robert. *The Great Cat Massacre*. New York: Random House, 1984.

Davis, Charles Michael. *Contemporary Reactions to Smallpox Inoculation in Eighteenth-Century France*. Ottawa: National Library of Canada, 1979. Text-fiche.

de Dainville, F., S.J. *L'éducation des Jésuites (XVIe–XVIIIe siècles)*. Paris: Editions de Minuit, 1978.

de Viguerie, J. *Une oeuvre d'éducation sous l'ancien égime: Les pères de la doctrine chrétienne en France et en Italie, 1592–1792*. Paris: Éditions de la nouvelle aurore aville, 1985.

de Villeray, Pierre-François Le Coq. *Réponse ou critique des Lettres Philosophiques de Monsieur de V***., par le R.P.D.P.B.* Reims, 1735.

Dennett, Daniel C. *Brainstorms: Philosophic Essays on Mind and Psychology*. Cambridge, Mass.: MIT Press, 1981.

Descartes, René. *Discours de la méthode*. Text and commentary by E. Gilson. Paris: J. Vrin, 1966.

———. *Oeuvres*. 11 vols. Edited by Charles Adam and Paul Tannery. Paris: J. Vrin, 1964–1974.

———. *The Philosophical Works of Descartes*. 2 vols. Translated by Elizabeth S. Haldane and G. R. T. Ross. Cambridge: Cambridge University Press.

———. *The Philosophical Writings of Descartes*. 2 vols. Translated by John Cottingham, Robert Stoothoff, and Dugald Murdoch. Cambridge: Cambridge University Press, 1984–1985.

———. *The Philosophical Writings of Descartes, Vol. 3: The Correspondence*. Translated by John Cottingham, Robert Stoothoff, Dugald Murdoch, and Anthony Kenny. Cambridge: Cambridge University Press, 1991.

———. *Regulae ad directionem ingenii*. Edited by Giovanni Crapulli. The Hague: Martinus Nijhoff, 1966.

Diderot, Denis. *Jacques the Fatalist and His Master*. Translated by J. Robert Loy. New York: Norton, 1978.

———. *Oeuvres philosophiques*. Edited by Paul Vernière. Paris: Editions Garnier Frères, 1964.

Dodds, E. R. "Progress in Classical Antiquity." In *Dictionary of the History of Ideas*, vol. 3, edited by Philip P. Wiener. New York: Charles Scribner's Sons, 1973.

Dretske, F. *Knowledge and the Flow of Information*. Cambridge, Mass.: MIT Press, 1981.

Dummett, Michael. "Can Analytical Philosophy Be Systematic, and Ought It to Be?" In *Truth and Other Enigmas*. Cambridge, Mass.: Harvard University Press, 1978.

Durzak, Manfred. *Poesie und Ratio. Vier Lessing-Studien*. Bad Homburg: Athenäum, 1970.

Eigeldinger, Marc. "*Les Rêveries*, solitude et poésie." In *Jean-Jacques Rousseau: Quatre études*. Neuchâtel, Switzerland: Editions de la Baconnière, 1978.

Ferrari, Jean. *Les sources françaises de la philosophie de Kant*. Paris: Klincksieck, 1979.

Ferry, Luc. *Homo aestheticus*. Paris: Bernard Grasset, 1990.
Fittbogen, G. *Die Religion Lessings*. Leipzig: Mayer and Müller, 1923.
Fodor, Jerry A. *Psychosemantics: The Problem of Meaning and the Philosophy of Mind*. Cambridge, Mass.: MIT Press, 1987.
Foucault, Michel. *The Archeology of Knowledge*. Translated by A. M. Sheridan Smith. New York: Pantheon Books, 1972.
———. *An Introduction*. Vol. 1 of *The History of Sexuality*. Translated by Robert Hurley. New York: Pantheon Books, 1978.
———. "What Is Enlightenment?" In *The Foucault Reader*, edited by Paul Rabinow. New York: Pantheon Books, 1984.
Freudenthal, Jacob. *Die Lebensgeschichte Spinozas*. Leipzig: Veit, 1899.
———. "On the History of Spinozism." *Jewish Quarterly Review* 8 (1895–1896).
Frijhoff, W., and D. Julia. *Ecole et société dans la France de l'ancien régime*. Paris: Armand Colin, 1975.
Fukuyama, Francis. *The End of History and The Last Man*. New York: Free Press, 1992.
Gadamer, Hans Georg. *Truth and Method*. Translated and edited by Garrett Barden and John Cumming. New York: Seabury Press, 1975.
Gadoffre, Gilbert. "La chronologie des six parties." In *Le Discours et sa méthode*, edited by Nicolas Grimaldi and Jean-Luc Marion. Paris: Presses universitaires de France, 1987.
Gadoffre, Gilbert, ed. *Discourse de la méthode, précedé d'une introduction historique, suivi d'un glossaire et une chronologie*, by René Descartes. Manchester, U.K.: Manchester University Press, 1941.
Garland, Henry B. *Lessing: The Founder of Modern German Literature*. London: Macmillan, 1962.
Gillispie, Charles Coulston. *The Edge of Objectivity: An Essay in the History of Scientific Ideas*. Princeton, N.J.: Princeton University Press, 1960.
Gilson, Etienne. *La liberté chez Descartes et la théologie*. Paris: J. Vrin, 1913.
———. *Methodical Realism*. Translated by Philip Tower. Front Royal, Va.: Christendom Press, 1990.
———. *Thomist Realism and "The Critique of Knowledge."* Translated by Mark A. Wauk. San Francisco: Ignatius Press, 1986.
Ginsberg, Morris. "Progress in the Modern Era." In *Dictionary of the History of Ideas*, vol. 3, edited by Philip P. Wiener. New York: Charles Scribner's Sons, 1973.
Goguet, Antoine-Yves. *De l'origine des loix, des arts, et des sciences*. Paris, 1758.
Greenberg, Daniel S. *The Politics of Pure Science*. New York: New American Library, 1976.
Guénée, S. *Bibliographie de l'histoire des universités françaises des origines à la révolution*. 2 vols. Paris: Picard, 1978.
Gueroult, Martial. *Descartes selon l'ordre des raison*. Vol. 2, *L'âme et le corps*. Paris: Aubier-Montaigne, 1968.
———. *Leibniz: Dynamique et métaphysique*. Paris: Aubier-Montaigne, 1967.
———. *Malebranche*. Vol. 1, *La vision en Dieu*. Paris: Aubier-Montaigne, 1955.
———. *Malebranche*. Vol. 2, *Le cinq abîmes de la Providence*, Part 1, *L'ordre et l'occasionnalisme*. Paris: Aubier-Montaigne, 1959.
———. *Spinoza*. Vol. 1, *Dieu*, Part 1, *Ethique*. Paris: Aubier-Montaigne, 1968.
Guitton, Jean. *Pascal et Leibniz: Étude sur deux types de penseurs*. Paris: Aubier, 1951.
Guthke, Karl, and Heinrich Schneider. *Gotthold Ephraim Lessing*. Stuttgart: J. B. Metzler, 1967.

Guthrie, W. K. C. *The Fifth Century Greek Enlightenment.* Vol. 3 of *A History of Greek Philosophy.* Cambridge: Cambridge University Press, 1969.
Habermas, Jürgen. *Theorie des Kommunikativen Handelns.* Frankfurt am Main: Suhrkamp, 1981.
Hall, Marie Boas. *Robert Boyle on Natural Philosophy: An Essay with Selections of His Writings.* Bloomington: Indiana University Press, 1965.
Haller, Rudolf. *Questions on Wittgenstein.* London: Routledge, 1988.
Hamilton, Alexander, James Madison, and John Jay. *The Federalist.* Edited by Jacob Cooke. New York: Meridian Books, 1965.
Hampshire, Stuart. "A New Philosophy of the Just Society." *New York Review of Books.* February 24, 1972.
Harrington, Thomas More. *Verité et méthode dans le "Pensées" de Pascal.* Paris: J. Vrin, 1972.
Harris, Errol. "Is There an Esoteric Teaching in the *Tractatus theologico-politicus?*" *Mededelingen Vanwege het Spinozahuis* 38 (1978).
Hartle, Ann. *Death and the Disinterested Spectator.* Albany: State University of New York Press, 1986.
Hazard, Paul. *La pensée européenne au XVIIIéme siècle de Montesquieu à Lessing.* Paris: A. Fayard, 1963.
Hegel, G. W. F. *Introduction to the Lectures on the History of Philosophy.* Translated by T. M. Knox and A. V. Miller. Oxford: Oxford University Press, 1985.
———. *Phenomenology of Spirit.* Translated by A. V. Miller. Oxford: Oxford University Press, 1977.
Heidegger, Martin. *Die Grundbegriffe der Metaphysik: Welt-Endlichkeit-Einsamkeit.* Frankfurt am Main: Vittorio Klostermann Verlag, 1983.
———. *Hölderlins Hymnen "Germanien" and "Der Rhein."* Frankfurt am Main: Vittorio Klostermann Verlag, 1980.
———. *Kant und das Problem der Metaphysik.* 4th ed. Frankfurt am Main: Vittorio Klostermann Verlag, 1973.
———. *Nietzsche.* 2 vols. Pfullingen: Verlag Günter Neske, 1961.
———. *Nietzsche, Vol. 4: Nihilism.* Translated by F. Capuzzi. Edited by D. Krell. San Francisco: Harper and Row, 1982.
———. *Sein und Zeit.* Tubingen: Max Niemeyer Verlag, 1979.
Hobbes, Thomas. *De corpore.* In *The English Works of Thomas Hobbes of Malmesbury,* 11 vols., edited by Sir William Molesworth. London: John Bohr, 1839–1845.
———. *Leviathan.* Edited by C. B. Macpherson. Harmondsworth, U.K.: Penguin Books, 1968.
———. *Leviathan; or, The Matter, Forme and Power of a Commonwealth Ecclesiastical and Civil.* Edited by Michael Oakeshott. New York: Collier Books, 1962.
Holbach, Paul Henri Thiry d', Baron. *La morale universelle; ou, Les devoirs de l'homme fondés sur sa nature.* 3 vols. Amsterdam, 1776.
———. *Le bon sens.* Paris: Editions rationalistes, 1971.
Hölderlin, Friedrich. "Rousseau" and "Der Rheinn." In *Sämtliche Werke,* vol. 2. Stuttgart: Kohlhammer Verlag, 1953.
Humbert, Pierre. *L'oeuvre scientifique de Pascal.* Paris: Albin Michel, 1947.
Hume, David. *Dialogues Concerning Natural Religion.* Edited with an introduction by Norman Kemp Smith. Oxford: Oxford University Press, 1935.
———. *Dialogues Concerning Natural Religion.* Edited by Wayne A. Colver and J. V. Price. Indianapolis, Ind.: Bobbs-Merrill, 1976.
———. *Enquiries Concerning the Human Understanding and Concerning the Principles*

of Morals. 2d ed. Edited by L. A. Selby-Bigge. Oxford: Oxford University Press, 1966.
———. *Letters of David Hume.* 2 vols. Edited by J. Y. T. Greig. Oxford: Oxford University Press, 1932.
———. *The Natural History of Religion.* Edited by H. E. Root. Stanford, Calif.: Stanford University Press, 1967.
———. *A Treatise of Human Nature.* 2d ed. Edited by L. A. Selby-Bigge and P. H. Nidditch. Oxford: Oxford University Press, 1978.
Husserl, Edmund. *The Crisis of the European Sciences and Transcendental Phenomenology.* Translated by David Carr. Evanston, Ill.: Northwestern University Press, 1970.
Jacob, Margaret C. *Living the Enlightenment: Freemasonry and Politics in Eighteenth-Century Europe.* New York: Oxford University Press, 1991.
———. *The Radical Enlightenment: Pantheists, Freemasons, and Republicans.* London: George Allen & Unwin, 1981.
Jacobs, Struan. *Science and British Liberalism: Locke, Bentham, Mill, and Popper.* London: Avebury, 1991.
Jacobi, F. H. *Sendschreiben an Fichte.* In *Werke,* vol. 3, edited by G. Fleisher. Leipzig, 1812–1825.
Jaki, Stanley L. *The Road of Science and the Ways to God.* Chicago: University of Chicago Press, 1978.
Kant, Immanuel. *Anthropology from a Pragmatic Point of View.* Translated by Mary J. Gregor. The Hague: Martinus Nijhoff, 1974.
———. *Critique of Aesthetic Judgment.* Translated by J. C. Meredith. Oxford: Oxford University Press, 1911.
———. *"Critique of Practical Reason" and Other Writings in Moral Philosophy.* Translated by L. W. Beck. Chicago: University of Chicago Press, 1949.
———. *"Critique of Practical Reason" and Other Works on the Theory of Ethics.* Translated by T. K. Abbot. London: Longmans Green, 1960.
———. *Critique of Pure Reason.* Translated by Norman Kemp Smith. London: Macmillan, 1956.
———. *Critique of Teleological Judgment.* Translated by J. C. Meredith. Oxford: Oxford University Press, 1928.
———. *The Doctrine of Virtue. Part 2 of the Metaphysics of Morals.* Translated by Mary J. Gregor. Philadelphia: University of Pennsylvania Press, 1971.
———. *Education.* Translated by Annette Churton. Ann Arbor: University of Michigan Press, 1960.
———. *Eine Vorlesung Kants über Ethik.* Edited by Paul Menzer. Berlin: Pan Verlag, 1924.
———. *First Introduction to the Critique of Judgment.* Translated by James Haden. Indianapolis, Ind.: Bobbs-Merrill, 1965.
———. "Fragmente aus Kants Nachlass." In *Immanuel Kants sammtliche Werke,* vol. 8, edited by G. Hartenstein. Leipzig: Leopold Voss, 1867–1868.
———. *Gesammelte Schriften.* Edited by the Preussischen Akademie der Wissenschaften. Berlin: Walter De Gruyter, 1902–1983.
———. *Lectures on Ethics.* Translated by Louis Infield. London: Methuen, 1930.
———. *The Moral Law, or Kant's Groundwork of the Metaphysics of Morals.* Translated by H. J. Paton. New York: Harper and Row, 1964.
———. *On History.* Translated by L. W. Beck, R. E. Anchor, and E. L. Fackenheim. Edited by L. W. Beck. Indianapolis, Ind.: Bobbs-Merrill, 1963.

———. *On the Old Saw: That May Be Right in Theory But It Won't Work in Practice.* Translated by E. B. Ashton. Philadelphia: University of Pennsylvania Press, 1974.
———. *Religion within the Limits of Reason Alone.* Translated by T. M. Greene and H. H. Hudson. New York: Harper and Row, 1960.
Kaplan, Francis. "Deux attitudes face au problème philosophique de l'existence de Dieu."*Revue des sciences philosophiques et théologiques* 75 (1991).
Kennington, Richard. "Descartes." In *History of Political Philosophy,* 3d ed., edited by Leo Strauss and Joseph Cropsey. Chicago: Rand McNally, 1987.
———. "Descartes and Mastery of Nature." In *Organism, Medicine, and Metaphysics,* edited by Stuart Spicker. Dordrecht, Holland: D. Reidel, 1978.
———. "The 'Teaching of Nature' in Descartes' Soul Doctrine." *Review of Metaphysics* 26 (1972).
Kierkegaard, Sören. *Fear and Trembling.* Translated by Walter Lowrie. Princeton, N.J.: Princeton University Press, 1969.
———. *A Kierkegaard Anthology.* Edited by R. Bretall. New York: Modern Library, 1936.
Klein, Jacob. *Greek Mathematical Thought and the Origin of Algebra.* Translated by Eva Brann. Cambridge, Mass.: MIT Press, 1968.
———. *Lectures and Essays.* Edited by Robert B. Williamson and Elliot Zuckermann. Annapolis, Md.: St. John's College Press, 1985.
Kojève, Alexandre. *Introduction to the Reading of Hegel.* Translated by James H. Nichols Jr. Edited by Allan Bloom. New York: Basic Books, 1969.
Kors, Alan Charles. *D'Holbach's Coterie: An Enlightenment in Paris.* Princeton, N.J.: Princeton University Press, 1976.
Kraus, Pamela A. "*Mens humana:* res cogitans and the Doctrine of Faculties in Descartes' *Meditationes.*" *International Studies in Philosophy* 18 (1986).
———. "'Whole Method': The Thematic Unity of Descartes' *Regulae.*" *Modern Schoolman* 63 (1986).
Kraynak, Robert P. *History and Modernity in the Thought of Thomas Hobbes.* Ithaca, N.Y.: Cornell University Press, 1990.
Kripke, Saul. *Wittgenstein on Rules and Private Language.* Oxford: Blackwell, 1982.
Kristol, William. "The Problem of the Separation of Powers: Federalist 47–51." In *Saving the Revolution: The Federalist Papers and the American Founding,* edited by Charles Kesler. New York: Free Press, 1987.
Krüger, Gerhard. "Die Herkunft des philosophischen Selbstbewusstseins." *Logos: Internationale Zeitschrift für Philosophie der Kultur* 22 (1933). Reprint, Darmstadt: Wissenschaftliche Buchgesellschaft, 1962.
Kryger, Edna. *La notion de liberté chez Rousseau et ses répercussions sur Kant.* Paris: Nizet, 1979.
Kuhn, Thomas S. "Mathematical versus Experimental Tradition." In *The Essential Tension: Selected Studies in Scientific Tradition and Change.* Chicago: University of Chicago Press, 1977.
La Mettrie, Julien Offray de. "Discours préliminaire." In *Oeuvres philosophiques.* Berlin, 1750.
La Peyrère, Issac. *Men before Adam.* London, 1656.
Lachterman, David R. *The Ethics of Geometry: A Genealogy of Modernity.* New York: Routledge, 1989.
Lanson, Gustave. *L'art de la prose.* Paris: Fayard, 1909.
Launay, Michel. "L'art de l'ecrivain politique dans le *Contrat Social.*" In *Actes du*

colloque de Dijon sur le Contrat Social, mai 1962. Dijon: Publications de l'Université de Dijon, 1964.
Le Guern, Michel. *Pascal et Descartes.* Paris: A. G. Nizet, 1971.
Lebrun, François, et al. *De Gutenberg aux Lumières.* Vol. 2. of *Histoire générale de l'enseignement et de l'éducation en France.* Paris: Nouvelle Librairie Française, 1981.
Lecercle, Jean-Louis. *Rousseau et l'art du roman.* Paris: Armand Colin, 1969.
Leibniz, Gottfried Wilhelm. *Die philosophischen Shriften.* Edited by C. I. Gerhardt. Hildesheim: Georg Olms, 1960.
———. *Philosophical Papers and Letters.* 2d ed. Translated and edited by Leroy E. Loemker. Dordrecht, Holland: D. Reidel, 1969.
———. *Theodicy: Essays on the Goodness of God, the Freedom of Man, and the Origin of Evil.* Translated by E. M. Huggard. New Haven, Conn.: Yale University Press, 1952.
Leisegang, H. *Lessings Weltanschauung.* Leipzig: Meiner, 1931.
Lelièvre, J. *L'éducation en France du XVIe au XVIIe siècles.* Bruxelles: 1975.
Lessing, Gotthold E. "Ernst and Falk, Dialogues for Freemasons." Translated by Channinah Maschler. *Interpretation: A Journal of Political Philosophy* 14 (1986).
———. *Gesammelte Werke.* 2 vols. Leipzig: Göschen'sch, 1855.
———. *Gesammelte Werke.* 10 vols. Edited by Paul Rilla. Berlin: Aufbau Verlag, 1954–1958.
———. *Sämtliche Schriften.* 23 vols. Edited by Otto F. Lachmann and Franz Muncker. Stuttgart: Göschen, 1886–1924.
———. *Theological Writings.* Translated by Henry Chadwick. London: Adam and Charles Black, 1956.
———. *Werke.* 25 vols. Edited by Julius Petersen and W. von Olshausen. Berlin: 1925–1935.
Locke, John. *An Essay Concerning Human Understanding.* Edited by P. H. Nidditch. Oxford: Oxford University Press, 1975.
———. *Two Treatises of Government.* Rev. ed. Edited by Peter Laslett. New York: New American Library, 1965.
Loeb, Louis E. "Is There Radical Dissimulation in Descartes' *Meditations?*" In *Essays on Descartes' "Meditations,"* edited by A. O. Rorty. Berkeley and Los Angeles: University of California Press, 1986.
Loofs, Friedrich. *Lessings Stellung zum Christentum.* Halle: Strien, 1910.
Lord, Carnes. *Education and Culture in the the Political Thought of Aristotle.* Ithaca, N.Y.: Cornell University Press, 1982.
Lowenthal, David. "Montesquieu and the Classics." In *Ancients and Moderns,* edited by Joseph Cropsey. New York: Basic Books, 1964.
Löwith, Karl. *Meaning in History.* Chicago: University of Chicago Press, 1949.
Lytotard, Jean-François. *The Post-Modern Condition: A Report on Knowledge.* Translated by Geoff Bennington and Brian Massumi. Minneapolis: University of Minnesota Press, 1984.
Machiavelli, Niccolo. *The Prince.* Translated by Harvey C. Mansfield Jr. Chicago: University of Chicago Press, 1985.
McCarthy, John C. "Desire, Recollection, and Thought: On Augustine's *Confessions* I, 1." *Communio: International Catholic Review* 14 (1987).
McDonough, Richard. "Wittgenstein's Critique of Mechanistic Atomism." *Philosophical Investigations* 14 (1991).
McGinn, Colin. "Can We Solve the Mind-Body Problem?" *Mind* 97 (1989).
Magee, Bryan. *Men of Ideas.* New York: Oxford University Press, 1982.

Magnard, Pierre. "Descartes inutile et incertain." *Revue des sciences philosophiques et théologiques* 75 (1991).
Mann, Otto. *Lessing. Seine und Leistung.* Hamburg: Schröder, 1948.
Mansfield, Harvey C. Jr. *America's Constitutional Soul.* Baltimore: Johns Hopkins University Press, 1991.
Marion, Jean-Luc. "Cartesian Metaphysics and the Simple Natures." In *The Cambridge Companion to Descartes,* edited by John Cottingham. Cambridge: Cambridge University Press, 1992.
———. "Générosite et phénoménologie: Remarques sur l'interpretation du *cogito* cartésien par Michel Henry." *Les études philosophiques,* 1988.
———. *L'ontologie grise de Descartes.* Paris: J. Vrin, 1975.
———. "La situation métaphysique du *Discours de la méthode.*" In *Le Discours et sa méthode,* edited by Nicolas Grimaldi and Jean-Luc Marion. Paris: Presses universitaires de France, 1987.
Maritain, Jacques. "The Political Ideas of Pascal." In *Ransoming the Time,* translated by H. L. Binsse. New York: Charles Scribner's Sons, 1948.
Marshall, Terence. "Art d'écrire et pratique politique de Jean-Jacques Rousseau." *Revue de métaphysique et de morale* 89 (1984).
———. "John Locke et la philosophie constitutionelle." *Revue de synthése* 106 (1985).
———. "La raison pratique et le constitutionnalisme américan." *Revue française de science politique* 38 (1988).
———. "Les droits de l'homme et la politique constitutionelle: Un dialogue franco-américain à l'époque révolutionnaire." In *La philosophie et la révolution française,* edited by B. Bourgeois and J. D'Hondt. Paris: J. Vrin, 1993.
———. "Perception politique et théorie de la connaissance dans l'oeuvre de Jean-Jacques Rousseau." *Revue française de science politique* 29 (1979).
———. "Poésie et praxis dans l'*Emile* de J. -J. Rousseau: Les droits de l'homme et le sentiment de l'humanité." *Revue des sciences philosophique et théologiques* 76 (1992).
———. "Rousseau Translations: A Review Essay." *Political Theory* 1 (1982).
Marx, Karl. *Economic and Philosophical Manuscripts.* In *Marx's Concept of Man,* edited by Erich Fromm. New York: Frederick Ungar, 1966.
Marx, Karl, and Friedrich Engles. *The German Ideology.* Edited by C. J. Arthur. New York: International Publishers, 1972.
Masson, Pierre-Maurice. "Contribution à l'étude de la prose métrique dans la *Nouvelle Héloise.*" *Annales de la Societé Jean-Jacques Rousseau* 5 (1910).
Miller, Genevieve. *The Adoption of Inoculation for Small Pox in England and France.* Philadelphia: University of Pennsylvania Press, 1957.
Molinier, Jean-Baptiste, Abbé. *Lettres servant de réponse aux 'Lettres philosophiques' de M. de V***.* Paris: 1735.
Montesquieu, Charles de Secondat, Baron de. *Oeuvres complètes.* Edited by Daniel Oster. Paris: Seuil, 1970.
Morrisoe, Michael. "Hume's Rhetorical Strategy." *Texas Studies in Literature and Language* 11 (1970).
———. "Rhetorical Method in Hume's Works on Religion." *Philosophy and Rhetoric* 2 (1969).
Mossner, E. C. "Hume's Four Dissertations: An Essay in Biography and Bibliography." *Modern Philosophy* 48 (1950).
———. "The Religion of David Hume." *Journal of the History of Ideas* 39 (1978).

Nadler, Stephen. *Arnauld and the Cartesian Philosophy of Ideas*. Princeton, N.J.: Princeton University Press, 1989.
Neurath, Otto. "Through War Economy to Economy in Kind." In *Empiricism and Sociology*. Dordrecht, The Netherlands: Reidel, 1973.
———. "Unified Science as Encyclopedic Integration." In *International Encyclopedia of Unified Science*. Chicago: University of Chicago Press, 1938.
Niebuhr, Reinhold. *An Interpretation of Christian Ethics*. New York: Harper and Row, 1935.
Nietzsche, Friedrich. *The Advantage and Disadvantage of History for Life*. Translated by Peter Preuss. Indianapolis, Ind.: Hackett, 1980.
———. *The Antichrist*. In *The Portable Nietzsche*, translated and edited by W. Kaufmann. New York: Viking Press, 1968.
———. *Beyond Good and Evil*. Translated by W. Kaufmann. New York: Vintage Books, 1989.
———. *The Birth of Tragedy*. Translated by W. Kaufmann. New York: Vintage Books, 1967.
———. *The Gay Science*. Translated by W. Kaufmann. New York: Vintage Books, 1974.
———. *Unmodern Observations*. Part 1, *David Strauss: Writer and Confessor*. Edited by William Smith. New Haven, Conn.: Yale University Press, 1990.
———. *The Will to Power*. Translated by W. Kaufmann and R. J. Hollingdale. Edited by W. Kaufmann. New York: Vintage Books, 1967.
Nigg, W. *Das Buch der Ketzer*. Zurich: Artemis Verlag, 1949.
Norman, Buford. "L'idée de règle chez Pascal." In *Méthodes chez Pascal: Actes du colloque tenu â Clermont-Ferrand 10–13 juin 1976*. Paris: Presses universitaires de France, 1979.
Noxon, James. "Hume's Agnosticism." *Philosophical Review* 73 (1964).
———. "Hume's Concern with Religion." *Southwestern Journal of Philosophy* 7 (1976).
Ozouf, Mona. *L'homme régénéré: Essais sur la révolution française*. Paris: Gallimard, 1989.
Pangle, Thomas. *Montesquieu's Philosophy of Liberalism*. Chicago: University of Chicago Press, 1973.
———. "The Political Psychology of Religion in Plato's *Laws*." *American Political Science Review* 70 (1976).
Pascal, Blaise. *Oeuvres complètes*. Edited by Jacques Chevalier. Paris: Bibliothèque de la Pléiade, 1954.
———. *Pensées sur la religion et sur quelques autres sujets*. Vol. 1, *Textes*. Edited by Louis Lafuma. Paris: Éditions du Luxembourg, 1951.
Paterson, Timothy. "Bacon's Myth of Orpheus: Power as a Goal of Science in *Of the Wisdom of the Ancients*." *Interpretation: A Journal of Political Philosophy* 16 (1989).
Penelhum, Terence. *Hume*. London: Macmillan, 1975.
———. "Natural Beliefs and Religious Beliefs in Hume's Philosophy." *Philosophical Quarterly* 33 (1983).
Pieper, Josef. *Guide to Thomas Aquinas*. Translated by Richard Wilson and Clara Wilson. San Francisco: Ignatius Press, 1991.
Pons, Georges. *Gotthold Ephraim Lessing et le christianisme*. Paris: Didier, 1964.
Popkin, Richard. *The History of Scepticism*. New York: Humanities Press, 1964.
———. "Spinoza and La Peyrère." In *Spinoza: New Perspectives*, edited by J. I. Biro and R. W. Shahan. Norman: University of Oklahoma Press, 1978.

Popper, Karl. *Conjectures and Refutations: The Growth of Scientific Knowledge.* New York: Harper and Row, 1962.
———. *The Open Society and Its Enemies.* Princeton, N.J.: Princeton University Press, 1950.
Price, J. V. "Empirical Theists in Cicero and Hume." *Texas Studies in Language and Literature* 5 (1963).
———. "Sceptics in Cicero and Hume." *Journal of the History of Ideas* 25 (1964).
Prufer, Thomas. "Notes for a Reading of Augustine, *Confessions,* Book X." In *Recapitulations: Essays in Philosophy.* Washington, D.C.: The Catholic University of America Press, 1993.
Przywara, Erich. "St. Augustine and the Modern World." In *A Monument to Saint Augustine,* by M. C. D'Arcy et al. London: Sheed and Ward, 1945.
Putnam, Hilary. "After Empiricism." In *Post-Analytic Philosophy,* edited by John Rajchman and Cornel West. New York: Columbia University Press, 1985.
Ratzinger, Joseph. "Originalität und Überlieferung in Augustins Begriff der *confessio.*" *Revue des études augustiniennes* 3 (1957).
Rawls, John. *A Theory of Justice.* Cambridge, Mass.: Harvard University Press, 1971.
Raynaud, Philippe. *Max Weber et les dilemmes de la raison moderne.* Paris: Presses universitaires de France, 1987.
———. "Nietzsche, la philosophie et les philosophes." In Friedrich Nietzsche, *Oeuvres,* vol. 2, edited by Jean Lacoste. Paris: R. Laffont, 1993.
———. "Théodicée." In *Dictionnaire de philosophie politique,* edited by Philippe Raynaud and Stéphane Rials. Paris: Presses universitaires de France, 1996.
Reedy, Gerard, S. J. "Spinoza, Stillingfleet, Prophecy, and 'Enlightenment.'" In *Deism, Masonry, and the Enlightenment: Essays Honoring Alfred Owen Aldridge,* edited by J. A. Leo Lemay. Newark: University of Delaware Press, 1987.
Rees, G. "Francis Bacon's Semi-Paracelsian Cosmology." *Ambix* 22 (1975).
Rees, G., and Christopher Upton. *Francis Bacon's Natural Philosophy: A New Source.* London: British Society for the Advancement of Science, 1984.
Reichenbach, Haus. *The Rise of Scientific Philosophy.* Berkeley and Los Angeles: University of California Press, 1951.
Révah, I. S. *Spinoza et le Dr. Juan de Prado.* Paris: Mouton and Co., 1959.
Ricoeur, Paul. *Le mal: Un défi à la philosophie et à la théologie.* Geneva: Labor et Fides, 1986.
Rigault, G. *Histoire générale de l'Institut de Frères des Ecoles Chrétiennes.* 8 vols. Paris: Plon, 1937–1953.
Rist, John M. *Epicurus.* Cambridge: Cambridge University Press, 1972.
Rist, John M., ed. *The Stoics.* Berkeley and Los Angeles: University of California Press, 1978.
Rivelaygue, Jacques. "La *Monadologie* de Leibniz." In *De Leibniz à Hegel,* vol. 1 of *Leçons de métaphysique allemande.* Paris: Grasset, 1990.
Rodis-Lewis, Geneviève. "Doute et certitude chez Descartes et Pascal." *Europe* 59 (1978).
Rohrmoser, Günther. "Lessing und die religionsphilosophische Fragestellung der Aufklärung." In *Lessing und die Zeit der Aufklärung.* Gottingen: Vandenhoeck and Ruprecht, 1968.
Romanos, George D. *Quine and Analytic Philosophy.* Cambridge, Mass.: MIT Press, 1983.
Root, H. E., ed. "Editor's Introduction." In *The Natural History of Religion,* by David Hume. Stanford, Calif.: Stanford University Press, 1967.

Rorty, Richard. "Habermas and Lyotard on Postmodernity." In *Essays on Heidegger and Others*, Vol. 2 of *Philosophical Papers*. Cambridge: Cambridge University Press, 1991.
———. "The Priority of Democracy to Philosophy." In *Objectivity, Relativism, and Truth*, Vol. 1 of *Philosophical Papers*. Cambridge: Cambridge University Press, 1991.
———. "Solidarity or Objectivity?" In *Post-Analytic Philosophy*, edited by John Rajchman and Cornel West. New York: Columbia University Press, 1985.
Rosen, Stanley. *Nihilism*. New Haven, Conn.: Yale University Press, 1969.
Roth, Leon. *Descartes' "Discourse on Method."* Oxford: Oxford University Press, 1948.
Rousseau, Jean Jacques. *Correspondance générale de J.-J. Rousseau*. 20 vols. Edited by Théophile Dufour. Paris: Armand Colin, 1924–1934.
———. "De l'imitation théâtrale, essai tiré des dialogues de Platon." In *Oeuvres complètes*, vol. 1. Paris: L. Hachette et Cie, 1862.
———. *Dictionnaire de musique*. 2 vols. Paris: Art et Culture, 1977.
———. *Emile*. Paris: Edition Garnier Frères, 1964.
———. *First and Second Discourses*. Translated by Judith R. Masters. Edited by Roger D. Masters. New York: St. Martin's Press, 1964.
———. *Lettres à d'Alembert sur les spectacles*. Paris: Garnier-Flammarion, 1967.
———. *Letter on Providence*. Translated by Terence Marshall. In *The Collected Writings of Rousseau*, vol. 3, edited by Roger Masters and Christopher Kelly. Hanover, N.H.: University Press of New England, 1992.
———. *Oeuvres complètes*. Edited by Jean Fabré and Michel Launay. Paris: Seuil, 1971.
———. *Oeuvres complètes*. Edited by Bernard Gangebin and Marcel Raymond. Paris: Bibliothèque de la Pléiade, 1959–1969.
Rowbotham, Arnold H. *The "Philosophes" and the Propaganda for the Inoculation of Smallpox in Eighteenth-Century France*. Berkeley and Los Angeles: University of California Press, 1935.
Russell, Bertrand. *History of Western Philosophy*. New York: Simon and Schuster, 1945.
Salmon, W. "A New Look at Hume's *Dialogues*." *Philosophical Studies* 33 (1978).
Scheler, Max. "Erkenntnis und Arbeit." In *Die Wissensformen und die Gesellschaft*. 2d ed. Bern: Franke, 1960.
Schilpp, Arthur, ed. *The Philosophy of Rudolf Carnap*. Library of Living Philosophers, 11. LaSalle, Ill: Open Court, 1963.
Schilpp, Paul. *Kant's Pre-Critical Ethics*. Chicago: Northwestern University Press, 1960.
Schmitz, Kenneth L. "The Geography of the Person." *Communio: International Catholic Review* 13 (1986).
———. "Is Liberalism Good Enough?" In *Liberalism and the Good*, edited by R. Bruce Douglass et al. New York: Routledge, 1990.
———. "Natural Religion, Morality, and Lessing's Ditch." In *Proceedings of the American Catholic Philosophical Association*, vol. 65. Washington, D.C.: American Catholic Philosophical Association, 1991.
Schneider, Johannes. "Lessings Stellung zur Theologie." In *Wege der Forschung*, vol. 21. Darmstadt: Wissenschaftliche Buchgesellschaft, 1968.
Schrempf, C. *Lessing als Philosoph*. 2d ed. Stuttgart: Frommann, 1921.
Schuster, John. "Whatever Should We Do with Cartesian Method? Reclaiming

Descartes for the History of Science." In *Essays in the Philosophy and Science of René Descartes*, edited by Stephen Voss. New York: Oxford University Press, 1993.
Searle, John. *Minds, Brains, and Science*. Cambridge: Cambridge University Press, 1984.
Sellier, Phillipe. *Pascal et Saint Augustin*. Paris: Armand Colin, 1970.
Serres, Michel. *Le système de Leibniz et ses modèles mathématique*. Paris: Presses universitaires de France, 1967.
Sève, René. *Leibniz et l'école moderne du droit naturel*. Paris: Presses universitaires de France, 1989.
Shell, Susan Meld. *The Rights of Reason: A Study of Kant's Philosophy and Politics*. Toronto: University of Toronto Press, 1980.
Shelley, Percey. "Defense of Poetry." In *Shelley's Poetry and Prose*. New York: Norton, 1977.
Shulsky, Abram. "The 'Infrastructure' of Aristotle's *Politics:* Aristotle on Economics and Politics." In *Essays on the Foundations of Aristotelian Political Science*, edited by Carnes Lord and David O'Connor. Berkeley and Los Angeles: University of California Press, 1991.
Silber, John R. "The Copernican Revolution in Ethics: The Good Reexamined." *Kant Studien* 51 (1959–1960).
———. "The Ethical Significance of Kant's *Religion*." In *Religion within the Limits of Reason Alone*, translated by T. M. Greene and H. H. Hudson. New York: Harper and Row, 1960.
———. "The Importance of the Highest Good in Kant's Ethics." *Ethics* 73 (1963).
———. "The Metaphysical Importance of the Highest Good as the Canon of Pure Reason in Kant's Philosophy." *University of Texas Studies in Literature and Language* 1 (1959).
———. "Procedural Formalism in Kant's Ethics." *Review of Metaphysics* 28 (1974).
———. "Verfahrens Formalismus in Kants Ethik." *Akten des 4. Internationalen Kant-Kongresses* 3 (1974).
Slade, Francis. "Rule as Sovereignty: The Universal and Homogeneous State." In *The Truthful and the Good: Essays in Honor of Robert Sokolowski*, edited by John J. Drummond and James G. Hart. Boston: Kluwer Academic, 1996.
———. "Was ist Aufklärung? Notes on Maritain, Rorty, and Bloom." In *The Common Things: Essays in the Thomistic Philosophy of Education*, edited by Daniel McInerny. Washington, D.C.: American Maritain Association, forthcoming.
Snyders, G. *La pédagogie en France aux XVIIe et XVIIe siècles*. Paris: Presses universitaires de France, 1972.
Sokolowski, Robert. *Pictures, Quotations, and Distinctions: Fourteen Essays in Phenomenology*. South Bend, Ind.: University of Notre Dame Press, 1992.
Solmsen, Friedrich. *Intellectual Experiments of Greek Enlightenment*. Princeton, N.J.: Princeton University Press, 1975.
Sparshott, F. E. "Zeno on Art: Anatomy of a Definition." In *The Stoics*, edited by John Rist. Berkeley and Los Angeles: University of California Press, 1978.
Spicker, G. *Lessings Weltanschauung*. Leipzig: Wigand, 1883.
Spinoza, Baruch. *Spinoza Opera*. 4 vols. Edited by Carl Gebhardt. Heidelberg: Carl Winters Universitaetsbuchhandlung, 1925.
———. *Tractatus theologico-politicus*. Translated by Samuel Shirley. Leiden: E. J. Brill, 1989.
Starobinski, Jean. *Jean-Jacques Rousseau: La transparence et l'obstacle*. Paris: Gallimard, 1971.

Stephen, Leslie. *The History of English Thought in the Eighteenth Century*. 2 vols. London: Smith, Elder, and Co., 1876.
Stich, S. *From Folk Psychology to Cognitive Science: The Case against Belief*. Cambridge, Mass.: MIT Press, 1983.
Strauss, Leo. *The City and Man*. Chicago: Rand McNally, 1964.
———. *Das Erkenntnisproblem in der Philosophischen Lehre Fr. H. Jacobi*. Ph.D. dissertation, Hamburg, 1921.
———. *Natural Right and History*. Chicago: University of Chicago Press, 1953.
———. *On Tyranny*. Rev. ed., including the Strauss-Kojève correspondence. Edited by Victor Gourevitch and Michael S. Roth. New York: Free Press, 1991.
———. *Persecution and the Art of Writing*. Glencoe, Ill.: Free Press, 1952
———. *The Political Philosophy of Hobbes*. Translated by E. M. Sinclair. Oxford: Oxford University Press, 1936.
———. *The Rebirth of Classical Political Rationalism*. Edited by Thomas L. Pangle. Chicago: University of Chicago Press, 1989.
———. *Six Essays*. Edited by H. Gilden. Indianapolis, Ind.: Bobbs-Merrill, 1975.
———. *Spinoza's Critique of Religion*. Translated by E. M. Sinclair. New York: Schocken Books, 1965.
———. *Thoughts on Machiavelli*. Glencoe, Ill.: Free Press, 1958.
———. *What Is Political Philosophy?* Glencoe, Ill.: Free Press, 1959.
Sutherland, Stewart. "Penelhum on Hume." *Philosophical Quarterly* 33 (1983).
Taton, René. "Sur l'invention de la machine arithmetique." In *L'oeuvre scientifique de Pascal*, edited by P. Costabel et al. Paris: Presses universitaires de France, 1964.
Thielicke, Helmut. "Vernunft und Existenz bei Lessing. Das Unbedingte in der Geschichte." In *Lessing und die Zeit der Aufklärung*. Gottingen: Vandenhoeck and Ruprecht, 1968.
Thomson, Ann, ed. *Materialism and Society in the Mid-Eighteenth Century: La Mettrie's "Discours préliminaire."* Geneva: Droz, 1981.
Tindal, Matthew. *Christianity as Old as the Creation; or, The Gospel, a Republication of the Religion of Nature*. London, 1730.
Tocqueville, Alexis de. *L'ancien régime et la révolution*. In *Oeuvres complètes*, vol. 2, edited by G. Lefebvre and J. P. Mayer. Paris: Gallimard, 1952.
Todorov, Tzevetan. *Frêle bonheur: Essai sur Rousseau*. Paris: Hachette, 1985.
Topliss, P. *The Rhetoric of Pascal: A Study of His Art of Persuasion in the "Provinciales" and the "Pensées."* Leicester, U.K.: Leicester University Press, 1966.
Turgot, Anne Robert Jacques, Baron d'Aulne. *Turgot on Progress, Sociology, and Economics*. Edited by Ronald L. Meek. Cambridge: Cambridge University Press, 1973.
Tweyman, Stanley. *Scepticism and Belief in Hume's Dialogues Concerning Natural Religion*. Dordrecht, The Netherlands: Kluwer, 1986.
Vamos, Mara. "Pascal's *Pensées* and the Enlightenment: The Roots of a Misunderstanding." *Studies on Voltaire and the Eighteenth Century* 97 (1972).
Velkely, Richard. *Freedom and the End of Reason: On the Moral Foundation of Kant's Critical Philosophy*. Chicago: University of Chicago Press, 1989.
Vink, A. G. "The Literary and Dramatic Character of Hume's *Dialogues Concerning Natural Religion*." *Religious Studies* 22 (1986).
Voltaire. *Candide; or, Optimism*. Translated by John Butt. Harmondsworth, U.K.: Penguin Books, 1947.
———. *Lettres philosophiques; ou, Lettres anglaises*. Edited by Raymond Naves. Paris: Garnier, 1962.

———. *Philosophical Letters*. Translated by Ernest Dilworth. Indianapolis, Ind.: Bobbs-Merrill, 1961.
Wade, Ira O. *The Structure and Form of the French Enlightenment*. Princeton, N.J.: Princeton University Press, 1977.
———. *The Intellectual Development of Voltaire*. Princeton, N.J.: Princeton University Press, 1969.
Wedberg, Anders. *A History of Philosophy*. 3 vols. Oxford: Oxford University Press, 1982–1984.
Weinberger, Jerry. *Science, Faith, and Politics: Francis Bacon and the Utopian Roots of the Modern Age*. Ithaca, N.Y.: Cornell University Press, 1985.
Wernle, Paul. *Lessing und das Christentum*. Tubingen: Mohr, 1912.
White, Howard B. *Antiquity Forgot: Essays on Shakespeare, Bacon, and Rembrandt*. The Hague: Martinus Nijhoff, 1978.
———. *Peace among the Willows: The Political Philosophy of Francis Bacon*. The Hague: Martinus Nijhoff, 1968.
Yandell, Keith. "Hume on Religion." In *Hume: A Re-evaluation*, edited by D. W. Livingston and J. T. King. Brooklyn, N.Y.: Fordham University Press, 1976.
Yates, Frances A. *The Rosicrucian Enlightenment*. London: Routledge and Kegan Paul, 1972.
Yovel, Yirmiyahu. *Spinoza and Other Heretics*. Vol. 1, *The Marrano of Reason*. Princeton, N.J.: Princeton University Press, 1989.
Zammito, John. *The Genesis of Kant's Critique of Judment*. Chicago: University of Chicago Press, 1992.
Zscharnak, L. "Einleitung und Lessings theologischen Schriften." In *Lessings Werke*, vol. 20, edited by Julius Petersen and W. von Olshausen. Berlin: Deutsches Verlagshaus, 1925–1935.

Index

Aaron, 83
Abel, 45–46
Abraham, 24, 95, 190
Achilles, 185
Adam, 44–46, 159
Alembert, Jean le Rond d', 2, 7, 10n, 11, 26n, 257, 259, 260, 266
Allison, Henry, 218n, 219n, 220n, 229n, 233n
Alquié, Ferdinand, 56n, 60n, 161
Aner, K., 224n
Apollo, 198n
Aristophanes, 198n, 236
Aristotle, 1n, 8, 10, 15, 18, 26, 32, 45, 47n, 48–49, 53, 64n, 69, 71n, 77n, 80, 81n, 99n, 101n, 108, 150, 151, 153, 156, 165–66, 180, 205n, 206n, 207n, 211n, 212n, 219n, 249, 257–58, 267, 272
Arnauld, Antoine, 94n
Augustine, Saint, 18, 84n, 95, 104, 156, 156–63, 176n, 186, 228n, 238
Avicenna, 196n

Bachelard, Gaston, 194n
Bacon, Francis, 3–4, 5, 7, 9, 11–12, 11n, 16, 17, 25, 26–27, 40–54, 125, 182n, 188, 192, 195n, 197, 198n, 234, 259, 260, 261, 281n
Baillie, J., 263n
Baird, A. W. S., 98n, 114n, 116n, 120n
Balthasar, Hans Urs von, 96n, 109n, 114n, 116n, 118n, 220n
Barny, Roger, 189n, 193n
Barth, Karl, 218, 219n, 220n, 224
Baudin, Émile, 94n
Bayle, Pierre, 126n, 127, 155, 193, 200n
Beccaria, Cesare, 38–39
Beck, Lewis White, 249
Becker, Carl, 233–35, 236, 237n, 238, 257n
Béguin, Albert, 193n, 197n
Beitzinger, Alfons J., 101n
Bentham, Jeremy, 276–77, 281n
Bergson, Henri, 211

Berkeley, George, 236
Berman, David, 11n, 183n
Bernard, Saint, 228n
Berns, Laurence, 206n
Beyssade, Jean-Marie, 57n, 60n
Blackburn, Simon, 176n
Blijenbergh, Willem van, 127
Bloom, Allan, 188n
Blount, Charles, 127, 128n
Blumenberg, Hans, 1n
Boleyn, Anne, 249
Borinski, Karl, 223n
Boulainvilliers, Henrie, comte de, 127
Boyle, Robert, 27, 33, 87n
Brahe, Tycho, 153
Brann, Eva, 205n, 211n
Brewster, David, 235
Bricke, John, 177n, 178n, 182n
Brocklis, L. W. B., 25n
Broome, J. H., 110n
Browne, Thomas, 127n
Brunschvicg, Léon, 94n
Buckley, Michael, 230n
Buddha, 1–2
Buffon, Georges-Louis Leclerc, comte de, 260n
Bultmann, Rudolf, 243
Burghley, William Cecil, Lord, 11
Burke, Edmund, 89
Burns, Timothy, 4n
Burton, John Hill, 237n
Burtt, Edwin A., 90n
Bury, J. B., 263n
Butler, Joseph, 29, 31–32, 34, 178n

Cain, 45–46
Calvin, John, 35
Carnap, Rudolf, 263n, 266, 271, 279–80, 281n
Carr, E. H., 263n
Carraud, Vincent, 122n
Cassirer, Ernst, 79n, 187n, 188n, 192n, 193n, 259n, 262n
Caton, Hiram, 92n, 121n

Index

Chadwick, Henry, 221n, 224n, 225n
Chartier, Roger, 25n
Chastellux, François-Jean, chevalier de, 28
Chomsky, Noam, 274
Chiron, 199, 209n
Churchland, Patricia S., 272n
Churchland, Paul M., 272n
Cicero, Marcus Tullius, 171n, 178n, 184, 182, 185n
Circe, 198n
Clarke, Samuel, 178n
Cleopatra, 108n
Climacus, Johannes, *see* Sören Kierkegaard
Colie, Rosalie L., 128n
Collins, James, 172n
Compère, Marie-Madeleine, 25n
Comte, Auguste, 227n, 261, 266
Condillac, Étienne de Bonnot, 257, 259, 260n, 266, 268n, 269
Condorcet, Jean-Antoine-Nicolas, marquis de, 21, 84n, 257, 261–62, 276
Copernicus, Nicolas, 40, 153, 187, 272
Corneille, Pierre, 219
Cotoni, Marie-Hélène, 204n
Cromwell, Oliver, 108n
Crosson, Frederick J., 95n, 186n
Curley, Edwin, 57n

Dampier, William, 236n
Dante Alighieri, 233
Darnton, Robert, 193n
Darwin, Charles, 253
Davis, Charles Michael, 23n,
de Dainville, François, S.J., 25n
de Viguerie, Jean, 25n
de Villeray, Pierre-François le Coq, 24n
Democritus, 50
Dennett, Daniel, 271n
Descartes, René, 7, 8n, 9–10, 11, 17–18, 26, 27, 40–41, 55–76, 79, 90, 92–123, 125, 150–54, 156–57, 164–66, 183, 188, 193n, 196n, 200n, 212, 228, 233, 234, 259, 260, 261, 281n
Diderot, Denis, 29, 30, 183, 192, 204, 237–38, 241, 244, 250–51, 257, 260, 265
Dilthey, Wilhelm, 223
Dionysus, 198n
Dodds, E. R., 263n
Dretske, E., 272n
Dumarsais, César Chesneau, 127
Dummett, Michael, 266n
Durkheim, Émile, 274
Durzak, Manfred, 218n, 219n, 225, 226n, 227n

Dworkin, Ronald, 280, 281n

Eichholz, Georg, 226
Eigeldinger, Marc, 194n
Einstein, Albert, 90n, 253
Engels, Friedrich, 208n
Epictetus, 108
Epicurus, 64n, 108, 170n, 172n, 181n
Euclid, 135
Euripedes, 234
Eurydice, 198

Faust, 220–21
Ferrari, Jean, 188n
Ferry, Luc, 211n
Feuer, Lewis Samuel, 281n
Feuerbach, Ludwig, 184, 227n, 266
Feyerabend, Paul, 267, 276n
Filmer, Robert, 125n
Fittbogen, G., 224n
Fodor, Jerry, 271n, 272
Fontanelle, Bernard Le Bouvier de, 127
Foucault, Michel, 6n, 8
Fourier, François Marie Charles 260
Frank, Philip, 265n
Franklin, Benjamin, 2n
Frederick II (the Great), 13
Fréret, Nicolas, 127
Freud, Sigmund, 167, 253, 274, 276
Freudenthal, Jacob, 126n, 132n
Frijhoff, Gottfried, 25n
Fukuyama, Francis, 4n, 84

Gadamer, Hans Georg, 149n
Gadoffre, Gilbert, 57n
Galilei, Galileo, 26–27, 33, 262
Garland, Henry B., 218, 219n
Gide, André, 211n
Gilbert, William, 27, 33, 46
Gildon, Charles, 128n
Gillispie, Charles Couston, 27n
Gilson, Etienne, 11, 41n, 57n, 61n, 74n, 91, 157n
Ginsberg, Morris, 263
Glazenmaker, Jan, 126
Goeze, Johann Melchior, 213
Goguet, Yves, 260n
Gourevitch, Victor, 4n
Gödel, Kurt, 267, 271, 273
Grassi, Orazio (pseud. Lothario Sarsi), 26
Greenberg, Daniel S., 41n
Gregory, Brad, 126n
Guénée, Simonne, 25n
Gueroult, Martial, 152n, 153n, 157n, 158n, 159n, 163n

Guthke, Karl, 218n, 219n, 223n
Guthrie, W. K. C., 1n

Habermas, Jürgen, 208n
Hall, Mary Boas, 87n
Haller, Rudolf, 265n
Halley, Edmund, 33
Hamilton, Alexander, 211n
Hampshire, Stuart, 281n
Hardenberg, Friedrich Leopold Freiherr von (pseud. Novalis), 126n
Harrington, Thomas More, 112n
Harris, Errol, 144n
Hartle, Ann, 95n
Harvey, William, 27, 33
Hazard, Paul, 223n
Hegel, Georg Wilhelm Friedrich, 4, 19, 84, 94, 154, 157, 162, 163, 194n, 197n, 203n, 216, 272, 281n
Heidegger, Martin, 41–42, 57n, 75, 189n, 195n, 196n, 202n
Helvétius, Claude-Adrien, 257, 278
Henri, M., 72n
Herder, Johann Gottfried, 206n
Hitler, Adolf, 255n
Hobbes, Thomas, 5, 8, 17, 18, 34–36, 41, 42, 77–91, 100n, 125, 132, 150, 184, 193n, 201, 259, 268, 281n
Holbach, Paul Henri Thiry, baron d', 29, 183n, 193, 257, 259, 260, 269
Homer, 185, 192
Hooke, Robert, 27
Horace, 197n
Hölderlin, Friedrich, 195n
Humbert, Pierre, 98n
Hume, David, 19, 168–86, 236–37, 259, 268
Husserl, Edmund, 14n
Huyghens, Christian, 27, 33

Ibn Izra, Abraham, 131, 132n
Isaac, 95

Jacob, 95
Jacob, Margaret C., 10n, 128n
Jacobi, Friedrich Heinrich, 189n, 218n
Jacobs, Struan, 276n
Jaki, Stanley, 8on
Jay, John, 211n
Jefferson, Thomas, 2n, 34, 39
Jelles, Jarig, 126
Jeremiah, 122n
Jesus (Christ), 37, 134n, 142, 156, 190, 215, 217n, 227
Job, 181

Jonah, 274
Julia, Dominique, 25n

Kant, Immanuel, 19, 20, 40–41, 78–79, 84n, 90–91, 145, 149, 154,, 155, 157, 163, 183, 187–88, 191, 192n, 193n, 194n, 195n, 199n, 202n, 205n, 206n, 207n, 208, 211n, 232–56, 259
Kaplan, Francis, 122n
Kennington, Richard, 14n, 41n, 98n, 103n, 108n, 111n, 207n
Kepler, Johannes, 27, 33, 36
Kierkegaard, Sören (pseud. Johannes Climacus), 213, 216, 217n, 226, 228, 231, 242, 248n
Klein, Jacob, 13n, 62n, 103n, 117n
Knippenberg, Joseph, 4n
Korah, 83
Kojève, Alexandre, 4n, 84n
Kors, Alan Charles, 31n, 37n
Kraus, Pamela, 103n, 112n
Kraynak, Robert P., 78n, 84n, 107n
Kripke, Saul, 275
Kristol, William, 210n
Krüger, Gerhard, 108n
Kryger, Edna, 188n
Kuhn, Thomas S., 51n, 267
Kühnrath, Henry, 126

La Mettrie, Julien Offray de, 6, 29, 257, 259, 260, 269
La Peyrère, Isaac, 131
Lachterman, David, 9n, 62n, 93n,
Lanson, Gustav, 204n
Launay, Michel, 204n
Lawler, Peter Augustine, 4n
Le Guern, Michel, 94n
Lebrun, François, 25n
Lecercle, Jean-Louis, 204n
Lelièvre, J., 25n
Leibniz, Gottfried Wilhelm, 10, 18, 49, 125, 150–67, 190, 218, 223n, 229, 231, 259
Leisegang, Hans, 225n
Lenin, Vladimir Illych, 255
Lessing, Karl, 219, 221, 222, 224
Lessing, Gotthold Ephraim, 10n, 20, 163, 213–31,
Lévesque de Burigny, Jean, 127
Locke, John, 5, 26, 36, 41, 90, 125, 150, 184, 186, 192n, 257n, 259, 268, 269, 278–79, 281n
Loeb, Louis E., 92n
Loofs, Friedrich, 220n, 223n
Lord, Carnes, 193n, 206n
Lowenthal, David, 210n

306   *Index*

Löwith, Karl, 41
Luther, Martin, 224
Lyotard, Jean-François, 2n
Lysenko, Trofim Denisovich, 16

McCarthy, John C., 95n
McDonough, Richard, 271n
McGinn, Colin, 272n, 275n
Mach, Ernst, 90n, 265n
Machiavelli, Niccolò, 6n, 8, 9, 14, 53–54, 103, 106
Madison, James, 211n
Magee, Brian, 281n
Magnard, Pierre, 94n
Maimonides, Moses, 137n
Malebranche, Nicolas, 151, 152, 157–59, 161–62
Mann, Otto, 225
Mansfield, Harvey C., Jr., 210n
Mansvelt, Regner van, 126
Mary (Virgin), 173n
Mao Tse-tung, 255
Marion, Jean-Luc, 57n, 72
Maritain, Jacques, 101n
Marshall, Terence E., 187n, 190n, 191n, 192n, 206n, 210n
Marx, Karl, 4, 5n, 184, 203n, 208n, 255, 266, 274, 276, 281n
Maschler, Channinah, 10n
Masson, Pierre-Maurice, 204n
Mill, John Stuart, 276n
Miller, Genevieve, 23n
Mirabaud, Jean-Baptiste de, 127
Molinier, Jean-Baptiste, abbé, 24n
Montaigne, Michel de, 94n, 170n, 261
Montesquieu, Charles Secondat, baron de, 27, 28, 37–38, 210–11
Morrisoe, Michael, 177n
Moses, 83, 131–32, 132n, 133n, 142
Mossner, Ernest Campbell, 169n, 170n, 177n, 182, 184n
Musaeus, Johann, 126

Neurath, Otto, 265–66, 281n
Newton, Isaac, 26, 27, 33, 36, 90n, 125, 178n, 188, 233, 234–38, 241, 258, 259
Niebuhr, Reinhold, 243–44, 248n, 251
Nietzsche, Friedrich, 9n, 13, 19, 41–42, 78, 91, 101n, 107, 167, 184, 192, 197n, 198n, 207n, 211, 212n, 219
Nigg, Walter, 224n
Norman, Buford, 112n
Novalis, *see* Hardenberg, Friedrich Leopold Freiherr von
Noxon, James, 175n, 177n, 179n

Nozick, Robert, 280, 281n

Odysseus (Ulysses), 185, 193n, 209n
Oldenburg, Henry, 136
Oostens, Jacob, 126n
Orpheus, 196–98, 212
Ovid, 11n, 92n, 197n
Ozouf, Mona, 189n, 193n

Paine, Thomas, 2n
Pangle, Thomas, 196n, 198n, 210n
Pascal, Blaise, 10, 17, 27, 92–123
Paterson, Timothy, 197n
Paul, Saint, 44, 101n, 122n, 142, 252
Penelhum, Terence, 176n, 179n
Pentheus, 250
Périer, Gilberte, 93
Petrarch, 219
Pieper, Josef, 80n
Pindar, 198n
Plato, 1n, 11, 20, 47–48, 52–53, 64n, 80, 81n, 96n, 101n, 105, 124, 149, 150, 155–56, 169, 189n, 190n, 192, 194n, 196, 197n, 198, 199n, 209n, 212n, 253–55
Pons, Georges, 219n, 221n
Pope, Alexander, 27, 190n, 233, 235, 236
Popkin, Richard, 132n, 261n
Popper, Karl, 254n, 263n, 267, 276, 282n
Prado, Juan de, 132n
Price, J. V., 178n, 182n
Proclus, 190n
Proteus, 50
Prufer, Thomas, 95n
Przywara, Erich, 115n
Ptolemy, 153, 272
Putnam, Hilary, 273n
Pyrrho, 115, 200n
Pythagoras, 47n

Quine, Willard van Orman, 21, 266n, 267, 275n
Quixote, Don, 116

Rajchman, John, 258n
Rappolt, Friedrich, 126
Ratzinger, Joseph, 95n
Rawls, John, 278, 280, 281n
Raynaud, Philippe, 150n, 162n, 163n, 167n
Reedy, Gerard, S.J., 128n
Rees, Graham, 51n
Reichenbach, Hans, 281n
Reimarius, Hermann Samuel, 213, 216, 219n, 224n

Ress, Johann Dietrich, 213
Révah, I. S., 132n
Ribera, Daniel, 132n
Ricoeur, Paul, 161n
Rigault, G., 25n
Rist, J. M., 64n
Rivelaygue, Jacques, 162n
Robespierre, Maximillien, 189n
Rodis-Lewis, Geneviève, 94n
Rohrmoser, Günther, 217n
Romanos, George D., 276n
Root, H. E., 169n
Rorty, Richard, 7n, 8, 258n
Rosen, Stanley, 189n
Roth, Leon, 57n
Rousseau, Jean Jacques, 7n, 19, 20, 29–30, 83–84, 187–212, 278
Rowbotham, Arnold H., 23n
Russell, Bertrand, 266n, 267, 272, 273, 281n

Sade, marquis de, 29, 193n, 197n
Saint-Simon, Claude-Henri de Rouvroy, comte de 260–61
Salmon, W., 178n
Sarsi, Lothario, *see* Orazio Grassi,
Satan, 160
Scheler, Max, 41–42
Schilpp, Paul, 192n
Schmitz, Kenneth L., 217n, 228n, 230n
Schneider, Heinrich, 218n, 219n, 223n
Schneider, Johannes, 218n, 219, 219n, 220n, 221n, 223n, 224n, 225n
Schopenhauer, Arthur, 167
Schrempf, Christof, 218n
Schuster, John, 55n
Schweitzer, Albert, 243
Searle, John, 271n
Sellier, Philippe, 101n
Seneca, 185, 198n
Serres, Michel, 153n
Sève, René, 164n
Shell, Susan Meld, 211n
Shelley, Percy, 197n
Shulsky, Abram, 211n
Sieyès, Emmanuel Joseph, comte de, 279
Silber, John R., 240n, 244n, 247n, 255n
Simon, Richard, 128n
Slade, Francis, 15n
Smith, Adam, 176n, 259
Smith, Norman Kemp, 170n, 182
Snyders, G., 25n
Socrates, 1–2, 11, 14, 20, 44, 80, 83, 95–96, 99, 169, 196n, 200, 208n, 217n
Sokolowski, Robert, 8n

Index 307

Solmsen, Friedrich, 1n
Sparshott, Francis Edward, 64n
Spencer, Herbert, 266
Spicker, G., 218n, 219n
Spinoza, Baruch, 18, 81n, 124–49, 151, 152, 157, 218, 232, 269n, 281n
Spitzelius, T., 126
Stalin, Joseph, 16, 255
Starobinski, Jean, 191n, 201n, 202n
Stephen, Leslie, 128,
Stillingfleet, Edward, 128n
Stitch, S., 272n
Strauss, Leo, 4n, 8n, 10n, 11n, 41–42, 81n, 88, 91, 101n, 102, 114n, 125n, 129n, 132n, 189n, 208n
Sutherland, Stewart, 179n

Tacitus, 186
Talmon, J. L., 280
Taton, René, 98
Tawney, R. H., 281n
Telemachus, 193n
Tertullian, 234
Thielicke, Helmut, 214n, 217n, 219n, 220n, 225, 228–29
Thomas Aquinas, Saint, 19, 31–35, 119, 137n, 180, 184–86, 233
Thomasius, Jacob, 126
Tillich, Paul, 243
Tindal, Matthew, 31–32, 35
Titmus, Richard, 281n
Tocqueville, Alexis de, 10n
Todorov, Tzevetan, 201n
Toland, John, 128n
Topliss, Patricia, 109n
Torricelli, Evangelista, 27, 33
Turgot, Anne Robert Jacques, baron de L'Aulne, 257, 260, 266
Tweyman, Stanley, 182n

Ulysses. *See* Odysseus

Vamos, Mara, 100n
Velleius, 172n
Velkley, Richard L., 187n, 193n, 205n, 211n
Velthuysen, Lambert van, 126n, 127
Veteler, Jacob, 126
Vink, A. G., 177n
Voltaire, François-Marie Arouet de, 7n, 16, 23–24, 26n, 27, 28–29, 30, 37–38, 128n, 162, 190, 193, 204, 223n

Wade, Ira, 127, 127–28
Weber, Max, 167

Wedberg, Anders, 281n
Weinberger, Jerry, 50n, 197n
Wernle, Paul, 223n
West, Cornel, 258n
White, Howard, 50n, 197n, 207n
Whitehead, Alfred North, 243
Wiese, Benno von, 223n
Wittgenstein, Ludwig, 271, 273
Wolff, Christian, 229n

Yandell, Keith, 174n, 175n
Yates, Frances A., 10n
Yovel, Yirmiyahu, 144n

Zammito, John, 195n
Zeno, 64n
Zeus, 210, 236
Zoroaster, 1
Zscharnak, L., 225

www.ingramcontent.com/pod-product-compliance
Lightning Source LLC
Chambersburg PA
CBHW031407290426
44110CB00011B/297